LANGUAGE AND LINGUISTICS

The new edition of this highly successful A–Z guide explores the main concepts and terms used in the study of language and linguistics. Containing over 300 entries, thoroughly updated to reflect the latest developments in the field, this book includes entries in:

- Cognitive linguistics
- Discourse analysis
- Phonology and phonetics
- Psycholinguistics
- Sociolinguistics
- Syntax and semantics

Beginning with a brief definition, each entry is followed by a comprehensive explanation of the origin and usage of the term. The book is cross-referenced throughout and includes further reading for academics and students alike.

R.L. Trask (1944–2004) was the highly regarded Professor of Linguistics at the University of Sussex. His numerous publications included *Language: The Basics* (1995) and *A Dictionary of Phonetics and Phonology* (1995).

Peter Stockwell is Professor of Literary Linguistics at the University of Nottingham and the editor of the *Routledge English Language Introductions Series*.

Language: The Basics (Second Edition)
R.L. Trask

Semiotics: The Basics
Daniel Chandler

Psycholinguistics: The Key Concepts
John Field

The Routledge Companion to Semiotics and Linguistics
Paul Cobley

LANGUAGE AND LINGUISTICS

The Key Concepts

Second Edition

R.L. Trask
Edited by Peter Stockwell

Routledge
Taylor & Francis Group

LONDON AND NEW YORK

First published as *Key Concepts in Language and Linguistics* 1999

This edition published 2007
by Routledge
2 Park Square, Milton Park, Abingdon, Oxon OX14 4RN

Simultaneously published in the USA and Canada
by Routledge
711 Third Avenue, New York, NY 10017

Routledge is an imprint of the Taylor & Francis Group, an informa business

First edition text © 1999 R.L. Trask
Second edition © 2007 R.L. Trask and Peter Stockwell

Typeset in Times by
Taylor & Francis Books

British Library Cataloguing in Publication Data
A catalogue record for this book is available from the British Library

Library of Congress Cataloging in Publication Data
A catalog record for this book has been requested

ISBN 978-0-415-41358-9 (hbk)
ISBN 978-0-415-41359-6 (pbk)
ISBN 978-0-203-96113-1 (ebk)

CONTENTS

ALPHABETICAL LIST OF KEY CONCEPTS

(Listed alphabetically, as they appear in this book)

accent
adjacency pair
adjective
adverb
affix
affricate
agreement
airstream mechanism
alternation
ambiguity
analogy
anaphor
animal communication
anthropological linguistics
aphasia
apparent time
applied linguistics
arbitrariness
argument
artificial language
aspect
autolexical grammar
autonomy
auxiliary
basic word order
behaviourism
bilingualism
bioprogram hypothesis
Black English
borrowing

case
clause
clitic
cloze
code-switching
cognitive linguistics
cohesion
colligate
communicative competence
community of practice
comparative reconstruction
competence
complement
computational linguistics
conceptual integration
conjunction
connotation
consonant
constituent structure
construction grammar
control
conversation analysis
conversational implicature
cooperative principle
coordinate structure
copula
creole
critical discourse analysis
critical period hypothesis
dead language

deep structure
deficit hypothesis
deictic category
denotation
dependency
derivation
descriptivism
design features
determiner
diachrony
dialect
diglossia
direct object
discourse
discourse analysis
displacement
distinctive feature
distribution
duality of patterning
dyslexia
elicitation techniques
ellipsis
entailment
ethics
ethnicity
ethnography of
  communication
etymology
euphemism
finite
focus
folk linguistics
foregrounding
forensic linguistics
formal grammar
frame
functionalism
functions of language
gap
gender
generative grammar
genetic hypothesis of language

genetic relationship
genre
given/new
government
Government-and-Binding
  Theory
grammar
grammatical category
grammatical relation
grapheme
head
historical linguistics
iconicity
identity
ideology
idiom
indicator
indirect object
Indo-European
infinitive
inflection
innateness hypothesis
integrationalism
internal reconstruction
international language
International Phonetic
  Alphabet
intertextuality
intonation
intuition
irrealis
kinship terms
landmark
language
language acquisition
language acquisition device
language areas
language change
language contact
language death
language disability
language faculty

language family
language instinct
language myths
language planning
language processing
langue
lateralization
lemma
Lexical-Functional Grammar
lexicography
lexicon
lingua franca
linguistic area
linguistic relativity hypothesis
linguistic sign
linguistics
literacy
loan word
localization
logonomic rules
manner of articulation
markedness
markers
meaning
medium
mental space
mentalism
metalanguage
metaphor
minimal pair
minimalist program(me)
minority language
mirror neurons
modality
modifier
mood
morpheme
morphology
motherese
movement
name
narrative

national language
natural class
natural-language processing
neurolinguistics
neutralization
nominalization
non-verbal communication
notational convention
noun
noun phrase
number
number of languages
observer's paradox
official language
onomastics
open-endedness
optimality theory
oracy
origin and evolution of
 language
orthography
paradigm
paradigmatic relation
paralanguage
parole
parsing
part of speech
perceptual strategy
performance
performative
person
philology
philosophy of language
phonation type
phoneme
phonetics
phonology
phonotactics
phrase
phrase-structure grammar
pidgin
place of articulation

politeness
polysynthesis
possible worlds theory
power
pragmatics
predicate
preposition
prescriptivism
prestige
presupposition
productivity
pronoun
prosody
proto-language
proto-language hypothesis
prototype
psycholinguistics
punctuation
purism
qualitative approach
quantitative approach
raising
rank scale
reconstruction
recursion
reference
relevance
rhetoric
root
rule
Saussurean paradox
schema
segment
selection restriction
semantic role
semantics
semiotics
sense
sense relation
sentence
sex differences in language
sexist language

sign language
slang
social history of language
social network
social stratification of language
sociolinguistics
sound symbolism
speech
speech act
speech community
speech event
speech sound
speech therapy
spelling
standard language
stem
stereotype
stimulus-freedom
stress
structuralism
structure
structure-dependence
stylistics
subcategorization
subject
subordination
suprasegmental
surface structure
syllable
symbolic system
synchrony
syntactic category
syntagmatic relation
syntax
system
systematic correspondence
Systemic Linguistics
tagmemics
tense
text
text linguistics
text world theory

textuality
tone language
topic
traditional grammar
trajector
transcription
transformational grammar
transitivity
tree
trope
turn-taking
typology
universal
universal grammar
usage

utterance
variable
variation
verb
verb phrase
vernacular
vocal tract
voice
voicing
vowel
well-formedness
word
word-formation
writing system
X-bar

LIST OF KEY CONCEPTS

(Arranged according to the linguistic sub-discipline: some items therefore appear repeatedly)

Phonetics and phonology

accent
affricate
airstream mechanism
alternation
consonant
distinctive feature
distribution
grapheme
iconicity
International Phonetic
 Alphabet
intonation
lateralization
manner of articulation
markedness
medium
minimal pair
neutralization
notational convention
phonation type
phoneme
phonetics
phonology
phonotactics
place of articulation
prosody
rule
segment
sound symbolism
speech

speech sound
stress
suprasegmental
syllable
tone language
transcription
vocal tract
voice
voicing
vowel

Morphology

affix
aspect
case
copula
derivation
finite
grammar
grammatical category
grammatical relation
grapheme
infinitive
inflection
markedness
morpheme
morphology
paradigm
paradigmatic relation
person
polysynthesis

pronoun
root
rule
spelling
stem
syllable
tense
word
word-formation

Lexicology

aspect
case
clitic
colligate
copula
derivation
determiner
idiom
infinitive
inflection
irrealis
kinship terms
lemma
lexicography
lexicon
loan word
modality
modifier
noun
orthography
predicate
preposition
pronoun
verb
word
word-formation

Syntax

adjective
adverb

agreement
anaphor
aspect
auxiliary
basic word order
case
clause
clitic
complement
conjunction
constituent structure
control
coordinate structure
deep structure
dependency
derivation
determiner
direct object
distribution
ellipsis
finite
frame
gap
given/new
government
grammar
grammatical category
grammatical relation
head
iconicity
indirect object
infinitive
intuition
markedness
modality
modifier
mood
movement
nominalization
notational convention
noun
noun phrase

number
paradigm
paradigmatic relation
parsing
part of speech
person
phrase
phrase-structure grammar
predicate
preposition
pronoun
raising
recursion
root
rule
sentence
structure
subcategorization
subject
subordination
surface structure
syntactic category
syntagmatic relation
syntax
tense
topic
transformational grammar
transitivity
tree
verb
verb phrase
X-bar

Semantics and pragmatics

ambiguity
analogy
anaphor
arbitrariness
argument
aspect
clause

cohesion
colligate
connotation
conversational implicature
copula
deictic category
denotation
entailment
euphemism
focus
frame
gender
given/new
iconicity
idiom
irrealis
kinship terms
lemma
linguistic sign
markedness
meaning
metaphor
modality
mood
name
paralanguage
politeness
possible worlds theory
power
pragmatics
presupposition
prototype
reference
relevance
selection restriction
semantic role
semantics
sense
sense relation
speech
stereotype
transitivity

trope
usage
utterance
verb
verb phrase

Text and discourse analysis

adjacency pair
anaphor
clause
cohesion
cooperative principle
discourse
discourse analysis
ellipsis
focus
frame
functionalism
genre
intertextuality
logonomic rules
narrative
natural-language processing
non-verbal communication
oracy
politeness
possible worlds theory
rank scale
rhetoric
schema
semiotics
speech
speech act
speech community
speech event
stylistics
Systemic Linguistics
text
text linguistics
text world theory
textuality

topic
turn-taking
usage
utterance
writing system

Applied linguistics and sociolinguistics

accent
aphasia
apparent time
applied linguistics
bilingualism
bioprogram hypothesis
Black English
cloze
code-switching
colligate
community of practice
computational linguistics
conversation analysis
creole
critical discourse analysis
deficit hypothesis
dialect
diglossia
elicitation techniques
ethics
ethnicity
ethnography of communication
forensic linguistics
gender
identity
ideology
indicators
international language
International Phonetic
    Alphabet
kinship terms
language change
language contact

language death
lingua franca
linguistic area
literacy
markers
minimal pair
minority language
motherese
narrative
national language
number of languages
observer's paradox
official language
oracy
parole
performance
performative
pidgin
politeness
power
prestige
sex differences in language
sexist language
sign language
slang
social history of language
social network
social stratification of
    language
sociolinguistics
speech community
speech therapy
standard language
stereotype
synchrony
tone language
transcription
turn-taking
usage
variable
variation
vernacular

**Psycholinguistics and cognitive
linguistics**

bilingualism
cloze
cognitive linguistics
communicative competence
competence
conceptual integration
critical period hypothesis
deictic category
dyslexia
foregrounding
frame
given/new
irrealis
landmark
language acquisition
language acquisition device
language areas
language disability
language faculty
language instinct
language planning
language processing
literacy
localization
mental space
mentalism
metaphor
mirror neurons
motherese
natural-language processing
neurolinguistics
oracy
perceptual strategy
possible worlds theory
prototype
psycholinguistics
qualitative approach
quantitative approach
schema
speech therapy

text world theory
trajector

Historical linguistics and philology

borrowing
comparative reconstruction
dead language
diachrony
etymology
genetic relationship
grapheme
historical linguistics
Indo-European
internal reconstruction
language change
language contact
language death
language family
loan word
onomastics
origin and evolution of language
orthography
philology
proto-language
proto-language hypothesis
punctuation
reconstruction
social network
standard language
typology
writing system

Theoretical linguistics and aspects of language theory

animal communication
anthropological linguistics
arbitrariness
artificial language
autolexical grammar

autonomy
behaviourism
construction grammar
critical period hypothesis
descriptivism
design features
displacement
duality of patterning
folk linguistics
forensic linguistics
formal grammar
functionalism
functions of language
generative grammar
genetic hypothesis of language
Government-and-Binding Theory
innateness hypothesis
integrationalism
language
language myths
langue
Lexical-Functional Grammar
linguistic relativity
linguistics
mentalism
metalanguage
minimalist program(me)
natural class
open-endedness
optimality theory
parole
philosophy of language
prescriptivism
productivity
purism
qualitative approach
quantitative approach
rank scale
Saussurean paradox
stimulus-freedom
structuralism

structure-dependence
surface structure
symbolic system
synchrony
system
systematic correspondence
Systemic Linguistics

tagmemics
traditional grammar
transformational grammar
typology
universal
universal grammar
well-formedness

PREFACE TO THE REVISED EDITION

The book in your hand is neither a dictionary nor an encyclopedia, but something in between. As its title suggests, it provides fairly detailed coverage of over 300 key concepts in the study of language. The named concepts selected for inclusion are all among the most important in the field and among those which every beginning student is likely to encounter.

The concepts are taken from every area of language study, from traditional grammar to contemporary grammatical theory, from child language to language and brain, from lexicography to the linguistic study of literary texts, from men's and women's speech to language and power. Each entry provides a brief definition of the term entered and then goes on to explain the concept in some detail – often with numerous examples – and it also introduces and explains related terms. Wherever possible, the historical origins of the concept are described, including the time of introduction and the names of individuals who have made the concept prominent. When a concept is controversial, the entry says so.

These words were written by Larry Trask in 1997, when he had completed the first edition of this *Key Concepts* book; seven years later, he died after a long battle with motor-neurone disease. His book has proven to be very popular: it is being used around the world by the sort of new students that Trask envisaged, and it is also regarded as a quick reference work by academics and researchers. More surprisingly, the book has found a ready audience amongst those readers who are neither professional linguists nor full-time students but who are simply interested in language and our recent theories about this most definingly human characteristic.

When the publishers asked me to produce a revised edition of this book, it was therefore with a combination of anticipation and apprehension that I agreed. Larry Trask's *Key Concepts* captures a serious engagement with the discipline of linguistics together with an infectious enthusiasm for language study: this produces its characteristic style, which is authoritative, readable, sophisticated, friendly, informative and occasionally scurrilous. Updating the entries involved removing some areas that were perhaps not as 'key' in the new century as in the old and adding some others that have shown a rapid development in recent years. The rewriting has been more interventionist and thorough than I expected, though I have tried throughout to keep faith with Trask's style. I have altered only a few of his acerbic comments and have enjoyed adding some of my own.

Larry Trask trained as a chemist, and left the Allegheny mountains in upstate New York for Peace Corps work in Turkey. From there he took a degree in linguistics and a doctorate in Basque in London, before taking up a lecturing post in Liverpool. As a student at Liverpool University in the mid-1980s, I sat in on a few of Larry Trask's lectures. His desire to enlighten and enthuse was inspiring; he was one of several colleagues there at that time who were unwittingly responsible for the broadness of my interests in language study over the intervening years. Of course he would be unaware that the callow face in his audience twenty years ago would be given the responsibility of adapting his book.

This revised edition, then, has been thoroughly updated and expanded. It presents the key concepts that a newcomer to the field is likely to come across: some of these concepts are quite complex and advanced. I have emphasised the broadness of the title in encompassing the slightly different concerns of 'language' study and 'linguistics'. There is, perhaps inevitably, a leaning towards English-language examples, as there was in the original, though I have tried to show where English has continuities with other languages as well as where it is different. Unfortunately, all of the references contained in the Bibliography at the end are published works in English, since it is the only language that I can be sure the reader of this book understands.

The key concepts are listed alphabetically through the book. This list is given at the beginning, and the entries are also listed systemically according to their linguistic sub-discipline. I have assumed you will be dipping into the book here and there like a hypertext rather than reading it like a conventional textbook, so each entry aims to be both self-contained and intertextual. Cross-references to other entries are given in **bold face** on first mention. Other terms which are explained in context but which do not merit their own entry are marked in **bold italics**. All of these items are listed in the Index, together with the names of key linguists mentioned in the book. Every entry has a short list of Further Reading: I have tried to combine introductory texts with the standard and challenging works. It should be clear from the titles which is which, but part of the appeal of linguistic study is the shortness of the journey from introduction to expertise, so I am happy for this book to lead the reader into a library or catalogue and leave you to find your own way from there.

Few people are genuinely expert in all of the areas covered by this book. Even Larry Trask thanked Nicola Woods, Lyn Pemberton and Richard Coates for assistance in the original composition. In turn, I am grateful to my colleagues at the University of Nottingham, where the broad range of the School of English Studies offers many chance encounters with diverse experts. Svenja Adolphs, Ron Carter, Kathy Conklin, Zoltan Dörnyei, Louise Mullany, Norbert Schmitt, and Violeta Sotirova were witness and assistants to the tuning up of my linguistic knowledge in the course of compiling this book. Sara Whiteley did an excellent job of compiling the index for me. Thanks to Joanna Gavins and Ada for reading for clarity and demanding playtime respectively.

I am grateful to Larry Trask's wife, Jan, for permission to revise this *Key Concepts in Language and Linguistics*. I hope it appears in a form that Larry would have approved.

Peter Stockwell

CONSONANTS (PULMONIC)

	Bilabial	Labiodental	Dental	Alveolar	Post alveolar	Retroflex	Palatal	Velar	Uvular	Pharyngeal	Glottal
Plosive	p b			t d		ʈ ɖ	c ɟ	k ɡ	q ɢ		ʔ
Nasal	m	ɱ		n		ɳ	ɲ	ŋ	N		
Trill	B			r					R		
Tap or Flap		ⱱ		ɾ		ɽ					
Fricative	ɸ β	f v	θ ð	s z	ʃ ʒ	ʂ ʐ	ç ʝ	x ɣ	χ ʁ	ħ ʕ	h ɦ
Lateral fricative				ɬ ɮ							
Approximant		ʋ		ɹ		ɻ	j	ɰ			
Lateral approximant				l		ɭ	ʎ	L			

Where symbols appear in pairs, the one to the right represents a voiced consonant. Shaded areas denote articulations judged impossible.

CONSONANTS (NON-PULMONIC)

Clicks	Voiced implosives	Ejectives
⊙ Bilabial	ɓ Bilabial	ʼ Examples:
ǀ Dental	ɗ Dental/alveolar	pʼ Bilabial
! (Post)alveolar	ʄ Palatal	tʼ Dental/alveolar
ǂ Palatoalveolar	ɠ Velar	kʼ Velar
ǁ Alveolar lateral	ʛ Uvular	sʼ Alveolar fricative

OTHER SYMBOLS

ʍ Voiceless labial-velar fricative   ɕ ʑ Alveolo-palatal fricatives

w Voiced labial-velar approximant   ɺ Voiced alveolar lateral flap

ɥ Voiced labial-palatal approximant   ɧ Simultaneous ʃ and x

ʜ Voiceless epiglottal fricative

ʢ Voiced epiglottal fricative

ʡ Epiglottal plosive

Affricates and double articulations can be represented by two symbols joined by a tie bar if necessary.   k͡p t͡s

VOWELS

Where symbols appear in pairs, the one to the right represents a rounded vowel.

SUPRASEGMENTALS

ˈ Primary stress
ˌ Secondary stress   ˌfoʊnəˈtɪʃən
ː Long   eː
ˑ Half-long   eˑ
˘ Extra-short   ĕ
| Minor (foot) group
‖ Major (intonation) group
. Syllable break   ɹi.ækt
‿ Linking (absence of a break)

DIACRITICS

Diacritics may be placed above a symbol with a descender, e.g. ŋ̊

̥ Voiceless	n̥ d̥	̤ Breathy voiced	b̤ a̤	̪ Dental	t̪ d̪
̬ Voiced	s̬ t̬	̰ Creaky voiced	b̰ a̰	̺ Apical	t̺ d̺
ʰ Aspirated	tʰ dʰ	̼ Linguolabial	t̼ d̼	̻ Laminal	t̻ d̻
̹ More rounded	ɔ̹	ʷ Labialized	tʷ dʷ	̃ Nasalized	ẽ
̜ Less rounded	ɔ̜	ʲ Palatalized	tʲ dʲ	ⁿ Nasal release	dⁿ
̟ Advanced	u̟	ˠ Velarized	tˠ dˠ	ˡ Lateral release	dˡ
̠ Retracted	e̠	ˤ Pharyngealized	tˤ dˤ	̚ No audible release	d̚
̈ Centralized	ë	̴ Velarized or pharyngealized	ɫ		
̽ Mid-centralized	e̽	̝ Raised	e̝	(ɹ̝ = voiced alveolar fricative)	
̩ Syllabic	n̩	̞ Lowered	e̞	(β̞ = voiced bilabial approximant)	
̯ Non-syllabic	e̯	̘ Advanced Tongue Root	e̘		
˞ Rhoticity	ɚ a˞	̙ Retracted Tongue Root	e̙		

TONES AND WORD ACCENTS

LEVEL			CONTOUR		
e̋ or	˥	Extra high	ě or	˩˥	Rising
é	˦	High	ê	˥˩	Falling
ē	˧	Mid	e᷄	˦˥	High rising
è	˨	Low	e᷅	˩˨	Low rising
ȅ	˩	Extra low	e᷈	˧˦˧	Rising-falling
↓		Downstep	↗		Global rise
↑		Upstep	↘		Global fall

The International Phonetic Alphabet (revised to 2005)
© *International Phonetic Association*

LANGUAGE AND LINGUISTICS

The Key Concepts

Second Edition

ACCENT

A particular way in which a group of people collectively pronounce a language. For any language with more than a handful of speakers, there are prominent regional, social and individual differences in the way the language is pronounced by different people, and the pronunciation of many words usually changes quite radically over time. Sometimes these differences are dramatic. Each distinguishable type of pronunciation is called an *accent*. Depending on where we come from and what experience we have, we will be able to identify accents different from our own with more or less precision: in the case of English this may be an American accent, a Deep South accent, a Scottish accent, a working-class London accent, a French accent (from a non-native speaker) and so on. Speakers of all languages can do the same.

It is important to realize that *everybody* has an accent: it is not possible to speak the sounds of a language without using some accent pattern. Of course, every one of us regards some accents as more familiar than others, or as more prestigious than others, but that is a different matter: we are merely more sensitive to accents which differ strongly from our own. In the early days of cinema, for example, British audiences were unable to understand the American voices in the 'talkies', simply because they had little experience of hearing Americans.

In Britain, the single most prestigious accent is *Received Pronunciation*, or RP, an accent which seems to have arisen in the prestigious 'public schools' (private schools) in the nineteenth century, and was adopted as the 'voice of the BBC' in the 1920s. This accent is not associated with any particular region, though it is structurally most similar to certain accents of the south-east of England. No more than 3 per cent of Britons speak with an RP accent, though many more have a near-RP accent which differs only in a few particulars. RP is the accent usually taught to foreign learners of English in Britain. Nevertheless, regional and social variation in accents within the small islands of Britain and Ireland is very great, probably greater than anywhere else in the English-speaking world: this density is largely due to the fact that English-speaking has its oldest history there.

In the USA, with its more recent English-speaking history, the most distinctive accents occur down the east coast and in the south, the areas which have been settled longest. West of the Appalachians, the differences level out somewhat, with less local variation apart from a few large cities. Regional accents of English are less prominent in the Caribbean, still less so in Canada, and least prominent of all in the southern-hemisphere countries such as South Africa, Australia and New Zealand, the most recent to be settled.

The writing system of English was largely formulated in the late medieval period with the influence of printing; since then, pronunciations have changed a great deal (consider *though*, *knight*, *came*, for example). Though this causes problems for foreign learners of English, the advantage is that English can be read in any accent. Writers and journalists often use *nonce-forms* of spelling to indicate specific accents of English (*y'all know wadda mean?*), but linguists can use the **International Phonetic Alphabet** to express differences in pronunciation very precisely.

Observe that, in the USA, an **accent** is usually considered to be just one aspect of a **dialect**; in Britain, the two are regarded as largely independent, at least in principle.

See also: **dialect**; **International Phonetic Alphabet**; **phonology**

Further reading: Ball and Rahilly 1999; Chambers and Trudgill 1998; Chambers *et al.* 2002; Foulkes and Docherty 1999; Hughes and Trudgill 1996; Ladefoged and Maddieson 1996; Llamas *et al.* 2007; Trudgill and Hannah 1994; Wells 1982.

ADJACENCY PAIR

In **conversation analysis**, often two utterances produced by different interlocutors will be closely related, such as in the form question/answer, accusation/defence, greeting/reply, farewell/reply, apology/acceptance and so on. These two utterances are often syntactically, semantically, lexically and cohesively linked, so they are termed *adjacency pairs*. Note that adjacency pairs are not always adjacent: they can be interrupted by intervening utterances. For example, here is a full exchange:

1 *Peter* (to Nick): Can you give me a hand?
2 *Peter* (before Nick has a chance to answer, shouts across the road): BOB! Any chance of a hand here?
3 *Bob*: Yeah, be there in a minute.
4 *Nick*: Well, will it take long – it's just that I'm in a rush and—

5 *Peter*: No, a couple of seconds. Can you?
6 *Nick*: Sure. I've got to be at the station soon.
7 *Peter*: Thanks.
8 *Nick*: What do I do?
9 *Peter*: If you could just push, I'll be able to jump-start it.
10 *Nick*: OK.

There are two main adjacency pairs here: 1 and 6, and 8 and 9. Each of these pairs has an acknowledgement follow-up (6 and 10 respectively) which is known as *feedback*. The first adjacency pair is interrupted by another adjacency pair (2 and 3) which functions as a *side-sequence*: it is unconnected directly with the main discourse. Nick begins an intervening question/answer adjacency pair (4 and 5) which functions as an *insertion-sequence*: the answer of the surrounding adjacency pair (1 and 6) depends upon this one. Another common feature of conversation appears here: Nick begins to explain he is in a rush (4), but is interrupted (5–6) and he *skip-connects* back to his explanation (6). The distance that skip-connecting is tolerated can be quite large, and skip-connects are especially prominent in online chat-room exchanges, where other users intervene before an interlocutor can return to 'their' topic.

See also: **conversation analysis**; **turn-taking**

Further reading: Holmes 1992; Duranti 1997.

ADJECTIVE

The **part of speech** which includes words like *big* and *beautiful*. English and many other languages have a large and growing class of adjectives, though in some languages the class of adjectives is tiny and closed or absent altogether. (In these languages, the meanings expressed by adjectives in English are expressed by other parts of speech.)

In English, adjectives may be identified by a number of criteria. Not every adjective exhibits every single one of the typical adjectival properties, but a word that exhibits most of them must still be classed as an adjective. Here are some tests for adjectives.

Distribution: An adjective can typically appear in each of the following slots to produce a good sentence: *This is a(n) – book*; *This book is –; – though this book is, it's not what we want.* (Try this with *new, interesting, expensive, beautiful.*)

Comparison: An adjective can be compared in one of the following two ways: *big/bigger/biggest; beautiful/more beautiful/most beautiful.* It can also appear in the *as … as* construction: *as pretty as Lisa.*

Degree: An adjective can be modified by a **degree modifier** like *very, fairly, too, so* or *rather*: *very big, fairly nice, so good, rather interesting.*

Affixation: An adjective may take the prefix *un-* or *in-* to form another adjective, the suffix *-ly* to form an **adverb**, or the suffix *-ness* or *-ity* to form a **noun**, among other possibilities: *happy/unhappy/ happily/happiness*; *possible/impossible/possibly/possibility.*

Negative properties: An adjective cannot be marked for **number** (singular versus plural) or for **tense** (past versus non-past), nor can it take the suffix *-ing* which goes onto **verbs**.

Note that these tests are grammatical in nature. Adjectives such as *big, wise, large* can be adapted in deviant ways for poetic and creative effects (*big him up, wise up, larging it*) but in the process the words themselves cease being adjectives and become other parts of speech, since they are defined grammatically not semantically.

The meaning of an adjective is most typically a temporary or permanent state or condition: *big, human, young, red, happy, drunk, shiny, intelligent, asleep.* Many adjectives express subjective perceptions, rather than objective facts: *interesting, beautiful, disgusting.* A few adjectives express very unusual types of meaning: *mere, utter,* the *heavy* of *She's a heavy smoker.* In English, adjectives are placed as **pre-modifiers** or **post-modifiers**, and the extent of this choice is often stylistically significant: consider the differing force and purpose of *the thick students* and *the students who are thick.*

See also: **adverb**; **part of speech**

Further reading: Collins Cobuild 1990; Crystal 1996; Greenbaum and Quirk 1990; Hurford 1994.

ADVERB

The **part of speech** which includes words like *soon* and *slowly.* English has a fairly large class of adverbs. Most commonly, an **adverb** describes the circumstances of an action: where it is done (*here, elsewhere, overhead*), when it is done (*tomorrow, often, rarely, never*) or how it is done (*fast, well, carefully, dramatically, resentfully*). But some adverbs have less usual kinds of meaning, and, as always, we can only identify adverbs with confidence by their grammatical properties. A typical property of adverbs is their position in the sentence. Consider the sentence *She poured the wine*. A typical adverb like *carefully* can be inserted into any one of three positions: *Carefully she poured the wine*; *She carefully poured the wine*; *She poured the wine carefully*; note that *She poured carefully the wine* sounds oddly poetic, and *She poured the carefully wine is plain ungrammatical (the asterisk marks ungrammaticality). The same is true of many other adverbs, like *often, angrily* and *skilfully*. But not all adverbs are so flexible: *yesterday* and *downstairs* can only fit into the first and third of the three typical positions, while *fast* can only fit into the last. (Naturally, some adverbs, such as *uphill*, have meanings which do not allow them to fit sensibly into this example, but consider another example like *She threw the ball*.) Adverbs with negative or interrogative meanings do something odd when they come first: we can't say *Seldom she poured the wine or *Why she poured the wine? but must say instead *Seldom did she pour the wine* and *Why did she pour the wine?*

Two other typical properties of adverbs are their ability to be compared (with *more* or *most*) and their ability to be **modified** by words expressing degree, such as *very, rather, too* and *so: more carefully, most often, very skilfully, rather casually, too fast, so well*. This is usually only possible with adverbs describing how something is done, though there are a few exceptions, like *often*. These adverbs can also appear in the *as ... as* construction, as in *Susie drives as well as Esther*.

Adverbs have few other grammatical properties. They never change their form: for example, they cannot be marked for **tense**, and they have no separate plural form (except, as always, in special poetic deviant uses, in new dialect forms or to indicate infantile speech: *seldoming, carefuller, tomorrowed, laters*).

English has a subclass of adverbs, called **sentence adverbs**, which are rather different from ordinary adverbs. While ordinary adverbs describe some aspect of the action, the sentence adverbs express the speaker's view of the whole rest of the sentence. For example, in *She probably poured the wine*, the sentence adverb *probably* says nothing about her pouring of the wine, but rather expresses the speaker's view of the likely truth of the statement *She poured the wine*. Other sentence adverbs are *maybe, certainly, frankly, mercifully, honestly,* *hopefully* and *fortunately.* Some of these can also be used as ordinary adverbs: compare the meaning of *Frankly, she must tell us about it* (sentence adverb expressing the speaker's view) with *She must tell us about it frankly* (ordinary adverb describing her telling). Some **prescriptivists** would regard a sentence like *Hopefully the ticket-office will be open* as unacceptable, since offices cannot hope, but in fact there is almost never any ambiguity.

Observe that many adverbs describing how something is done (the **adverbs of manner**) are derived from **adjectives** by means of the suffix *-ly: eager/eagerly, furious/furiously.* But other adverbs, including **adverbs of time** and **adverbs of place**, are usually simple words, not derived from anything.

Earlier grammarians often had the bad habit of assigning the label 'adverb' to almost any troublesome word they didn't know what to do with, such as *not, almost* and *very.* Some dictionaries and other books still continue this unfortunate practice today, but in fact these words do not behave like adverbs and are not adverbs: some of them (like *very*) belong to other parts of speech entirely, while others (like *not*) exhibit unique behaviour and cannot be sensibly assigned to any part of speech at all.

See also: **adjective**; **part of speech**

Further reading: Collins Cobuild 1990; Crystal 1996; Greenbaum and Quirk 1990; Hurford 1994.

AFFIX

A grammatical element which cannot form a word by itself. Affixes are **bound morphemes**, in the sense that they are meaningful units (**morphemes**) which cannot exist independently of another morpheme to which they must be attached. Most (but not all) of the world's languages contain grammatical **affixes** used for various purposes. English has fewer affixes than some other languages, but it still has some. For example, English usually expresses plurality in nouns with the sounds /s/ or /z/ as in *cats* and *dogs*, or the older *-en* affix as in *oxen, children, women.* English of course also borrows some plural systems from other languages in the fossilized forms *datum/data, octopus/octopi*, and though we keep the *-i* plural in *spaghetti*, we anglicize *pizzas*. I was once behind someone in a queue buying ice cream 'Magnums' who asked for 'three mint

Magna'! Modern linguists have debated whether the medieval 'strong' plural *mice* (inflected with an internal vowel change) should apply to multiple examples of a computer *mouse*, and have decided that *mouses* ought to be the right form. Other meanings expressed by affixes in English include the comparative affix *-er* (*wider*) and the superlative affix *-est* (*widest*), the vagueness of *-ish*, the abstraction of *-ness*, the various oppositenesses of *anti-*, *un-*, *non-*, *dis-* and *de-*, the repetition of *re-*, the emptiness of *-less*, and the anticipation of *pre-*(even somewhat redundantly in words like *pre-warn*, *pre-plan*, and *pre-book*).

Verbs in English can also exhibit affixes, as shown by *paint*, which has grammatical forms like *paints* (*She paints pictures*), *painted* (*She painted a picture* and the quite different *She has painted a picture*) and *painting* (*She is painting a picture*). Other affixes can be added to the verb *paint* to obtain the verb *repaint* and the nouns *painter* and *painting* (as in *This is a nice painting*).

An affix that goes on the end, like *-s* and *-ing*, is a **suffix**, while one that goes on the beginning, like *re-*, is a **prefix**. Other types of affix exist, such as **infixes**: observe that the Tagalog verb *sulat* 'write' has inflected forms *sumulat* 'wrote' and *sinulat* 'was written', with infixes *-um-* and *-in-* inserted into the middle of the verbal **root**. English only has infixing deviantly, whether creative (*abso-bloodylutely*) or poetic (*pity this poor monster manunkind*). There are also **superfixes**, which are placed 'on top of' a word in the sense of stress or pronunciation variation: note the English nouns '*record* (a vinyl music disc) and '*contest* (a competition), distinguished from the related verbs re'*cord* and con'*test* only by a change in the placement of the stress.

See also: **derivation**; **inflection**; **morpheme**

Further reading: Bauer 1988; Katamba 1994.

AFFRICATE

A term relating to the **manner of articulation of consonants**. When the air behind a closure is gradually released, friction of the airstream results. The sounds made by this sustained friction are **affricates**: /s/, /z/, /ʃ/, /ʒ/, /θ/, /ð/ and so on. Even when a **plosive** is produced (/t/, /d/), there is often a very brief affrication that follows the release: this can be sustained in certain **accents** such as London Cockney /tˢ/ in Tuesday. Affricates are distinguishable in **phonetics**, but cause problems in **phonology**, where the phonemic value of the sounds is debatable. For example, /tʃ/ could be treated contrastively in English (*chip/ship*, *match/mats*) since it alters the meaning wherever it occurs in the word, and is clearly phonologically permitted in any position. However, /pr/ cannot occur at the end of an English word (*print*, *leprosy*) and /tθ/ can only occur at the end (*fifth* in most accents that pronounce the second /f/, and *eighth*). So should these examples be treated as single phonological units or as separate sounds consisting of a plosive plus an affricate?

See also: **accent**; **phonology**

Further reading: Ball and Rahilly 1999; Collins and Mees 2003; Ladefoged and Maddieson 1996.

AGREEMENT

The grammatical phenomenon in which the form of one word in a sentence is determined by the form of another word which is grammatically linked to it. *Agreement*, which is also called *concord*, is an exceedingly common phenomenon in languages generally, but it is not present equally in all of them. Swahili, Russian, Latin and German have a great deal of agreement; French and Spanish have somewhat less; English has very little; Chinese has none at all.

Certain types of agreement are especially frequent. A finite verb may agree in **person** and **number** with its subject. This happens in Basque; here are the present-tense forms of *joan* 'go' (the pronouns are in brackets since they are optional):

(*ni*) *noa*	'I go'	
(*hi*) *hoa*	'you go'	(singular intimate)
Ana doa	'Ann goes'	
(*gu*) *goaz*	'we go'	
(*zu*) *zoaz*	'you go'	(singular polite)
(*zuek*) *zoazte*	'you go'	(plural)
Neskak doaz	'The girls go'	

In each case, the form of the verb marks the subject as first, second or third person and as singular or plural, and we say that the verb-form *agrees* with the subject in person and number. As you can see from the English glosses, English has only a tiny amount of agreement of this kind: only the third-person singular *goes* is explicitly distinguished, all other persons and numbers taking an invariable *go*.

Much less frequently, a verb may agree in person and number with its *object*. This also happens in Basque. The form *(zuk) (ni) ikusi nauzu* 'you saw me' carries agreement both for the subject 'you' (*-zu*) and for the object 'me' (*n-*); compare *(zuk) (gu) ikusi gaituzu* 'you saw us' and *neskek (ni) ikusi naute* 'the girls saw me'.

Adjectives and **determiners** may agree in number with their **head** noun. Basque does not have this, but Spanish does: compare *la casa vieja* 'the old house' with *las casas viejas* 'the old houses', in which both the determiner *la(s)* 'the' and the adjective *vieja(s)* 'old' show agreement with singular *casa* 'house' and plural *casas* 'houses'. As the English glosses suggest, this kind of agreement is generally absent from English, but we do have a trace of it in cases like *this old house* versus *these old houses*, in which the determiner agrees (but not the adjective).

A determiner or an adjective may also agree in **case** with its head noun. This occurs in German: in *mit diesem Mann(e)* 'with this man' (the *e* is optional and is therefore in brackets), the noun *Mann(e)* stands in the dative case, and the determiner *diesem* 'this' agrees with it in case, while in *für diesen Mann*, *Mann* stands in the accusative case, and the determiner now agrees with that.

The Spanish and German examples also illustrate what might be called agreement in **gender**. For example, the Spanish noun *casa* 'house' is feminine in gender; if we use instead a masculine noun, such as *libro* 'book', we get *el libro viejo* 'the old book' and *los libros viejos* 'the old books', showing that the determiner and the adjective are 'agreeing' in gender as well as in number. Such gender matching is traditionally regarded as another variety of agreement; strictly speaking, however, this is not agreement but **government**, since a single noun like *casa* or *libro* has only one possible gender, and hence in these cases it is not the *form* of the noun which determines the forms of the other words, but its very *presence* – the defining criterion for government. Some linguists apply to such cases the label *governmental concord*.

See also: **government**

Further reading: Greville 2006; Hurford 1994.

AIRSTREAM MECHANISM

Any way of producing a stream of air for use in speech. We produce speech by using our vocal organs to modify a stream of air flowing through some part of the vocal tract, and all speech sounds require this airstream for their production. There are several very different ways of producing an airstream, only some of which are used in languages, and only one of which is used in all languages.

To begin with, an airstream may be either *egressive* (flowing out of the mouth) or *ingressive* (flowing into the mouth). Further, the air which is moving may be lung air (this is the *pulmonic* mechanism), pharynx air (the *glottalic* mechanism) or mouth air (the *velaric* mechanism). This gives six possible combinations, only four of which are used in speech.

In the *pulmonic egressive* airstream mechanism, air is squeezed out of the lungs by the diaphragm and the rib muscles and passes out through the mouth (and possibly the nose). This is the principal mechanism in all languages and the only one used in most languages (including English). In the *pulmonic ingressive* mechanism, air is drawn in from the outside through the mouth into the lungs; no language uses this, but you may hear it intermittently from a child sobbing and talking at the same time.

In the *glottalic egressive* mechanism, the glottis is closed and the larynx is driven up in the throat like a piston, pushing the air of the pharynx out through the mouth. The sounds produced are *ejectives*, which occur in only a few languages. If the larynx is driven downward instead, outside air is pulled into the mouth and pharynx, and we have the *glottalic ingressive* mechanism. The sounds produced are *injectives* (or *voiceless implosives*); these are very rare in their pure form, but, if the glottis is left open slightly, so that air can leak out from the lungs, we get a complex ingressive-egressive mechanism, producing *voiced implosives*, which are much commoner.

In the *velaric egressive* mechanism, the back of the tongue is pressed against the velum and another closure is made in front of this; the tongue body is pushed up, so that, when the front closure is released, mouth air is driven outward. The resulting sounds are *reverse clicks*, which do not occur in any language. If, instead, the tongue body is pulled downward, when the front closure is released, air is pulled into the mouth; this is the *velaric ingressive* mechanism, and the resulting sounds are *clicks*. Clicks occur as speech sounds in some languages of southern Africa; elsewhere, these sounds occur only paralinguistically, as in the English *tsk-tsk* noise of disapproval or the *clack-clack* noise for geeing up a horse. All speech sounds can be described in these ways by their manner of articulation, even non-linguistic sounds: a velaric ingressive bilabial plosive is a kiss.

There is one other airstream mechanism, which is very unusual. Persons who have had their larynxes removed surgically can learn to produce an airstream by swallowing air and then forcing it up through the oesophagus; this *oesophagic egressive* airstream is effectively a controlled belch.

See also: **phonation type**

Further reading: Ball and Rahilly 1999; Collins and Mees 2003; Crystal 1997; Ladefoged and Maddieson 1996; Laver 1994.

ALTERNATION

A variation in the form of a linguistic element depending on where it occurs. Certain English nouns ending in the consonant /f/ form their plurals with /v/ instead: *leaf* but *leaves*, *knife* but *knives*. We say that such items exhibit an /f/–/v/ alternation. For most (not all) speakers a similar alternation occurs in singular *house* (with /s/) but plural *houses* (with /z/), though here our spelling system does not represent the alternation explicitly.

A somewhat different sort of alternation is found in related words like *electric* (which ends in /k/) and *electricity* (which has /s/ instead of /k/ in the same position).

More subtle is the three-way alternation occurring in the English plural marker. The noun *cat* has plural *cats*, pronounced with /s/, but *dog* has plural *dogs*, pronounced with /z/ (though again the spelling fails to show this), and *fox* has plural *foxes*, with /z/ preceded by an extra vowel. This alternation is regular and predictable; the choice among the three *alternants* (as they are called) is determined by the nature of the preceding sound.

Alternations are exceedingly common in the world's languages, and they are often of great interest to linguists trying to produce elegant descriptions of languages. Where pronunciation changes at a grammatical boundary, as in the examples at morpheme boundaries above, these are called *sandhi*, a term deriving from the ancient Sanskrit grammarians. Changes to morpheme pronunciation within a single word are *internal sandhi*; *external sandhi* also

13

occurs across word boundaries, as in the introduction of an 'intrusive /r/' between 'law and order', a /w/ between 'mellow elephant', or the merging of word-final /t/ and word-initial /j/ in 'don't you' into a single affricate /tʃ/.

See also: **phonetics**; **phonology**; **phonotactics**

Futher reading: Ball and Rahilly 1999; Bloomfield 1933; Hockett 1958; Lass 1984; Matthews 1991; Sommerstein 1977.

AMBIGUITY

Two or more sharply distinct meanings for a single string of words. The simplest type of ambiguity is a *lexical ambiguity*, which results merely from the existence of two different meanings for a single word. Example: *The sailors enjoyed the port.* Here *port* can mean either 'fortified wine' or 'town by the sea', and the entire string of words accordingly has two different interpretations, but the structure of the sentence is exactly the same in both cases. Where intentional, such ambiguity often has humorous, ironic or subversive effects.

More interesting are *structural ambiguities*, in which the words have the same meanings, but quite different structures can be assigned to the entire string of words, producing different meanings. Examples: *Small boys and girls are easily frightened*; *Exploding mines can be dangerous*; *The shooting of the hunters was appalling*; *Anne likes horses more than Mark.* In the first two of these, the different structures can be easily represented by **tree** diagrams, and such cases are called *surface-structure ambiguities*. In the last two, the tree structures appear to be identical in both readings (interpretations), and we need to appeal to more abstract levels of representation to identify the differences in structure; these are *deep-structure ambiguities.*

Complex cases are possible, involving both lexical and structural ambiguities, as in the classic *Janet made the robot fast*, which has an astonishing number of quite different readings.

The concept of ambiguity can be extended to cases which are only ambiguous when spoken, and not when written. Simple cases of this are *an ice-box* versus *a nice box* or *a slide-rule* versus *a sly drool.* The mishearing of song lyrics demonstrates the phenomenon, where they are known as *mondegreens* after a *Harper's* magazine columnist in 1954 confessed to mishearing a folk-ballad lyric *They ha'e slain the Earl of Murray, and they laid him on the Green* as *They ha'e slain the Earl of Murray and Lady Mondegreen.* Other examples include: *all eyes and chest* for Simon and Garfunkel's *all lies and jest*; *The ants are my friends, they're blowin' in the wind* for Dylan's *The answer, my friend, is blowin' in the wind*; *I'm a turtle crawlin' out of Michelle* for Shaggy's *I'm a turtle crawlin' outta me shell*; and *In the meadow we can build a snowman; then pretend that he is sparse and brown* for the actual *In the meadow we can build a snowman; then pretend that he is Parson Brown*, from 'Winter Wonderland'.

See also: **meaning**; **structure**

Further reading: Cruse 1986; Kempson 1977.

ANALOGY

A type of **language change** in which some forms are deliberately changed merely to make them look more like other forms. The ordinary processes of language change, including perfectly regular changes in pronunciation, have the effect of introducing irregularities. Speakers sometimes react to the presence of irregularities in their language by eliminating them and making the irregular forms regular; this is one kind of *analogy*.

For example, when Latin was changing into French, the pronunciation of stressed /a/ and that of unstressed /a/ developed differently, in a perfectly regular manner: stressed /a/ became the *diphthong* /ai/, while unstressed /a/ remained /a/. This led to apparently irregular variations in the stems of certain verbs, as with the verb meaning 'love'; compare the first two columns in the following table (here an acute accent marks the position of the Latin stress):

	Latin	Old French	Mod. French
1Sg	ámo	aim	aime
2Sg	ámas	aimes	aimes
3Sg	ámat	aimet	aime
1Pl	amámus	amons	aimons
2Pl	amátis	amez	aimez
3Pl	ámant	aiment	aiment

15

As you can see, the stem of the verb fluctuated between *aim-* and *am-* in Old French in a seemingly unpredictable way (the Latin stress was also lost in Old French). As a result, speakers subjected the forms in *am-* to analogy, producing the modern French forms shown in the third column (there have been further changes in pronunciation, of course, but these are not relevant here). Analogy can be far less systematic than this, and it can even turn regular forms into irregular ones. Many formerly irregular English verbs have been turned into regular verbs by the analogy of cases like *love/loved*; an example is *work/wrought*, which has been analogized to *work/worked*. On the other hand, in Early Modern English, the past tense of *catch* was the regular *catched*, but this has been replaced by *caught*, apparently by analogy with *taught*, and many Americans have replaced *dive/dived* with *dive/dove*, by analogy with verbs like *drive/drove*.

See also: **language change**; **semantics**

Further reading: Trask 1996.

ANAPHOR

A linguistic item which takes its interpretation from something else referred to in the same sentence or discourse. In the sentence *Susie wants to get a job in Paris, but she needs to improve her French first*, the item *she*, in the most obvious interpretation, means Susie. We say that *she* is an **anaphor**, and that *Susie* is the **antecedent** of *she*; the relationship between these two items is one of **anaphora**, or **binding**, and *she* is **bound** by *Susie*. Further examples of anaphors include *herself* in *Susie injured herself* (antecedent *Susie*) and *each other* in *Susie and Mike are seeing a lot of each other* (antecedent *Susie* and *Mike*). Anaphoric reference involves 'pointing back' to the antecedent, where the antecedent is often the most fully realized lexical item. Sometimes the less full item occurs first (*She needs to improve her French, Susie does*, or *He knew something was wrong when he arrived. Henry looked around himself anxiously*). This phenomenon of 'pointing forward' is called **cataphora**. Likewise, the antecedent of an anaphor need not be in the same sentence. Consider this: *Susie is looking run-down. I think she needs a holiday.* Here the antecedent *Susie* is in a different sentence from the anaphor *she* which points to it.

16

It is possible for a *zero-element* (a null element) to be an anaphor: instead of saying *Susie needs a new car but she doesn't have the money*, we can say *Susie needs a new car but doesn't have the money*. In the second version, instead of the overt anaphor *she*, we have only a piece of silence, but the interpretation is the same. For linguistic purposes, we often write the second version with the symbol ø (meaning 'zero') or e (for 'empty') in the appropriate place: *Susie needs a new car but* e *doesn't have the money*. The zero anaphor represented as e is often called an *empty category*.

In linguistic descriptions, it is common practice to use *referential indices*, usually subscript letters, to indicate explicitly which anaphors have which antecedents; items which are *coindexed* (have the same subscripts) are *coreferential* (refer to the same thing), while those which have different subscripts refer to different things. So, for example, *Mike$_i$ has found his$_i$ dog* means 'Mike has found his own dog', while *Mike$_i$ has found his$_j$ dog* means 'Mike has found somebody else's dog' (here the preceding context must make it clear who owns the dog).

Anaphora in general, and empty categories in particular, pose many intricate problems of linguistic analysis, and in recent years they have been the object of intensive investigations. Theoretical linguists are fascinated by the seemingly complex nature of the rules governing the use of anaphors, and grammatical theorists have often seen the elucidation of these rules as a matter of fundamental importance. At the same time, **functional** linguists are deeply interested in the ways in which anaphors are used to structure discourses. **Psycholinguists** are interested in whether anaphoric reference is to the pre-text or to the situation modelled mentally out of that text, and linguists with **typological** or anthropological interests have devoted considerable attention to the various ways in which anaphors are employed in different languages.

See also: **gap**; **pronoun**

Further reading: Barss 2003; Huddleston 1984.

ANIMAL COMMUNICATION

The signalling systems used by non-human creatures. Most of the other creatures on the planet can communicate with other members of their species in one way or another, and often by specialized vocal noises termed *calls*. But the signalling systems of these creatures are vastly different from human language. First, they lack **duality of patterning**: they are based on the principle of 'one sound, one meaning', and neither sounds nor meanings can be modified or combined. Consequently, they lack **open-endedness**: only a tiny number of different meanings can be expressed. They lack **displacement**: 'utterances' are confined to the here and now. They lack **stimulus–freedom**: a call is produced always and only when the appropriate stimulus is present, and there is no choice.

Hence non-human creatures live in a communicative world which is alien to us: it is bounded by the horizon, lacking a past or a future, consisting only of the endless repetition of a few familiar messages about what's going on at the moment. Moreover, unlike human languages, with their ceaseless and rapid changes, the signals used by other species never change by any process faster than evolutionary change.

There are marginal exceptions: honeybee dances contain a limited amount of displacement; bird songs possibly contain an element of duality; whale songs change from year to year; a fox may occasionally give a danger call in the absence of any danger merely to distract her cubs from a meal she is trying to eat. But these exceptions are inconsequential: animal signals do not remotely approximate to human language, and they cannot be regarded as simpler versions of it.

Since all these statements are true of our closest living relatives, the apes, it follows that our non-human ancestors of a few million years ago also had such a limited system. Attempts at teaching scaled-down versions of human language to apes and other creatures have often been vitiated by poor procedure, but there is now a small amount of evidence suggesting that these creatures, when intensively trained under laboratory conditions, can learn at least the rudiments of a human language, though no more.

See also: **design features; origin and evolution of language; protolanguage hypothesis**

Further reading: Crystal 1997; Malmkjær 2004; Steinberg 1993; Trask 1995; Wallman 1992.

ANTHROPOLOGICAL LINGUISTICS

The study of the relation between language and culture. Anthropologists generally find it necessary to learn the languages of the people they are studying, and they realized early that the languages themselves might provide valuable clues about the cultures under investigation. In the late nineteenth century, the anthropologist Franz Boas in the USA laid particular stress upon the importance of Native American languages in the study of Native American cultures and, thanks to his influence and that of his student Edward Sapir, American linguistics was largely born out of anthropology. As a result, American linguistics long retained an anthropological orientation, and indeed most linguists worked in anthropology departments until the middle of the twentieth century. In Britain, the anthropologist Bronislaw Malinowski drew comparable attention to the study of languages in the early twentieth century, and his ideas greatly influenced J.R. Firth, widely regarded as the founder of linguistics in Britain.

The explosive growth of areas like **sociolinguistics**, **psycholinguistics** and linguistic theory during the past few decades has not obliterated interest in anthropological linguistics, which is now recognized as a distinctive discipline in its own right; it is sometimes also called *linguistic anthropology*. Anthropological linguists have been greatly interested in such topics as **kinship** systems, colour terms, **metaphors**, systems for conferring **names** upon people and places, connections between languages and myths, *folk taxonomies* (systems for classifying animals and plants), the treatment of space and time in languages, the expression of **sex differences** and **social** differences in speech, and the structure of **narratives**; more than most linguists, they have been intrigued by the **linguistic relativity** hypothesis.

See also: **cognitive linguistics**; **ethnography of communication**; **linguistic relativity**

Further reading: Bonvillain 1993; Crystal 1997; Duranti 1997; Foley 1997; Palmer 1996.

APHASIA

Disordered language resulting from brain damage. Strictly speaking, we should say *dysphasia* (which means 'disordered speech') for damage to the language faculties and reserve *aphasia* (which means 'absence of speech') for cases in which the victim's language faculties are totally destroyed. However, in practice the two terms are used interchangeably, and the most profound and severe cases are distinguished as *global aphasia*.

That damage to the head can produce language disorders has been known since ancient times. But it was only in the mid-nineteenth century that scientists began to investigate the problem systematically, by studying the symptoms of brain-damaged patients and then, after the victims' deaths, by carrying out *postmortem* examinations to see which areas of the brain had been damaged. The French surgeon Paul Broca found that damage to a particular area of the brain, with a high degree of consistency, produced an aphasia characterized by painful, halting speech and a near-total absence of grammar; today the area he identified is called *Broca's area*, and the associated aphasia is called *Broca's aphasia*. A few years later, the German neurologist Carl Wernicke identified a second area of the brain, damage to which consistently produces a different aphasia, characterized by fluent but senseless speech and grave difficulties in comprehension: we now speak of *Wernicke's area* and *Wernicke's aphasia*. Broca's area and Wernicke's area are now known to be two of the most important **language areas** in the brain, each with responsibilities for specific aspects of language.

In practice, no victim ever suffers damage exclusively to one neatly defined area of the brain, and consequently every sufferer exhibits a somewhat distinctive range of symptoms. The complexity of aphasia rather discouraged further research during much of the twentieth century. However, in the middle of that century the American neurologist Norman Geschwind revived interest in the subject, confirmed the existence of distinct language areas in the brain, and developed a classification of aphasias which is now more or less standard. For example, Broca's and Wernicke's areas are connected by a bundle of fibres called the *arcuate fasciculus*, and damage to this produces a third type of aphasia, *conduction aphasia*, with specific symptoms of its own. Recent evidence from *magnetic resonance imaging* (MRI scans) of the brain is confirming many of the hypotheses of early **neurolinguistics**.

It has also been discovered that brain damage affects users of **sign language** in precisely the same way as it affects users of spoken language. This confirms that what is damaged is **language**, and not merely the ability to speak or to perceive speech. It is crucial to distinguish aphasia from *speech defects*, which result merely from damage to the nerves or muscles controlling the speech organs, and have no consequences for the language faculty itself.

See also: **language areas**; **language disability**; **neurolinguistics**; **speech therapy**

Further reading: Crystal 1997; Malmkjær 2004; O'Grady *et al.* 1996.

APPARENT TIME

A technique for studying **language change** in progress. One way of studying language change in a community is to examine the speech of that community at intervals over several generations. But such *real-time* studies are often not practical: several generations of researchers might be involved; universities are unlikely to fund such long-term projects; and techniques of fieldwork and analysis will change so radically that early data become unreliable.

An alternative is the use of *apparent time*. In this approach, we begin by assuming that individuals normally acquire their speech habits early in life and thereafter rarely change them. If this is so, then a comparison of the speech of elderly, middle-aged and younger speakers in a community will reveal any linguistic changes which are in progress: the younger the speakers, the more conspicuously their speech will be affected by any changes in progress.

Pioneered by the American linguist William Labov in the 1960s, apparent-time studies have proved to be a powerful tool in examining language change, even though it has been found that, in certain circumstances, older speakers actually *do* change their speech later in life.

See also: **language change**; **quantitative approach**; **sociolinguistics**

Further reading: Labov 1994; Llamas *et al.* 2007.

APPLIED LINGUISTICS

The application of the concepts and methods of **linguistics** to any of various practical problems involving language. The term *applied linguistics* is most often encountered in connection with foreign-language teaching. Linguistic concepts find a number of uses here, for example in *contrastive linguistics* – the systematic comparison of the sounds, the words and the grammatical systems of the mother tongue and the language being learned – with the intention of bringing out the important differences which need to be mastered. But linguistics has also proved useful in a variety of other practical domains, such as mother-tongue teaching, **lexicography**, translation, the teaching of reading, **forensic linguistics**, and the diagnosis and treatment of **language disability**. Today all these are understood as forming part of applied linguistics, such that the term is used by many simply in contrast with *theoretical linguistics* to emphasize its practical, fieldwork-based, data-driven and empirical nature.

See also: **language planning**; **sociolinguistics**; **stylistics**

Further reading: Cook 2003; Corder 1975; Cotterill 2002; Crystal 1997; Davies 1999; Emmitt *et al.* 2006; O'Grady *et al.* 1996; Pennycook 2001; Richards *et al.* 1992; Schmitt 2002.

ARBITRARINESS

The absence of any necessary connection between the form of a **word** and its meaning. Every language typically has a distinct word to denote every object, activity and concept its speakers want to talk about. Each such word must be formed in a valid manner according to the phonology of the language. But, in most cases, there is absolutely no reason why a given meaning should be denoted by one sequence of sounds rather than another. In practice, the particular sequence of sounds selected in a given language is completely arbitrary: anything will do, so long as speakers agree about it.

Speakers of different languages, of course, make different choices. A certain large snouted animal is called a *pig* in English, a *Schwein* in German, a *cochon* in French, a *cerdo* in Spanish, a *mochyn* in Welsh, a *txerri* in Basque, a *numbran* in Yimas (a language of New Guinea), and so on across the world. None of these names is more suitable than any other: each works fine as long as speakers are in agreement.

Such agreement need not be for all time. The animal was formerly called a *swine* in English, but this word has dropped out of use as a name for the animal and been replaced by *pig*.

Arbitrariness can be demonstrated the other way round. Many languages allow a word to have the phonetic form [min], but there is no earthly way of predicting the meaning of this word if it should exist. In English, [min] (spelled *mean*) exists and has several unrelated meanings: 'tight-fisted', 'cruel', 'average', 'signify'. French *mine* means '(coal) mine'; Welsh *min* is 'edge'; Irish *min* is 'meal'; Basque *min* is 'pain'; Arabic *min* is 'from'. There is nothing about this sequence of sounds that makes one meaning more likely than another. Arbitrariness is pervasive in human languages (and also in **animal communication**), but there does nonetheless exist a certain amount of **iconicity**: cases in which the relation between form and meaning is not totally arbitrary.

Unfortunately, even with some iconicity, it is the presence of massive arbitrariness which makes impossible the **universal translator** beloved of science-fiction films, unless the machine worked by telepathy rather than linguistics. Because of arbitrariness, even the most powerful computer program can have no way of guessing the meaning of a word it has not encountered before.

Linguists have long realized the importance of arbitrariness, but it was particularly stressed by the Swiss linguist Ferdinand de Saussure in the early twentieth century, with his concept of the **linguistic sign**.

See also: **design features**; **iconicity**; **linguistic sign**; **semantics**; **sound symbolism**

Further reading: Trask 1995.

ARGUMENT

Any one of the **noun phrases** required by a particular **verb**. Each verb requires some number of noun phrases (NPs) to accompany it in a sentence, if the result is to be grammatical; these NPs are its *arguments*, and the number of NPs required by a verb is the *valency* of that verb. For example, the simple intransitive verbs *smile* and *arrive* are **monovalent**, requiring only one argument, the subject, as in *Susie smiled*. (Note that **Susie smiled Natalie* is ungrammatical; the asterisk marks this). In contrast, a simple transitive verb like *kiss* or *slap* is **divalent**, requiring a subject and one object, as in *Susie kissed Natalie*. (Note that **Susie kissed* is ungrammatical). But a ditransitive verb like *give* or *show* is **trivalent**, requiring a subject and two objects, as in *Susie gave Mike a present*. A given English verb usually requires between one and three arguments, but note the unusual behaviour of the verb *rain*, which neither requires nor permits any arguments at all, except for the 'dummy' subject *it*, as in *It's raining*. This verb arguably has a valency of zero.

In addition to its arguments, a verb very often permits some further phrases which are optional. These optional phrases are **adjuncts**, and adjuncts in English are most often expressed as **prepositional phrases** or as **adverbial phrases**. For example, the minimal sentence *Susie kissed Natalie* can be expanded with some optional adjuncts to yield *Susie kissed Natalie on the neck in the kitchen this morning* (there are three adjuncts here).

See also: **complement**; **grammatical relation**; **transitivity**

Further reading: Butt and King 2000; Kroeger 2004; van Valin 2001.

ARTIFICIAL LANGUAGE

A language deliberately invented by a particular person. Since the seventeenth century, hundreds of artificial languages have been invented; some of them were no more than sketches, while others were provided with extensive grammars and large vocabularies. Only a handful of these have ever gained any use.

Many of the earlier attempts were made by philosophers, and these were often *a priori* in nature, meaning that they paid no attention to existing languages but were put together according to whatever principles seemed good to the inventors. More than a few were intended to be 'universal' or 'logical' languages and were based on some grand scheme for classifying all human knowledge. All were deeply impractical. Among the more notable attempts were those of the Frenchman Descartes, the Scot Dalgarno and the Englishman Wilkins.

Since the nineteenth century, artificial languages have more usually been *a posteriori*, that is, derived in some way from existing languages, and they have been constructed by linguists, logicians, priests, politicians, oculists and businessmen. The German philosopher Leibniz had much earlier proposed a kind of regularized Latin with only a small number of endings, and the French politician Faiguet had likewise sketched out a kind of regularized French, in both cases to no effect. In 1880 the German priest Schleyer published Volapük, an enormously awkward and complex mixture of bits of several European languages with cumbersome grammatical endings of his own devising; the result resembled a kind of demented

Swedish, but it attracted hundreds of thousands of followers for a few years. Then in 1887 the Polish oculist Zamenhof published Esperanto, a much simpler language also stitched together from bits and pieces of several European languages, and this has ever since been the world's single most widely learned and used artificial language.

Esperanto still has a number of cumbersome features, and simplified versions called Ido, Esperantido, Espido, Esperantuisho and Modern Esperanto have been constructed, with minimal success. The Danish linguist Jespersen constructed a greatly modified offshoot called Novial, which attracted little interest. The Italian logician Peano invented Latino Sine Flexione, a kind of simplified and regularized Latin, and the American writer Hogben followed with Interglossa, essentially a version of classical Greek with no wordendings at all. A kind of regularized common Romance called Interlingua was constructed by a group of people and has found some limited use, especially for scientific purposes. A modified and expanded version of Interglossa now called Glosa has recently been published. And dozens of other twentieth-century projects have been put forward only to sink without trace.

Worthy of mention is Basic English, a stripped-down version of English employing only 850 words and published in 1930 by the British scholar C.K. Ogden; this was popular for a while, but it proved unworkable and has disappeared.

All of these *conlangs* (constructed languages) are of the *auxlang* (auxiliary language) type. However, there are many *artlangs* developed for artistic purposes. The fantasy writer J.R.R. Tolkien invented not one but several languages for his novel *The Lord of the Rings*, and he even provided some of them with histories, sound changes, family trees and writing systems (most of which draw on Finnish, Old Icelandic and Welsh). The linguist Marc Okrand was commissioned to invent a Klingon language for the *Star Trek* films, and there are now Klingon translations of the Bible and Shakespeare. Lastly, *loglangs* (logical languages) such as computer-programming languages can have a practical purpose, though most (like 'Loglan' and its descendant 'Lojban' maintained by the Logical Language Group) display a fundamental wrong-headedness about what a language is and what it is used for.

See also: **language**; **natural-language processing**

Further reading: Bodmer 1944; Crystal 1997; Large 1985; Malmkjær 2004.

ASPECT

The **grammatical category** representing distinctions in the temporal structure of an event. Quite independently of its location in time, an event may be viewed as having any of a number of different temporal organizations: it may be seen as having internal structure or as consisting of an unanalysable whole; it may be seen as extending over a period of time or as occurring in a single moment; it may be seen as a single occurrence or as a series of repeated occurrences; it may be seen as beginning, continuing or ending. All these and others are types of *aspect*.

Compared with many other languages, English has a rather modest aspectual system, but aspect is still important in English. Here are some examples. The sentence *She smoked* illustrates **perfective** aspect (the event is viewed as an unanalysable whole); *She was smoking* shows **continuous** (or **progressive**) aspect (the event is viewed as extending over time); *She used to smoke* exhibits **habitual** aspect (the event is viewed as a customary or habitual one); *She kept smoking* illustrates **iterative** aspect (the action is viewed as a series of repeated events); *She started smoking* exhibits **inchoative** aspect (the event is viewed as just beginning); and *She quit smoking* exhibits **conclusive** aspect (the event is viewed as drawing to a close). The second, third and fourth of these all represent differing types of **imperfective** aspect (the action is viewed as having some kind of internal structure).

Some other languages display further aspectual forms, such as the **punctual** aspect (the event is viewed as occurring in a single moment); English has no special form for this, and we use our perfective form, as in *She sneezed*. But compare Basque, which distinguishes *Agertu zen* 'She appeared' (for a moment) from *Agertzen zen* 'She appeared' (over a period of time). The African-American variety of English has a **completive** aspect (*She done talked*) and Jamaican English has a **narrative** aspect (*She bin talked*).

English has another distinctive form, the **perfect**, which has several functions but most typically expresses a state resulting from an earlier event. For example, the perfect form *She had finished the wine* most obviously means 'There was no wine then because she drank the last of it earlier'. The perfect is often classed as an aspect, although it is decidedly unusual among aspects. (Note that **perfective** and **perfect** have very different meanings; even some textbooks get these two confused).

Aspect must be carefully distinguished from **tense**, even though the formal expression of the two categories is often deeply intertwined in languages. All of the English examples above are in the past tense, and all of them have corresponding non-past ('present') forms, except that the perfective *She smoked* and the habitual *She used to smoke* both have the same present-tense counterpart, *She smokes*, which most often has the habitual sense. Crudely, English has only two tenses (past and present) marked morphologically; all other time characteristics are expressed by aspect.

Certain types of aspect-like distinctions may be expressed by lexical means, rather than grammatically; an example is the contrast among English *nibble, eat, devour*. A distinction expressed in this way is called an ***Aktionsart*** or ***lexical aspect***. Similarly, a verb can carry a sense of its own duration: *to make a table* carries its own completion in a way that *to sit at a table* does not (it would be odd to talk of *finishing sitting*): a verb like the former with a natural ending is ***telic***, and the latter verb is ***atelic***.

See also: **grammatical category**; **tense**

Further reading: Binnick 1991; Comrie 1976; Dahl 1985.

AUTOLEXICAL GRAMMAR

A model of grammar proposed by Jerrold Sadock in the 1980s, in which **morphology**, **syntax** and **semantics** are regarded as independent modules with a **phrase-structure grammar**. The modules are brought together at the ***interface*** by the **lexicon**, which matches up the three modules. Only sentences which do not violate the rules of all three modules are regarded as well-formed sentences. Autolexical grammar was developed from the viewpoint of languages which feature morphosyntactic mismatches (such as the Kalaallisut of Western Greenland), and then subsequently applied to English, where it accounts particularly well for spoken forms.

See also: **lexicon**; **phrase-structure grammar**

Further reading: Sadock 1991.

AUTONOMY

The view that the human **language faculty** is independent of general mental and cognitive abilities. A young child is obliged to spend years learning to make sense of the world it is born into, and at the same time it must learn its first language. For decades there has been a controversy, sometimes called the **nature-nurture debate** or the **content-process debate**, over whether children are born with a distinctive and largely independent faculty for learning language, or whether they simply acquire a language in the same way they acquire other kinds of understanding and skills, by using their general all-purpose cognitive abilities.

The first view – represented by such proposals as the **genetic hypothesis of language** and the **innateness hypothesis** – is probably supported by a majority of theoretical linguists. The second has been supported by a number of psychologists, and has recently been most strongly articulated within **cognitive linguistics**. The first view holds that children are born with specialized structures or areas in their brains which are dedicated to the learning and use of languages; Chomsky's version further holds that important information about the nature of human languages is already present at birth. The second view denies this, and sees language acquisition as not different in kind from, say, learning to judge size and distance; some versions go further and claim that learning a first language is not different from learning to ice skate or to drive a car.

This last, extreme, view can probably be disposed of: the abundant evidence for the **critical period hypothesis**, demonstrating that first-language acquisition is rapid in children but impossible in adults, surely demonstrates that learning a first language is very different from learning to ice skate. Otherwise, though, the debate is still very much alive.

Linguists like to support the first view by pointing to the evidence from **language disability**: some disabilities, such as the *Williams syndrome*, appear to leave the language faculties intact while severely damaging other mental faculties; others, such as *Specific Language Impairment*, chiefly affect only linguistic behaviour while leaving other mental faculties largely unscathed. Supporters of the second view point to continuities and common properties between language and other visual, aural, tactile and spatial development.

See also: **cognitive linguistics**; **critical period hypothesis**; **genetic hypothesis of language**; **innateness hypothesis**; **language disability**; **language faculty**

Further reading: Bates 1976; Bates *et al.* 1979, 1988; Jackendoff 1993; Macwhinney and Bates 1989; Pinker 1994.

AUXILIARY

A specialized grammatical item, most often part of a **verb phrase**, which serves to express any of several **grammatical categories**. The English auxiliaries are specialized verbs; they chiefly serve to express **aspect**, **voice** and **modality**, and they commonly also carry markers of **tense** and **agreement**. The English auxiliary verbs possess several properties not shared by ordinary verbs.

- Negation: *She is running; She isn't running/She is not running.* Compare *She smokes*; **She smokesn't*; **She smokes not* (the asterisk marks ungrammaticality).
- Inversion: *She is running; Is she running?* Compare *She runs*; **Runs she?*
- Ellipsis: *Susie is running, but Janet isn't.*
- Emphasis: *She did run.*
- Tagging: *She did run, didn't she?*

The English auxiliaries are of two types. The ***primary*** (or ***nonmodal***) ***auxiliaries*** are *be* and *have*. These resemble ordinary main verbs in having a full set of inflected forms (*have, has, had, having*), and a primary auxiliary can be the only verb in a sentence: *She is British*; *He has brown eyes.* The ***modal auxiliaries*** have only one or two forms each; most of them come in pairs, which can to some extent be regarded as differing in tense: *can/could, will/would; shall/ should; may/might; must.* These lack the -*s* ending of the third-singular present: **She cans speak French.*

The verbs *need, dare* and *ought* sometimes exhibit some (but not all) of the properties of modal auxiliaries; these are called the ***semimodals***. Examples: *Need she come? She dare not do it, but she ought to.* The verb *do* serves as a 'dummy' auxiliary, inserted to carry the auxiliary properties when no other auxiliary is present. Examples: *She doesn't smoke; Does she smoke?*; *Janet doesn't smoke, but Susie does; She does smoke.*

In some other languages, such as Australian languages, the auxiliaries are not verbs at all, but an entirely distinct part of speech. Some linguists prefer to take the same view of the English auxiliaries.

See also: **subcategorization**; **verb**; **verb phrase**

Further reading: Coates 1983; Frawley 2006; Hurford 1994; Palmer 2001.

BASIC WORD ORDER

The most typical order of elements in the sentences of a language. Almost every language shows a strong preference to put the words of a sentence into a particular order; this preferred order may be virtually rigid – with almost no departures allowed – or it may be little more than a statistical preference. This preference is the *basic word order* of the language.

A convenient and widely used way of characterizing basic word order is in terms of just three major elements: **Subject**, *Object* and **Verb**, or S, O and V. The basic word order of English, in these terms, is SVO: we normally say *The Turks love backgammon*, while *Backgammon the Turks love* is unusual, and other orders, such as **Love the Turks backgammon* or **Backgammon love the Turks* are impossible. SVO order is also typical of French, Swahili and Chinese, among others.

Other languages have different basic word orders. VSO is found in Irish and Welsh, SOV in Japanese, Turkish, Basque and Quechua, and VOS in Malagasy (in Madagascar). The Amazonian language Hixkaryana is OVS, and there are reports that another Amazonian language, Apuriña, may be OSV.

It appears that SOV order is the most frequent on the planet, followed closely by SVO and more distantly by VSO. VOS is decidedly uncommon, and OVS and OSV are, at best, very rare. No one knows if these observations represent important human preferences in grammatical structure or if they are merely historical accidents resulting from the survival and spread of some languages at the expense of others.

See also: **typology**

Further reading: Comrie 1989; Whaley 1997.

BEHAVIOURISM

The view that psychology should invoke only observable and measurable phenomena. Early in the twentieth century, psychology had become somewhat obscurantist and even metaphysical. Behaviourism originated as a healthy reaction to this state of affairs: the early behaviourists wanted to sweep away what they saw as empty speculation and the endless postulation of undetectable concepts. They therefore resolved to deal with nothing except what could be directly observed and preferably measured. Along with their rejection of the excess baggage of earlier approaches, they often went so far as to reject such intangible concepts as 'emotions', 'intentions', 'purposes' and even 'minds'.

Behaviourism exercised great influence over the linguist Leonard Bloomfield and the *American structuralists* who followed him: they, too, preferred to concentrate on directly observable linguistic behaviour and to refrain from abstract theorizing.

In 1957 the American psychologist B.F. Skinner published *Verbal Behavior*, an attempt at interpreting **language acquisition** strictly in terms of behaviourism, and by far the most radical attempt ever at treating language in a behaviourist framework. Skinner's book was savagely (some would say unfairly) reviewed by the young Noam Chomsky, who argued vigorously that Skinner's approach not only explained nothing but could not possibly explain anything of interest. (More recent work on acquisition has reinforced Chomsky's arguments by demonstrating that first-language acquisition is clearly not, as Skinner had maintained, an essentially passive affair, but that young children actively construct their language as they go). Fair or not, Chomsky's review persuaded a whole generation of linguists that the essentially atheoretical behaviourist approach had nothing to offer linguistics. As a result, the linguists influenced by Chomsky abandoned behaviourism and embraced **mentalism** instead, and linguistics was eventually integrated into the emerging discipline of **cognitive science**.

See also: **language acquisition**; **language instinct**; **mentalism**

Further reading: Malmkjær 2004; Pinker 1994; Trask 1995.

BILINGUALISM

The ability to speak two languages. In modern western society, the ability to speak two languages is often seen as something of a remarkable achievement, particularly in the English-speaking countries. However, over 70 per cent of the Earth's population are thought to be bilingual or *multilingual* (able to speak three or more languages), and there is good reason to believe that bilingualism or multilingualism has been the norm for most human beings at least for the past few millennia. There is evidence that children raised bilingually tend to be more expressive, more original and better communicators than children raised with only one language.

In New Guinea, in south-east Asia, in India, in the Caucasus, in the Amazon rainforest, people routinely learn two or three neighbouring languages as well as their own, and the same was true of Australia before the European settlement. Even today, many millions of Europeans are at least bilingual, speaking both their own mother tongue and the national language of the country they live in, and many of them can additionally speak a *global language* or *world language* like English or French.

Bilingualism can be the property of an individual, but equally it can be the property of an entire **speech community** in which two or more languages are routinely used. The existence of bilingual and multilingual societies raises a number of important social, political and educational issues. In what languages should education be delivered, and at what levels? What languages should be accepted for publication and broadcasting? In what languages should laws be written, and what languages should be accepted in court proceedings? Differences of opinion may lead to *language conflict*, as speakers jostle for the right to use their own mother tongues in the widest possible domain, possibly to the exclusion of other languages.

It is also possible for an individual to speak two different **dialects** of a single language – for example, her own regional dialect and the **standard language**. In this case, we speak of *bidialectalism*.

See also: **code-switching**; **diglossia**; **minority language**

Further reading: Bonvillain 1993; Crystal 1997; Edwards 1994, 2004; Heller 2007; Li 2000; Romaine 1995; Steinberg 1993; Zentella 1997.

BIOPROGRAM HYPOTHESIS

The hypothesis that human beings are born with a 'default' structure for language built into their brains. Human languages differ rather substantially in their grammatical structures (for example, in their **basic word order**). However, **creoles** all over the world appear to be strikingly similar in their grammar: all creoles look pretty much alike, regardless of where they came into existence or of which languages provided most of the input into them.

The linguist Derek Bickerton has proposed an explanation for this observation. Since creoles are newly created languages, built out of the reduced **pidgins** which preceded them, and since the children who create a creole are obliged to build its grammar for themselves, Bickerton argues that there must be some kind of innate machinery which determines the nature of that grammar. He calls this machinery the *bioprogram*, and he sees the bioprogram as an innate default structure for language which is always implemented by children unless they find themselves learning an adult language with a different structure, in which case they learn that instead. The bioprogram hypothesis therefore represents a rather specific and distinctive version of the **innateness hypothesis**.

See also: **genetic hypothesis of language**; **innateness hypothesis**

Further reading: Bickerton 1981, 1984; Holm 1988–9, 2000.

BLACK ENGLISH

The distinctive varieties of English used by many native speakers of African or Caribbean origin, and now more usually called *African-American (Vernacular) English*. Several important English-speaking countries have sizable populations of black people whose ancestry lies largely in Africa or the Caribbean; most prominent here are Britain and the USA. For various historical reasons, the majority of British and American black people, as well as many ethnically white people living in connected areas of the southern and eastern USA, speak varieties of English which are quite distinctive, differing from other varieties in vocabulary, pronunciation, grammar and modes of discourse.

These varieties of English exhibit characteristics which are often of considerable linguistic interest: for example, many have highly unusual verbal systems which make distinctions unknown in other types of English. It is possible that some of these features may continue characteristics of the **creoles** once used by the ancestors of the present-day speakers, and a few may even continue features present in the mother tongues of Africans sold into slavery long ago.

But the primary reasons for the recent interest in black varieties are not linguistic, but rather social, political and educational. Like speakers of other distinctive varieties, speakers of Black English often regard their mother tongue as a badge of identity and a matter of pride: abandoning it may be seen as an act of betrayal. At the same time, just as with other groups, failure to acquire a command of standard English is a serious obstacle to making a career in all but a few professions, and Black English itself may be strongly stigmatized among white speakers in formal settings, though it has been extremely influential and prestigious amongst younger speakers of English of all races in Britain and the USA.

Consequently, politicians, academics, teachers and school administrators, both black and white, are faced with some difficult questions of how to regard Black English. Some people advocate the extreme position of recognizing and teaching only standard English and of attempting to stamp out Black English. Most linguists, and some others, would see this stance as unworkable and destructive, and would advocate the encouragement of **bidialectalism**: competence in both Black English and standard English.

Recently, however, a number of influential commentators, particularly in the USA, have been vigorously advocating another position: Black English, now renamed **Ebonics**, should be recognized not only as the equal of standard English but even as a totally separate language, and it should be the language of instruction in schools and even a school subject itself, a policy already adopted (though only briefly) by at least one American school board. These debates continue, not only amongst politicians and observers but within **sociolinguistics**.

See also: **creole**; **sociolinguistics**

Further reading: Holmes 1992; Llamas *et al.* 2007.

BORROWING

Whenever **speech communities** come into contact, languages often take elements from each other, even if the extent of their mutual influence does not develop further (into **pidginization**, for example). Such *borrowing* is most commonly at the lexical level: words are borrowed where the source language has lexicalized a concept that has become useful in the target language. Examples from English include the useful words *schadenfreude* (from German), *chic* (from French), *spaghetti* (from Italian), *juggernaut* (from Persian), *curry* (from Tamil), and many others. Sometimes these words retain their foreign pronunciation and connotations; sometimes they are thoroughly assimilated. Innovations in politics, science, technology, education, culture, emigration and so on are often signalled by *loan-words* being borrowed from other languages: Latin and Greek for scientific terms, French for culinary and administrative terms, for example. Grammatical words (like modal **auxiliaries, pronouns** and **determiners**) are very rarely borrowed, and the borrowing of syntactic structures is also unusual; where they are borrowed, it is usually an indication of a major sociolinguistic upheaval in the history of the language (as when English lost its Germanic case system, or borrowed many words from French for which words already existed in English).

See also: **language change**; **language contact**

Further reading: Crowley 1997; Fennell 2000.

CASE

The **grammatical category** by which the form of a **noun phrase** varies for grammatical or semantic reasons. Case is indicated **morphologically** usually in the form of **affixing** to **nouns**; where such case-marking exists, the language relies less on word-order to signify relations between the participants in the verbal process. Affixes indicating case are called **inflections**. Not all languages have case, but quite a few do. Consider Basque. The Basque noun phrase *etxea* 'the house' has a number of different case-forms, such as:

Name	Form	Function
Absolutive	*etxea*	intransitive subject; direct object
Ergative	*etxeak*	transitive subject
Dative	*etxeari*	'to the house' (abstract relation)
Genitive	*etxearen*	'of the house' (possessor)
Instrumental	*etxeaz*	'by means of the house'
Comitative	*etxearekin*	'with the house'
Locative	*etxean*	'in the house' (location)
Ablative	*etxetik*	'from/out of the house'
Allative	*etxera*	'to the house' (motion)

A case-language must have at least two case-forms; most have three to six distinct cases, and some, like Basque and Finnish, have a dozen or more. English in its Anglo-Saxon and early Middle English varieties used to distinguish *nominative* (subject), *accusative*

35

(direct object), *genitive* (possessive relations) and *dative* (abstract relations) by attaching case-suffixes to nouns. Now English only has remnants of its case ancestry, in the **pronoun** forms *I/me, yours/ mine, he/him/his* and *she/her/hers*, in *who* and *whom*, and in the genitive case-ending *-es* which is now ellipted with an apostrophe: *Peter's book, the reader's eyes.*

Many different cases have been identified in the world's languages. Here are the most common and their typical functions, though these vary across different languages:

Nominative: subject participant, these nouns are typically unmarked or have a null-inflection.

Accusative: the direct object.

Dative: indirect object.

Genitive: indicating a possessive relationship between one noun and another.

Ablative: indicating motion or movement, sometimes called the adverbial case.

Vocative: used where the noun is a direct address.

Abessive: used to indicate absence, as in the Finnish inflection *-tta*: *rahatta* 'without money'.

Comitative: shows accompaniment or instrumentality, as in the Estonian *-ga: ninaga* 'with a nose'.

Allative: indicates motion or positioning 'onto' or 'on top of'.

Essive: used for a temporary state, as in the Finnish *-na*: *pikku-lapsena* 'as a baby'.

Temporal: used to indicate points in time, as in the Hungarian *-kor*: *karácsonykor* 'at Christmas'.

Aversive: where the noun is something to be feared.

A special case is the *ergative*, which defines the relationship of agency between nouns in a sentence. A very general distinction can be made between *ergative* languages and *nominative* languages, based on how they treat these differences in **transitivity**. Roughly, ergative languages focus their articulation on the agency of the utterance, while nominative languages focus on the subject of the sentence. More specifically, in nominative languages like English the subject of a sentence with a transitive verb and the subject of a sentence with an intransitive verb are treated alike, while direct objects of transitive verbs are treated differently; in ergative languages, the subject of an intransitive verb is treated the same as the direct object of a transitive verb, and it is the subject of transitive verbs that are treated differently. In English for example, the grammar in the two sentences *Helen opened the door* and *The door opened* is quite different, though the agency of the event might be thought of as being the same. A language with an ergative case would articulate these relationships very differently. Examples of ergative languages include Basque, Inuit, Kurdish, Tagalog, Tibetan and many native Australian languages like Dyirbal.

In the **Government-and-Binding Theory**, the idea of case has been generalized and made abstract, and a *Case* (with a capital letter) is assumed to belong to every noun phrase in every grammatical sentence. In this approach, the linguistic realization of Case in the surface structure of the language is a matter of the transformational rules local to the language.

See also: **morphology**; **transitivity**

Further reading: Blake 2001; Dixon 1994; Hurford 1994.

CLAUSE

The largest grammatical unit smaller than a **sentence**. The clause is a traditional and fundamental unit of sentence structure, though the term is not used by all grammarians in exactly the same way.

Traditionally, a clause is a grammatical unit consisting of a **subject** and a **predicate**, and every sentence must consist of one or more clauses. In the following examples, each clause is marked off by brackets.

A *simple sentence* consists only of a single clause: [*Susie has bought a skirt*].

A *compound sentence* consists of two or more clauses of equal rank, usually joined by a connecting word like *and*, *or* or *but*: [*Susie wants children*], but [*her career won't allow them*].

A *complex sentence* consists of two or more clauses where one outranks the others, which are subordinated to it: [*After she got her promotion*], [*Susie bought a new house*].

A clause which is the highest-ranking, or only, clause in its sentence is a *main clause*; a clause which is subordinated to another is a *subordinate clause*. Traditional grammarians usually regarded a subordinate clause as entirely separate from the higher-ranking clause it is attached to, but today linguists normally regard a subordinate clause as forming a part of its higher clause, and the examples below show this.

There are several types of subordinate clause:

An **adverbial clause** is related to its higher clause like an **adverb**: [*Susie develops a rash [whenever she eats strawberries]*].

A **complement clause** is attached to a preceding word (usually a verb or a noun) and 'completes' the sense of that word: [*Susie has decided [that she will look for a new job]*]; [*The rumour [that Susie is quitting] is not true*].

An **embedded question** is a question buried in a larger sentence: [*Susie has not decided [what she is going to do]*].

A **relative clause** modifies a noun: [*The skirt [that Susie bought] is too short*].

Recently some grammarians have been extending the term **clause** to every unit containing a **verb**, including many units traditionally regarded only as **phrases**. Examples: [*Susie's heavy smoking*] is *affecting her health*; *Susie wants* [*to buy a new car*]; [*Having finished her dinner*], *Susie reached for her cigarettes*. This extended usage is not standard, but it is now very widespread. Note that the bracketing system adopted here is convenient for linear text, but expressing syntax in a **tree** diagram is much clearer and more common.

See also: **phrase; sentence; subordination; tree**

Further reading: Collins Cobuild 1990; Crystal 1996; Hurford 1994; Jackson 2002; Jeffries 2006.

CLITIC

A **clitic** is attached to a word (its **host**) and the two are pronounced together but the two are treated separately at the level of syntax. For example, the contractions *'s*, *'ll* and *'m* in *he's running*, *I'll be there*, and *I'm not playing* are all clitics. A clitic is never stressed, even when its host is, which is why it has been argued that *n't* (*couldn't*, *won't*) is not a clitic, since the *not* of the full form (*could not*, *will not*) can never be unstressed. **Determiners** (*the* pronounced both as /ðə/ and /ði/, *a* and *an*) are also treated as clitics, since they cannot appear on their own but must accompany a head noun. Those which precede the host are known as *proclitics*; those which follow the host are *enclitics*; and those (as in Portuguese) which are inserted into the word are *mesoclitics*. *Cliticization* in different languages provides important data on the rules of constituent structure and phonology.

See also: **auxiliary**; **syntax**

Further reading: Heggie and Ordóñez 2004.

CLOZE

A *cloze test* or *cloze procedure* was a popular method in **language testing**, which involved presenting learners with a text from which certain words had been deleted. The student must then fill in the blanks in a way that preserves linguistic well-formedness and demonstrates comprehension. It was popular in the 1970s and 1980s since it was easy to design and assess (it could even be automated), and it could be graded for difficulty from the deletion of simple content words to test understanding, or the deletion of words requiring grammatical **agreement** or *declension*, up to the deletion of **auxiliaries**, **determiners** or **prepositions** to test precise linguistic competence in the second language. However, it came to be criticized on the basis that it actually tested clause-level ability rather than text-level skills, and the cloze-spaces could be guessed at more readily by students with cultural framing knowledge rather than linguistic knowledge. It was also often the case that native-speakers did not score 100 per cent, since they were using more idiomatic or register choices that evaded the cloze design.

Cloze tests continue to be used in the second-language classroom, nevertheless. They have also proven useful in **psycholinguistics** as tests of comprehension, and in **sociolinguistics** as a means of eliciting dialect words from informants.

See also: **applied linguistics**; **sociolinguistics**

Further reading: Buckingham and Yorkey 1984; Oller and Jonz 1994.

CODE-SWITCHING

Changing back and forth between two language varieties, especially in a single conversation. Sociolinguists use the term *code* to denote any identifiable speech variety, including both a particular language and a particular variety of a language. Many speakers have control over at least two varieties of their language (for example, a German-speaker may speak both his local variety of German and standard German), and many more have control over two languages (for example, Welsh/English bilinguals in Wales). Such speakers will shift back and forth between these varieties, depending on such factors as who they are talking to, where they are, and what they are talking about. This is *code-switching*.

Speakers switch between languages, dialects, styles or accents during a conversation usually because the setting itself has changed and demands a different variety: this is *situational code-switching*. Alternatively, speakers can deliberately switch to another code in order to force a new perception of the situation on the other participants: this is called *metaphorical code-switching*. Switching can happen at thematic boundaries in a conversation, between sentences, between clauses, or even as tag-phrases at the end of utterances.

See also: **bilingualism**

Further reading: Auer 1998; Crystal 1997; Holmes 1992; Li 2000; Romaine 1994; Stockwell 2002a.

COGNITIVE LINGUISTICS

An approach to the study of language which is based upon human perception and conceptualization of the world. During the twentieth century the most influential approach to the study of language has been **structuralism**: linguists have largely devoted themselves to the purely structural aspects of language systems themselves, such as sound systems and grammatical systems. A key feature of structuralism is that it concentrates on the internal structure of a language and not on the way in which the language relates to the non-linguistic world.

Naturally, links between languages and the world have not been neglected, and **anthropological linguistics** in particular has been devoted to studying links between language and culture. Since about 1980, however, a growing number of linguists have been devoting serious attention to a more ambitious project: the elucidation of the ways in which linguistic objects and structures reflect the manner in which human beings perceive, categorize and conceptualize the world. This is *cognitive linguistics*: together with *cognitive psychology* and **neurolinguistics** they constitute the field of *cognitive science*.

Among the early contributors to the cognitive approach was the American theoretical linguist George Lakoff, who has written extensively on the importance of **metaphor** in shaping languages. More recently, a number of people with diverse backgrounds have been attempting to analyse linguistic structures in terms of conceptual and perceptual categories like *figure and ground*, **landmark** and **trajector** (something which moves), location in space, events and states, **frames** and **schemas** (*scripts* or *mental models* of real and hypothetical world objects and events), and categories and hierarchies. The American linguist Ronald Langacker has constructed a theory of grammar, called *cognitive grammar*, on the basis of these ideas.

See also: **foregrounding**; **metaphor**; **mentalism**; **schema**

Further reading: Hickmann and Robert 2006; Hiraga 2005; Hofstadter 1979; Johnson-Laird 1983, 1993; Kövecses 2005; Lakoff 1987; Lakoff and Johnson 1980; Langacker 1987–91, 1990; Palmer 1996; Stillings *et al.* 1987; Stockwell 2002b; Ungerer and Schmid 1996.

COHESION

The presence in a **discourse** of explicit linguistic links which provide structure. Among these devices are **anaphors** like *she*, *they*, *this* and *one another*, temporal connectives like *after* and *while*, and logical connectives like *but* and *therefore*. Every one of these items serves to provide some kind of specific link between two other smaller or larger pieces of discourse.

Consider a pair of examples. In the first, the cohesion has gone wrong: *The Egyptians and the Assyrians were carrying standards some 5,000 years ago. They were poles topped with metal figures of animals or gods.* Here the reader might naturally take *they* as referring to the Egyptians and the Assyrians, and is likely to be flummoxed by the continuation. The second version is different: *Some 5,000 years ago, the Egyptians and the Assyrians were carrying standards. These were poles topped with metal figures of animals or gods.* This time the item *these* immediately makes it clear that it is *the standards* which are being referred to, and the continuation is smooth and effortless.

Naturally, the proper use of cohesive devices has long been recognized as a fundamental aspect of good writing, but in recent years linguists have been turning their attention to the analysis of these devices. The term *cohesion* was coined by the British linguist Michael Halliday, and the study of cohesion is especially prominent within Halliday's **Systemic Linguistics**, but it is also now a familiar part of most linguistic analyses of texts and discourses. An important aspect of this is *lexical cohesion*, which describes the ways in which words are related semantically or in relation to the experiential *schemas* which people accumulate through their lives.

Note that cohesion and *coherence* are not necessarily the same thing. A text can be lexicogrammatically cohesive while being utterly incoherent for understanding. Cohesion is a linguistic property, while coherence is a combined linguistic and **cognitive** property.

See also: **Systemic Linguistics**; **text**

Further reading: Halliday 2004; Halliday and Hasan 1976; Masterman and Wilks 2005, Thompson 2004; Wolf and Gibson 2006.

COLLIGATE

Two words display *colligation* if they are related syntagmatically and grammatically: in other words, if they occur close to one another and are significant at the grammatical level. For example, infinitive forms of a verb would colligate with each other, present progressive -*ing* forms would colligate together, phrasal verbs which take the particle *up* (*run up*, *throw up*, *catch up*) would all be colligates. The term is usefully contrasted with *collocation* which is a lexical rather than grammatical relationship. For example, *fat* typically *collocates* with *man*, *lady*, *chance*, *cheque* but not with *brick*, *wine* or *car*. This is not to say that the latter sort of collocations never occur, but collocation is a relatively predictable relationship, and the range of collocational possibilities is known as a word's *collocability*. Both of the terms *colligate* and *collocate* are used extensively in *corpus linguistics*.

See also: **computational linguistics**; **semantics**

Further reading: McEnery and Wilson 2001; McEnery *et al.* 2006.

COMMUNICATIVE COMPETENCE

The ability to use language appropriately in social situations. In order to speak a language successfully, you need to have purely *linguistic competence* in that language: mastery of pronunciation, of grammar and of vocabulary. But you need more than that: you also need *sociolinguistic competence*, knowledge of such things as how to begin and end conversations, how and when to be polite, and how to address people. In addition, you further need *strategic competence*, knowledge of how to organize a piece of speech in an effective manner and how to spot and compensate for any misunderstandings or other difficulties.

The concept and the term were introduced by the American linguist Dell Hymes in the 1970s. Hymes was dismayed by what he saw as the excessively narrow concern of many linguists with nothing but internal linguistic structure, at the expense of communication, and he wished to draw attention to the importance of *appropriateness* in language use.

Today linguists of a theoretical orientation still prefer to focus on the purely structural aspects of language, but those with an interest in **anthropological linguistics**, in **functionalism**, in **sociolinguistics**, in language teaching, or in communication generally typically attach great importance to the examination and elucidation of communicative competence.

See also: **ethnography of communication; sociolinguistics**

Further reading: Bonvillain 1993; Foley 1997.

COMMUNITY OF PRACTICE

A notion from **sociolinguistics** which goes beyond the definition of a **speech community** by encompassing all the cultural and behavioural practices of a group (including linguistic practices), which together serve to define that group. The idea has been particularly fruitful in relation to the study of **gender** and language, since it takes a contextual view of the power relations and ideologies which influence the language practices within a group. The *CoP* approach also suggests that linguistic behaviour is adaptable and variable when the individual moves between different groups in her life, and so it has refocused linguists' minds on the online, provisional and transitory nature of much language usage.

See also: **gender**; **social network**; **sociolinguistics**; **speech community**

Further reading: Eckert and McConnell-Ginet 1992, 1995, 1999, 2003; Wenger 1998.

COMPARATIVE RECONSTRUCTION

The principal method used to find information about an unattested language which is the ancestor of several known languages. Every living language changes over time, but it does not change everywhere in the same way. A language spoken over a sizable area may therefore break up, first into regional **dialects**, and eventually into several quite diverse daughter languages. When we find several languages, either spoken today or abundantly recorded in written texts, which clearly share a common ancestor, we have ways of working backwards to figure out what that unrecorded ancestor was like. Chief among these is *comparative reconstruction*, or the *comparative method*.

The comparative method deals with the phonological forms of words, and its successful use in a given case depends upon the correctness of three assumptions. First, we assume that a significant proportion of the words of the ancestral language still survive in the recorded daughter languages. Second, we assume that those surviving words in most cases have not changed their meanings too dramatically. Third, we assume that phonological change (change in the pronunciations of those words) is generally *regular* – that is, that a given sound in a given environment has consistently changed in exactly the same way in a single daughter language. Only when these three assumptions are substantially correct can we apply the comparative method.

Below is a modest example, showing the words for certain meanings in four European languages for which we have excellent reasons for believing that they share a common ancestor.

English	Latin	Greek	Irish Gaelic
fish	piscis	ikhthys	iasg
father	pater	pater	athair
foot	ped-	pod-	troigh

English	Latin	Greek	Irish Gaelic
for	pro	para	do
six	sex	hexa	sé
seven	septem	hepta	seacht
sweet	suavis	hedys	milis
salt	sal	hal	salann
new	novus	neos	nua
night	noct-	nykt-	(in)nocht 'tonight'
nine	novem	(en)nea	naoi

The key point here is the **systematic correspondences** which we can see in many cases. For the first set, we observe that a native English word beginning with /f/ is matched by a Latin word beginning with /p/ and a Greek word beginning with /p/. The Irish case is a little more difficult, but examination of further data reveals that the usual Irish correspondence here is zero: no initial consonant at all, as in the words for 'fish' and 'father'. The reason that the Irish words for 'foot' and 'for', and also the Greek word for 'fish', do not match is that the ancestral words for these senses have been replaced in these cases by different words. (Remember our first assumption: not too many ancestral words have been lost and replaced.)

Likewise, in the second set, we find initial /s/ consistently in all the languages except Greek, where instead we find initial /h/ with equal consistency. Again, the word for 'sweet' has been lost and replaced in Irish.

The third set exhibits initial /n/ in all four languages, though the Greek word for 'nine' has acquired a prefix absent elsewhere. The Irish word for 'night' does not fit, but the Irish word for 'tonight' does fit, and we may reasonably assume that the word for 'tonight' contains an earlier word for 'night', now itself lost and replaced. (Recall our second assumption: we can tolerate a certain amount of change in meaning, but not too much.)

Now the explanation for these correspondences resides crucially in our third assumption: change in pronunciation has mostly been *regular* in all four languages. So, we conclude, the words in the first group all began with the same sound in the ancestral language, and that sound has developed regularly into /f/ in English, into /p/ in Latin and Greek, and into zero in Irish. Similarly, all the words in the second group began with a *different* same initial sound in the ancestral language, one which has regularly developed into /h/ in

45

Greek but into /s/ in all the others. And all the words in the third group began with yet another same sound in the ancestral language, one which has developed into /n/ in all four languages.

It remains only to decide what the ancestral sounds were in each case, and this is the central step in comparative reconstruction. By examining all the available evidence, and by knowing what kinds of phonological changes are frequent and natural in languages, specialists have determined that, in the ancestral language, all the words in the first group originally began with */p/, those in the second with */s/, and those in the third with */n/. (The asterisk denotes a reconstructed sound.) The original */p/ has changed to /f/ in English and been lost in Irish, and the original */s/ has changed to /h/ in Greek, all of these being changes which are frequent in languages and easy to understand. Apart from these cases, the three ancestral sounds, in initial position, have remained unchanged in all four languages.

Of course, we do not apply the comparative method only to word-initial sounds: we must figure out, as far as possible, what the entire words looked like in the ancestral language. Specialists have managed to determine that the forms of these words in the ancestral language were approximately as follows (endings omitted): *pisk-, * pəter, *ped-, *per, *sweks, *septm, *swad-, *sal-, *newo-, *nekwt- and *newn. The change in pronunciation in each of the four daughter languages has been largely regular, though naturally with a few complications here and there. And the unrecorded ancestral language in this case, of course, is **Proto-Indo-European**, the ancestor of the **Indo-European** family, to which all four languages belong.

The comparative method consists of the entire business of deciding that certain languages probably share a common ancestor, identifying systematic correspondences, and working backwards to identify the forms of the words in the ancestral language, and this method is the cornerstone of work in **historical linguistics**. If we can't find systematic correspondences, then we can't do comparative reconstruction, and any miscellaneous resemblances that we come across are very likely only the result of chance, or perhaps even of ancient **language contact**.

See also: **internal reconstruction**; **reconstruction**; **systematic correspondence**

Further reading: McMahon 1994, 2000; Trask 1996.

COMPETENCE

Our ability to use language, viewed in the abstract. When we use our language, we commit all sorts of errors. We make slips of the tongue, we sometimes can't think of a word or name we know perfectly well, we interrupt ourselves, we mishear or misunderstand what others are saying, we may even lose the thread of what we ourselves are saying, there are limits upon our memories, and so on. There are also sociological factors that affect the language we use. In the early 1960s, the American linguist Noam Chomsky began arguing that such errors should be dismissed from consideration in examining our ability to use language. Chomsky argued that every one of us possesses an abstract linguistic *competence* which is independent of the errors we sometimes make, and he argued further that the elucidation of this competence was, or should be, the principal business of linguistic theory. The errors and social context he relegated to the quite different domain of **performance**, which he considered to be the proper subject-matter of different disciplines.

Chomsky's position here has been enormously influential in linguistics, and it has formed the basis of his research programme, dedicated to the identification of the highly abstract principles which he sees as making up our competence. Interestingly, Chomsky's distinction is strikingly reminiscent of the distinction between **langue** and **parole** introduced generations earlier by the Swiss linguist Ferdinand de Saussure, though not quite identical to it. Nevertheless, there are critics who see Chomsky's conception of competence as far too abstract, and who are inclined to doubt whether such a sharp line should or can be drawn between our ability to use language and our actual behaviour. **Sociolinguists**, **applied linguists** and **cognitive linguists**, for example, are interested in what would be classified here as aspects of **performance**.

See also: **langue**; **language faculty**; **performance**; **universal grammar**

Further reading: Harris 1993; Newmeyer 1983; Matthews 1979.

COMPLEMENT

A grammatical unit which contains a **verb** and which forms part of a larger unit. The term *complement* has in fact been used by linguists in a variety of senses, but it is most commonly applied to a grammatical unit which contains a verb and which, in some sense, completes a larger grammatical unit which begins with some other words. Consider the sentence *The rumour that John is a Chinese spy amuses me*. Here everything before *amuses* is a single **noun phrase**, the subject of the sentence, and it contains a ***noun-complement clause***, which is *that John is a Chinese spy*; this is attached to the noun *rumour*, and it completes the subject noun phrase.

Slightly different are *Susie told me that she would come* and *I don't know whether she's coming*, in which *that she would come* and *whether she's coming* are **verb-complement clauses** attached to the verbs *told* and *know*, respectively. The items *that* and *whether*, which introduce complement clauses, are assigned to a **part of speech** called ***complementizers***. (Traditional grammarians called them **conjunctions**.)

The complements illustrated above are all **finite**. But we also have ***non-finite*** complements: the sentence *Susie wants to buy a car* contains the non-finite complement *to buy a car*, which is attached to the verb *wants*. Note, however, the big difference between *Susie wants to earn some extra money*, in which *to earn some extra money* is a ***direct complement*** attached to *wants*, and *Susie moonlights to earn some extra money*, in which *to earn some extra money* is a ***purpose complement***; the second, but not the first, is equivalent to *in order to earn some extra money*.

The term complement is also applied to a variety of other things which appear to 'complete' a sentence in some sense. For example, in *Susie is considered clever*, the item *clever* is sometimes called a ***subject-complement*** (it applies to *Susie*, the subject of the sentence), and, in *Susie finds Mike tiresome*, the item *tiresome* is sometimes called an ***object-complement*** (it applies to *Mike*, the object of the verb).

See also: **argument**

Further reading: Greenbaum and Quirk 1990; Hurford 1994.

COMPUTATIONAL LINGUISTICS

The use of computers to perform various tasks involving language. The introduction of digital computers has made possible a number of approaches to descriptive and practical problems of language which could not previously be addressed adequately or at all.

One obvious use of computers is to store a *corpus* of spoken or written texts. Such a machine-readable corpus can be rapidly searched and interrogated in order to obtain such information as the frequency of occurrence of certain words, forms or constructions. In this way we can obtain hard data about real language use which would not otherwise be accessible, and we can further make comparisons between, say, spoken and written English, or between American and British English. This is *corpus linguistics*, which has had enormous success in recent years in the creation of new grammars based on spoken usage as well as on writing. *Concordances* are used extensively in the field: a concordance is a computed list of every occurrence of an individual word in the corpus. A corpus can be anything from a small set of texts parsed and tagged right up to multi-million word digitized collections of spoken and written data. Both grammarians and lexicographers today routinely base their grammatical descriptions and their dictionaries on the data extracted from vast corpora.

Computational linguistics has also been influential in *machine translation* (the development of computer programs which can take a text written in one language and convert it into a different language), *speech synthesis* and *voice recognition* (converting written input into an intelligible imitation of human speech), *computer-assisted language learning* (CALL), and in the **stylistic** analysis of texts.

See also: **colligate**; **natural-language processing**

Further reading: Barnbrook 1996; Biber 2006; Crystal 1997; Garside *et al.* 1997; Mahlberg 2005; McEnery and Wilson 2001; McEnery *et al.* 2006; O'Grady *et al.* 1996; Sampson and McCarthy 2005; Sinclair 1991; Sinclair and Carter 2004; Tognini-Bonelli 2001.

CONCEPTUAL INTEGRATION

A theory within **cognitive linguistics** which places the human capacity for dealing with **metaphor** at the heart of our linguistic ability. Developed in the late 1990s by Gilles Fauconnier and Mark Turner out of Fauconnier's earlier work in *mental spaces*, *CI* theory explains individuals' ability to understand novel situations which go beyond anything comparable in their experience. Early cognitive linguistic theory saw a metaphor as a mapping from a *source domain* of familiar semantic content onto a *target domain* of unfamiliar and new information (JULIET IS THE SUN, LIFE IS A JOURNEY). This target domain was then restructured in terms of the source, to produce a new (metaphorical) understanding. However, it became clear that the products of such mappings often went beyond a simple restructuring on the basis of existing knowledge: domains were *blended* to take on an emergent logic of their own.

The theory has been productive especially in relation to creative, literary and expressive metaphors in the field of *cognitive poetics*.

See also: **cognitive linguistics**; **metaphor**

Further reading: Fauconnier and Turner 2002; Stockwell 2002b.

CONJUNCTION

The **part of speech** which includes words like *and* and *or*. Today the label *conjunction* is normally only applied to a very small group of words, chiefly *and* and *or*, which were traditionally called the *coordinating conjunctions*. Most usually, a conjunction *conjoins* (joins) two or more instances of the same category. Examples: *Would you like a doughnut or a piece of pie?* (conjoined noun phrases); *Susie sipped her drink, lit a cigarette and opened her book* (conjoined verb phrases).

Traditional grammarians also included among the conjunctions another group of words, the *subordinating conjunctions* or *subordinators*. These are the words like *if, whenever, although* and *after*, which introduce adverbial clauses. Examples: *After she finished her essay, she headed for a shower; If she arrives in time, she can come with us.* But these words behave very differently from the true conjunctions, and today they are normally placed in a class by themselves.

Traditional grammarians also counted as conjunctions the *complementizers* like *that* and *whether*, as in *She said that she would come* and *I don't know whether she's coming*. But these words behave differently again, and today they are placed by themselves in yet a third class.

See also: **coordinate structure**

Further reading: Collins Cobuild 1990; Crystal 1996; Hurford 1994; Jeffries 2006.

CONNOTATION

The meaning of a word that is broader than its central and primary sense, often acquired through frequent associations. The word *rugby* has as its central sense (its **denotation**) a particular type of football game, but, depending on your experience of rugby, it may also conjure up in your mind such associations as 'large men', 'manliness', 'boorish and bawdy behaviour', or 'public schools' (that is, expensive and prestigious private schools); it may remind you of your pride in your local or national team, or it may remind you of a present or former boyfriend. All these associations are part of the *connotation* of the word. Even more loose are the meanings by *association*, which tend to be even more personal and idiosyncratic.

See also: **denotation**; **meaning**

Further reading: Jeffries 2006.

CONSONANT

A **speech sound** produced by significantly obstructing the flow of air through the **vocal tract**. All speech sounds are produced by manipulating the vocal tract while air is flowing through it. If this manipulation does not produce any significant obstruction of the airstream, the result is a **vowel**; if it does produce obstruction, the result is a *consonant*.

Consonants are classified into several types, differing in the kind of obstruction involved. If the vocal tract is blocked completely, and then the closure is released suddenly, the result is a *plosive*, like [p] or [d]. If the vocal tract is blocked completely and the closure is released slowly, producing friction noise, the result is an **affricate**, like [ts] or [ʃ]. If the vocal tract is not completely blocked, but is reduced instead at some point to a tiny opening through which the air is forced, producing friction noise, the result is a *fricative*, like [f] or [z]. These three types together are *obstruents*; all other consonants are *resonants*.

If a complete closure is made in the mouth, but the velum is lowered so that air can flow out freely through the nose, the result is a *nasal*, like [m] or [n]. If a complete closure is made along the centre-line of the vocal tract, but space is left for the air to flow out along one or both sides, the result is a *lateral*, like [l]. If a speech organ is 'flicked' rapidly against another one, touching it briefly and then returning immediately to its starting point, the result is a *tap*, like the sound [ɾ] in Spanish *pero* 'but'. If a similar flicking movement is made, but the moving organ ends up in a different place from where it started, the result is a *flap*, as in the unusual kind of /r/-sound found in some languages of India. (Many books, especially in the USA, do not distinguish between taps and flaps, but it seems helpful to do so.) If a small opening is made in such a way that air forced through the opening causes some organ to vibrate vigorously, the result is a *trill*, as in the [r]-sound of Spanish *perro* 'dog'.

There is one more class of consonants, but these do not really fit our definition. The [j]-sound at the beginning of English *yes*, the [w]-sound in *wet*, and most of the several different sounds used by English-speakers to pronounce the /r/ of *red* are all strictly vowels by the definition, since they involve no significant obstruction. But the point is that these sounds *behave* like consonants in English and other languages, in spite of their vowel-like nature, and hence they are commonly regarded as a distinct group of consonants, the *approximants*. See the remarks under **vowel** for an explanation.

See also: **speech sound**; **vowel**

Further reading: Ashby 1995; Ball and Rahilly 1999; Ladefoged 1993.

CONSTITUENT STRUCTURE

A type of hierarchical grammatical structure in a sentence. Consider the sentence: *The little girl washed her doll*. In the view of most linguists, this consists of two pieces, or grammatical units: *the little girl* and *washed her doll*. The first of these in turn consists of *the* plus *little girl*, and this last consists of *little* plus *girl*. The second likewise consists of *washed* plus *her doll*; of these, the first consists of *wash* plus *-ed* and the second of *her* plus *doll*.

This is the sort of grammatical (syntactic) structure exhibited by all sentences in English and in most other languages, and we call it *constituent structure*. Constituent structure is hierarchical: a sentence consists of a couple of large pieces, each of which consists of some smaller pieces, each of which in turn consists of some still smaller pieces, and so on, until we reach the smallest pieces of all, the **words** or **morphemes**. And every one of these pieces is a *constituent* of the sentence. Moreover, every constituent must belong to some particular **syntactic category**: that is, the grammar of English (or of any language) allows only constituents belonging to certain categories to be combined into certain larger categories. An attempt at using a constituent of the wrong category produces an ungrammatical result, as in *The under the bed washed her doll* (the asterisk marks ungrammaticality).

Sentence structure, or **syntax**, is thus a very orderly affair: every grammatical sentence is built up from smaller constituents combined into larger constituents, according to certain rigid **rules**, the rules of grammar for that particular language. The resulting structure of a sentence can be revealingly exhibited by a **tree**.

Some languages, including many Australian languages, seem not to have this sort of sentence structure; instead, they exhibit a much looser type of structure in which smaller units do not have to be combined into larger ones in such an orderly way. These are called *non-configurational languages*, or *W-star languages*. Languages like English, in contrast, are *configurational languages*.

See also: **phrase**; **phrase-structure grammar**; **syntax**; **syntactic category**; **tree**

Further reading: Brown and Miller 1991; Burton-Roberts 1986; Kroeger 2004; van Valin 2001.

CONSTRUCTION GRAMMAR

A set of related approaches to grammar that treat constructions at clause level as the units of grammar, rather than the syntactic unit. The construction has an abstract conceptual content (such as 'X moves over Y' or 'A causes B to die'), which is then related to various stylistic realizations: so construction grammars have been seen as the point where **generative semantics** shifted into **cognitive linguistics** in the 1980s. An example of a construction grammar would be Ronald Langacker's *cognitive grammar* which understands prepositions as being the surface realization of a set of spatial image-schemas with a mental origin in physical experience.

Crucially, construction grammars are not derivational. So for example, the **active** and the **passive** forms of a sentence are regarded as having different conceptual structures rather than one being a transformation of the other. Since construction grammars depend on the conceptual meaning in context, they can be seen as approaches to linguistics that collapse the classical distinctions between **semantics, syntax** and **pragmatics**. The construction is the unit of language, which cuts across these other aspects. So, for example, in *They laughed him out of the room*, the normally intransitive verb receives a transitive reading and the situation can be interpreted on the basis of the 'X cause Y to move' construction rather than the syntactic deviance alone. As a result, construction grammars are proving most useful in understanding **language acquisition** and are being used for second-language teaching, since it is the meaningfulness of the situation which is of primary importance, and syntax and semantics are treated holistically.

See also: **cognitive linguistics; language acquisition**

Further reading: Croft and Cruse 2004; Goldberg 2006; Lakoff 1987; Langacker 1987–91.

CONTROL

The phenomenon in which a **verb phrase** (VP) with no subject is interpreted as having some subject. In sentences like *John wants to go home* and *John promised Mary to go home* (the second is not grammatical for all speakers), we understand that it is John who is going home. That is, *John* is the 'understood' subject of the subjectless VP *go home*, and so we say that *John*, the subject of *wants* and of *promised*, *controls* the VP *go home*. This is an example of *subject-control*. However, in the sentence *John persuaded Mary to go home*, it is Mary who is going home; this time *Mary*, the object of *persuaded*, controls the VP *go home*, and we have an instance of *object-control*.

There is one more possibility, illustrated by the sentence *Going home sounds like a good idea*. This time there is no **noun phrase** available at all to be interpreted as the subject of the VP *going home*, and we call one an instance of *arbitrary control*. Control phenomena can be rather intricate, and many current theories of grammar devote a good deal of machinery to their treatment. Note that some writers refer to control as *sharing*.

Note that the term control has a second sense. In a number of languages, intransitive sentences are divided into two different grammatical types, distinguished by the degree of control exercised over the action by the subject. In such languages, sentences like *He went home* and *He stood up*, in which the subject has a high degree of control, are expressed with one construction, while others, like *He died* and *He sneezed*, in which the subject has a low degree of control, are expressed with a different construction.

See also: **anaphor**; **raising**

Further reading: Borsley 1991; Palmer 1994.

CONVERSATION ANALYSIS

A particular and highly empirical approach to examining the structure of **discourse**. The term *conversation analysis*, which came into prominence in the 1970s, sounds straightforward enough, but it is used in two rather different ways. Some people use it in a very broad sense, to include all possible approaches to the study of conversational structure. Much more commonly, however, the term is used more narrowly to denote an approach which rejects the use of traditional and widely used grammatical concepts and terms and attempts instead to work out from observation what speakers are doing and how they are doing it, with any required concepts and terms being derived purely from observation. The leading figure in the development of this approach was the American sociologist Harvey Sacks.

The approach is particularly associated with a general approach to social sciences called ***ethnomethodology***, whose proponents argue that the proper object of sociological study is the set of techniques that the members of a society use to interpret their world and to act within it. In practice, this means a minimum of theorizing and a strong emphasis upon raw data and on the patterns that emerge from the data. Consequently, conversation analysis, in this narrow sense, contrasts most obviously with **discourse analysis**, which operates from the beginning with the familiar concepts and terms of general linguistics and attempts to examine the role of these concepts in discourses, including conversations.

See also: **discourse analysis**; **turn-taking**

Further reading: Duranti 1997; Eggins and Slade 2004; Levinson 1983; Mey 1993; Pridham 2001; Schiffrin 1994; Wooffitt 2005; Yule 1996.

CONVERSATIONAL IMPLICATURE

A certain type of inference. Suppose Alice asks Bill *Is Susie coming to Mike's party on Saturday?*, and Bill replies *Dave wants to go to a concert.* On the face of it, this is an idiotic response to a simple question: Bill has declined to mention Susie at all and has instead brought up Dave and a concert, neither of which was being asked about. And yet this is a perfectly normal and satisfactory answer to the question: providing that Alice knows that Dave is Susie's boyfriend, she can reason as follows: 'Bill doesn't know whether Susie is coming to the party, or he would simply have told me, but Dave is Susie's boyfriend, and Bill tells me he wants to go to a concert; doubtless he will want Susie to come with him, and the concert must be on Saturday, or Bill wouldn't have mentioned it, and therefore I can conclude that Susie will probably be going to the concert with Dave, and hence that she won't be coming to the party'.

Alice's conclusion that Susie probably won't be coming to the party is an example of a ***conversational implicature***. This conclusion has not been asserted by Bill, and it does not logically follow from what Bill has said, and yet it is reasonable, and Alice will surely draw it. How can this be so?

The first key point here is the ***context*** of Bill's utterance. Alice knows that Dave and Susie are a couple, and she knows that people like their partners to accompany them to social events, or at least that Dave does, and this contextual knowledge is crucial: without it, Alice would have little chance of making sense of Bill's response. This is typically the case with an implicature: it can only be drawn by a hearer who has an adequate knowledge of the context.

A second key point is that Alice assumes that Bill is being ***cooperative***. If Bill had known for certain that Susie was or was not coming to the party, Alice would have expected him to say so, and failure to do this would be uncooperative. Moreover, Alice has every right to assume that the concert in question must be on the Saturday; had it been on the Friday, Bill's behaviour would have been very uncooperative indeed, not merely irrelevant but positively misleading. Alice therefore assumes that Bill is cooperating, and draws her conclusion accordingly.

A notable property of implicatures is that they are ***defeasible*** – they can be explicitly denied without producing anomaly. Suppose Bill's reply had been *Well, Dave wants to go to a concert, but Susie has decided to come to Mike's party anyway.* Here Bill is expressly denying the implicature 'Susie probably won't be coming to the party', but the result is still fine. This demonstrates that implicatures are not logically valid. Nevertheless, they are powerful inferences, and an implicature which is not denied will be assumed by the hearer to be true.

Now it is certainly not possible to assert that Bill's response actually *means* 'Susie is probably not coming to the party'. Suppose Alice asks Bill a quite different question: *I'd like to go to one of the outdoor concerts in the park next week. Is anybody else interested?* Bill replies *Dave wants to go to a concert.* This time Alice is hardly likely to conclude that Susie is probably not coming to Mike's party, since such an inference would make no sense in this very different context.

Implicatures are therefore very different in nature from the two other major kinds of inference, **entailment** and **presupposition**; among other things, neither of these two can be denied without producing anomaly.

Implicatures therefore belong squarely to the domain of **pragmatics**, the study of how meanings are extracted from context. Their existence was uncovered by the British philosopher Paul Grice in the 1960s, and Grice's **cooperative principle** represents the major attempt at explaining how speakers are successful in communicating such meanings. A more recent development claims that all such inferences are the product of a principle of **relevance**.

See also: **cooperative principle**; **entailment**; **pragmatics**; **presupposition**; **relevance**

Further reading: Cutting 2002; Hurford and Heasley 1983; Levinson 1983; Thomas 1995; Yule 1996.

COOPERATIVE PRINCIPLE

A fundamental principle governing conversational exchanges. In the 1960s, the British philosopher Paul Grice undertook an examination of the way people behave in conversation. His fundamental conclusion was that conversational exchanges were governed by an overarching principle, which he named the *cooperative principle*. Essentially, this principle holds that people in a conversation normally cooperate with one another, and, crucially, that they assume that the others are cooperating. That is, when you say something, and another person makes a response, you assume that the response is intended as a maximally cooperative one, and you interpret it accordingly. Note that this term is not used in an ideological sense: participants in arguments, deliberate deception, lying, fiction, hypothesizing and making errors are still 'cooperating' in the pragmatic sense.

It is this principle which is responsible for the existence of **conversational implicatures**, powerful inferences which are not logically valid but which are derived from the assumption that the other person is cooperating to a maximum extent.

Grice further decomposed his principle into a number of more specific components, the **maxims of conversation**, such as 'Make your contribution as informative as is required', 'Be relevant', and 'Do not say that for which you lack adequate evidence'. These maxims are there to be broken, but when they are obviously broken (*flouted*), the hearer can generate certain implicatures from that fact.

See also: **conversational implicature**; **relevance**

Further reading: Blakemore 1992; Cutting 2003; Hurford and Heasley 1983; Sperber and Wilson 1995; Thomas 1995; Yule 1996.

COORDINATE STRUCTURE

A grammatical structure consisting of two or more units of equal rank joined by a connecting word. In English, a coordinate structure most usually consists of some grammatical units connected by a **conjunction** like 'and' or 'or'. As a rule, the two units, or *conjuncts*, which are combined, or *conjoined*, must belong to the same **syntactic category**. Here are some examples, in which the coordinate structures are bracketed and so are the conjuncts they consist of: [[*Susie*] *and* [*her parents*]] *are coming* (conjoined noun phrases); *Susie* [[*undressed*] *and* [*took a shower*]] (conjoined verb phrases); *Hungarian is spoken* [[*in Hungary*], [*in much of Romania*] *and* [*in part of Serbia*]] (conjoined prepositional phrases); *Does she drive* [[*well*] *or* [*badly*]]? (conjoined adverbs).

In certain circumstances, we can conjoin two units of different categories: *She polished the table* [[*lovingly*] *and* [*with great care*]] (adverb conjoined with prepositional phrase). But in most cases this is not possible: **She smokes* [[*Marlboros*] *and* [*too much*]] (noun phrase wrongly conjoined with adverb phrase) (the asterisk marks ungrammaticality).

A few coordinate structures exhibit more complex patterns, as in *Susie is [neither [Irish] nor [Welsh]]*. And a few constructions that look broadly like coordinations have decidedly unusual structures, such as *[Janet prepared] and [Zelda served] [the sandwiches]* (this is called **right-node raising**), and *[Esther ordered chicken Kashmir] and [Larry, lamb rogan josh]* (this is called **gapping**); such constructions present formidable difficulties of analysis. Note that the bracketing system adopted here is convenient for linear text, but expressing syntax in a **tree** diagram is much clearer and more common.

See also: **conjunction; tree**

Further reading: Collins Cobuild 1990; Crystal 1996; Hurford 1994; Jeffries 2006.

COPULA

A specialized grammatical item, often a **verb**, which serves only to express identity or class membership. The English copula is *be*, and this verb has two main functions. First, as the verb in an *equational sentence*, it expresses identity and functions rather like an equal sign in mathematics: *The largest planet in our solar system is Jupiter*. Such a sentence can be readily reversed: *Jupiter is the largest planet in our solar system*. Second, as the verb in an *ascriptive sentence*, it ascribes some property to its subject, or, in other words, it assigns its subject to membership in some class: *Susie is clever; Susie is sleepy; Susie is a woman with a red car*. Here certain properties are being ascribed to Susie (cleverness, sleepiness, having a red car), or, equivalently, Susie is being assigned to the class of clever people, to the class of sleepy people, or to the class of car-owners. Such sentences become unnatural or worse when reversed: *??Clever is Susie; ??A woman with a red car is Susie*.

Of course, English *be* can also function as an **auxiliary**, and in that case it is not serving as a copula.

See also: **auxiliary; verb**

Further reading: Hurford 1994; Jackson 2002.

CREOLE

A language developed from a **pidgin**. A pidgin is a combination of two or more languages which sometimes occurs in trade contact, multi-ethnic or refugee situations, where participants need a functioning common language. It is usually reduced in complexity and function and is learned as a second language by all speakers. Sometimes the pidgin becomes stable and established and comes to be spoken as a mother-tongue by children: the language has then become a *creole*, which quickly develops in complexity and is used in all functional settings. The process of turning a pidgin into a creole is *creolization*.

Countless creoles have come into existence during the past few centuries, often because of the activities of European colonists. Speakers of English, French, Spanish, Portuguese and Dutch have established colonies in Africa, Asia and the Americas, in areas where the local languages were very different, and in many cases the Europeans imported African slaves speaking any of dozens of African languages. The Caribbean has been a particularly fertile area for creoles, as Europeans and Africans (and to a lesser extent Native Americans) were forced to construct innumerable local pidgins, very many of which went on to be converted to creoles.

When a creole remains in contact with the prestige language from which it was largely constructed, it may undergo significant *decreolization* – adjustment towards that prestige standard – and the result may be a *creole continuum*, a range of varieties from a highly conservative version of the creole (the *basilect*) through increasingly decreolized versions (the *mesolects*) to something more or less identical to the prestige standard (the *acrolect*). This stratification typically reflects the degree of education or a continuum between rural and urban speakers.

The study of creoles was pioneered by the Trinidadian John Thomas, the American Addison Van Name and the German Hugo Schuchardt in the late nineteenth century, and the topic has never since been really neglected, but it has prospered particularly since the 1970s, and it is now regarded as a major area of investigation. Linguists studying contemporary **language change** have found creolization to be a rich source of information, particularly from the point of view of the construction of new grammatical systems. The remarkable similarities in grammar among creoles all over the world have led to the proposing of the **bioprogram hypothesis**. At one time, there was a widespread belief that all creoles were descended from a single ancestral creole by massive vocabulary replacement (*relexification*), but this idea in its simple form is no longer taken seriously. A variation on the notion is that syntactic similarities in unrelated creoles can be ascribed to the similarities in social setting and function of those situations, and these structures are then relexified by the local influential language.

See also: **bioprogram hypothesis**; **pidgin**

Further reading: Chaudenson 2001; Holm 1988–9, 2000; Kouwenberg and Singler 2005; Romaine 1988; Sebba 1997.

CRITICAL DISCOURSE ANALYSIS

The analysis of **texts** within their social context. It is possible, of course, to examine a text from a purely structural point of view: the vocabulary and constructions it employs, the linguistic devices it uses to relate one part to another, and so on. But the approach called *critical discourse analysis* is rather different. This approach is primarily interested in the social context in which a text is written. (Critical discourse analysis is particularly associated with the work of the British sociolinguist Norman Fairclough, and it has become particularly influential in Europe and Australasia.)

Why was this text constructed at all? To whom is it addressed, and why? Does the writer or speaker have concealed purposes, and, if so, what are they? What hidden assumptions and biases underlie the text? These are the sorts of questions pursued in critical discourse analysis. The linguistic techniques involved in such analysis are often called *critical linguistics*, and the educational policy of teaching people to be alert to such matters is *critical language awareness*.

A simple example is provided by headlines and stories in different newspapers reporting the same story. Compare the following possible headlines for the same real-world event: *Police shoot demonstrators*; *Demonstrators are shot*; *Shooting at demo*; *Demo ends in violence*; *2 dead at demo*; *Police make arrests as 2 die in demo riot*. A critical discourse analyst would consider the different ideologies encoded by these different linguistic forms, such as the implicit assignment of blame and the shifting of emphasis.

See also: **discourse**; **text**

Further reading: Carter 1997; Chilton 2003; Fairclough 1992, 1995, 2001, 2003; Pennycook 2001; Wodak 1996; Wodak and Chilton 2005.

CRITICAL PERIOD HYPOTHESIS

The hypothesis that a first language can only be acquired during the first few years of life. Young children learn perfectly any language to which they are adequately exposed, and they do this without explicit teaching. Few adults can perform the same feat. In the 1960s the American neurologist Eric Lenneberg proposed an explanation: we are born with a singular ability to learn languages, but this ability is 'shut down', probably by some genetic programming, at around age thirteen, the *cut-off age* for first-language acquisition.

Strong support for Lenneberg's hypothesis comes from the observation of *feral children*: children who, for some reason, have been denied normal access to language in early life. In the eighteenth century, a young teenage French boy later named Victor was discovered living wild. He had no language and failed to learn much after being taken into care. More recently, a French girl known as Isabelle and an American girl known as Genie were prevented by psychopathic parents from hearing any language. After discovery and rescue, Isabelle, who was six, learned French rapidly, and quickly caught up with other children of her age, but Genie, nearly fourteen when discovered, never learned more than a minimal amount of English, in spite of intensive therapy. An American woman known as Chelsea was born nearly deaf, but was misdiagnosed as mentally retarded. Only at age thirty-one was she correctly diagnosed and given a hearing aid; she then began learning English but she too never made more than minimal progress.

See also: **language acquisition**; **language instinct**

Further reading: Aitchison 1989; Field 2003; Steinberg 1993.

DEAD LANGUAGE

A language which is no longer spoken. The term *dead language* is applied to two quite different cases, which you should be careful to distinguish.

In the first case, a dead language is a language which has disappeared as a mother tongue because its speakers abandoned it in favour of some other language (or, sometimes, because its speakers were all killed). This has happened countless times. A number of languages of ancient Anatolia and the Middle East have disappeared in this way, including Hittite, Sumerian and Akkadian. An unknown number of European languages disappeared in favour of Latin during the Roman Empire, including Etruscan in Italy, Gaulish in Gaul and Iberian in Spain. In Britain, Cornish and Manx have vanished in modern times in favour of English. And hundreds of indigenous languages in Australia and the Americas have been abandoned in favour of English, Spanish and Portuguese.

A slight complication is that one or two of these truly dead languages, such as Cornish, have today a few speakers; these people speak the dead language as a second language, having learned it from books. Whether we continue to regard such a language as dead is a matter of taste, but most linguists would probably regard Cornish as dead, since it perhaps has no native speakers. A few dead languages may continue to find some use as religious or literary languages, but again, in the absence of native speakers, they may be regarded as dead.

In the second case, the language in question never ceases to be spoken as a mother tongue, but over a period of time it changes so substantially that its later forms are so different from the earlier form (and often from one another) that it no longer makes sense to apply the same name. This has happened to Latin. Latin has never ceased to be spoken in Portugal, Spain, France and Italy, but the modern forms of Latin are so different from the language of the Romans, and from one another, that we no longer find it convenient to call them 'Latin'. Hence we speak of *French* rather than 'Paris Latin', *Catalan* rather than 'Barcelona Latin', and so on.

See also: **language death**

Further reading: Crystal 2000; Holmes 1992; Romaine 1994.

DEEP STRUCTURE

An abstract representation of the structure of a sentence posited by a linguist for analytical purposes. The concept of deep structure was a central part of the first versions of **transformational grammar**, introduced by Noam Chomsky in the 1950s. Chomsky's idea was that certain important generalizations about the structures of the sentences in a particular language were difficult to state in terms of the **surface structure** of sentences, but that these generalizations could be readily expressed in a theoretical framework in which sentences were assumed to have abstract underlying forms which were very different from their surface forms.

Chomsky defended his idea by appealing to examples like *John is eager to please* and *John is easy to please*. On the surface, these may appear to have identical structures, but, crucially, they receive very different interpretations. Using the symbol NP for a **noun phrase** which is in some sense 'missing' on the surface, we might therefore posit deep structures for these two sentences of approximately the following forms: *John is [eager to please NP]*, but *[NP to please John] is easy*. These representations now allow us to explain the meaning of each sentence, but they must be modified by the action of powerful rules called *transformations* in order to produce the correct surface forms in each case.

The conception of deep structure has changed substantially over the years, as Chomsky and his colleagues have continued to modify their ideas, and the several successive versions of transformational grammar (and its successor **Government-and-Binding Theory**) have involved very different views of deep structure, which has more recently been called *D-structure*. Consequently, different textbooks will present significantly different versions of it, and the most recent versions are often very abstract indeed. Most theories of grammar other than transformational grammar have declined to recognize a concept of deep structure, preferring instead to work solely with surface structures.

When deep structure was first introduced, there was some enthusiasm for seeing it as representing a mental reality, something actually present within speakers' brains. This idea has gradually been abandoned, and today only a minority of linguists would want to see D-structure as anything more than an analytical convenience.

See also: **ambiguity**; **surface structure**; **transformational grammar**

Further reading: Kroeger 2004; Lyons 1991; van Valin 2001.

DEFICIT HYPOTHESIS

The hypothesis that a group of speakers has an inadequate command of grammar and vocabulary to express complex ideas. In the 1960s, the British educational theorist Basil Bernstein proposed that a given language can be regarded as possessing two fundamentally different styles, or *codes*. A *restricted code*, in this view, has a limited vocabulary and a limited range of grammatical constructions; it is adequate for talking to people with very similar backgrounds about everyday experiences, but it is highly inexplicit and depends for success upon a large degree of shared experience. It is too inexplicit and too limited to express complex and unfamiliar ideas in a coherent manner. An *elaborated code*, in contrast, possesses a large vocabulary and a wide range of grammatical constructions, and it is entirely suitable for communicating complex ideas, in a fully explicit manner, to people who do not share the speaker's background. Bernstein's *deficit hypothesis* holds that, while middle-class children have full control over both codes, working-class children have access only to the restricted code. Hence working-class children cannot communicate effectively in the manner expected in educational institutions, and so they cannot hope to succeed in schools which are largely predicated on elaborated code.

This hypothesis has generated a storm of discussion and debate. Linguists, led by William Labov, have mostly been critical and dismissive of it. They defend instead the *difference hypothesis* – by which working-class speech is merely different from middle-class speech, and not inferior to it in expressiveness – and, hence, that working-class children in school are penalized only for being different, and not for being incompetent. The notion of *deficit* has been debated also in relation to linguistic differences ascribed to gender and ethnicity.

See also: **standard language**

Further reading: Emmitt *et al.* 2006; Holmes 1992; Stockwell 2002a.

DEICTIC CATEGORY

Any **grammatical category** which expresses distinctions pertaining to the time and place of speaking or to the differing roles of participants. The word *deixis* means 'pointing', and deictic expressions serve to anchor the speaker in relation to their surroundings and other participants. *Egocentric* deixis refers to linguistic markers whereby person, place and time are used in relation to the speaker (*I, here, now*). Clearly, **person, tense** and *locative* **adverbials** are the main carriers of these three deictic dimensions.

Further deictic categories have been proposed that extend the notion or try to adapt it to situations where speakers imagine other viewpoints (as in narratives and fiction, for example). So *textual, compositional* and *relational deixis* have also been explored in relation to social marking, and delineating the different 'voices' in split narratives. **Cognitive linguists** in particular have been interested in the ways that the *deictic centres* expressed by consistent deictic choices are maintained and shifted.

See also: **cognitive linguistics**; **grammatical category**

Further reading: Duchan *et al.* 1995; Green 1995; Levinson 1983; Lyons 1968; Rauh 1983; Stockwell 2002b.

DENOTATION

The central meaning of a linguistic form, regarded as the set of things it could possibly refer to. The study of **meaning** is a complex affair, and several quite different kinds of meaning have to be carefully distinguished before we can hope to make much progress. For example, when you say *The cat is scratching the sofa*, you clearly have some particular, individual cat in mind, and the relation between the cat and that animal is one of **reference**. Now the word *cat* itself cannot normally refer to any particular entity in this way. However, one way of looking at the central meaning of *cat* is to see this as consisting of all the cats in the (real or conceptual) world – that is, as the totality of things to which the word *cat* might reasonably be applied. This interpretation is called the *denotation* of the word *cat*.

Denotation is a difficult concept to work with, since concepts like 'all the cats in the world' are almost impossible to pin down. Among 'all the cats in the world', should we include all those cats which have not yet been born, and all those which died millions of years ago? Nevertheless, denotation is often invoked in **semantics**, and formal versions of semantics often try to formalize denotation as what is called *extension*: the extension of *cat* is the *set* (in the formal mathematical sense) of all the entities in the universe of discourse (the totality of things we can talk about) to which *cat* can be applied.

Denotation is most frequently contrasted with **connotation**, but it has important similarities to **sense**, which is essentially a more directly linguistic way of interpreting the same kind of meaning. (And some writers have a habit of using *denotation* almost interchangeably with **reference**, but this is inappropriate.)

See also: **connotation**; **reference**; **sense**

Further reading: Frawley 1992; Hofmann 1993; Saeed 1997.

DEPENDENCY

A grammatical link between two (or more) different points in a sentence. In a *dependency*, the presence, absence or form of an item at one point in a sentence is directly linked to the presence, absence or form of a second item at a different point in the same sentence. There are several types of dependency. When the presence of one item requires the presence or absence of another, we have **subcategorization** (for example, the verb *slap* requires an object noun phrase, while *smile* does not allow one). When the presence of one item requires a particular form on a second item, we have **government** (for example, the German preposition *mit* 'with' requires its object to take the dative case). When the form of one item requires a particular form on a second item, we have **agreement** (for example, a plural subject requires a plural verb-form).

All these are *local dependencies*, in which the two ends of the dependency are not allowed to be separated by more than a certain amount. In an *unbounded dependency* (or *extraction*), there is no limit on how far apart the two ends can be. The example *Susie slapped* is ungrammatical (marked by the asterisk), since the verb lacks the object it requires. Likewise, *Who did Susie slap Louise?* is ungrammatical, since *who* cannot be used unless there is a suitable **gap**, or 'hole', elsewhere in the sentence. But *Who did Susie slap e?* is fine, since *who* and the missing object (marked by the symbol *e*) permit each other to occur. And the question word and the gap can be arbitrarily far apart: *Who did Archie say* *that Bill thought that Claire believed that Donna suspected Susie slapped* e?

See also: **agreement**; **government**; **subcategorization**

Further reading: Brown and Miller 1991; Greville 2006.

DERIVATION

Constructing new words by adding **affixes** to existing words. In most languages, *derivation* is one of the principal ways of obtaining new words from existing words, and its study is one of the major branches of **morphology**.

The key point is to distinguish **derivation** from **inflection**. When we add certain affixes to a **lemma** like *write*, producing forms like *writes*, *writing* and *written* (and also, in a more complex manner, *wrote*), we do not get any new words, but only grammatically distinct forms of the same word: this is **inflection**. You wouldn't expect to find different dictionary entries for all these forms: there would just be the one entry for all of them, under *write*. However, other affixes produce genuinely different words, such as *rewrite*, *underwrite* and *writer*, and these are examples of derivation. This time you *would* expect to find separate dictionary entries for these words, though a small dictionary might not bother with *rewrite*, since its meaning is so obvious.

Like many languages, English is rich in both derivational prefixes and derivational suffixes. Examples of the first are *re-*, *anti-*, *syn-*, *counter-*, *non-*, *un-*, *trans-*, *pre-* and *mis-*. Examples of the second are *-ness*, *-ity*, *-less*, *-wise*, *-ize*, *-dom*, *-ly* (two different ones), *-er* and *-(at)ion*. Multiple affixes are possible, though normally there are strict rules governing the order in which affixes may be added. Starting from *happy*, we can derive first *unhappy* and then *unhappiness*. Starting with *derive*, we can obtain first *derivation*, then *derivational*, and finally the very obscure technical term in linguistics *transderivational*. Starting with *exist*, we can successively derive *existent*, *existence*, *existential* and *existentialism*. In every case, at every stage, the result is a new word which deserves its own entry in the dictionary.

In **transformational grammar**, the complete set of stages linking the **deep structure** of a sentence to its **surface structure** is also called derivation. Among the various theories of grammar, transformational grammar is distinguished by its claim that the syntactic structure of a sentence is not a single **tree**, but rather a series of trees. The most fundamental level of structure is the deep structure of the sentence, and the most superficial, the **surface structure**. These two levels of representation are typically linked by a whole series of trees, each one resulting from the application of a *transformation* to the preceding one. The ordered series of trees which results is the derivation of that particular sentence.

In this sense, the term derivation is also applied to the series of stages involved in process-based theories of **phonology** like *generative phonology* in converting an *underlying form* into a surface form.

See also: **affix**; **inflection**; **morphology**; **phonology**; **transformational grammar**; **word-formation**

Further reading: Brown and Miller 1991; Epstein and Seely 2002; Katamba 1994.

DESCRIPTIVISM

The policy of describing languages as they are found to exist. A prominent feature of **traditional grammar** is the frequent presence of **prescriptivism**: identifying and recommending forms and usages favoured by the analyst and condemning others not favoured by the analyst. Excepting only in certain educational contexts, modern linguists utterly reject prescriptivism, and their investigations are based instead upon *descriptivism*. In a descriptivist approach, we try to describe the facts of linguistic behaviour exactly as we find them, and we refrain from making value judgements about the speech of native speakers. Of course, our descriptions sometimes include the observation that speakers themselves regard certain usages as good or bad, but that is a very different thing from expressing our own opinions.

Descriptivism is a central tenet of what we regard as a scientific approach to the study of language: the very first requirement in any scholarly investigation is get the facts right. Prescriptivism, in great contrast, is not a scientific approach. The strong opinions of prescriptivists may be variously regarded as recommendations about good style, as an aspect of social mores, as a consequence of our educational system, or perhaps even as a matter of morality, but they are not statements about actual behaviour, and hence they are not scientific.

See also: **prescriptivism**

Further reading: Pinker 1994; Trask 1995.

DESIGN FEATURES

An informal list of the seemingly universal properties of human languages. The idea of *design features* was introduced by the American linguist Charles Hockett in 1960; both Hockett and others have occasionally proposed revisions to the original list, and several versions are in print. All contain the fundamental features of **arbitrariness**, **duality of patterning**, **displacement**, **open-endedness** and **stimulus-freedom**. Of these five, only the first is also normally found in **animal communication**.

Sign languages present a few complications. They clearly do not possess the secondary design feature of using the *vocal-auditory channel* as their primary medium, and it is debatable whether they possess duality of patterning.

See also: **animal communication**; **arbitrariness**; **duality of patterning**; **displacement**; **open-endedness**; **stimulus-freedom**

Further reading: Crystal 1997; Hockett 1960; Trask 1995.

DETERMINER

The **part of speech** which includes words like *the* and *my*. The English determiners are a smallish class of chiefly grammatical items which have only a single function: they typically occur as the first item in a **noun phrase**. Here is a simple test for determiners. Any single word which can fit into the blank in the following frame to produce a noun phrase is a determiner: – *new book*. Examples: *the, a, this, that, some, every, no, my, her, which*. There are some further determiners which can only fit into plural noun phrases, as in: – *new books*. Examples: *these, most, both, all, few, several*. But be careful here: certain words which are not determiners will also fit into this second blank (*entirely, attractive, other*), but these items require entirely different syntactic structures to fit into this string of words. The two most highly grammatical determiners, *the* and *a(n)*, are called *articles*. The ones like *my* and *her* are traditionally called *possessive pronouns*, but grammatically they are determiners, not **pronouns**. Normally a noun phrase contains only one determiner. But certain noun phrases appear to contain two: *all my children, both these books*. In such cases, the first item is often called a *predeterminer*. A noun phrase which is headed by a singular uncountable noun or by any plural noun need not have an overt determiner: *French wine, new books*. Some linguists prefer to say that such noun phrases contain a *zero determiner*. Some (not all) determiners have meanings involving quantity, such as *many, several* and *all*. These are called *quantifiers*, and some linguists prefer to separate the quantifiers into a separate part of speech from determiners, but there is little or no grammatical justification for this.

See also: **noun phrase**

Further reading: Collins Cobuild 1990; Greenbaum and Quirk 1990; Jackson 2002.

DIACHRONY

The time dimension in language. It was the Swiss linguist Ferdinand de Saussure, in the early twentieth century, who first emphasized the fundamental difference between **synchrony** and *diachrony* in the study of language. In a *diachronic* approach, we look at how a language has changed over some period of time. Most work in **historical linguistics** is diachronic in nature, but not all of it: a linguist might well be interested in constructing a purely synchronic description of, say, the Old English of King Alfred's day or the Latin of Caesar's day, without considering how the language had developed from an earlier form or what happened to it later.

See also: **historical linguistics**; **language change**; **Saussurean paradox**; **synchrony**

Further reading: Fennell 2000; McMahon 1994.

DIALECT

A more or less identifiable regional or social variety of a language. Every language that is spoken over any significant area is spoken in somewhat different forms in different places; these are its *regional dialects*. Moreover, even in a single community, the language may be spoken differently by members of different social groups; these different forms are *social dialects* or *sociolects*. For example, the English of London is noticeably different from the English of Birmingham, Liverpool, Glasgow, New York, New Orleans or Sydney, and even within London stockbrokers tend not speak like motor mechanics.

It is important to realize that everybody speaks some dialect or other; it is not possible to speak a language without using some dialect. (In fact, you might say that dialects exist but **language** is merely an abstract term for a collection of dialects.) Informally, we often reserve the label *dialect* for a speech variety which is noticeably different from our own, or which is lacking in prestige, but this is not the way the term is used in linguistics. In British usage, the term dialect includes only features of grammar and vocabulary, while features of pronunciation are treated under the quite different heading of **accent**. In American usage, an accent is usually considered to be just one part of a dialect.

The study of regional dialects, known as *dialect geography* or *dialectology*, has been a major part of linguistics since the late nineteenth century; there have been many studies of regional variation, often resulting in the publication of *dialect atlases* containing a series of *dialect maps*, each showing the variation in respect of a single feature (the lines which separate features on the map are known as *isoglosses*). *Dialectology* has had a distinctively historical dimension, with researchers often using historical documents, place names and archaeological evidence to investigate dialectal change and *diffusion*, and also using dialect evidence for historical research in return. In contrast, social dialects (in the form of *urban dialectology*) have only been seriously studied since the 1960s; the pioneering work here was done by the American linguist William Labov. While this **sociolinguistic** work has also provided insight into long-term language change, its main focus has been **synchronic**, and it has tended to regard dialect as simply one type of social language variation.

A **standard language** is a rather special dialect of some language, one which has been *codified* (standardized in dictionaries and published grammars, and used in the education system and for prestigious texts) and elaborated for use in a wide variety of domains.

Linguistically unsophisticated people sometimes apply the term dialect to a regional language of low prestige, but the term is never so used in linguistics, in which a dialect is always a variety of a language which has other varieties.

See also: **accent**; **onomastics**; **standard language**

Further reading: Auer *et al.* 2005; Chambers and Trudgill 1998; Crystal 1997; Foulkes and Docherty 1999; Llamas *et al.* 2007.

DIGLOSSIA

Marked specialization of function between two language varieties in a single speech community. It is by no means rare for two or more distinct languages or language varieties to be used side by side within a single community, with or without a high degree of **bilingualism**. For example, many citizens of Spain routinely switch between Basque, Catalan or Galician on the one hand and Castilian Spanish on the other, depending on the circumstances; German-speakers in Germany, Switzerland and Austria likewise switch between standard German and their own local varieties of German, which are often not comprehensible to other speakers; all of English, Malay, Cantonese Chinese and Tamil are widely spoken in Singapore, though very few people there can speak all four. In most such cases, people naturally prefer to speak their own mother tongue whenever they can, and they switch to another language or variety only when they have to. In a few communities, however, something very different happens: the languages or language varieties come to be perceived as having different functions in the community as a whole, and hence each variety is used more or less exclusively for those functions in which it is deemed appropriate. Normally only two language varieties are involved in such a case, and the result is *diglossia*.

Diglossia was first identified as a distinctive phenomenon by the American linguist Charles Ferguson in the 1960s. Ferguson's initial characterization has since been modified very slightly, but the characteristics of a diglossic society are essentially the ones he identified. There is a clear difference in prestige between the two language varieties: one, called **High** (or H), enjoys great prestige, while the other, called **Low** (or L), enjoys little or no prestige; in extreme cases, speakers may deny the very existence of L. In all cases, L is the mother tongue of all or most speakers, while H is learned only through formal education. Speakers of limited education may have a very inadequate command of H, and they may even have trouble understanding it.

The specialization of function is highly predictable from one diglossic society to another. The L variety is used for ordinary conversation and for the more popular types of entertainment (such as soap operas and commentary on sports events); it is rarely written, and may well lack a recognized written form. However, it may be used in comic strips, in captions to political cartoons, in scurrilous publications, and perhaps in personal letters. The H variety is used in newspapers and most other publications, for all serious literature, for university lectures, for news broadcasts and other formal types of radio and television broadcasts, and (usually) for religious purposes.

So well entrenched is this perceived specialization that using the 'wrong' variety for a particular purpose will be seen as comical or offensive: even speakers with a minimal command of H prefer to hear H when H is appropriate, since the use here of L, which they can understand perfectly well, is felt to be undignified or worse. In one famous incident, there were riots in the streets of Athens in 1901 upon the publication of a translation of the New Testament into the Low variety of Greek: thousands of Greeks were enraged by the use of L in such a solemn religious context, and they insisted upon an H version which many of them could not understand.

Among the diglossic societies identified several decades ago were:

- Greece – H = Katharévusa, a kind of reconstructed classical Greek, L = Dhimotikí, ordinary spoken Greek
- German Switzerland – H = standard German, L = Swiss German
- the Arab countries – H = the classical Arabic of the Koran, L = ordinary spoken Arabic
- Paraguay – H = Spanish, L = Guaraní, the mother tongue of most of the population and a Native American language.

Changing political circumstances have brought diglossia to an end in Greece, and there are signs that the Arab countries may be going the same way (though diglossia is far from dead here); Switzerland and Paraguay continue much as before. Other instances of diglossia have arisen in the past and have often proved highly stable. A good example is medieval Europe, in which Latin (H) was used for all serious purposes, while the innumerable local vernaculars (L) remained the everyday speech of the entire population, most of whom knew nothing of Latin. This state of affairs persisted for centuries before Latin finally gave way to the new national languages like French, Spanish, Italian and German, which had previously been regarded as unfit for serious purposes.

See also: **bilingualism**

Further reading: Ferguson 1959; Holmes 1992; Stockwell 2002a; Wardhaugh 2005.

DIRECT OBJECT

The grammatical status of a **noun phrase** which occurs inside a **verb phrase** and which is the second obligatory argument of a transitive verb. For example, *Susie threw the ball* features a **transitive** verb *threw* with the *direct object the ball*. The direct object here functions as the patient or beneficiary upon which the verb acts. Intransitive verbs (*die, go, fell*) cannot take direct objects (**He died her, *She went her mother's,* I fell the hill*), except in creative or deviant circumstances. Direct objects are marked for **case** in case languages as *accusative* in languages like Latin or Russian (or the English case-remnant accusative *me* in *He hit me* rather than the nominative **He hit I*), and are marked in the *absolutive case* in *ergative* languages like Basque.

Direct objects have the property of being able to become the subject of the *passive* form of the sentence (*The ball was thrown by Suzie*; compare **She was died, *The hill was fallen by me*). In **Government-and Binding theory**, indirect objects are not recognized so direct objects are simply classified as *objects*.

See also: **case**; **transitivity**

Further reading: Blake 2001; Jackson 2002.

75

DISCOURSE

In **sociolinguistics** and **critical discourse analysis**, *discourse* is any connected piece of speech or writing in its social context (this last circumstance sets discourse apart from **text**). In **applied linguistics**, discourse refers more narrowly to the interactive and communicative dimension of language, and involves **conversation analysis**, **semiotics**, and the dynamic processes of text production and understanding. While usage varies, we most commonly apply the label **discourse analysis** to an approach which is based heavily upon traditional grammatical concepts, **conversation analysis** to an empirical approach which rejects traditional concepts and seeks to extract patterns from data, and **text linguistics** to the study of large units of language each of which has a definable communicative function.

See also: **cohesion**; **critical discourse analysis**; **discourse analysis**

Further reading: Allen and Guy 1974; Carter 1997; Coulthard 1985; Cutting 2002; Mills 2004; Nofsinger 1991; Renkema 2004; Schiffrin 1994; Sinclair and Carter 2004; Sinclair and Coulthard 1975.

DISCOURSE ANALYSIS

An approach to the study of **discourse** which is based upon traditional grammatical concepts and terms. In principle, we might apply the label *discourse analysis*, or DA, to any kind of investigation of the structure of discourse, but in practice the label is most commonly reserved for an approach based upon familiar grammatical concepts. That is, a proponent of discourse analysis comes to the analytical task with a complete battery of grammatical concepts and terms of the sort familiar to any student of grammar and attempts to see how these concepts are involved in structuring discourses. To put it another way, DA is an attempt to extend our highly successful analysis of sentence structure to units larger than the sentence.

Though there is considerable variation in practice, DA often begins by trying to identify minimal units of discourse and then by looking for rules governing how these minimal units can be strung together in sequence to produce well-formed discourses, much as smaller syntactic units are combined into sentences according to the rules of syntax. DA thus contrasts strongly with the alternative approach known as **conversation analysis**. Proponents of DA complain that conversation analysis is hugely inexplicit and *ad hoc*, and lacking in any identifiable underpinning, while the practitioners of the other approach in turn accuse DA of being excessively *a priori* and of paying too little attention to real texts, as opposed to deliberately constructed ones.

DA has been prominent since the 1970s; it is particularly important in Germany and the Netherlands, where it is often almost indistinguishable from **text linguistics**, but it has also been pursued with some vigour in the English-speaking countries. More recently, discourse analysis has been invigorated by the use of *corpus linguistics* and the availability of large corpora of spoken discourse transcriptions.

See also: **computational linguistics**; **conversation analysis**; **text linguistics**

Further reading: Brown and Yule 1983; Carter 1997; Eggins and Slade 2004; Fairclough 1995, 2003; Levinson 1983; McCarthy 1991; Renkema 2004; Wooffitt 2005.

DISPLACEMENT

The ability to speak about things other than the here and now. With just a single known exception (see below), every signal used by a non-human creature to communicate pertains wholly and directly to the immediate time and place of signalling. No non-human signal, with the marginal exception of scent markings left to define territory or to provide a trail, ever refers to the past or the future, to hypothetical or counterfactual states of affairs, or to anything not directly perceptible to the creature signalling. To put this more picturesquely, mice do not swap stories about their close encounters with cats, nor do bears soberly discuss the severity of the coming winter; rabbits do not engage in heated discussions about what might lie on the far side of the hill, nor do geese draw up plans for their next migration.

Human language is utterly different. We have not the slightest difficulty in talking about last night's football game, or our own childhood, or the behaviour of dinosaurs which lived over 100 million years ago; with equal ease, we can discuss political events in Peru or the atmosphere of the planet Neptune. And, of course, we can discuss what might have happened if the South had won the American Civil War, and we can produce fables and fantasies involving hobbits, dragons, talking animals and intergalactic wars.

All this is *displacement*: the ability to talk about things other than what we can see, hear, feel and smell at the moment.

This displacement, which we take utterly for granted, is one of the most momentous differences between human languages and the signalling systems of all other species. They can't do it at all; we do it almost every time we open our mouths.

There is just one striking exception. A honeybee scout which has discovered a source of nectar returns to its hive and performs a dance, watched by the other bees. This *bee dance* tells the watching bees what direction the nectar lies in, how far away it is, and how much nectar there is. And this is displacement: the dancing bee is passing on information about a site which it visited some time ago and which it now cannot see, and the watching bees respond by flying off to locate the nectar. Startling though it is, the bee dance is, so far at least, absolutely unique in the non-human world: no other creatures, not even apes, can communicate anything of the sort, and even the bee dance is severely limited in its expressive powers: it cannot cope with the slightest novelty.

The importance of displacement was first pointed out by the American linguist Charles Hockett in 1960.

See also: **design features**; **open-endedness**; **stimulus-freedom**

Further reading: Trask 1995.

DISTINCTIVE FEATURE

Any one of a number of minimal phonological elements of which **speech sounds** or **phonemes** are composed. For decades after the **phoneme** concept was introduced into linguistics, linguists tended to assume that each phoneme was an independent unit which could not be analysed into any smaller units. But this view, while profitable, ran into serious difficulties in some respects. Most obviously, it provided no basis for recognizing the **natural classes** of phonemes which often need to be singled out in describing languages.

Eventually, therefore, phonologists ceased to regard phonemes as indivisible, and to treat them instead as *bundles*, or *matrices*, of smaller components. These smaller components are *distinctive features*, or *features* for short. In most cases, the features invoked are *binary*, meaning that a feature can only be either present (marked by [+]) or absent (marked by [–]).

For example, all sounds which are produced with **voicing**, such as [a m z d], carry the *feature specification* [+ voice], while voiceless sounds, such as [p f h], are [– voice]. Similarly, sounds produced with the velum lowered, like [m n ã], are [+ nasal], while all others are [– nasal]. A suitable set of such features, typically around fifteen or so, is adequate both to distinguish every phoneme in a language from every other, and also to characterize the required natural classes: for example, the set /p t k/, which is a natural class in English, might be singled out as [– continuant, – friction, – voice], the class of voiceless frictionless stops.

The set of feature specifications identifying a particular segment or class was long regarded as a mere unordered collection of items with no internal structure, but, since the 1980s, there has been a marked tendency to assign to each set of features a kind of hierarchical structure, in which some features are treated as subordinate to other features; this approach is called *feature geometry*.

The idea of distinctive features was first developed by the European linguists of the Prague School in the 1930s, first by the Russian Nikolai Trubetzkoy, but most prominently by Roman Jakobson. Jakobson later emigrated to the USA, and there, in collaboration with the Swede Gunnar Fant and the American Morris Halle, put together the first complete theory of distinctive features, in the 1950s. This first effort was formulated in terms of *acoustic features* reflecting things that could be seen in a sound spectrogram, but in the 1960s Halle and Noam Chomsky proposed a very different set of *articulatory features*, based chiefly on the activities of the speech organs. Features of this sort have predominated in phonology ever since, though phonologists continue to propose modifications to the system even today.

See also: **natural class**; **phoneme**

Further reading: Ball and Rahilly 1999; Clark and Yallop 1995; Collins and Mees 2003; Giegerich 1992; Hawkins 1984; Katamba 1989.

DISTRIBUTION

The set of positions in which a given linguistic element or form can appear in a language. The notion of *distribution* is a central feature of the approach to language study called **structuralism**, and it was outstandingly important in the version called *American structuralism*.

79

Distribution is a simple notion. Any given linguistic element which is present in a language, whether a speech sound, a phoneme, a morpheme, a word, or whatever, can occur in certain positions but not in other positions. A statement of its possible positions is its distribution, and this distribution is usually an important fact about its place in the language.

For example, distribution is important in identifying **parts of speech**. In English, any word which can occur in the slot in *This – is nice* must be a **noun**, because English allows only nouns to occur in this position. And larger **syntactic categories** can be partly identified in the same way: anything that can occur in the slot in *– is nice* must be a **noun phrase**.

But distribution is perhaps most prominent in **phonology**. Consider the English labiodental fricatives [f] and [v]. Simplifying slightly, in Old English, the sound [v] could only occur between vowels, while [f] could never appear between vowels. Hence Old English allowed words like [fiːf] 'five', [fæːt] 'fat', [livian] 'live' (verb), and [ovər] 'over', but no words like *[væːt] or *[ofər]. We say that, in Old English, [f] and [v] were in *complementary distribution*, meaning that there was no position in which both could occur. Since the two sounds are phonetically similar, we can therefore assign both to a single **phoneme**, usually represented as /f/. Indeed, the Old English spellings of the four words were *fif*, *fatt*, *lifian* and *ofer*, reflecting the fact that only one phoneme existed.

In modern English, however, the distribution of these two sounds is very different: they can both occur in the same positions to make different words. We thus have **minimal pairs** like *fat* and *vat*, *fine* and *vine*, *rifle* and *rival*, and *strife* and *strive*. We therefore say that [f] and [v] are in *contrastive distribution*, and they must now be assigned to separate phonemes, /f/ and /v/, just as the modern spelling suggests.

See also: **phoneme; phonotactics**

Further reading: Giegerich 1992.

DUALITY OF PATTERNING

A type of structure in which a small number of meaningless units are combined to produce a large number of meaningful units. Non-human creatures have signalling systems based upon 'one sound, one meaning', and hence they can express only a tiny number of meanings. Since we can scarcely produce more than 100 distinguishable speech sounds, and if our languages worked in the same way, it would follow that we would not be able to produce more than 100 distinct units of meaning.

But human languages are organized differently. Each spoken language possesses a small number of basic speech sounds: its **phonemes**. The number varies from a minimum of ten to a maximum of around 100, with the average being around thirty. Crucially, these phonemes are themselves meaningless, but they can be combined into sequences which are meaningful.

English has around forty phonemes (the precise number depending on the **accent**). Among these are /p/, /t/, /k/, and /æ/ (as in *cat*). Even just these four phonemes can be combined variously to produce a large number of words with very different meanings: /æt/ *at*, /ækt/ *act*, /kæt/ *cat*, /pæt/ *pat*, /tæp/ *tap*, /kæp/ *cap*, /pæp/ *pap*, /pækt/ *pact* or *packed*, /tækt/ *tact* or *tacked*, /kæpt/ *capped*, /tæpt/ *tapped*, and so on. Adding one more phoneme, the **diphthong** /eɪ/, we can now get /peɪ/ *pay*, /keɪ/ *Kay*, /teɪp/ *tape*, /keɪk/ *cake*, /teɪk/ *take*, /keɪp/ *cape*, /teɪpt/ *taped*, and so on. With forty-odd phonemes, English can produce a huge number of one-syllable words, but of course English also has words that are several syllables long.

Duality thus allows a language to form many tens of thousands of different words, all of which can be produced by a **vocal tract** which can produce no more than a few dozens of distinguishable speech sounds. Duality is therefore of crucial importance in facilitating the existence of spoken languages. Together with the grammatical property of **recursion**, duality allows human languages the ability to produce an infinite number of utterances, all with different meanings, and hence makes **open-endedness** possible.

Sign languages perhaps lack duality; this has been much debated. It is not in doubt that the signs of sign languages can be decomposed into smaller meaningless elements, but it is not clear at present that these smaller elements form a system analogous to a set of phonemes in a spoken language.

The importance of duality was first pointed out by the French linguist André Martinet in the 1950s (he called it *double articulation*) and by the American linguist Charles Hockett in 1960; it was Hockett who coined the term *duality*.

See also: **animal communication**; **design features**; **phoneme**; **phonotactics**

Further reading: Trask 1995.

DYSLEXIA

A certain disability affecting reading and writing. Strictly, *dyslexia* (often informally called *word blindness*) is a disability with reading, while the related disability with writing is *dysgraphia*, but the two very commonly occur together. (The terms *alexia* and *agraphia* are often preferred in North America.) A *dyslexic* has difficulty in perceiving a printed page: the words on the page often appear distorted, as though viewed through a misshapen lens; both the order and the shapes of the letters may be perceived wrongly or appear to 'jump'. Similar problems affect writing: letters may be put down in the wrong order or turned upside-down or backwards. Both in reading and in writing, mirror-image letters like b, d, g and q may be confused. In more severe cases, called *deep dyslexia*, words may be confused with totally unrelated words, even those of very different appearance, which are somehow similar in sound, meaning or grammatical class: for example, *saw* with *was*, *dinner* with *food*, *rib* with *ride*, *bun* with *cake*, *saucer* with *sausage*, *for* with *and*.

As is usual with linguistic disfluencies such as *stammering* (*stuttering* in the USA), individuals vary significantly in the particular symptoms they exhibit, and treatment or management varies correspondingly. Also, as with other disabilities, dyslexia and dysgraphia may be present from early childhood in children showing no sign of brain damage, or they may be acquired in adulthood as a result of brain damage; the two cases are called *developmental dyslexia* and *acquired dyslexia*, respectively. The former belief that dyslexia could be traced to a single uniform cause is now known to be false: dyslexia can in fact result from any of a number of different causes, and many specialists suspect that any given case of dyslexia probably results from the interaction of several distinct factors. Though linguistic disfluencies have in the past been taken as signs of low intelligence, research has shown this is not the case.

See also: **aphasia**; **language disability**

Further reading: British Dyslexia Association 1996; Crystal 1997; Malmkjær 2004.

ELICITATION TECHNIQUES

In most branches of **applied linguistics** such as **sociolinguistics**, **psycholinguistics** and other sub-disciplines which are based on empirical data rather than intuition, a key problem for the fieldwork researcher is obtaining naturalistic data from language users. Where **anthropological linguists** are investigating newly discovered languages, there is often no alternative but to learn the language by spending an extended period of time living in the speech community. This sort of *participant observation* produces an intimate encounter with the language under investigation, but it also runs the risk of falling foul of the **observer's paradox** (that the data will be altered by the presence of the observer). Even in researching familiar and well-documented languages like English, sociolinguistic researchers have developed a large range of ingenious *elicitation techniques* designed to gain access to natural language data without raising the awareness of the informants.

Techniques include asking informants emotionally involving questions (the 'danger of death' scenario) to produce unselfconscious narratives; starting an interview session with casual conversation and gradually increasing awareness through a formal setting, a reading passage, and a list of **minimal pairs**; routinely ignoring the first few minutes of recorded data so that informants become relaxed with the recording equipment; surreptitious recording in a public place (see also **ethics**); using a *sense relation network* – a diagram that links semantically related words to elicit dialect terms; and many others.

Similar methods have to be used when the researcher is interested in the intuitions, attitudes and opinions of the informants. Even theoretical linguists are on safer ground when they base their *acceptability* judgements for well-formedness on informants' opinions rather than exclusively on their own intuitions. In **sociolinguistics**, a *matched guise test* is used in which a recording of the same person speaking in different accents is played to informants, in order to evaluate the informants' attitudes to the accent as a token for their personality and values. Certain accents – typically urban and working-class – are evaluated negatively in terms of educational level, wealth, trustworthiness and even good looks.

See also: **ethics**; **sociolinguistics**

Further reading: Llamas *et al.* 2007.

ELLIPSIS

The omission from a sentence or an utterance of material which is logically necessary but which is recoverable from the context.

Traditional grammarians have for centuries applied the term *ellipsis* to a wide range of phenomena in which some part of a sentence or an utterance appears to be 'missing' or 'understood'. Contemporary linguists, however, generally prefer to use the term more narrowly to denote only the omission of material which can be unambiguously recovered from the context.

So, for example, consider the following exchange. Mike: *Where's Susie?* Sarah: *In the library.* Here, Sarah's response is unambiguously interpretable in the context as meaning *Susie is in the library,* and hence we speak of the ellipsis of the material *Susie is.* But now consider another exchange. Mike: *Here's the book I promised you.* Sarah: *Thanks.* This time Sarah's response cannot be specifically identified as a reduced form of any particular longer utterance, and so we would probably not speak of ellipsis here.

Various particular types of ellipsis can occur within a single utterance, and these often have individual names. Example: *Susie wants me to come to Greece with her, but I can't.* Here the missing continuation is clearly *come to Greece with her,* and this construction is called **VP-deletion**. Another example: *Somebody wants me out, and I know who.* The missing material is *wants me out,* and this construction is **sluicing**.

Ellipsis must be carefully distinguished from **elision**, which is the removal of sounds, as when we pronounce *fish and chips* as *fish 'n' chips*, or when a British speaker pronounces *library* as *libry*. Sounds are elided; words are ellipted.

See also: **cloze**; **syntax**

Further reading: Jackson 2002.

ENTAILMENT

A particular type of inference. If I say to you *Booth assassinated Lincoln*, then, assuming my statement is true, you may safely draw certain conclusions, including *Lincoln is dead* and *Booth killed somebody*. These are among the several **entailments** of my original sentence.

We say that *statement P entails statement Q* whenever the following inference holds: if *P* is true, then *Q* must also be true. Note that any entailment of *P* never contains more information than *P*, and in fact it usually contains less.

Normally, if P entails Q, then Q does not entail P (check this with the examples). But it is possible for P and Q to entail each other, and in this case we are looking at *paraphrases*. Examples: *Sally sold a car to Mike*; *Mike bought a car from Sally*. An entailment differs in several respects from a **presupposition** or a **conversational implicature**. For one thing, an entailment is destroyed by negation: the sentence *Booth did not assassinate Lincoln* does not entail either *Lincoln is dead* or *Booth killed somebody* (presuppositions are different here). For another, an entailment is totally independent of any context (conversational implicatures are different in this respect).

See also: **conversational implicature**; **presupposition**

Further reading: Hurford and Heasley 1983; Levinson 1983; Verschueren 1999.

ETHICS

The *ethics* of data collection have become particularly important in those branches of linguistics which are based on **eliciting** natural-language examples from non-professional informants. It was once thought acceptable to record and collect examples of language from people, and even live amongst them as a friend or visitor, without a thought given to the cultural impact of the fieldwork and without telling them – even after the research was completed – what the researcher was doing at the time. Since the 1980s, especially in **sociolinguistics** and **anthropological linguistics**, there has been a greater emphasis on gaining the consent of speech communities for the research. Where this is not possible because the **observer's paradox** would affect the data collected, then permission and disclosure is effected after the study is finished. There are particular problems involved in gaining access to **vernacular** speech and intimate conversations, and, for different reasons, business and legal discourse. Covert recording, even in a public place, would be largely regarded as illicit. Many universities now have *ethics committees* (an extension of their role in biomedical research) which determine the ethical standards of proposed research projects.

See also: **elicitation techniques**; **observer's paradox**; **sociolinguistics**

Further reading: Cameron 1995; Llamas *et al.* 2007.

ETHNICITY

The relation between language use and ethnic background, especially in a mixed community, has become an important area of study in linguistics. In modern urban societies, it is now commonplace to find speakers of a variety of ethnic backgrounds living together and interacting in various ways. Examples include Anglos, Latinos and black people in western American cities and speakers of Anglo-Saxon, Caribbean and Asian origin in British cities. Especially since the 1980s, some linguists have begun turning their attention to the links between language and ethnic background.

In some cases, of course, some speakers are bilingual (for example, Spanish–English bilinguals in the USA and Punjabi–English bilinguals in Britain). It is of interest to see how and in what circumstances such speakers change back and forth between their languages (this is **code-switching**) and also to find out what influence each language has on the other. The British sociolinguist Ben Rampton has identified the phenomenon of *crossing*, in which a member of one ethnic group deliberately adopts the language or usage of another ethnic group for specific social purposes. Linguists are interested in determining the extent to which a given language or variety serves as a badge of identity for a particular ethnic group, and how that group's variety of a language differs from varieties of the same language used by other speakers.

The study of language and ethnicity has thus become a major strand in sociolinguistics. Specifically, the study of language and ethnicity is sometimes called *ethnolinguistics*.

See also: **Black English**; **code-switching**; **identity**

Further reading: Edwards 1994; Fishman 1999; Fought 2007; Harris 2006; Rampton 1995; Saville-Troike 2003; Stockwell 2002a; Wardhaugh 1987, 2005.

ETHNOGRAPHY OF COMMUNICATION

The study of the norms of communication in a **speech community**, including verbal, non-verbal and social factors. **Anthropological linguists** have long stressed the importance of examining communicative behaviour in the context of a culture, though the term *ethnography of communication* itself was not coined until the 1970s, by the American anthropological linguist Dell Hymes. Investigators have looked at a broad range of variables in a number of speech communities: loudness of voice, pitch of voice, distance between speakers, expressions and postures, eye contact, terms of address, rules for initiating conversations, and many others.

For example, Mexicans in conversation prefer to stand much closer together than do Americans, which can lead to comical results when a Mexican is talking to an American. English-speakers who meet each other but have nothing in particular to say will begin talking about the weather, since silence is considered unacceptable; but Chinese-speakers in the same position may choose to remain silent without giving offence. Hungarian speakers offer less **back-channel** noises (*yes, mmm, uh-huh*) than British speakers require. In Japanese and in Javanese, even the simplest utterance may assume any of a number of very different forms, depending on the relative status of the speaker, the addressee and the person being talked about, and also on the circumstances in which the conversation takes place. Gesticulations accompanying speech differ from one extreme (Italians) to the other (Swedes), and vary enormously in form. Such gestures can contribute to the pragmatics not only of emphasis but also of **denotation**.

See also: **non-verbal communication; paralanguage**

Further reading: Bonvillain 1993; Duranti 1997; Foley 1997; Schiffrin 1994.

ETYMOLOGY

The origin and history of a particular word, or the branch of linguistics that studies this. Every language has a vocabulary containing many thousands of words, and every one of those words has its own particular origin and history, that is its own *etymology*. Sometimes the word in question has been in the language as long as the language has existed; in this case, the word has simply been inherited from some ancestral language. For example, English *three* derives from Old English *threo*, which in turn derives from Proto-Germanic **thrijiz*, which in turn derives from Proto-Indo-European **treyes*, which in turn probably derives from the word for 'three' in the unknown ancestor of Proto-Indo-European (the asterisk denotes a reconstructed form). The same Germanic source yields

Gothic *threis*, Danish and Swedish *tre*, Dutch *drie*, German *drei*, and so on. The same Indo-European source yields Latin *tres*, itself the ancestor of Spanish *tres*, Italian *tre*, French *trois*, Romanian *trei*, and so on. Also from the same Indo-European source come Sanskrit *trayas*, Russian *tri*, Polish *trzy*, Lithuanian *trys*, Albanian *tre*, Irish *tri*, Welsh *tri*, and, less obviously, Persian *se* and Armenian *erek*. The last two may look dubious, but generations of patient and careful etymological work have established the histories of all these words beyond dispute.

In other cases the word in question has not been inherited from an ancestral language, but has instead entered the language at some point in time; it may simply have been 'borrowed' (copied) from a neighbouring language, or it may have been coined by speakers using the resources of the language. In these cases etymologists will be deeply interested in finding out, as far as they can, just when the word was first used, where and by whom, and in what sense. Without such evidence, etymology can be little more than guesswork.

Many thousands of English words have been (directly or indirectly) borrowed from other languages in which they already existed: *angel* from ancient Greek, *lettuce* from Latin, *knife* from Old Norse, *face* from Norman French, *cigarette* from modern French, *skunk* from Massachusett, *shampoo* from Hindi, *brandy* from Dutch, *mosquito* from Spanish, *poodle* from German, *umbrella* from Italian, *alcohol* from Arabic, *ski* from Norwegian, *yogurt* from Turkish, *ukulele* from Hawaiian, *whisky* from Scots Gaelic, *kayak* from an Inuit language, *kangaroo* from the Guugu-Yimidhirr language of Australia, and so on. In such cases, etymologists may be interested in going further, and in tracing the history of the word within the foreign language from which it is borrowed.

Many other English words have been constructed by English-speakers in any of a large number of ways. Such words as *ginger-bread*, *paperback*, *scarecrow*, *spaghetti western*, *strip-tease*, *baby-sit*, *laptop*, *word processor*, *underfunding*, *bewitch*, *megastar*, *non-magnetic*, *miniskirt*, *edit*, *deli*, *flu*, *smog*, *burger*, *love-in*, *laser*, *giggle*, *bang*, *scrooge*, *quixotic*, *gothic* and *malapropism* have all been coined in English by one means or another – some of them centuries ago, others very recently – and etymologists are interested in all of them.

See also: **loan word**; **onomastics**

Further reading: Crowley 1997; Hock and Joseph 1996; Trask 1996.

EUPHEMISM

The use of a word or phrase as a *synonym* for another word which is avoided because of its taboo status or because of its negative political or ideological connotations. Famous examples of euphemism include the huge number of terms for the *lavatory* (itself a word that focuses on washing rather than defecating): *w.c., toilet, restroom, loo* (from the French *lieu* 'place'), *netty* (from the French *nettoyer* 'to wash' or possibly the Italian *gabinetto* 'cabin', i.e., toilet), *little boys/girls room, cloakroom, ensuite, convenience,* and euphemistic phrases such as *powder my nose, pay a visit, freshen up* and many many more. Sex, death, race, drug abuse and the jargon of intimate groups are other areas of *overlexicalized* euphemism.

Political and military euphemism has been a particularly productive area of *lexicalization* as governments have become more democratically accountable and sensitive to adverse public opinion of their wars: the USA–Vietnam war produced *collateral damage* (civilian casualties); the Balkan war turned genocide into *ethnic cleansing*; the USA–Iraq war produced *surgical strikes* (supposedly precise bombing); the Israeli–Hezbollah war refined this as a *needle strike*; soldiers are *assets*; wars are *campaigns*; deadly weapons are *systems*, and so on.

In **critical discourse analysis**, the linguist Paul Chilton has claimed that *euphemism* in discourse is the opposite of **metaphor** as far as ideology is concerned: where metaphor replaces words and is coercive and legitimizing, euphemism is suppressive and dissimulating. He suggests that the linguistic strategies that effect euphemism include not only the sort of lexical replacement listed above but also omission, passivization and nominalization.

See also: **critical discourse analysis**; **metaphor**

Further reading: Chilton 2003; Stockwell 2002a.

FINITE

Marked for **tense**. In many (not all) languages, a single **verb** may exhibit a number of different forms serving different grammatical functions, and these forms are often divided into two types called *finite* and *non-finite*. English, with its small number of grammatical markings, is not the ideal language to illustrate the difference, since some of the non-finite forms look just like some of the finite forms. But let's try.

A finite form is always marked for tense, and it also carries **agreement**, insofar as English has any agreement. Consider the verb *smoke*. Now this **citation form** (or **lemma**) of the verb, the form we use to name it and to enter it in a dictionary, is a non-finite form, the so-called **infinitive**. But the form *smokes*, as in *Susie smokes*, is finite: that *-s* on the end tells us that this form is marked for present tense and that it agrees with a third-person singular subject. Moreover, it is the only verb-form in the sentence, and only a finite form can stand as the only verb in a sentence. By the same reasoning, the form *smoke* which occurs in *I smoke* and *they smoke* is also finite, even though it carries no overt marking at all.

Also finite is the *smoked* of *Susie smoked*, which bears the past-tense suffix *-ed* and is again the only verb in the sentence. But present-tense *smokes* and *smoke* and past-tense *smoked* are the only finite forms the verb *smoke* has.

A non-finite form is not marked for tense, it shows no agreement, and it cannot be the only verb in a sentence. An example is the form *smoking*, which has several functions. In *Susie is smoking*, it combines with the **auxiliary** *is*, which itself is finite. In *I have often seen Susie smoking*, it functions as a kind of **complement** (the finite form here is *have*). In *Smoking a guilty cigarette, Susie pondered the ruins of her love life*, it introduces a kind of **modifier** (the finite form here is *pondered*). In *Smoking is bad for you*, it functions as a kind of **nominalization**, the kind called a **gerund** (the finite form is *is*).

Also non-finite is *smoked* when it functions as a **past participle**, as in *Susie has smoked since she was fifteen* (the finite forms are *has* and *was*), or as a **passive participle**, as in *Cigars are rarely smoked by women* (the finite form is *are*). The infinitive *smoke*, also non-finite, occurs in constructions like *Susie can't smoke in her office* (the finite form is *can*) and *Susie wants to smoke* (the finite form is *wants*).

If, as is sometimes done, we choose to regard sequences like *is smoking* (as in *Susie is smoking*) and *has smoked* (as in *Susie has smoked since she was fifteen*) as single verb-forms, then these are finite, since the first element is finite. It is more usual, though, to analyse such sequences into their finite and non-finite components. But not all such sequences are finite: in *Wanting to smoke a quick cigarette, Susie made a rush for the balcony*, the sequence *wanting to smoke* contains no finite forms at all (the only finite form in the sentence is *made*).

A clause or a sentence containing a finite verb-form is itself finite. Thus, *Susie smokes* is a finite sentence, while both clauses are finite in

Susie always smokes a cigarette after she finishes dinner. But, in *Having finished her dinner, Susie decided to smoke a cigarette,* only *Susie decided to smoke a cigarette* is finite, while *having finished her dinner* and *to smoke a cigarette* contain no finite forms and are non-finite.

See also: **tense**

Further reading: Hurford 1994; Jackson 2002; Jeffries 2006.

FOCUS

Singling out some particular element of a sentence or an utterance as representing the most important new information. Consider the utterance *Susie needs a holiday.* Here it is not obvious that attention is being drawn to any particular part of the utterance. But now add **stress**: *SUSIE needs a holiday.* Now the utterance clearly means 'The one who needs a holiday is Susie, and not somebody else', and we say that *Susie* is in *focus*. If we stress something else, then that element is placed in focus: *Susie needs a HOLIDAY* (it's not something else that Susie needs).

In spoken English, we can always put a particular element in focus by stressing it. But both spoken and written English have another device for placing an element in focus: the use of any of several types of *cleft*. So, we might say, or write, *It's Susie who needs a holiday* (placing *Susie* in focus), or *What Susie needs is a holiday* (placing *a holiday* in focus). Also common, especially in traditional music lyrics and in spoken discourse like sports commentaries, is **topic** *headlining* to create focus: *My true love he is handsome*; *Their defending is atrocious, the Londoners.* However, focus must be clearly distinguished from **topic**: even professional linguists have been known to confuse these terms.

See also: **given/new**; **topic**

Further reading: Greenbaum and Quirk 1990.

FOLK LINGUISTICS

Speakers' beliefs about their language or about language generally. In any given speech community, speakers will usually exhibit many beliefs about language: that one language is older, more beautiful, more expressive or more logical than another – or at least more suitable for certain purposes – or that certain forms and usages are 'correct' while others are 'wrong', 'ungrammatical' or 'illiterate'. They may even believe that their own language was a gift from a god or a hero.

Such beliefs rarely bear any resemblance to objective reality, except insofar as those beliefs *create* that reality: if enough English-speakers believe that *ain't* is unacceptable, then *ain't* is unacceptable, and, if enough Irish-speakers decide that English is a better or more useful language than Irish, then they will speak English, and Irish will die.

It is because of facts like these that some, especially socio-linguists, are now arguing that folk-linguistic beliefs should be taken seriously in our investigations – in great contrast to the usual position among linguists, which is that folk beliefs are no more than quaint bits of ignorant nonsense.

See also: **language myths; prescriptivism**

Further reading: Crystal 1997.

FOREGROUNDING

A **psycholinguistic** term used in **stylistics** to refer to the sense that certain elements in a discourse are more prominent than others. Foregrounding often depends on stylistic *deviance*, which in turn involves a sense of a default or background norm from which the foregrounded element can emerge. Foregrounding is partly a function of linguistic patterning and partly a matter of perception, of course.

In **cognitive linguistics**, the phenomenon of foregrounding is described in terms of *figure* and *ground* relationships. Most pre-positional meanings are reducible to *image-schemas* involving the movement of a **trajector** against a **landmark** (figure and ground, respectively). However, foregrounding is an important feature in cognitive linguistics at the higher levels of text comprehension as well.

See also: **landmark; trajector**

Further reading: Langacker 1987–91; Stockwell 2002b; van Peer 1986.

FORENSIC LINGUISTICS

A relatively recent discipline that applies linguistic techniques as a means of establishing facts in criminal or detective cases. For example, criminals have been tracked down on the basis of their accent signalling where they come from; semantic ambiguities have been highlighted to introduce doubt into criminal convictions; patterns in written texts have been used as part of the psychological profiling of suspects. Forensic linguists explore the language of the criminal court system, policing, and also matters of authorial attribution.

See also: **applied linguistics**

Further reading: Cotterill 2002; Gibbons 2003; McMenamin 2002; Shuy 2005, 2006.

FORMAL GRAMMAR

A grammar which is expressed in terms of notational rules and transformational algorithms. **Generative grammars** are the best-known examples of formal grammar. The rules of the grammar must be self-contained (that is, they should not reach outside their own parameters to point to extraneous or social knowledge), the notational system must consist of a finite set of elements, and the algorithmic rules for transforming strings into other strings should be finite and complete. Working in reverse, a computer program which is based on these formal rules constitutes a *parser* of the language. No computer program yet exists which is able to parse a language with the absolute accuracy of a human being; this possibly points to a fundamental theoretical flaw in the notion of formal grammars.

See also: **generative grammar; grammar**

Further reading: Antony and Hornstein 2003; Chomsky 1977, 2000.

FRAME

A term with a number of senses in different sub-disciplines of linguistics. In various grammars, a *frame* refers to the syntactic framing of a class of words as a structural context: *Suzie found – packet* can frame a word from the class of determiners (*the*, *a*, *her*), for example. In setting out the **case** system of a verb in a case language, the list of possible cases for a verb is a *case frame*. In **semantics** and **cognitive linguistics**, frames are sets of knowledge that are used to provide interpretive information about a piece of language, sometimes called *knowledge frames* or **schemas**.

See also: **case**; **cloze**; **schema**

Further reading: Chafe 1970, 1994; Duchan 2003; Fillmore 1987.

FUNCTIONALISM

Any approach to the description of language structure which attaches importance to the purposes to which language is put. Many approaches to linguistics focus entirely on the purely structural characteristics of languages, ignoring the possible functions of language, and this approach has been very rewarding. But a large number of linguists have preferred to combine the investigation of structure with the investigation of function; an approach which does this is a *functionalist* approach.

There are very many functionalist approaches which have been put forward, and they are often very different from one another. Two prominent ones are **Role-and-Reference Grammar** (RRG), developed by William Foley and Robert Van Valin, and **Systemic Linguistics** (SL), developed by Michael Halliday. RRG approaches linguistic description by asking what communicative purposes need to be served and what grammatical devices are available to serve them. SL is chiefly interested in examining the structure of a large linguistic unit – a **text** or a **discourse** – and it attempts to integrate a great deal of structural information with other information (social information, for example) in the hope of constructing a coherent account of what speakers are doing.

Functionalist approaches have proved fruitful, but they are usually hard to formalize, and they often work with 'patterns', 'preferences', 'tendencies' and 'choices', in place of the explicit **rules** preferred by non-functionalist linguists.

See also: **structuralism**; **Systemic Linguistics**

Further reading: Bloor and Bloor 2004; Givón 1995; Halliday 2004; Siewierska 1991; Thompson 2004.

FUNCTIONS OF LANGUAGE

The various purposes to which language may be put. We often tend to assume that 'the function of language is communication', but things are more complicated than that. Language serves a number of diverse functions, only some of which can reasonably be regarded as communicative. Here are some of the functions of language which we can distinguish:

1 We pass on factual information to other people.
2 We try to persuade other people to do something.
3 We entertain ourselves or other people.
4 We express our membership in a particular group.
5 We express our individuality.
6 We express our moods and emotions.
7 We maintain good (or bad) relations with other people.
8 We construct mental representations of the world.

All of these functions are important, and it is difficult to argue that some of them are more important, or more primary, than others. For example, studies of conversations in pubs and bars have revealed that very little information is typically exchanged on these occasions and that the social functions are much more prominent. Of course, a university lecture or a newspaper story will typically be very different.

This diversity of function has complicated the investigation of the **origin and evolution of language**. Many particular hypotheses about the origin of language have tended to assume that just one of these diverse functions was originally paramount, and that language came into being specifically to serve that one function. Such assumptions are questionable, and hence so are the hypotheses based upon them.

Proponents of **functionalism** are often interested in providing classifications of the functions of languages or texts; see under **Systemic Linguistics** for a well-known example.

See also: **qualitative approach**; **Systemic Linguistics**

Further reading: Bloor and Bloor 2004; Crystal 1997.

GAP

The absence in a sentence of a linguistic element which is in some sense logically required. Though linguists had long been aware of the existence of **ellipsis**, in the 1960s the American linguist Noam Chomsky and his students began to pay particular attention to certain types of 'missing' elements in the syntactic structures of sentences. These missing elements were dubbed *gaps*. Here are a few examples of English sentences containing gaps; as is conventional, the position of each gap is marked with the symbol *e* (for 'empty'): *Susie wants* e *to buy a car* (*to buy* has no subject); *Susie is hard to please* e (*please* has no object); *Who were you talking to* e*?* (*to* has no object); *Susie bought a necklace and Zelda* e *a bracelet* (the second clause has no verb); *Rod gave the museum a T-shirt and Elton* e e *a pair of glasses* (the second clause lacks both a verb and the phrase *the museum*).

The behaviour of gaps has increasingly been seen as crucial in formulating adequate theories of grammar, and recent theories of grammar often provide specific machinery for treating them. Recently the name *empty category* has often been preferred to gap, at least for those cases in which the 'missing' element is a **noun phrase**.

See also: **anaphor**

Further reading: Barss 2003; Huddleston 1984.

GENDER

The classification of **nouns** into two or more classes with different grammatical properties. In many of the world's languages, all the nouns are divided into two or more classes which require different grammatical forms on the noun and/or on certain other words grammatically linked with the noun or nouns in particular sentences. German, for example, has three gender classes (termed **masculine**, **feminine** and **neuter**), which require different forms for associated **determiners** and **adjectives**. Thus, 'the table' is *der Tisch*, 'the pen' is *die Feder*, and 'the book' is *das Buch*, where *der, die*, and *das* are all different forms of 'the'; 'an old table' is *ein alter Tisch*, 'an old pen' is *eine alte Feder*, and 'an old book' is *ein altes Buch*.

It is important to realize that grammatical *gender* need have nothing to do with sex. The word comes from the Latin *genus*, meaning 'kind'. In German (and other European languages), there is a noticeable (but imperfect) correlation between sex and gender assignment, but also some oddities (French feminine *la barbe* 'beard'); however, most nouns denote things that have no sex, and yet they must still be assigned to a gender. In many other gender languages, sex plays no part at all in gender assignment.

A gender language must have at least two gender classes, but it may have more – eight, ten, or possibly even more. The native Australian Dyirbal, for example, has four classes: masculine and animate objects; feminine and dangerous objects; edible objects; others. In some gender languages, we can often guess from the form of a noun which gender it belongs to; in others, we can often guess from its meaning which gender it belongs to; in very many languages, however, we cannot guess, because gender assignment is arbitrary. In German, for example, a noun which denotes a male or a female *usually* (not always) goes into the *der* gender or the *die* gender, respectively, and nouns with certain endings usually go into a predictable gender. After that, though, the gender of the remaining nouns is impossible to guess. In Navaho, nouns denoting humans usually go into one gender, nouns denoting round things into a second gender, nouns denoting long stiff things into a third gender, and so on, but not all nouns can have their gender guessed in this way.

English, it is worth pointing out, has no gender. We have a few sex-marked pronouns like *he* and *she*, and a few sex-marked nouns like *duke* and *duchess* (and many that are becoming disused: *baker/ baxter*; *actor/actress*; *jew/jewess*), but we have no grammatical gender.

Sociolinguists (and others) often use the term gender in a very different way, to indicate the socially performed roles of masculinities and femininities, with only an indirect relationship to biological sex. This usage must be carefully distinguished from the strictly grammatical sense of the term.

See also: **grammatical category**

Further reading: Corbett 1991; Hurford 1994; Trask 1995; and on the sociolinguistic sense: Cameron and Kulick 2003; Coates 1998, 2004; Connell 1995; Holmes and Meyerhoff 2003; Mills 2003.

GENERATIVE GRAMMAR

A grammar of a particular language which is capable of defining all and only the grammatical sentences of that language. The notion of generative grammar was introduced by the American linguist Noam Chomsky in the 1950s, and it has been deeply influential. Earlier approaches to grammatical description had focused on drawing generalizations about the observed sentences of a language. Chomsky proposed to go further: once our generalizations are accurate and complete, we can turn them into a set of **rules** which can then be used to build up complete grammatical sentences from scratch.

A generative grammar is mechanical and mindless; once constructed, it requires no further human intervention. The rules of the grammar, if properly constructed, automatically define the entire set of the grammatical sentences of the language, without producing any ungrammatical garbage. Since the number of possible sentences in any human language is infinite, and since we do not want to write an infinitely long set of rules, a successful generative grammar must have the property of **recursion**: a single rule must be allowed to apply over and over in the construction of a single sentence.

Chomsky himself defined several quite different types of generative grammar, and many other types have more recently been defined by others. A key characteristic of any generative grammar is its *power*: the larger the number of different kinds of grammatical phenomena the grammar can handle successfully, the more powerful is the grammar. But – and this is a fundamental point – we do not want our grammars to have limitless power. Instead, we want our grammars to be just powerful enough to handle successfully the things that actually happen in languages, but not powerful enough to handle things that do not happen in languages.

Within certain limits, all the different kinds of generative grammar can be arranged in a hierarchy, from least powerful to most powerful; this arrangement is called the *Chomsky hierarchy*. The goal of Chomsky's research programme, then, is to identify that class of generative grammars which matches the observed properties of human languages most perfectly. If we can do that, then the class of generative grammars we have identified must provide the best possible model for the grammars of human languages.

Two of the most important classes of generative grammars so far investigated are (context-free) **phrase structure grammar** and **transformational grammar**. The second is far more powerful than the first – and arguably too powerful to serve as an adequate model for human languages – while the first is now known to be just slightly too weak (and has been modified).

(Special note: in recent years, Chomsky and his followers have been applying the term *generative grammar* very loosely to the framework called **Government-and-Binding Theory** [GB], but it should be borne in mind that GB is not strictly a generative grammar in the original sense of the term, since it lacks the degree of rigorous formal under-pinning which is normally considered essential in a generative grammar.)

See also: **phrase-structure grammar**; **transformational grammar**

Further reading: Antony and Hornstein 2003; Bach 1974; Cook and Newson 1996; Lyons 1991.

GENETIC HYPOTHESIS OF LANGUAGE

The hypothesis that the human language faculty is rooted in our genes. This hypothesis holds that our distinctive language faculty is a trait which we have evolved over time, just like our upright posture and our opposable thumb. According to this view, language just *grows* in children, much as their teeth grow, except that language learning requires exposure to speech; that is, the hypothesis sees our language faculty as a distinct and specific part of our genetic endowment. It is seemingly supported by the nature of certain genetically based disabilities, which disrupt language while affecting little else, or which leave language largely unaffected while disrupting most other cognitive abilities. It is perhaps further supported by the existence of the astonishing **language instinct** in children. While controversial, this hypothesis is now widely accepted by linguists. The **innateness hypothesis** is a more specific version of it.

Nevertheless, the genetic hypothesis has been vigorously criticized by the British linguist-turned-computer-scientist Geoffrey Sampson and by the American psychologist Elizabeth Bates and her colleagues.

See also: **autonomy**; **innateness hypothesis**; **language instinct**

Further reading: Bates 1976; Bates *et al.* 1979; Bates *et al.* 1988; Crowley 1997; Macwhinney and Bates 1989; Pinker 1994; Sampson 1997.

GENETIC RELATIONSHIP

The relationship between languages which share a common ancestor. Living languages are always changing, and, when a single language extends over a significant geographical area, different changes inevitably occur in different places. Over time, then, the original language breaks up, first into a continuum of regional **dialects**, then eventually into several quite distinct languages. The several languages which result are the *daughter languages* of their common ancestor, and these daughters are *genetically related*.

Over millennia, this splitting may be repeated again and again, and that single ancestral language may thus give rise to a sizable **language family**. All the languages in the family are genetically related; those which share a more recent common ancestor are more closely related than those whose last common ancestor is more distant.

One of the principal goals of **historical linguistics** is the identification of genetic relationships. This is often easy when the languages in question are closely related – that is, when their last common ancestor was spoken not more than two or three millennia ago. More distant genetic links, resulting from more remote common ancestry, are more difficult to identify with certainty and require careful analytical procedures to avoid being misled by chance resemblances and ancient instances of **language contact**. Eventually, at some time-depth, genetic links become impossible to identify at all, because the ceaseless processes of linguistic change will obliterate all traces of a common origin, or at least render them unrecognizable amid the background noise. Features of language change such as **borrowing**, **language planning** and **prescriptivism** also serve to disrupt the neat family-tree metaphor involved here.

It is possible that all languages are ultimately descended from a single common ancestor – the ancestral speech of the first humans – and hence that all are genetically related, but we will never know about it.

See also: **historical linguistics**; **language family**; **proto-language**; **reconstruction**

Further reading: Lehmann 1992; McMahon 1994; Trask 1994, 1996.

GENRE

A historically stable variety of **text** with conspicuous distinguishing features. The concept of *genre* is shared by (at least) linguistics, anthropology and literary criticism. Its study is well established but contentious, and figures ranging from the Russian linguist Roman Jakobson to the Russian Marxist literary critic Mikhail Bakhtin have made important contributions.

The key fact about a given genre is that it has some readily identifiable distinguishing features that set it off markedly from other genres, and that those features remain stable over a substantial period of time. In most cases, a particular genre also occupies a well-defined place in the culture of the people who make use of the genre.

Among the genres familiar to most of us are lyric poetry, religious liturgy, legal documents, proverbs, fairy tales, scholarly monographs, and news stories. Other societies may present further types, such as the illness-curing chants of Mayan shamans and the oral epic poems of Serbian or ancient Greek bards. Very often mastery of a particular genre is seen as a requirement for a certain profession; this is so for lawyers, bards, academics, shamans, scientists and physicians, among others.

It is characteristic of every genre that the outward form of expression is of vital significance, and at least as important as the content; in some cases the form may actually be more important than the content, as is true of many types of poetry, such as French villanelles and Japanese haiku. In many communities, song and verse genres are characterized by such features as the use of totally different words from the everyday ones and the requirement that no word may ever be repeated. But even a scientific paper is subject to rigid rules of form: the order of presentation must be background/procedure/results/interpretation/conclusions; the paper must be written in an impersonal third person; and all mistakes, accidents and dead ends that cropped up during the work must be silently omitted. A chemist who volunteered in a paper 'At this point I dropped the beaker on the floor and had to start over' would not get his or her paper published.

See also: **text**

Further reading: Bakhtin 1968, 1984; Bhatia 1993; Foley 1997.

GIVEN/NEW

A way of classifying the elements of a sentence according to their information content. Most utterances are not produced in isolation:

instead, each is produced in some context involving what has been said previously and what is known to, or believed by, the speaker and the listener. As a result, it is often the case that some part of an utterance serves only to tie it to this context, while another part introduces some kind of new information. We therefore speak of the *given/new* distinction.

The *given* part of an utterance represents the part which is already familiar to the listener in one way or another, while the *new* part represents the main contribution of the utterance. Consider the following exchange. *Mike: I don't know the woman in the white dress. Susie: Oh, she's the new Professor of Psychology.* Here Susie's reply can be analysed into the given part *she* and the new part *is the new Professor of Psychology.*

The analysis of sentences and utterances in terms of their organization of information was pioneered by the linguists of the **Prague School** in the early twentieth century, especially by the Czech Vilém Mathesius, under the name *functional sentence perspective.* Instead of *given* and *new*, Mathesius used the terms *theme* and *rheme*, and these are still in use today, especially by the proponents of **Systemic Linguistics**, though the terms are used here in a slightly specialized way. Still other linguists prefer the terms **topic** and *comment* in the same senses.

See also: **topic**

Further reading: Brown and Miller 1991; Greenbaum and Quirk 1990; Thompson 2004.

GOVERNMENT

The grammatical phenomenon in which the *presence* of a particular word in a sentence requires a second word which is grammatically linked with it to appear in a particular *form*. Most English personal pronouns occur in two different **case** forms, the *nominative* and the *objective*. Examples: *I/me, she/her, they/them.* When a preposition takes one of these pronouns as its object, that pronoun must appear in its objective form: *with me*, not **with I; for her*, not **for she.* We say that the preposition *governs* the case of its object, or simply that the preposition governs its object. What this means is that it is the very presence of the preposition which requires the objective case. This is not **agreement**: it makes no sense to say that the pronoun is 'agreeing' with the form of the preposition, because an English preposition has only a single form. Government can be more complex. In German, for example, there are several different cases, and some prepositions govern one case, others another. For example, *mit* 'with' governs the dative case, and so German requires *mit mir* 'with me', with the dative caseform *mir* of the pronoun *ich* 'I'. But the preposition *für* 'for' governs the accusative case, and so 'for me' is *für mich*, with accusative *mich*. Each preposition in German governs some particular case, and a learner simply has to learn which prepositions require which cases.

Verbs can also govern case-forms. In Basque, for example, a particular verb may govern objects in any of several cases. Most govern the absolutive case; for example, *ikusi* 'see' does so: *neska ikusi dut* 'I saw the girl' (*neska* 'the girl', absolutive). But some govern the dative, such as *lagundu* 'help': *neskari lagundu diot* 'I helped the girl' (*neskari*, dative). And a few govern the instrumental, such as *gogoratu* 'remember': *neskaz gogoratu naiz* 'I remembered the girl' (*neskaz*, instrumental). In English, all verbs govern objects in the objective case.

For the somewhat special case of gender government, see under **agreement**. In the **Government-and-Binding Theory**, the concept of government is generalized and extended in certain ways that are central to the machinery of that framework.

See also: **agreement**; **dependency**; **subcategorization**

Further reading: Gleason 1961.

GOVERNMENT-AND-BINDING THEORY

A particular theory of grammar, the descendant of **transformational grammar**. During the 1960s and 1970s, Noam Chomsky's transformational grammar went through a number of substantial revisions. In 1980, Chomsky gave a series of lectures in Pisa outlining a dramatic revision of his ideas; these lectures were published in 1981 as a book, *Lectures on Government and Binding*. The new framework presented there became known as the *Government-and-Binding Theory* (GB) or as the *Principles-and-Parameters* approach.

GB represents a great departure from its transformational ancestors; while it still retains a single transformational rule, the framework is so different from what preceded it that the name 'transformational grammar' is not normally applied to it.

As the alternative name suggests, GB is based squarely upon two ideas. First, the grammars of all languages are embedded in a **universal grammar**, conceived as a set of universal *principles* applying equally to the grammar of every language. Second, within universal grammar, the grammars of particular languages may differ only in small and specified respects; these possible variations are conceived as *parameters*, and the idea is that the grammar of any single language will be characterized by the use of a particular *setting* for each one of these parameters. The number of available settings for each parameter is small, usually only two or three.

GB is a *modular* framework. Its machinery is divided up into about eight distinct *modules*, or *components*. Each of these modules is responsible for treating different aspects of sentence structure, and each is subject to its own particular principles and constraints. A sentence structure is well formed only if it simultaneously meets the independent requirements of every one of the modules. Two of those modules – those treating **government** and **binding** (the possibility that two **noun phrases** in a sentence refer to the same entity) – give GB its name.

Just like transformational grammar, GB sees every sentence as having both an abstract underlying structure (the former **deep structure**, now renamed *D-structure*) and a superficial structure (the former **surface structure**, now renamed *S-structure*). There is also a third level of representation, called *logical form* (LF). Certain requirements apply to each one of these three levels, while further requirements apply to the way in which the three of them are related.

The motivation for all this, of course, is the hope of reducing the grammars of all languages to nothing more than minor variations upon a single theme, the unvarying principles of universal grammar. But the task is far from easy, and Chomsky, confronted by recalcitrant data, has been forced into the position of claiming that the grammar of every language consists of two quite different parts: a *core* – which alone is subject to the principles of universal grammar – and a *periphery* – consisting of miscellaneous language-specific statements not subject to universal principles. This ploy has been seen by critics as a potentially catastrophic retreat from the whole basis of the Chomskyan research programme.

GB was an abstract framework to begin with, but it has become steadily more abstract, as its proponents, confronted by troublesome data, have tended to posit ever greater layers of abstraction, in the hope of getting their universal principles to apply successfully at some level of representation. Critics have not been slow to see this retreat into abstraction as a retreat from the data altogether, that is as an attempt to shoehorn the data into *a priori* principles which themselves are sacrosanct. The more outspoken critics have declared the GB framework to be more a religious movement than an empirical science. Nevertheless, GB has for years been by far the most influential and widely practised theory of grammar in existence.

Recently, however, Chomsky has, to general surprise, initiated the **Minimalist Program** (original US spelling), in which almost all of the elaborate machinery of GB is rejected in favour of a very different approach.

See also: **transformational grammar**

Further reading: Antony and Hornstein 2003; Cook and Newson 1996; Cowper 1992; Culicover 1997; Haegeman 1994; Horrocks 1987; Ouhalla 1994; Sells 1985.

GRAMMAR

The rules for constructing words and sentences in a particular language, or the branch of linguistics studying this. Every language has a *grammar*. Where this is set out explicitly in published linguistic descriptions, in textbooks, and taught through the school system, it can be said to be *codified* and *standardized*. Of course, those many languages which have never been subject to professional linguists' detailed scrutiny also operate according to their grammars. The linguistic study of grammar is conventionally divided into two parts: **morphology** – the study of word structure – and **syntax** – the study of **sentence** (or **utterance**) structure.

The tradition of studying grammar is venerable: the ancient Indians, the ancient Greeks and Romans, and the medieval Chinese, Arabs and Jews all did important grammatical work on their favourite languages, and the Port-Royal grammarians in seventeenth-century France were already contemplating grammar from a universalist point of view. But the rise of modern linguistics in the early twentieth century gave new impetus to the study of grammar; by the 1930s and 1940s the American Leonard Bloomfield and his successors were doing important work in morphology, and in the 1950s Noam Chomsky made the study of syntax one of the most prominent of all areas of linguistics, by introducing the new approach called **generative grammar** and by reviving the search for **universal grammar**.

Approaches to the study of grammar are many and various. Pre-twentieth-century approaches represent **traditional grammar**, while most twentieth-century approaches are varieties of **structuralism**. The more formal approaches developed since the 1950s are known as *theories of grammar*; among the more prominent ones are the several versions of **phrase-structure grammar**, Lexical-Functional Grammar, and **transformational grammar** with its descendant **Government-and-Binding Theory**. Among the approaches embedded within **functionalism**, the most prominent is **Systemic Linguistics**.

See also: **generative grammar**; **morphology**; **syntax**; **universal grammar**

Further reading: Brown and Miller 1991; Hurford 1994; Kroeger 2005; Pinker 1994.

GRAMMATICAL CATEGORY

A linguistic category which has the effect of modifying the forms of some class of words in a language. The words of every language are divided up into several *word classes*, or **parts of speech**, such as **nouns**, **verbs** and **adjectives**. It often happens that the words in a given class exhibit two or more forms used in somewhat different grammatical circumstances. In each such case, this variation in form is required by the presence in the language of one or more *grammatical categories* applying to that class of words.

English **nouns** are affected by only one grammatical category, that of **number**: we have singular *dog* but plural *dogs*, and so on for most (but not all) of the nouns in the language. These forms are not interchangeable, and each must be used always and only in specified grammatical circumstances. And here is a key point: we must *always* use a noun in either its singular form or its plural form, even when the choice seems irrelevant; there is no possibility of avoiding the choice, and there is no third form which is not marked one way or the other. This is typically the case with grammatical categories.

English **pronouns** sometimes vary for **case**, as with *I/me*, *she/her* and *they/them*, and again only one of the two forms is generally possible in a given position. English nouns lack the category of case, but nouns in Latin, German, Russian and many other languages do vary in form for case.

English **adjectives** vary for the grammatical category of *degree*, as with *big/bigger/biggest*, and yet again only one of the three forms is possible in a given position.

English **verbs** exhibit the category of **tense**, as with *love/loved*, *work/worked*, *see/saw*, *take/took*, *sit/sat* and *drive/drove*. (Quite a few of these are irregular, but that does not matter: what matters is that the first form is required in certain circumstances but the second in others, and so we have *I see her* [now] but *I saw her* [in the past].) (English verbs have other forms, of course, but these other forms are either not marked for tense, or not just for tense; instead they are marked for other grammatical categories like **aspect** and **voice**.)

Some grammatical categories, like number and tense, are extremely widespread in the world's languages (though by no means universal), while others are unusual and confined to a few languages. For example, some North American languages have a grammatical category of *visibility*, by which nouns and pronouns must be explicitly marked to indicate whether or not the speaker can see the things they refer to at the moment of speaking. And many languages have the category of *evidentiality*, by which every statement must be overtly marked to show the source of the speaker's information: 'I saw it myself', 'Somebody told me', 'I have inferred this from evidence', and sometimes further distinctions.

See also: **aspect**; **case**; **deictic category**; **gender**; **mood**; **number**; **person**; **tense**; **voice**

Further reading: Crystal 1997; Gleason 1961; Lyons 1968; Palmer 1971.

GRAMMATICAL RELATION

Any one of the ways in which a **noun phrase** may be related to a **verb** in a particular sentence. Grammatical relations have been recognized as fundamental since ancient times. Though they were noticeably ignored during the early days of **generative grammar**, they have once again come to be viewed as an essential part of the grammatical structure of a sentence.

Grammatical relations, which are sometimes called *grammatical functions*, are also surprisingly difficult to define explicitly. The most familiar grammatical relation is that of **subject**. In English, the subject of the sentence usually comes first, or at least before the verb, and it is the only thing the verb ever agrees with (English doesn't have much **agreement**, of course). The subjects of the following sentences are bracketed: [*Susie*] *smokes*; *Carefully* [*she*] *poured the wine*; [*My girlfriend's parents*] *are visiting us*; [*Most of my students*] *drink*; [*That you are worried*] *is obvious*. The part of the sentence that follows the subject is the **predicate** (in one sense of that term).

A noun phrase that follows a verb is in most cases a **direct object**. Examples: *She likes* [*me*]; *Susie wants* [*a new car*]; *Susie has visited* [*most of the countries in Europe*]. But, if the verb is one of a small group including *be* and *become*, the following noun phrase is not a direct object but a **predicate nominal**. Examples: *Susie is* [*the cleverest person I know*]; *Susie became* [*an atheist*].

An **oblique object** is less directly connected to the verb. In English, an oblique object surfaces as the object of a **preposition**, though some other languages use case-endings for the same purpose. Examples: *I went to Spain with* [*Lisa*]; *The cat is under* [*the bed*].

Another traditional grammatical relation is the **indirect object**, but it is not clear whether or not indirect objects exist in English. Traditional grammarians would say that *Lisa* is an indirect object in both *Mike gave this book to Lisa* and *Mike gave Lisa this book*, and some linguists agree. However, in the first it is hard to see that *Lisa* is anything other than an ordinary oblique object. In the second, somewhat surprisingly, *Lisa* is arguably a direct object: note the corresponding passive *Lisa was given this book by Mike*.

See also: **grammar**; **parsing**; **syntax**

Further reading: Brown and Miller 1991; Hurford 1994.

GRAPHEME

A single character in a recognized **writing system**. Every established writing system necessarily makes use of some set of written characters. Depending both upon the nature of the system used and on the facts of the language being written, this number may range from a mere handful up to many thousands.

At the simplest level of analysis, for example, the version of the roman alphabet used for writing English makes use of some eighty-odd graphemes: the twenty-six capital letters <A>, <B>, <C>, ... , the twenty-six small letters <a>, <b>, <c>, ... , the ten digits <0>,

<1>, <2>, ..., an assortment of punctuation marks like <.>, <,>, <?> and <;>, and the blank space < >. (It is conventional to enclose a grapheme in angle brackets.)

A more sophisticated analysis of English writing might prefer to set up some additional graphemes, notably the *digraphs* used for writing single sounds, such as the <sh> of *ship*, the <ch> of *chip*, the <th> of both *thin* and *then*, the <ng> of *sing* and the <ea> and <ee> of *bread* and *reed*. Indeed, advocates of spelling reform (such as, most famously, Noah Webster, Mark Twain and George Bernard Shaw) have recommended single joined graphemes to represent these phonemes.

Some other languages using the roman alphabet have additional graphemes involving *diacritics*, such as <ç>, <ş>, <ñ>, <é>, <â> and <ø> (plus their capital versions); these are sometimes counted as distinct letters of the alphabet and sometimes not, but they are still distinct graphemes. A few languages even add further letters, like Icelandic and Old English <þ> and German <ß>. The Arabic alphabet has no capital letters, but most letters have two or even three different graphic forms, depending on where they occur in a word, and each of these different forms is a grapheme.

The non-alphabetic Chinese writing system uses several thousand graphemes for everyday purposes and thousands more for specialist purposes, and the complex mixed system represented by the Egyptian hieroglyphs used a total of nearly 5,000 graphemes.

The standard ASCII set of characters found on most computer keyboards contains ninety-five graphemes, including such symbols as <$>, <*>, <+>, <&> and <@>, which are not usually counted as graphemes in the English writing system. (Incidentally, in *lip-reading* as used by some deaf people, sounds which look the same in terms of mouth and face shape are called *visemes*: examples include the group /p b m/ and /l t d n/. Words like *pet*, *met*, *bet*, *bed*, *bell*, *Ben*, *men* and *pen* cause difficulty for lip-readers.)

See also: **orthography**; **writing system**

Further reading: Coulmas 1996.

HEAD

That element in a **phrase** which is chiefly responsible for the nature of that phrase. Every phrase in every language is built up from smaller units according to certain rather rigid rules. The several different types of phrase are distinguished from one another to some extent by differences in structure but mainly by the nature of the item (usually a word) around which it is constructed; that item is the *lexical head*, the **headword**, or simply the **head**, of the phrase, and it usually provides the name for the kind of *phrase* built up around it.

For example, the **noun phrase** *the little girl in the blue dress* is built up around the **noun** *girl* as its head; the whole phrase denotes some kind of girl. Likewise, the **verb phrase** *sang quietly to herself* is built up around the **verb** *sang* as its head; the whole phrase denotes some specific kind of singing. The adjective phrase *pretty as a picture* is headed by the adjective *pretty*; the adverb phrase *very slowly* is headed by the adverb *slowly*; and the prepositional phrase *under the bed* is headed by the preposition *under*.

The concept of heads is an ancient one, but it largely disappeared from linguistics during the earlier part of the twentieth century. Since the 1970s, however, heads have once again come to be seen as grammatically central, and many contemporary theories of grammar assign them a very prominent place; one or two theories even take headedness to be the most important grammatical notion of all.

See also: **constituent structure; modifier; phrase; phrase-structure grammar**

Further reading: Brown and Miller 1991; Hurford 1994.

HISTORICAL LINGUISTICS

The study of **language change** and of its consequences. Historical linguistics was the first branch of linguistics to be placed on a firm scholarly footing. It is traditional to date the founding of the discipline to 1786, when the British amateur linguist Sir William Jones famously pointed out the clear common ancestry of Greek, Latin and Sanskrit and hence of the existence of the vast **Indo-European** family of languages, all of which descend from a single common ancestor. At about the same time, however, several Hungarian linguists were establishing that Hungarian must likewise share a common origin with Finnish and several other languages, in a different family now called *Uralic*.

Historical linguistics was vigorously developed throughout the nineteenth century, chiefly by linguists who were German or trained in Germany. Most of the attention was on *comparative linguistics*: the business of deciding which languages shared a common ancestry and hence which **language families** existed, of performing **reconstruction** to work out the properties of unrecorded ancestral languages (**proto-languages**), and of identifying the various changes which had led each ancestral language to break up into its several divergent daughters.

In the latter part of the nineteenth century, a number of younger linguists decided that they had enough evidence to declare that sound change was invariably regular – that is, that a given sound in a given context in a given language always changed in the same way, without exception. This *Neogrammarian hypothesis* became the orthodoxy in the field for the next hundred years, and it proved very fruitful.

In the twentieth century, and especially in recent years, there has been an explosion of interest in all aspects of language change. In particular, linguists have been searching eagerly for principles governing language change: what makes some changes more likely than others? It has proved possible to study changes which are in progress in contemporary languages, including English, and such studies have turned up a number of startling phenomena, many of which are clearly incompatible with the Neogrammarian hypothesis. A key point has been the discovery of the crucial link between **variation** and change. Historical linguistics has once again become one of the liveliest areas in all of linguistics.

See also: **comparative reconstruction**; **internal reconstruction**; **language change**; **language family**; **Saussurean paradox**; **sociolinguistics**; **systematic correspondence**

Further reading: Crowley 1997; Fennell 2000; Hock and Joseph 1996; McMahon 1994; Trask 1996.

ICONICITY

A direct correlation between the form of a word and its meaning. The overwhelming norm in languages is **arbitrariness**, by which the form of a word bears no relation to its meaning. But there are certain exceptions, and these exceptions exhibit varying degrees of *iconicity*.

There are several types of iconicity. The most obvious is *pho-naesthetic* analogy, which includes *onomatopoeia*. An onomatopoeic word is one which denotes a sound and which has a linguistic form specifically designed to mimic that sound with some degree of recognizability. English examples include *clink, meow, hiss, bang, boom, hum, quack* and *woof*. But even onomatopoeic words exhibit a good deal of arbitrariness: the sound of a gunshot is represented as *bang* in English, but as *pum* in Spanish, *peng* in German, and *dzast* in Basque. Non-onomatopoeic phonaesthesia can be discerned perhaps in the Basque word *tximeleta* (roughly, chee-may-LAY-tah) 'butterfly', or the English word 'jittery', though these become debatable.

Other forms of iconicity include the *sequential order principle*, by which the order of events or the order of perceptual focus is reflected in the linguistic sequence; the *quantity principle*, which suggests that linguistic complexity is matched to conceptual complexity; and the *proximity principle*, which suggests that conceptual or emotional distance is mirrored in linguistic distance. This last form of iconicity includes 'distance' measured not just in terms of the length of the utterance but also in terms of distancing caused by modalization, hypothesis, negation, fictional narrativizing, and so on. The study of how experience and language are related iconically is part of **cognitive linguistics**.

See also: **arbitrariness**; **cognitive linguistics**; **sound symbolism**

Further reading: Anttila 1988; Hiraga 2005.

IDENTITY

Identity in relation to linguistics concerns the role of language in providing a speaker with individuality and group membership. Every time you open your mouth, you give other people important clues about what sort of person you are: where you come from, what social class you belong to, even your sex and age (for example, on the telephone). This information says something both about your individuality and about the social, national and ethnic groups to which you consider yourself to belong. For several decades now, sociolinguists have realized that providing each speaker with an individual and group identity is one of the most important **functions of language**.

An appreciation of this identifying function of language is crucial in understanding many types of social and linguistic behaviour. One of the most obvious of these is the seeming paradox that many people consistently describe their own speech as 'bad' or 'wrong' or 'inferior', and yet make no effort to change it towards the sort of speech they explicitly describe as 'better'. In fact, people have been observed asserting one view of their own variety's stigma, while simultaneously encouraging and correcting their children's speech towards that stigmatized vernacular. In these cases, the maintenance of a valued social identity overrides any other consideration.

The link between language and identity can involve entirely different languages. Welsh-speakers in Wales or Basque-speakers and Catalan-speakers in Spain may (and often do) regard their distinctive language as a central part of their identity and may deeply resent pressures to abandon their ancestral language in favour of the more prestigious English or Spanish. Rather than consenting to becoming anonymous if slightly quaint speakers on the fringes of the English-speaking or Spanish-speaking world, they prefer to see themselves as part of a distinct people, with their own nation, their own history, their own traditions, their own values and their own goals; the most obvious outward sign of this distinct identity is their language. The all-too-common failure to recognize or esteem this identifying effect of language has led countless times to grief and to major social, educational and political problems.

See also: **social stratification of language**

Further reading: Crystal 1997; de Fina 2003; Fishman 1999; Joseph 2004.

IDEOLOGY

In linguistics, *ideology* refers to the set of beliefs underlying an **utterance** or **discourse**. It is an especially important notion in **Systemic Linguistics** and in **critical discourse analysis**. In everyday language, 'ideology' and 'ideological' tend to have negative connotations, but these linguists regard every example of language in use as having an ideological dimension. For example, an utterance that describes an event in the world has to choose one of the many possible lexicogrammatical ways in which that event can be encoded: active, passive, focusing on one topic rather than another, foregrounding one perspective rather than another, choosing particular naming and address patterns rather than others, selecting a level for formality, register, politeness, and so on. All of these encode a range of ideological choices, and there is no neutral choice. Choices which are seen as natural and neutral are usually simply ideological realizations which the receiver agrees with.

See also: **identity**; **minority language**; **national language**; **official language**; **power**

Further reading: Bourne and Cameron 1989; Crowley 1996; Fairclough 1995; Simpson 1993.

IDIOM

An expression whose meaning cannot be worked out from the meanings of its constituent words. Even if you know the meanings of all the words in the phrase *let the cat out of the bag*, you cannot guess the idiomatic meaning of the whole expression: this you must learn separately. (It means, of course, to reveal something publicly which is supposed to be a secret.) Such an expression is an *idiom*, and English, like other languages, has lots of idioms. Among these are *buy a pig in a poke* (commit oneself to an irrevocable course of action without knowing the relevant facts), *the tip of the iceberg* (the small visible part of a large problem), *kick the bucket* (die), *three sheets to the wind* (drunk) and *stick to one's guns* (refuse to change one's mind or give up).

The meanings of all such idioms are unpredictable and must be learned separately. Many such idioms are so familiar that native speakers hardly realize they are using an idiom at all. Exposure to a foreign language quickly reveals the true position: for example, the Basque idiom *Ez kendu babak altzotik* is literally 'Don't take the beans out of your lap', but no non-speaker of Basque is likely to guess the idiomatic meaning. (It means 'Don't get up on your high horse', 'Don't lecture me', and perhaps you can now see the motivation for the idiom.)

Idioms usually derive from the social history of the language community and thus offer a good guide to the cultural concerns of that society. British English has many idioms from its seafaring past (*copper-bottom investment, money for old rope, cash on the nail, set off on a different tack, got him over a barrel, between the devil and the deep-blue sea,* and many others including *three sheets to the wind*). Idioms often, though not always, involve **metaphor**.

A linguistically fascinating fact about idioms is that some of them (though not all of them) can undergo the ordinary syntactic processes of the language. For example, *let the cat out of the bag* can appear in sentences like *The cat has been well and truly let out of the bag,* or *Several cats were let out of that particularly secret bag,* in which the idiom has been broken up and its parts scattered about the sentence, and yet the idiomatic sense is still present. Such findings pose interesting problems both of syntax and of **psycholinguistics**.

See also: **metaphor**; **vernacular**

Further reading: Fernando 1996; Huddleston 1984; Langlotz 2006.

INDICATOR

In **sociolinguistics**, an **indicator** is a linguistic variable which does not carry any social significance for the speaker, unless their attention is explicitly drawn to it. Such features are typically indicative of some social factor, though they are below the conscious awareness of speakers. As such, they are very useful for sociolinguists. Examples might include the systematic use of 'dark /l/' (a velarized /l/) for a 'light /l/' (alveolar or dentalized) in many Scottish accents, which most speakers can hear but are not normally explicitly aware of; or the use of the non-standard 'I'll be there while midnight' (= 'until midnight') which many north-western English speakers use without being conscious, until they travel elsewhere, that it is non-standard.

See also: **marker**; **stereotype**

Further reading: Chambers 2003; Llamas *et al.* 2007; Stockwell 2002a.

INDIRECT OBJECT

In a sentence *I gave him the ball,* there are three **arguments**: the subject (*I*), the **direct object** (*the ball*) and an **indirect object** (*him*) which receives the action of the verb and is additional to the

115

obligatory direct object. In **case** languages, the indirect object is usually marked in the **dative** case. In languages like English, it is indicated in the word-order, or sometimes with the particle 'to'. So the following are allowed: *I gave the ball to him, To him I gave the ball.* The following sound odd: **I him gave the ball, *I gave the ball him,* though the latter is possible in some dialects. There are disagreements in different grammars over what counts as an indirect object, and in **generative grammar**, only **direct objects** are recognized – all other **noun phrases** are treated separately.

See also: **argument; case; direct object**

Further reading: Blake 2001; Jackson 2002; Jeffries 2006.

INDO-EUROPEAN

A vast **language family**. People have long been aware that certain languages are strikingly similar to certain other languages. In the late eighteenth century a few linguists began to realize that certain ancient languages of Europe and Asia, notably Latin, Greek and Sanskrit (in India), were so remarkably similar in their grammars that they must share a common origin. This observation, famously made by Sir William Jones in 1786, marks the official beginning of the recognition of the Indo-European (IE) family. It was quickly realized that Gothic (and the other Germanic languages), Old Persian (and the other Iranian languages) and the Celtic languages also shared the same common origin, as well as the Baltic and Slavic languages, and Albanian and Armenian. Over a century later, texts written in several long-extinct languages were unearthed in Anatolia and central Asia; when deciphered, these too proved to be written in ancient Indo-European languages: Hittite (and several other Anatolian languages) in the first case and the Tocharian languages in the second. A very few other ancient Indo-European languages have turned up in inscriptions but are so poorly documented we know little about them.

By applying **comparative reconstruction** (which was largely developed and refined by its application here), linguists were eventually successful in carrying out a substantial reconstruction of the single language which was the remote ancestor of all these languages. This ancestor is called *Proto-Indo-European*, or PIE. The speakers of PIE were illiterate and left no records, but we nevertheless know a great deal about the phonology, grammar and vocabulary of PIE. For example, we are confident that a PIE root of the approximate form *kwel- 'revolve, turn' (the asterisk indicates a reconstructed form) is the source of Latin *collum* 'neck', Greek *polos* 'pole' – borrowed as English (*north*) *pole* – and Old Church Slavonic *kolo* 'wheel' (among others), and that a reduplicated form of this *kwekwlo-* is the source of Greek *kuklos* 'circle, wheel' – borrowed as English *cycle* – Sanskrit *cakra-* 'wheel' and English *wheel* (Old English *hweowol*). We think PIE was probably spoken around 6,000 years ago, but the place is unknown. Most people favour the south Russian steppes, but others have argued for the Balkans, Anatolia, the Middle East, the Caucasus, central Asia and other locations. In any case, the IE languages eventually spread over a huge area of Asia and most of Europe, repeatedly breaking up into clusters of daughter languages as they did so. In the process, the IE languages obliterated an unknown number of earlier languages, including all the earlier languages of Europe except for Basque in the west and Finnish and its relatives in the north. Until the eve of modern times, the Indo-European family extended from India to western Europe (hence its name), but the European colonial expansion has introduced IE languages like English, Spanish, French, Portuguese and Russian into vast areas of the globe, displacing many more languages in the process. Today about half the world's people speak IE languages, even though the number of living IE languages is below 200.

See also: **comparative reconstruction**; **language family**; **reconstruction**

Further reading: Baldi 1983; Beekes 1995; Lehmann 1967, 1993; Lockwood 1969, 1972; Mallory 1989; Szemerényi 1996; Trask 1996.

INFINITIVE

Traditional grammar has the unmarked form of a verb expressed as *to go*, *to be*, *to do* and calls these **infinitives**. However, no modern grammar follows this practice. The infinitive is the non-finite form of a verb, unmarked for tense, person, number or mood. Some languages have a separate form for the infinitive (Spanish *completar* 'to complete', French *venir* 'to come'); English uses an uninflected stem (*complete*, *come*, *be*, *do*, *go*). Infinitives are most often used as the complements of other verbs: *He wanted to go*, *I was going to be* *there by ten, To jump in the river would not be allowed*. In the sentence, *He was going to go boldly where no one had gone before*, any syntactic test would show that *go boldly where no one had gone before* is a constituent **verb phrase**, and there is no reason other than historical ignorance to outlaw the 'splitting of the infinitive' and say correctly *He was going to boldly go where no one had gone before*.

See also: **finite**; **verb**

Further reading: Jackson 2002; Hurford 1994.

INFLECTION

Variation in the form of a single word for grammatical purposes. In many (not all) languages, a single word can assume any of several different forms, or even dozens of different forms, the choice depending on the grammatical context in which it is used. This is *inflection*. A word may be inflected by adding **affixes** or by various types of internal change.

English has very little inflection, but it does have some. A typical **noun** has only two grammatical forms: singular and plural (*dog/dogs, child/children, foot/feet*). A typical **verb** has slightly more forms than a noun; for example, *write* has *write, writes, wrote, written, writing*, while *love* has only *love, loves, loved, loving*, and *put* has just *put, puts, putting*. (The number is larger if we count syntactic forms like *has written* as inflections, which we sometimes do but usually don't.) A typical **adjective** has three inflected forms: positive *big*, comparative *bigger*, superlative *biggest*.

Inflection is not universal. Vietnamese, for example, has no inflection at all, and every word is completely invariable in form. On the other hand, some North American languages have astonishingly complex inflectional systems, in which a single verb may appear in hundreds of different forms.

The key point about inflection is that applying it never gives you a new word, but only a different form of the same word (the **lemma**). But **derivation**, in contrast, does produce new words which have to be entered separately in a dictionary.

See also: **derivation**; **grammatical category**; **morphology**

Further reading: Bauer 1988; Brown and Miller 1991.

INNATENESS HYPOTHESIS

The hypothesis that children are born knowing what human languages are like. It is obvious that *particular* languages are not innate and must be learned. Any child, regardless of ethnic background, will learn perfectly whatever language it is exposed to, and an isolated child prevented from any exposure to language will learn no language at all. Nevertheless, modern linguists are often impressed by the striking resemblances among languages all over the globe. In spite of the obvious and seemingly dramatic differences among them, linguists are increasingly persuading themselves that the observed degree of variation in language structures is much less than we might have guessed in advance, and hence that there are important universal properties shared by all languages.

In the 1960s, the American linguist Noam Chomsky put forward a bold hypothesis to explain this apparent universality: according to his **innateness hypothesis**, a number of important characteristics of language are built into our brains at birth, as part of our genetic endowment, and hence we are born already 'knowing' what a human language can be like. In this view, then, learning a particular language is merely a matter of learning the details which distinguish that language from other languages, while the universal properties of languages are already present and need not be learned.

The innateness hypothesis was controversial from the start, and a number of critics, among them philosophers and psychologists, took vigorous issue with Chomsky's position, arguing that there is no evidence for innate linguistic knowledge, and that the acquisition of a first language could be satisfactorily explained in terms of the all-purpose cognitive faculties which the child uses to acquire other types of knowledge about the world. This controversy reached a head in 1975, when Chomsky debated the issue with one of his most distinguished critics, the Swiss psychologist Jean Piaget.

Chomsky and his supporters have responded in several ways. First, they attempt to point to identifiable universal properties of language, what they call **universal grammar** (itself a deeply controversial notion); these properties they claim to be arbitrary, unexpected and in no way deducible from general cognitive principles. Second, they point out that children *never* make certain types of errors which we might have expected. For example, having learned *The dog is hungry*, they can produce *They dog looks hungry*, yet, having learned *Susie is sleeping*, they *never* produce **Susie looks sleeping*. Third, they invoke the **poverty of the stimulus**. By this term they mean that the data available to the child are quite inadequate to account for the knowledge which the child eventually acquires. For example, the usual rules of question-formation in English seem to predict that a statement like *The girls who were throwing snowballs have been punished* should have a corresponding question **What have the girls who were throwing been punished?* In fact, every English-speaker knows that this is impossible, and no child or adult ever tries to construct such questions. However, there seems to be no way that this constraint could possibly be inferred from what the child hears, and Chomsky therefore invokes a universal principle, supported by comparable data from other languages, which he takes as part of our innate linguistic endowment.

See also: **genetic hypothesis of language**; **universal grammar**

Further reading: Aitchison 1989; Piattelli-Palmarini 1979; Sampson 1997; Steinberg 1993.

INTEGRATIONALISM

An approach to linguistics based on communicativeness, which argues that separating **langue** and **parole** is a mistake (or at least a misreading of the work of Ferdinand de Saussure). Integrationalists argue that the typical separation of language from its context in what they term *segregationalist* linguistics produces an object for analysis that can no longer be considered as language. Instead of being an 'add-on' factor, the pragmatic, psycholinguistic and social setting of an utterance is an inseparable part of its nature, and must be described holistically by the linguist. While persuasive as an idealization, it is difficult to see what an integrationalist practical analysis would actually look like, since every analysis would need to be unique and unrepeatable, and this strikes at the heart of any claim of linguistics to be scientific, generalisable or replicable.

See also: **langue**; **parole**

Further reading: Davis 2001; Harris 1998; Harris and Wolf 1998; Toolan 1996.

INTERNAL RECONSTRUCTION

A method in **historical linguistics** which can be applied to a single language to recover information about its past. The name *internal reconstruction* is given to several related but different procedures. What most of them have in common is this: we observe that a certain pattern exists in the language of interest, but that certain forms are exceptions to the pattern; we hypothesize that the exceptional forms were once regular, and we identify the changes which made them irregular.

A particularly famous example of internal reconstruction involves **Proto-Indo-European** (PIE), the unrecorded ancestor of the **Indo-European** languages. The young Ferdinand de Saussure observed that, while the vast majority of PIE verbal roots could be reconstructed with the general form *CeC-*, where *C* represents any consonant, there were a number with other forms: *eC-*, *aC-*, *oC-*, *Ce:-*, *Ca:-* or *Co:-*, the last three always with long vowels represented by a colon. Saussure therefore hypothesized that these exceptional roots had once been perfectly regular roots of the form *CeC-*, but that certain ancestral consonants had been categorically lost from the language, that some of these vanished consonants had first altered the quality of a neighbouring vowel *e* to *a* or *o*, and that all of them had, upon disappearance, induced lengthening of a preceding vowel. This analysis makes all the exceptional roots the result of regular phonological change applying to what were originally perfectly normal roots. These hypothetical lost consonants have become known as *laryngeals*, and Saussure's *laryngeal hypothesis* was eventually confirmed by the discovery that one Indo-European language, Hittite, actually preserves some of these consonants.

See also: **comparative reconstruction**

Further reading: Crowley 1997; Fox 1995; Hock 1986; Trask 1996.

INTERNATIONAL LANGUAGE

A language which is widely used, for a variety of purposes, by people in different countries, especially by people for whom it is not a mother tongue. As a consequence of various political and social circumstances, a single language may come to be used extensively by people in a number of countries, most of whom speak various other languages as their mother tongues. In medieval Europe, Latin was everywhere the language of scholarship, science, diplomacy, religion and (usually) the law, and people working in these areas could all write (and sometimes speak) Latin. In eighteenth- and nineteenth-century Europe, French was the international language of diplomacy, of fine arts and high culture, and of polite society generally; most educated people could and did speak French, even if their mother tongue was (say) Russian or German. Chinese and Arabic have likewise served at times as international languages, in east Asia and in the Muslim world, respectively.

Today, however, English is beyond dispute the premier international language throughout the world. English is everywhere the first language in such domains as business, science, technology, communications and popular culture. When a Swedish manufacturing company negotiates a business deal in Thailand, the negotiations are conducted in English. When a Brazilian geneticist publishes his latest research, he publishes in English. When an Egyptian pilot flies into Moscow, he speaks to the control tower in English. When the Secretary-General of the United Nations, the Chairman of the International Olympic Committee or the Commanding Officer of NATO makes an important announcement, he makes it in English. Even pop groups from Norway, Russia, France and Japan often sing in English.

This pre-eminence of English is rather recent; it largely dates from 1945. Though the British Empire had earlier introduced English, as a first or a second language, into huge areas of the world, it was chiefly the rise of American political and economic power, and the accompanying spread of American culture (hamburgers, jeans, Hollywood films, TV shows, rock music) after the Second World War which made a command of English such an attractive and valuable asset in the succeeding decades.

Indeed, English has now become the first *global language* or *world language* the planet has ever seen. That is, English now enjoys some kind of special status in almost every country in the world: as the sole official language, as a co-official language, or as the designated principal foreign language. Polyglot countries like Nigeria, India and Singapore use English for most administrative and commercial purposes; countries like Spain, Germany, Greece, Algeria, Korea and Japan have abandoned French or Chinese as the preferred foreign language in favour of English; many large German business firms now require their senior managers to conduct all internal business in English; Dutch universities have come close to adopting English as the sole language of instruction for all subjects, and may yet do so. It has been estimated that nearly one quarter of the Earth's population – approaching 1.5 billion people – are now competent in English, and the number is growing all the time. Nothing like this has ever happened before.

See also: **power**

Further reading: Brutt-Griffler 2002; Crystal 1997, 2003; Jenkins 2003; Wardhaugh 1987.

INTERNATIONAL PHONETIC ALPHABET

An agreed set of symbols for representing speech sounds. The languages of the world employ a rather large number of distinguishable speech sounds, and, for serious work in phonetics and linguistics, it is essential to have an agreed set of symbols for representing these sounds as explicitly as possible. The twenty-six letters (**graphemes**) of the roman alphabet are not nearly enough for the task, and consequently various systems have been invented for the purpose, most of them based upon the roman alphabet supplemented by various additional symbols and/or diacritics ('accents'). By far the most widely used system is the *International Phonetic Alphabet*, or **IPA**. The IPA was invented in 1888 by the International Phonetic Association, the professional body of phoneticians. The Association has frequently revised and expanded its alphabet, the most recent revision having taken place in 2005: this IPA table is reproduced at the beginning of this book.

The policy of the Association is to keep the use of diacritics to a minimum, and hence the IPA employs a very large number of specially designed characters, such as [ʃ] for the consonant in English *shy*, [ŋ] for the velar nasal in English *singing*, [ɬ] for the sound spelled <ll> in Welsh, as in *Llanelli*, and [ʎ] for the sound spelled <gl> in Italian, as in *figlio* 'son'. This makes the alphabet cumbersome to print, but nevertheless the IPA is the most widely used phonetic alphabet in the world; even many good dictionaries of English and of other languages now often use the IPA for representing pronunciations.

The ordinary roman letters often have obvious values, as with [k], [s], [m] and [i] (this last is the vowel of Italian *si* 'yes'), but a few of these have values which are unexpected for English-speakers: [j] for the initial consonant of English *yes*, [y] for the vowel of French *tu* 'you', [x] for the final consonant of German *Bach* and [r] for the trill of Spanish *perro* 'dog'.

Double characters are used for certain purposes: for example, [tʃ] for the affricate occurring twice in English *church*. Diacritics are used for a wide variety of purposes: for example, [tʷ] is a labialized (lip-rounded) version of [t], [tⁿ] is a nasally released version of [t] (released through the nose, not through the mouth), [b̰], is a creaky-voiced version of [b], and [i̠] is a retracted version of [i] (a vowel resembling [i] but pronounced a little further back in the mouth). Length is marked by a special colon, so that [iː] represents a long version of [i]. There are also symbols for representing various types of tones, pitches, boundaries and pauses.

Though they are primarily designed for representing speech sounds (objective physical events), the IPA symbols are naturally also widely used for representing the **phonemes** of particular languages. For example, the initial consonant of English *think* is phonetically the dental fricative [θ] for most speakers, and so the phoneme realized in this way is commonly represented as /θ/. But note carefully that a conventional phoneme symbol consisting of an IPA symbol in phoneme slashes may not in fact be pronounced in the way the IPA symbol would suggest; for example, the phoneme at the beginning of English *red* is customarily represented as /r/, for orthographical convenience, but probably no native speaker of English ever pronounces this word with the trill [r]: it's just that the IPA symbols that represent precisely what English-speakers say are awkward to print, and moreover different speakers of English use different pronunciations of /r/, pronunciations which would be represented by different IPA symbols (such as [ɾ], [ɽ], [ʀ], [ʁ] or even [ʋ], for example). An IPA symbol in square brackets is (or should be) intended to represent a real speech sound accurately; an IPA symbol in phoneme slashes is just a convenient way of representing some phoneme in some language and may not be a faithful guide to phonetic reality.

In the USA, many people have used a different phonetic alphabet, called ***American transcription***. This uses many different symbols from the IPA, with diacritics in preference to special characters; it was designed for people writing on a typewriter. With the increasing use of computers and word processors which can produce IPA characters, the American system is slowly giving way to the IPA, though you might still find it in older texts.

See also: **consonant**; **phonetics**; **speech sound**; **vowel**

Further reading: Ball and Rahilly 1999; Katamba 1989; Ladefoged 1993; Pullum and Ladusaw 1996.

INTERTEXTUALITY

Connections between **texts**. The concept of **intertextuality** was introduced in the 1960s by the French critic Julia Kristeva, drawing on work by the Russian critical theorist Mikhail Bakhtin. Most obviously, the term can be applied to the prominent allusions made in one literary work to another work, which serve to create counterpoint, continuity, or irony, or draw on authority, or increase artistic richness or resonance, for example. However, Kristeva sees every text as constituting an **intertext** in a succession of texts already written or yet to be written. A version of this idea has recently begun to be incorporated into the linguistic analysis of texts. The general idea is that a text does not exist in isolation and cannot be fully appreciated in isolation; instead, a full understanding of its origins, purposes and form may depend in important ways on a knowledge of other texts. A sonnet may depend upon the reader's familiarity with the sonnet-writing tradition; a newspaper story may depend upon previous news stories; a political speech may invoke earlier speeches and political statements; even a recipe may depend upon the reader's acquaintance with other recipes.

See also: **genre**; **text**

Further reading: Fabb 1997; Thibault 1994.

INTONATION

Variation in the pitch of the voice during speech. In science-fiction films, robots are often made to speak in a dead-level pitch, with no rises and falls. The (intended) effect is one of inhuman speech, for no healthy human being ever speaks in such a way. Instead, the pitch of our voice rises and falls in structured ways during each utterance, and the resulting pattern is the **intonation** pattern of the utterance.

Every utterance in every language, without exception, is produced with some intonation pattern imposed on it. These patterns are largely peculiar to individual languages and accents, though certain universal tendencies can be observed. For example, it is very common in languages for yes–no questions (as in *Are you coming with us?*) to be uttered with a final rise in pitch, while statements (as in *This is my wife*) tend more often to be uttered with a final fall – but Australians and Americans often utter statements with a final rise, a phenomenon which is highly conspicuous to other speakers of English, and which has popularly been dubbed 'uptalk' or the more technical **high-rising terminal**. This feature diffused rapidly across the English-speaking world in the 1990s, and has even found its way into other languages.

The intonation of English has been seriously studied since the 1920s, at least. The British tradition has been to analyse intonation in terms of **contours**, or **tunes**, superimposed on sizable chunks of an utterance; the American tradition, in contrast, prefers to decompose intonation patterns in terms of jumps between several discrete **levels**.

See also: **prosody**; **suprasegmental**

Further reading: Cruttenden 1986; Tench 1996; Yip 2002.

INTUITION

Your 'gut feeling' about the facts of your native language. We all have intuitions about our own language: about what is normal, acceptable, unusual, strange or impossible, or about what a given form means and when we might use it, if at all. The issue, and it is a central one, is how much trust (if indeed any at all) we should place in speakers' intuitions in compiling our descriptions of language.

The American linguists of the first half of the twentieth century, with their adherence to empiricism, generally preferred to base their descriptions entirely on the observed spontaneous usage of native speakers. At times they found it necessary (as we still do today) to interrogate speakers directly to obtain elusive information: 'How would you say X?'; 'Is Y a possible form?'; 'What does Z mean?' But, on the whole, they regarded speakers' judgements as a less secure source of information than spontaneous usage.

In the 1950s, the American linguist Noam Chomsky and his followers put forward a dramatic new proposal: that important facts about a language could be obtained directly from speakers' intuitions. That is, they proposed that you could find out important things about your own language by merely asking yourself questions like 'Is construction X possible, and, if so, what does it mean?' Since almost all the early Chomskyans were speakers of English, this meant that their descriptions of English were very largely based upon their own considered opinions about their own usage. And this policy has proved to be deeply controversial.

For one thing, it didn't take long for sceptical linguists to demonstrate conclusively that native speakers' intuitions were sometimes hopelessly wrong. Again and again, the sceptics found that native speakers of English and of other languages, on being asked 'Is construction X possible for you?', would assert strongly that X was not possible, and would sometimes further insist that they couldn't even understand X – and then, a few minutes later, these same speakers would use X in their own spontaneous speech. A good example is the north-eastern American locution 'They're a lousy team any more', which, on interrogation, is sometimes rejected as ungrammatical and incomprehensible by people who nevertheless use this form freely in their own speech. (The example means 'They used to be a good team, but now they're lousy'.)

For another thing, the linguists who were working on English often had a theoretical stake in the outcome of questions, and time and again a linguist pondering the status of a doubtful example would consult his (or her) own intuitions and find that those intuitions gave him just the answer he needed to make his current analysis work. For example, one linguist, pondering the case of 'I saw us in the mirror', reached the conclusion that this was ungrammatical – which was exactly the result he needed to make his new theory work. Yet most speakers of English who are unacquainted with the theoretical issue and have no stake in it not only agree that this sentence is perfectly grammatical but use such sentences freely in their spontaneous speech.

Consequently, many linguists not of a Chomskyan persuasion today reject intuitions as a reliable source of information and insist on verifiable and observable empirical evidence to test their theories. Much debate concerns methods of minimizing the **observer's paradox**, so that the fieldworkers themselves do not inadvertently alter the data. In **sociolinguistics** and **applied linguistics**, some skilful techniques for linguistic data collection have been developed as a result.

See also: **generative grammar**; **Government-and-Binding Theory**; **sociolinguistics**

Further reading: Labov 1975; Sampson 1975.

IRREALIS

Irrealis verb forms indicate a grammatical **mood** in which the sense expressed is non-actual, doubtful, speculative or is in some other way not real. For example, *If I were rich, I'd buy ten of them* contains two irrealis verbs: the second (*I would*) describes an imaginary state conditional on being rich; and the first (*I were*) expresses an unrealized possibility. Like many **Indo-European** languages, English expresses this latter sense using the *subjunctive* mood form of the verb (*were* rather than the *indicative* mood form *was*), though the subjunctive has been falling out of English usage across the world and is really only maintained in fossilized forms like this. Greek, Sanskrit and Georgian also possess an *optative* mood for irrealis senses, which express desired or hoped-for states. Irrealis forms are used for necessity, obligation, possibility, fears and any sort of counterfactual. In **cognitive linguistics**, irrealis forms are particularly interesting since they cue up parallel or alternate knowledge **frames** which the hearer has to monitor.

See also: **mood**

Further reading: Palmer 2001.

KINSHIP TERMS

The system of terms available in a given language for naming relatives. Kinship terminology varies widely among languages. Where English has only *uncle*, many other languages have different words for 'father's brother' and 'mother's brother'. English distinguishes *niece* and *nephew*, but some other languages have only a single word to cover both, and this same word sometimes covers also 'grandson' and 'granddaughter'. In English, both men and women have only *sisters*, but in Basque a man has an *arreba* while a woman has an *ahizpa*, while in Seneca there are different words for 'older sister' and 'younger sister'. German has a useful word *geschwister* which means 'sibling' but sounds more like the formality level of English 'brother' or 'sister'.

The scope for variation is enormous, but anthropological linguists have found that most kinship systems can be analysed into fairly orderly combinations of a few semantic features, such as [male/female ego], [male/female referent], [older/younger], [ascending/

descending generation]. Several particular systems are found to recur widely in the world's languages, such as the famous *Omaha system* found in certain North American languages and elsewhere.

See also: **anthropological linguistics**

Further reading: Foley 1997; Wardhaugh 2005.

LANDMARK

A term from *cognitive grammar* to explain how prepositions are conceptualized. Prepositions like *over*, *through*, *into*, *from*, *against*, *about* and so on are metaphorically derived from an idealized spatial concept which is called an *image-schema*. The notion of *over*, for example, involves one object in the focus of attention (the *figure*) describing a motion path over the top of an object that receives less attention (the *ground*). Figure and ground in image-schemas are termed **trajectors** and *landmarks* respectively.

See also: **cognitive linguistics; foregrounding; trajector**

Further reading: Croft and Cruse 2004; Langacker 1987–91, Ungerer and Schmid 1996.

LANGUAGE

The central object of study in linguistics. The term *language* covers several rather different concepts which need to be carefully distinguished.

To begin with, of course, we need to distinguish between an individual language – such as English or Swahili – and language in general. Most linguists believe that all individual languages necessarily possess important properties in common – otherwise, **linguistics** would be a somewhat unrewarding discipline – and every individual language is therefore a combination of these **universal** properties with a number of accidental and often idiosyncratic features. For many (not all) linguists, it is these universal properties which are of greatest interest, but the only way we can get at these properties is by scrutinizing individual languages.

In this enterprise, strategies differ. Some linguists prefer to analyse a few languages in exhaustive detail, in the hope of identifying subtle abstract principles concealed deep in the data; these principles constitute **universal grammar**. Others, though, dismiss this approach as narrow and misleading, and prefer to proceed by surveying large numbers of structurally different languages and looking for both generalizations and interesting diversity.

The ultimate goal of linguistics is the elucidation of the human **language faculty** (called *langage* by Saussure). To this end, linguists have usually found it essential to distinguish between the abstract mental system of rules, principles and constraints which are shared by speakers (called **langue** by Saussure and **competence** by Chomsky, though the terms are not quite equivalent) and the real utterances produced by individual speakers on particular occasions (Saussure's **parole**, Chomsky's **performance**). More recently Chomsky has introduced a further distinction: he suggests that an individual language may itself be viewed either as a set of rules and principles in the minds of speakers (his *I-language* – intensional, internal and individual – which is the object of linguistic study), or as a set of possible sentences in society (his *E-language* – external – which cannot be studied); this latter concept is still an abstraction, distinct from actual **utterances**.

One way of getting at the abstract properties of natural languages, championed by Chomsky in his early days and still pursued by others (though no longer by Chomsky), is to devise **formal grammars** which can characterize *formal languages*. The idea is to compare the properties of these formal languages with the observed properties of natural languages to see which kinds of formal grammars give the best fit. This is the motivation behind the construction of **generative grammars**.

By complete contrast, others have seen the formalist linguistic separation of language from its context as a fundamental mistake. **Sociolinguists** and **applied linguists**, for example, regard the collective performance of language by speech communities as the proper object of study. Those working in **pragmatics** or **discourse analysis** similarly work with the social and ideological aspects of language in use. **Integrationalists** regard the study of language as the study of communication, and no piece of language can be wrenched from its interpersonal, social and uniquely occurring situation without fundamentally altering the nature of the data. Though formalism continues to dominate theoretical linguistics, the field of linguistics should properly be seen as being at the centre of this rich and broad-based research movement.

See also: **competence**; **language faculty**; **natural-language processing**; **performance**

Further reading: Chambers 2003; Crystal 1997; Trask 1995.

LANGUAGE ACQUISITION

The process by which a child acquires its mother tongue. The acquisition of a first language is arguably the most wonderful feat we perform in our whole life, and we do it at an age when we can hardly do anything else. An explanation for this feat is now considered to be one of the central tasks of linguistics.

The serious linguistic investigation of acquisition dates mainly from the 1940s, when the Russian linguist Roman Jakobson published a pioneering study. In 1957, the American psychologist B.F. Skinner published *Verbal Behavior*, an attempt at explaining acquisition within the framework of **behaviourism**, but this book was savagely reviewed by the American linguist Noam Chomsky, who argued persuasively that Skinner's account was hopelessly inadequate to explain anything of interest.

From about the 1960s, intensive studies of children acquiring their first language became increasingly frequent; particularly influential was Roger Brown's 1973 book *A First Language*. This body of work quickly established that early acquisition proceeds through a sequence of well-defined stages, called *cooing*, *babbling*, the *one-word stage* and the *two-word stage*. After this, it becomes impossible to recognize well-defined stages, though particular constructions, such as questions and negation, are found to develop in a series of well-ordered stages which are highly consistent not only across children but across languages.

A further crucial observation is that acquisition of a first language seems to be possible only up to a certain age, the *cutoff age*, after which it is no longer possible, an observation formalized in the **critical period hypothesis** put forward by the neurologist Eric Lenneberg in the 1960s. Children deprived of exposure to language during this crucial period are *feral children*, and several such unfortunate cases have been studied.

We now know a great deal about what children can be observed to do as they acquire their first language, and attention has turned increasingly to theoretical interpretation of the raw data. Analysts have been impressed both by the speed of acquisition and by its fundamental orderliness. Many, like Chomsky, have been further impressed by the seeming observation that the data available to the child from adult utterances seem to be inadequate to account for the knowledge acquired. This *poverty-of-the-stimulus* argument led Chomsky to propose his **innateness hypothesis**, by which children are born already knowing what human languages are like, and only need to acquire the details of the language they are learning; to this end, Chomsky postulated a specific **language acquisition device** (LAD) in the human brain.

However, undoubtedly the greatest single advance in the study of acquisition has been the realization that language acquisition is not merely a passive affair in which the child soaks up bits of language that come her way. Instead, it is an *active* process: children *actively construct their language*. There is now no doubt about this: children take the clues available to them and use these clues to construct their own grammatical rules, rules which grow in sophistication as acquisition proceeds. This conclusion is strongly confirmed by the observation of acquisition in unusual circumstances, such as deaf children acquiring a **sign language** or children hearing only a **pidgin** and quickly turning it into a **creole**. This determination to acquire language is very powerful and must surely be part of our biological endowment; the Canadian psycholinguist Steven Pinker has dubbed it the **language instinct**.

See also: **bioprogram hypothesis**; **critical period hypothesis**; **genetic hypothesis of language**; **innateness hypothesis**; **language acquisition device**; **language instinct**

Further reading: Berko Gleason 1997; Crystal 1997; Fletcher and Macwhinney 1995; Goodluck 1991; Ingram 1989; Lust 2006; Owens 1996, 1991; Steinberg 1993.

LANGUAGE ACQUISITION DEVICE

A hypothetical mental organ dedicated to the acquisition of a first language. In the 1960s, the American linguist Noam Chomsky began developing his **innateness hypothesis**, by which we are born already knowing what human languages are like. Chomsky further elaborated his hypothesis by arguing that children must possess a *language acquisition device*, or LAD, a specific mental organ (a structure in the brain) which is dedicated to extracting from haphazard and often degenerate speech the generalizations required for the child to construct the necessary rules of phonology and grammar. Chomsky's argument was an argument from necessity: because of the seemingly formidable obstacles to **language acquisition** explained in that entry, there simply *must* be some specialized neurological structure which can extract generalizations and construct suitable rules, even rules which are not overtly illustrated by the speech the child hears. But the LAD is purely hypothetical: no one has yet identified any areas or structures in the brain which seem to have the required characteristics, and there is no shortage of critics who see the LAD as a fantasy.

In recent years, Chomsky himself has seemingly abandoned his claims for the LAD in favour of an even stronger claim: he now believes that so much information about the nature of human language is already present in our brains at birth that all the child has to do is to 'set a few switches' to the correct values for the language being acquired. This is his *parameter-setting model*, and it too is deeply controversial.

A contrary view from **cognitive linguistics** suggests continuities in humans' physically embodied condition, with connections between perceptual and motor skills development out of which language emerges and is distributed across the brain. However, the question of where language comes from – both individually and for our species – remains a difficult and controversial area.

See also: **innateness hypothesis**; **language acquisition**; **language instinct**

Further reading: Aitchison 1989; Lust 2006.

LANGUAGE AREAS

The regions of the brain which are devoted to particular aspects of the use of language. As part of their investigations into **aphasia** in the mid-nineteenth century, the French surgeon Paul Broca and the German neurologist Carl Wernicke identified two well-defined areas in the brain which play a crucial role in the use of language. Both are located in the left hemisphere of the cerebral cortex (the wrinkly grey outer layer of the brain) in the vast majority of people, though a few people have them on the right side or even on both sides.

Wernicke's area is located behind and above the ear. It is responsible for comprehension and also for access to ordinary vocabulary in speaking. *Broca's area* is located close to the temple. It is responsible for providing the necessary grammatical structure, including grammatical words and affixes; in speech, it also controls intonation and the fine muscular movements of the speech organs. Originally identified by post-mortems carried out on brain-damaged patients who had suffered from aphasia, these areas can also be observed to be functioning in normal, healthy, conscious subjects by the use of modern brain scanners.

Since Wernicke's area is close to the part of the brain which processes auditory input, and since Broca's area is close to the area controlling muscular movements, we require only one further link to make sense of the whole arrangement. This link, the *arcuate fasciculus*, was found long ago. It consists of a J-shaped bundle of fibres connecting Wernicke's area to Broca's area.

Consequently, we now have a good picture of the organization of language in the brain. During listening, speech signals are passed by the ears to the auditory part of the brain, which processes the sounds and sends the result to Wernicke's area for interpretation. During speech, Wernicke's area provides the ordinary vocabulary, via the arcuate fasciculus, to Broca's area, which embeds this vocabulary into the required grammatical structure and then sends its instructions to the organs of speech. With the necessary changes for switching from a sound medium to a visual medium, essentially the same things happen during the use of **sign language**. With a high degree of reliability, damage to any of these areas produces the expected **language disability** (though the brain has proven itself remarkably adept at routing skills around damaged areas to learn to talk again).

See also: **aphasia**; **language disability**; **neurolinguistics**

Further reading: Aitchison 1994, 1998; Akmajian *et al.* 1995; O'Grady *et al.* 1996; Steinberg 1993.

LANGUAGE CHANGE

Change in languages over time. One of the fundamental facts about living languages is that they are always changing. New words, new pronunciations, new grammatical forms and structures, and new meanings for existing words are always coming into existence, while older ones are always dropping out of use. It is absolutely impossible for a living language to avoid changing. The motivations for change are many and various, and only some of them are reasonably well understood. New objects, new concepts, new activities all require new names; at the same time, old objects and activities may cease to exist, and their names may die with them. Certain linguistic forms may acquire social prestige and spread to the speech of those who formerly did not use them. The physiological characteristics of the mouth may tend to favour certain changes in pronunciation, but such changes may disrupt formerly regular grammatical patterns, introducing irregularities which may later be removed in one way or another. Syntactic structures which come to be frequently used may be reduced to simpler grammatical forms. And **language contact** may induce speakers to import forms and usages from other languages.

Such constant change means that a language at any point in time is always significantly different from its direct ancestor of some centuries earlier, and often vastly different from its ancestor of one or two millennia earlier. Moreover, a language spoken over a sizable area does not change everywhere in the same way, and so, over time, it breaks up, first into regional **dialects** and then, eventually, into several very different languages, producing a **language family**. The *diffusion* of change happens irregularly and inconsistently, and it is largely this that is responsible for language variation (studied in **sociolinguistics**).

The study of language change itself is **historical linguistics**, and this discipline has enjoyed great success in working out the innumerable changes which have applied in the past to individual languages and families; it has also made progress in identifying, and sometimes explaining, principles of language change: some types of change, we now know, are more natural, more frequent and more readily explicable than others.

Not infrequently, speakers take exception to the presence in their language of certain changes, or even of *all* changes, and they campaign to 'stamp out' those innovations of which they particularly disapprove. Sometimes they even agitate to 'fix' their language into a particular form admired by them, like a dead butterfly in a specimen box, with no further changes to be tolerated except after protracted deliberation by suitable authorities. Well, it is true that certain changes may lead to a (temporary) reduction in the expressive power of a language (though most do not, and many changes actually increase its expressive power), and informed commentary on these matters may be valuable in educational contexts. On the whole, though, railing against language change is at best a waste of time and at worst a display of ignorance of the processes which make language a rich human achievement.

See also: **historical linguistics; language contact; language family; language myths; prescriptivism**

Further reading: Aitchison 2001; Auer *et al.* 2005; Chambers *et al.* 2002; Cooper 1989; Crowley 1997; Crystal 1997; Fennell 2000; McMahon 1994, 2000; Milroy 1992; Trask 1994, 1995, 1996.

LANGUAGE CONTACT

Changes in one language resulting from the influence of another language. The speakers of any given language are almost always in some kind of contact with the speakers of one or more other languages, for any of several reasons. When two different languages are spoken in adjacent areas, speakers on both sides of the boundary will be exposed to the other language, and may often gain some fluency in that other language, creating a ***dialect chain*** across political national boundaries Because of conquest or migration, speakers of two or more languages may be mixed together in a single community. Speakers of one language may travel and become exposed to different languages spoken elsewhere. And, of course, in modern times the mass media have brought awareness of a number of languages into regions in which these were formerly unknown.

In all such cases, speakers of one language may, deliberately or unconsciously, introduce into their language features of another language to which they have been exposed, and we therefore speak of ***language contact***, or simply ***contact***.

The consequences of contact may range from the trivial to the far-reaching. At the simplest level, speakers may merely take over a few words from their neighbours; this is called **borrowing**, and the words borrowed are **loan words** in the receiving language. This happens most readily because the words are the names of genuinely new things: for example, English-speakers had never seen coffee, or boomerangs, or tobacco, or chocolate, or pizzas until they encountered them being used by speakers of various other languages, and so took them over along with their foreign names. But it can also happen purely for reasons of prestige: the enormous prestige of Norman French in England after the Conquest brought thousands of Norman French words into English, where they often displaced their native equivalents (as when *face* displaced native English *andwlita*), or shifted their English counterparts into other meanings (which accounts for our *beef* from *cattle*, our *mutton* from *sheep*, and our *pork* from *pigs*).

But contact can go much further than this, affecting grammar and pronunciation. For example, the Celtic language Breton, spoken in Brittany, has acquired a French-style uvular /r/, and it has been losing its native phoneme /h/, absent from French. The Mayan languages of Mexico and Guatemala have acquired a number of new phonemes from the local prestige language, Spanish. Some varieties of Scottish Gaelic have lost the inflected prepositions of that language and replaced them with prepositional phrases comparable to English ones. Among the Semitic languages of Ethiopia, the original verb–subject–object word order of sentences has been largely changed to the subject–object–verb order typical of the neighbouring Cushitic languages.

Few languages are, or have ever been, sufficiently isolated to avoid some degree of contact, and hence virtually every language shows some evidence of ancient or modern contact with other languages. On occasion, speakers of a given language may react unfavourably to such contact by embracing **purism**, with variable results. In recent years, the world dominance of English has led to massive English influence upon languages from French to Japanese.

In extreme cases, the effects of contact may be so overwhelming that one language is abandoned entirely by its speakers in favour of another, in the process called **language death**.

See also: **language death**; **linguistic area**; **loan word**; **purism**

Further reading: Hock 1986; Hock and Joseph 1996; Kouwenberg and Singler 2005; McMahon 1994; Trask 1996.

LANGUAGE DEATH

The disappearance of a language as a mother tongue. A language, particularly a **minority language**, may come under enormous pressure from a more prestigious or more widely used language spoken nearby. Native speakers of the language under pressure may find themselves obliged, not only to learn the local prestige language, but to use it in an ever-greater number of contexts. Eventually, a time may come when many children are no longer learning the threatened language as their mother tongue, or are learning it only imperfectly. At this point we say the threatened language is *moribund* or dying, and the almost inevitable result is that, within a generation or two, no one will be able to speak the threatened language at all. This is *language death*, and the process which leads to it is *language shift*.

Language death is usually gradual. In any given place, at any given time, some children are still learning the dying language as their mother tongue, while others are learning it only imperfectly and still others not at all. The language may disappear completely from some areas while surviving in others. Occasionally, a language dies because its speech community is suddenly wiped out, whether by natural disaster (such as the 1998 Papua New Guinea earthquake which destroyed the populations speaking Arup, Malol, Sissano and Warapu) or by invasion and genocide (such as the eradication of native Caribbean languages by European colonizers, or the destruction of Moriori speakers in the Chatham Islands by invading Maoris from New Zealand over the nineteenth century). This form of language death is commonly called *linguicide*.

The language spoken by the last generation or so of native speakers may be very much changed from the language spoken by an earlier generation. Irregularities may be lost; the more complex or less frequent forms and sentence patterns may drop out of use; native words may be massively replaced by words taken from the prestige language; the pronunciation may change so as to become more similar to that of the prestige language; stylistic variation may be lost, leaving only a single unvarying style. The final outcome, of course, is a **dead language**. Later on, efforts may be made to reinvent and codify the dead language, and even resurrect it with native speakers: modern Greek Katharévusa, modern written Welsh, Manx and Cornish have all been reconstructed with varying degrees of success.

See also: **dead language**; **power**; **language contact**; **minority language**

Further reading: Crystal 2000; Dalby 2003; Hock and Joseph 1996; Krauss 1992; Llamas *et al.* 2007; McMahon 1994; Nettle and Romaine 2000.

LANGUAGE DISABILITY

Any pathological condition which has adverse consequences for the sufferer's ability to use language normally. Language disabilities must be carefully distinguished from *speech defects* like lisping and inability to produce a tapped /r/; these are purely mechanical problems with the nerves and muscles controlling the organs of speech, and they have no effect upon the **language faculty** itself (though *stammering*, or *stuttering* in the USA, does seem to involve some cognitive interference as well).

A true disability results either from a genetic defect or from damage to the **language areas** in the brain. Since the possible types of damage and defects are virtually limitless, individual sufferers naturally exhibit an enormous range of disabilities: we hardly ever find two individuals with exactly the same symptoms. Nevertheless, it has proved possible to identify a number of fairly specific disabilities and, in many cases, to associate these with particular genetic defects or with damage to particular areas of the brain.

The best-known disabilities are the several types of **aphasia**, all of which result from injury to more or less identifiable areas of the brain. But other types exist. For example, the *Williams syndrome* is known to result from a genetic defect in Chromosome No. 11; this defect causes both some highly specific physiological abnormalities and some rather consistent abnormalities in language use. Less well understood is *Specific Language Impairment*, or SLI, which devastates the ability to use the grammatically inflected forms of words correctly (such as *take, takes, took, taking*) but which has only a few non-linguistic consequences; the Canadian-based linguist Myrna Gopnik has recently uncovered evidence that this impairment too may result from a specific genetic disorder, though one which has not yet been identified.

But the known range of disabilities is positively startling. A bilingual sufferer may lose one language completely but retain the second perfectly, and then, after some time, may lose the second but regain the first. Many types of disability are characterized by greater or lesser degrees of *anomia*, the inability to remember words for things. But some sufferers exhibit astoundingly specific deficits, such as a total inability to use or understand words denoting fruits and vegetables, with *no other problems at all*. Some people lose verbs but retain nouns, and so they have no trouble with the noun *milk* (as in *a glass of milk*), but cannot handle the verb *milk* (as in *to milk a cow*). Some elderly sufferers from *Alzheimer's disease* find themselves reverting to languages, dialects and accents that they spoke in their youth, and lose abilities that they gained in later life. In spite of some impressive progress, we are still very far from understanding most types of language disability.

See also: **aphasia**; **language areas**; **neurolinguistics**

Further reading: Caplan 1992; Field 2003; Ingram 2007; Pinker 1994; Steinberg 1993; Trask 1995.

LANGUAGE FACULTY

Our biological ability to use language. Human beings are the only creatures on earth that use language, and many linguists and others have concluded that we must therefore have some kind of specific biological endowment for language, one which is totally absent, or nearly so, from all other living species: our *language faculty* (the Swiss linguist Ferdinand de Saussure used the term *langage* for this, but his label is now little used).

To be sure, this conclusion has been challenged from two directions. On the one hand, some experimenters have attempted to teach other species, usually apes, to use some simplified version of a human language (most often a version of a **sign language**) and, in spite of serious problems with their methodology and interpretations, a few observers are now prepared to accept that these creatures do indeed exhibit a (severely limited) capacity for using language – though critics of this conclusion are numerous and vigorous. On the other hand, psychologists like Jean Piaget and Jerome Bruner have argued that our language faculty, while admittedly real, is not at all an individual and distinctive part of our biological inheritance, but merely one more manifestation of our general all-purpose cognitive abilities.

Nevertheless, the majority view among linguists at present is that our language faculty is real, that it is at least largely distinct from all of our other cognitive abilities, and that it must be the biological result of some kind of distinctive evolution within the brains of our ancestors. This is the belief that underlies a number of celebrated attempts at giving an account of our language-using abilities, including the **genetic hypothesis of language**, Chomsky's **innateness hypothesis**, Bickerton's **bioprogram hypothesis**, and even the search for **universal grammar**.

A constant theme in these investigations is the issue of *modularity*. Chomsky and others have long argued that our language faculty must consist of a number of specialized and largely independent subcomponents which interact in specific ways to produce our overall linguistic behaviour. More recently, however, some people have begun to question whether our language faculty as a whole should itself be regarded as a distinctive part of our mental equipment. They suggest instead that various aspects of language use may have entirely separate evolutionary origins, and that what we call our language faculty is probably an epiphenomenon; that is, a purely superficial unity which in fact results from the interaction of diverse structures and processes within our brains, many of which are in no way confined to language behaviour. These debates will doubtless continue for some time.

The study of all the biological aspects of our language faculty is sometimes called *biolinguistics*.

See also: **animal communication; autonomy; bioprogram hypothesis; genetic hypothesis of language; innateness hypothesis; origin and evolution of language**

Further reading: Jackendoff 1993; Pinker 1994; Sampson 1997; Steinberg 1993.

LANGUAGE FAMILY

A group of languages all of which share a common ancestor. Every living language is constantly changing, and the changes which affect the language in one place do not necessarily affect it in other places. Consequently, if the language is spoken over any significant area, then, over time, it will tend to break up into rather distinct varieties. At first these are merely the *regional dialects* of the language, but, given sufficient time, these dialects may become so different from one another that we are forced to regard them as separate languages: the *daughter languages* of that single *ancestral language* or *mother language*.

The daughter languages may in turn break up into further daughter languages, eventually producing a sizable number of languages all of which started out as nothing more than regional varieties of that single ancestor. All the languages which share a common ancestor in this way constitute a single *language family*, and we say that all of them are *genetically related*. Around 300 such language families have been identified by linguists, some of them very large, others quite small.

English, for example, is fairly closely related to a group of other languages: Afrikaans, Danish, Dutch, Faroese, Frisian, German, Icelandic, Norwegian, Swedish, Yiddish and the extinct Gothic; we call these the *Germanic* languages, and we believe they are all descended from a single ancestor spoken perhaps around 500 BC, very likely in Scandinavia. But the Germanic languages in turn share a more remote common ancestor with a vast number of other languages, including Welsh, Spanish, Greek, Russian, Armenian, Persian and Bengali (to name just a few), and hence all of these languages belong to a single huge family called the *Indo-European* family.

See also: **historical linguistics**; **Indo-European**; **language change**

Further reading: Comrie *et al.* 1997; McMahon 1994; Trask 1996.

LANGUAGE INSTINCT

The powerful tendency of children to acquire language. Any physically normal child who is adequately exposed to a language will learn it perfectly, and a child exposed to two or three languages will learn all of them. A hearing child normally learns the surrounding spoken language. A deaf child exposed to a **sign language** will learn that. Children exposed only to a **pidgin** will turn that pidgin into a full language: a **creole**. A group of children exposed to no language at all will invent their own and use it.

For a long time, linguists were slow to appreciate the significance of these observations, and both creoles and sign languages were widely regarded as peripheral and even inconsequential phenomena scarcely deserving of serious study by linguists. But times have changed. Very gradually at first, and then, from about the 1970s, almost explosively, the examination of these phenomena convinced almost all working linguists that creoles and sign languages were every bit as central to the discipline as spoken languages with a long history.

We now realize that children are born with a powerful biological drive to learn language, and that only shattering disability or inhuman cruelty can prevent a child from acquiring language by one means or another. In the 1990s, the Canadian psycholinguist Steven Pinker coined the felicitous term *language instinct* to denote this remarkable aspect of our biological endowment. Our **language faculty**, we now strongly suspect, is built into our genes, and learning a first language may not be so different from learning to see: at birth, our visual apparatus is not working properly, and it requires some exposure to the visible world before normal vision is acquired.

Not infrequently, the term language instinct is applied more specifically to the **genetic hypothesis of language** and/or to the related **innateness hypothesis**.

See also: **creole**; **critical period hypothesis**; **genetic hypothesis of language**; **innateness hypothesis**; **language acquisition**; **sign language**

Further reading: Aitchison 1989; Pinker 1994.

LANGUAGE MYTHS

Widely held but false beliefs about individual languages or about language in general. For one reason or another, various absurdly false beliefs about languages have at times taken hold in the popular imagination and have often proved difficult to stamp out. Some of these misconceptions have even been maintained by knowledgeable linguists. Here are a few of these myths.

Primitive languages

Linguists as recent and eminent as Otto Jespersen have maintained that some languages spoken today are 'primitive' or 'savage' languages, characterized by strange grammatical systems supposedly reflecting a primordial human view of the world. Non-linguists have at times gone further and supposed that some languages have little or nothing in the way of grammar, and that they have tiny vocabularies lacking abstractions or generalizations and supplemented by grunts and gestures. All this is nonsense: every human language ever discovered has a rich and complex grammar and a vocabulary of many thousands of words, and is perfectly adequate for expressing anything its speakers want to express. When they need to express anything new, they borrow from other languages or innovate in their own language.

Stadialism

Many linguists formerly believed that every human language necessarily develops over time from a 'primitive' type through increasingly sophisticated types until finally (perhaps) reaching the most 'advanced' type possible. This idea was promulgated by European linguists who were inclined to see their European languages as representing the pinnacle of linguistic perfection, with significantly different languages, and especially those spoken by variously coloured folks, as necessarily representing some earlier stage of development. This blatantly racist idea is thankfully dead among linguists, though avowedly non-racist versions of it are still maintained in some quarters, and non-linguists sometimes still believe it is true. It is not. Languages admittedly differ markedly in their grammatical systems, and they can and do change those systems dramatically over time; however, there is no tendency for languages to change in one direction rather than another, and there is nothing special about European languages.

Those Eskimo words for 'snow'

By a comical series of events, the legend has grown up that the Eskimo (Inuit) languages have vast numbers of words for different kinds of snow. In fact, the several dialects of the two Eskimo languages variously exhibit between two and four distinct words for snow. This is about the same as English, with its *snow*, *slush*, *sleet*, *blizzard* (not to mention skiers' terms like *hard-pack*, *powder* and *crust*). However, it is generally true that sets of concepts that are ***overlexicalized*** and ***underlexicalized*** in a language (in comparison with other languages) can give clues as to cultural preoccupations and worldviews.

Basque

The Basque language of western Europe has no known relatives and it is noticeably different from other European languages, particularly from those (the great majority) which are related within the **Indo-European** family. Consequently, a number of myths have grown up about it: Basque is the most complex language on the planet; no outsider has ever managed to learn it; all the verbs are passive; and so on. In fact, of course, Basque is a perfectly unremarkable language. Its grammar is highly regular, and it is easy to learn: today thousands of people speak it as a second language. Its sentence structure is nearly identical to that of Japanese or Turkish.

It does have a **morphology** which is somewhat unusual in Europe, but similar systems are found in hundreds of languages outside of Europe. Of course, Basque people themselves are partly responsible for promoting this view of their own separateness and distinctiveness, with a nationalist political agenda.

The land that time forgot

Somewhere, runs the story, in the Ozarks, or in the Appalachians, or in Derbyshire in England, there's a village where the locals still speak perfect Elizabethan English, untouched by the vast changes which have transformed English everywhere else. No, there isn't: this is pure fantasy. There is no such thing as a living language which doesn't change. This myth crops up because people occasionally notice that the local English in some corner of the world preserves one or two old forms which have disappeared elsewhere. (For example, Appalachian English preserves the *a'doing* form, as in *I was a'shootin' at some squirrels*; this was once universal in English but has been lost everywhere else.) But *every* variety of English preserves a few forms lost in other varieties, and every variety also exhibits a few innovations not found elsewhere. (For example, Appalachian English has undergone a change in its vowels such that Appalachian *think* sounds to the rest of us rather like *thank*.)

Similar myths have been maintained by speakers of other languages. Until the eighteenth century, even some linguists believed that the ancestral language of all humankind was still spoken, in its pristine state, in some favoured corner of the world; much ink was spilt over deciding which corner this might be. (For example, one such linguist argued for the Netherlands, and claimed that Dutch was the uncorrupted ancestral tongue of all humans. He was Dutch, of course.) But all languages that are spoken change incessantly, and no language anywhere is closer than any other to the remote origins of human speech.

There's a moral here: don't believe everything you read. Many journalists, authors of popular books, and especially website writers are ignorant of the facts, and they tend to perpetuate eye-catching falsehoods in place of the more humdrum truth. Your critical sense should even extend to this book, of course!

See also: **folk linguistics**; **prescriptivism**

Further reading: Crystal 1997; Pullum 1991.

145

LANGUAGE PLANNING

Making deliberate decisions about the form of a language. Very commonly, a language 'just grows': it develops and changes in response to countless small decisions made more or less unconsciously by its speakers. But it is perfectly possible, and in some circumstances necessary, for the future of a language to be determined in important respects by deliberate, self-conscious decisions, often made on an official basis. This is *language planning*, sometimes also called *linguistic engineering*.

Consider the case of Finnish. For centuries, Finland had been a province of Sweden or of Russia; either Swedish or Russian had therefore been the **official language** of the country, and Finnish had remained merely the everyday language of most of the population. But, when Finland finally achieved independence in 1918, the Finns naturally chose to make Finnish their new **national language**.

But this decision required a great deal of work. First, there was no agreed standard form of Finnish: instead, there were only innumerable local varieties of it, differing in vocabulary, pronunciation and grammar. Second, since Finnish had never been used for such purposes as law, administration, science, technology and scholarship, there was a great dearth of technical vocabulary in all these fields: there simply *were* no Finnish equivalents for terms like *manslaughter, ministry, molecule, piston* and *linguistics*.

The Finns were therefore obliged to put these things right, and the task was carried out centrally, by bodies set up by the new Finnish Government. Specialists in Finnish language drew up a new standard form of the language, and specialists in a huge variety of disciplines met to agree on suitable Finnish technical terms in their fields. Their decisions were official, and they were imposed upon the Finnish taught in schools, published in books and magazines, and broadcast over the radio.

The task was completed satisfactorily, and today there exists a single standard form of Finnish, known and used by everyone, together with an adequate and uniform set of technical terms. But the work is never done, since new technical terms come into use every year, in fields ranging from physics to linguistics, most of them coined in English, and the Finns are constantly obliged to keep finding Finnish equivalents.

Language planning also includes the deliberate attempt to avoid sexist, homophobic or other discriminatory discourse (which is often then characterized by its reactionary opponents as 'political correctness').

See also: **national language**; **official language**; **sexist language**; **standard language**

Further reading: Bex and Watts 1999; Cooper 1989; Crystal 1997; Holmes 1992; Trask 1996; Wright 2004.

LANGUAGE PROCESSING

The mental activities involved in producing and comprehending language. Whenever we produce an utterance, or whenever we hear and understand one, there is a great deal of elaborate activity going on in our brains. This activity is *language processing*.

Psycholinguists have developed a battery of techniques for working out the stages involved in language processing. Subjects can be tested in a laboratory, to find out how the performance of linguistic tasks is affected by varying conditions, and evidence can be obtained from *speech errors*. The results, however, are not always easy to interpret. Nevertheless, linguists have enjoyed some success in working out the several distinct stages involved in *speech planning*, the mental processes which allow us to produce utterances. Comprehension is more difficult: a number of **perceptual strategies** have been proposed, and these are moderately successful at accounting for the understanding of simple utterances, but the comprehension of more complex utterances is still something of a mystery. Recently there have been several hypotheses advanced within **cognitive linguistics**, but most of these have yet to be empirically verified.

See also: **perceptual strategy**; **psycholinguistics**; **text world theory**

Further reading: Aitchison 1989; Akmajian *et al.* 1995; O'Grady *et al.* 1996.

LANGUE

The abstract language system shared by the speakers of a language. The term *langue* was introduced by the Swiss linguist Ferdinand de

Saussure in the early twentieth century; in Saussure's treatment, this term contrasts specifically with **parole**, actual utterances. A distinction along these lines has often been considered essential in linguistics since Saussure's day, and Noam Chomsky's more recent distinction between **competence** and **performance** is broadly analogous, but note that Saussure's langue is the property of a whole community of speakers, while Chomsky's **competence** is the property of a single speaker.

See also: **competence**; **language**; **parole**

Further reading: Culler 1986; Sampson 1980.

LATERALIZATION

Specialization between the two hemispheres (halves) of the brain. By a quirk of evolution, the left side of the brain controls the right side of the body and vice versa. But there are also notable differences in the responsibilities of the two hemispheres: the left side is chiefly responsible for analysis (breaking complex things up into smaller parts), and it handles things like doing arithmetic, solving equations and determining chronological sequences. The right hemisphere, in great contrast, is responsible for synthesis (combining pieces into integrated wholes), and hence it handles things like recognition and association, and also the enjoyment of music (though trained musicians learn to use their left hemispheres for this purpose as well).

In the vast majority of people, the **language areas** of the brain are in the left hemisphere, though a few people have them on the right or, rarely, even on both sides.

See also: **language areas**

Further reading: Akmajian *et al.* 1995; Ingram 2007; O'Grady *et al.* 1996; Steinberg 1993.

LEMMA

The least marked form of a word, sometimes called the ***citation form*** since it is the version most likely to be given as the indexed word in dictionaries. For example, *book* would be the lemmatized form of the set of words including *books, rebook, booked, bookish, booker* and *booking*. In relatively low inflected languages like English, it is usually easy to determine the lemma of a set of words (though consider *mouse* with *mice*, or *go* and *went*, or *am, are, is* and *be*, for example). In highly inflected languages, the situation is not so easy: Czech, for example, has various forms of *dobro* 'good' (*dobré ráno* 'good morning', *dobrý den* 'good day', *dobrý večer* 'good evening', *dobrou noc* 'good night' and even *mám se dobře* 'I'm good/fine'), such that selecting one is not straightforward. Or given a phrasal set, such as *pick yourself up, pick myself up, pick himself up* and so on, most people would give *pick oneself up* as the lemma, even though it would be the least used. Lemmas (*lemmata* to be pedantic) are particularly useful when setting concordance programs to search through linguistic corpora (*corpora*).

See also: **computational linguistics; lexicon**

Further reading: Adolphs 2006; Sinclair 1991.

LEXICAL-FUNCTIONAL GRAMMAR (LFG)

LFG was developed in the late 1970s by the American linguists Joan Bresnan and Ronald Kaplan. It differs from some other theories of grammar in holding that the syntactic structure of a sentence is something more than just the familiar **constituent structure** represented by a **tree** diagram. In LFG, the structure of a sentence consists of two distinct formal objects: *C-structure* of the familiar kind plus a *functional structure* (or *F-structure*) which displays certain additional kinds of information. Most important in the F-structure is the labelling of **grammatical relations** like **subject** and **object** (these are called *grammatical functions* in LFG).

The first part of the name reflects the fact that a great deal of work is done by the *lexical entries*, the 'dictionary' part of the framework. Lexical entries are usually rich and elaborate, and each one inflected from a lexical item (such as *write, writes, wrote, written* and *writing*) has its own lexical entry. Lexical entries are responsible for dealing with many relations and processes handled by different machinery in other frameworks; an example is the **voice** contrast between actives and passives.

149

LFG was designed to be convenient for work in computational linguistics and has found applications there. It was also designed in the hope that it would prove to be psychologically realistic, but overt psycholinguistic support has not been forthcoming.

See also: **generative grammar**; **Government-and-Binding Theory**; **phrase-structure grammar**

Further reading: Horrocks 1987; Kaplan and Bresnan 1982; Sells 1985.

LEXICOGRAPHY

The writing of dictionaries. Dictionaries of a sort have been around for a long time, but ancient and medieval efforts were mostly very different from our modern ones. To start with, the early ones were usually bilingual dictionaries, glossaries offering translations of words from one language into another. The medieval period saw the production of monoglot works, but these were not usually arranged alphabetically: instead, the words were grouped by meaning (words pertaining to farming, names of fruits, and so on). The first alphabetical dictionaries of English were not complete: instead, they were compendia of 'hard words', that is, of obscure and difficult words, often mainly of Latin origin.

By the eighteenth century, books that we can easily recognize as dictionaries of English were beginning to appear. By far the most prominent of these in Britain was Dr Samuel Johnson's great work published in 1755; Johnson's American counterpart, Noah Webster, published the first edition of his American dictionary in 1828. Other dictionaries followed, and lexicography became a recognized profession in the English-speaking countries.

In the second half of the nineteenth century, an enormous project was undertaken in Britain: the preparation of a huge dictionary of English recording every word, every spelling, and every sense attested in writing in English since the year 1000. Directed by the Scottish scholar James Murray, this project was carried out by methods that seem comically primitive today: an army of contributors noted down examples of words and sent them in on slips of paper, and Murray and his assistants simply built the dictionary out of these mountains of paper slips. The completed work was published in a series of volumes between 1884 and 1928, under the title *New English Dictionary on Historical Principles*. In 1933 it was republished, with a supplement, as the *Oxford English Dictionary*, or *OED*. Further supplements followed, and finally an expanded and updated second edition was prepared and published in 1989. Both editions are available on CD-ROM, making the *OED* an enormously valuable research tool. A third edition is in process. Throughout the twentieth century, English dictionaries have been published in numbers. In the last couple of decades, lexicography has been revolutionized by the introduction of *corpus*-based techniques, and modern dictionaries are now usually based upon huge corpora of English, from which words, forms, spellings, meanings and grammatical behaviour are extracted, thus allowing lexicographers to appeal directly to the observed facts of usage. Also noteworthy are the numerous innovations introduced by the COBUILD dictionaries in Britain and by other dictionaries written especially for advanced foreign learners of English. These describe words as they are observably used by the speech community, rather than as defined by the lexicographer alone or in prestigious texts.

See also: **computational linguistics**

Further reading: Green 1996; Ilson 1986; Jackson 2000; Landau 1984; McArthur 1986.

LEXICON

The vocabulary of a language. Every speaker of a language possesses a certain vocabulary, and this may be divided into his (or her) *active vocabulary*, the words which he uses himself, and his *passive vocabulary*, the words which he understands but doesn't normally use. In linguistics, however, we don't normally speak of the vocabulary of a particular language; instead, we speak of the *lexicon*, the total store of words available to speakers.

Very commonly, the lexicon is not regarded merely as a long list of words. Rather, we conceive of the lexicon as a set of lexical resources, including the **morphemes** of the language, plus the processes available in the language for constructing words from those resources. For example, given the existence of English verbs like *varnish* and *scratch*, and of the word-forming *affixes* *-able* and *un-*, it is perfectly possible for you to create the words *varnishable* and *unscratchable* whenever you need them, and to expect to be understood at once, even if you and the person you are speaking to have never encountered these words before.

Quite apart from the lexicon of a language as a whole, psycho-linguists are interested in the **mental lexicon**, the words and lexical resources stored in an individual brain. Evidence from a variety of sources, including **language disability**, has provided a great deal of information about this. There is good evidence that words of a single grammatical class, and also words of closely related mean-ings, are stored in the brain 'in the same place', whatever that means exactly; and it is perfectly clear also that words are not stored in isolation, but are instead stored with innumerable links to other words which are related in function, which are related in meaning, which have similar sounds, or which were even learned at the same experiential moment.

See also: **morphology**; **part of speech**; **word-formation**

Further reading: Aitchison 1994; Bauer 1998; Davis 2001; Hoey 2005; Katamba 1994; Schmitt and McCarthy 1997.

LINGUA FRANCA

A language which is widely used in some region for communication among people speaking a variety of languages. The original *lingua franca* (the name means 'Frankish language', though the sense is 'European language' or 'Christian language') was a variety of Ita-lian, strongly laced with words from French, Spanish, Greek, Arabic and Turkish, used as a trade language in the eastern Medi-terranean during the late Middle Ages. Since then, we have applied this label to any language which enjoys wide use among speakers of a variety of different languages in some region.

In the past, this term was applied very broadly, and many of the speech varieties called *lingue franchi* (this is the plural if you want to be pedantic) were **pidgins** or **creoles**. Today, though, we more commonly use the term for a language which is the long-established mother tongue of some influential group of speakers but which is none the less widely used for inter-group communication by speak-ers of several other languages, such as Swahili in East Africa, Hausa in West Africa, or English in Singapore.

See also: **creole**; **international language**; **pidgin**

Further reading: Holmes 1992; Kouwenberg and Singler 2005.

LINGUISTIC AREA

A geographical region in which several unrelated or distantly related languages have striking characteristics in common. With only a very few exceptions, speakers of a language are always in contact with neighbours speaking different languages, and they have dealings with those neighbours. The resulting **language contact** means that words, speech sounds and even grammatical forms may pass from some languages into neighbouring languages. This is exceedingly common.

In certain cases, however, this contact may be so intense that a number of striking characteristics diffuse throughout a geographical region, becoming prominent in a number of languages which are unrelated or only distantly related. As a result, the languages in question may, in some respects, undergo *convergence*: they come to resemble one another more closely than they resemble their closest linguistic relatives in other regions. This state of affairs we call a *linguistic area* or, using the German term, a *Sprachbund*.

Several linguistic areas have been identified by linguists, among them south-east Asia and the Balkans. South-east Asia is a particularly striking case. Many languages in this area – including Burmese, Thai and Vietnamese – are so similar in their structures that linguists believed for a while that they must all be related in a single family. But careful investigation has revealed that they are not discoverably related to each other at all; they all have true relatives elsewhere which are not very similar to them, and the striking resemblances result purely from convergence among neighbouring but unrelated languages.

In the Balkans, Greek and Albanian constitute distinct branches of the **Indo-European** family, while Bulgarian, Macedonian and Serbo-Croatian belong to the distinct Slavic branch of Indo-European, and Turkish is not Indo-European at all. Yet all these languages participate to varying degrees in a language area: they share with one another a range of grammatical characteristics which they do not share with their closest relatives elsewhere.

The study of language areas is called *areal linguistics*.

See also: **language contact**

Further reading: Hock and Joseph 1996; Trask 1996.

LINGUISTIC RELATIVITY HYPOTHESIS

The hypothesis that the structure of our language to some extent determines the way we perceive the world. For centuries, scholars have speculated on possible links between language on one hand and mind, perception and culture on the other; a prominent example is the eighteenth-century German linguist and philosopher Wilhelm von Humboldt.

Around the beginning of the twentieth century, linguistics began to emerge from anthropology as a distinct discipline in the USA, and American linguists, with their anthropological background, often took a keen interest in the links just mentioned. The American linguist Edward Sapir was particularly fascinated by possible connections between language and thought; he once wrote: 'Language and our thought-grooves are ... , in a sense, one and the same'. But it was Sapir's student, Benjamin Lee Whorf, who was to develop this idea into its most dramatic form.

Examining several Native American languages, Whorf was struck by the observation that different languages appeared to divide up the world differently, and that, further, a concept that was represented as a 'thing' in one language might be represented as an 'event' or a 'process' in another. These purely linguistic differences he was inclined to see as representing genuine differences in the way that speakers of different languages perceive the world. Though he himself never made such an explicit statement, his work soon came to be interpreted as supporting a remarkable conclusion: the structure of our language in large measure determines the way we perceive the world. This dictum is known as the *linguistic relativity hypothesis*, or equally as the *Sapir-Whorf hypothesis*.

The idea has been controversial from the start. In the 1960s, the anthropologists Brent Berlin and Paul Kay published a famous study of basic colour terms in a number of languages, concluding that, even though languages differ markedly in their linguistic systems for naming colours, there were important universal characteristics of colour terms, suggesting that universals of perception underlay the linguistic differences. But their conclusions were challenged on a number of grounds, most famously by the psychologists John Lucy and Richard Shweder, who in the 1970s reported some interesting differences in the behaviour of speakers of different languages.

Since then any number of linguists, anthropologists and psychologists have chipped in with fascinating data supporting one side or

154

the other, but at present there is still no consensus on the degree of validity which can be reasonably assigned to this hypothesis. However, psycholinguists have managed to demonstrate that, in memory tests, it is easier to remember things when we have explicit names for them. So, for example, it is easier to remember colours accurately if our language provides a wide range of specific colour terms. It may be that a weak version of the Sapir-Whorf hypothesis works, such that linguistic habits encourage a tendency to think in a particular customary way, but the language itself does not constrain thought.

See also: **anthropological linguistics**

Further reading: Berlin and Kay 1969; Duranti 1997; Gumperz and Levinson 1996; Lucy 1992; Lucy and Shweder 1979; Steinberg 1993; Whorf 1956; Wierzbicka 1996.

LINGUISTIC SIGN

A linguistic object possessing both form and meaning. The concept of the *linguistic sign* was introduced in the early twentieth century by the Swiss linguist Ferdinand de Saussure, in whose system it plays a central role. This concept is a very simple one: every linguistic object has two aspects, or facets: a linguistic form (called by Saussure the *signifiant*, or 'signifier') and a meaning (the *signifié*, or 'thing signified'). For example, the English word *dog* has a particular form (a sequence of three meaningless **phonemes**) and also a particular meaning (a specific kind of animal). The two together make up a single linguistic sign in English.

Saussure drew particular attention to the **arbitrariness** of each linguistic sign: there is no reason why any particular linguistic form should be associated with any particular meaning, and the pairing that exists in each case is an arbitrary one.

The recognition of linguistic signs lies at the heart of our view of any given language as a **symbolic system**. Saussure's idea of linguistic signs was also influential in shaping the discipline of **semiotics**.

See also: **arbitrariness; iconicity; semiotics; symbolic system**

Further reading: Culler 1986; Peirce 1991.

LINGUISTICS

The scientific study of language. There were significant traditions of language study in ancient India, in ancient China, in ancient Greece and Rome, among the medieval Arabs and Jews, and elsewhere. Most of these investigations, though, were solely confined to studying the local prestige language. Modern linguistics does not derive from these older traditions; instead, it grew up from fresh beginnings in Europe and the USA.

By the seventeenth century, a few European scholars and philosophers were beginning to interest themselves in general questions about the nature of language, and between the seventeenth and nineteenth century, scholars like Descartes, Locke and Humboldt made a number of significant contributions. But, with a few exceptions, these men typically knew nothing about any languages other than the major languages of Europe, and their work suffered from a lack of data, with the result that much of it was speculative and *a priori*.

By the end of the eighteenth century, **historical linguistics** had begun to be firmly established, and throughout the nineteenth century the historical study of language was for many people synonymous with the scientific study of language. Towards the end of the century, though, a number of linguists began turning their attention to the serious study of the structure of language from a non-historical point of view. Prominent among them were von der Gabelentz, Kruszewski and Baudouin de Courtenay. But the most influential figure, by far, was the Swiss linguist Ferdinand de Saussure.

Though he had been trained as a historical linguist, and though he had made major contributions to historical studies, Saussure began to focus on some more general questions of language structure and to reach some profound conclusions. He failed to publish this work, but, after his death, his former colleagues and students edited his lecture notes into a book, which was published under Saussure's name in 1916: this book is the famous *Cours*. So great has been the influence of the book that Saussure has been dubbed 'the father of linguistics'. The European linguistic tradition, with its heavy theoretical bias, largely derives from Saussure's work, though in Britain Bronislaw Malinowski and (especially) J.R. Firth independently developed a more strongly data-oriented descriptive approach born of anthropological fieldwork.

Meanwhile, in the USA, anthropologists were undertaking the study of the dying Native American languages. This study was keenly promoted by Franz Boas, who is often regarded as the founder of the American linguistic tradition; Boas's successors, such as A.L. Kroeber and (especially) Edward Sapir, went on to develop linguistics as an independent discipline in the USA. But the single most influential figure was Leonard Bloomfield, whose 1933 textbook *Language* effectively defined the field and set the agenda for American linguists. Bloomfield's successors, the *American structuralists* (or *post-Bloomfieldians*), drew their inspiration from Bloomfield, and they created a brand of linguistics which stressed hands-on experience with real data and often dismissed the contemporary European tradition as mere 'armchair theorizing'.

This is how things stood in the 1950s: a highly theoretical tradition in Europe, a highly anti-theoretical tradition in the USA, and something in between in Britain. But, in 1957, the young American linguist Noam Chomsky published *Syntactic Structures*, a brief and watered-down summary of several years of original research. In that book, and in his succeeding publications, Chomsky made a number of revolutionary proposals: he introduced the idea of a **generative grammar**, developed a particular kind of generative grammar called **transformational grammar**, rejected his American predecessors' emphasis on the description of data – in favour of a highly theoretical approach based upon a search for universal principles of language (later called **universal grammar**) – proposed to turn linguistics firmly towards **mentalism**, and laid the foundations for integrating the field into the as yet unnamed new discipline of **cognitive science**.

Chomsky's ideas excited a whole generation of students; since American universities were expanding rapidly in the early 1960s, these students quickly found jobs and began developing the field, and within a few years Chomskyan linguistics had become the new orthodoxy in the USA. Before long, Chomsky's ideas had crossed the Atlantic and established themselves also in many parts of Europe.

Today Chomsky's influence is undimmed, and Chomskyan linguists form a large and maximally prominent cohort among the community of linguists, to such an extent that outsiders often have the impression that linguistics *is* Chomskyan linguistics, that linguistics is by definition what the Chomskyans do. But this is seriously misleading.

In fact, the majority of the world's linguists would acknowledge no more than the vaguest debt to Chomsky, if even that. Investigators of **historical linguistics**, of **sociolinguistics**, of **anthropological** linguistics, of psycholinguistics and neurolinguistics, of language acquisition, of *dialectology*, of semantics and pragmatics, of conversation analysis, discourse and texts, of computational linguistics, and of a dozen other areas, all have their own agendas and priorities, and they are making progress – sometimes dramatic progress – without paying any attention to Chomsky's contributions. Indeed, it can reasonably be argued that the greatest advances in our understanding of language in recent years have come from the new field of sociolinguistics, in which pioneers like William Labov, Peter Trudgill, and Jim and Lesley Milroy have transformed our whole perception of what it means to speak a language.

Linguistics today is surely as lively a discipline as any on earth. In the past forty years or so we have probably learned more about language than our ancestors managed in 2,000 years, and there is no reason to believe that things are slowing down now.

See also: **language**

Further reading: Akmajian *et al.* 1995; Crystal 1997; Elgin 1983; Fromkin and Rodman 1998; Hudson 1984; O'Grady *et al.* 1996; Trask 1995.

LITERACY

The ability to read and write effectively. *Literacy* is the ability to read and write, and that sounds simple enough. But it isn't. Between the two extremes of a magisterial command of reading and writing on the one hand and total *illiteracy* on the other, we find any number of intermediate stages: literacy is a matter of degree. One person may be able to read a popular tabloid newspaper but unable to read a tax return or even the instructions on an aspirin bottle. Another may be able to read a fair range of material but be incapable of writing anything intelligible.

Attempts have been made since the 1940s at defining a level of *functional literacy* – the minimum level of reading and writing required to function effectively in a world dominated by written material – but this has proved exceedingly difficult to do. The United Nations defines it relative to the culture in which the individual lives, so the same functional literacy differs in absolute terms between a nomadic African tribesman and an accountant living in the print-rich West.

The term has also been extended to include notions such as *cultural literacy*, *visual literacy*, *design literacy*, *computer literacy* and others.

Throughout history, the acquisition of literacy has been regarded as conferring high prestige (in many cultures, it has been the qualification for movement from one social class to another, or the qualification for electoral voting rights). Today, perhaps 75 per cent of the world's population may be described as literate – an enormous advance, since it is not so many generations since a knowledge of reading and writing was the exclusive preserve of tiny elites. Mass literacy is largely a twentieth-century phenomenon.

An individual who lacks the reading and writing skills typical of his community is *illiterate*; an entire society which lacks a recognized writing system is *aliterate*, or sometimes in a historical context *preliterate*.

See also: **oracy**; **standard language**

Further reading: Crystal 1997.

LOAN WORD

A word copied into one language from another language. The speakers of almost every language are in contact with the speakers of other languages, and very often people take a liking to some of the words used by their neighbours and take those words into their own language. This process is called **borrowing**, and the words that are taken over are *loan words* in the receiving language.

There are several motivations for borrowing a word. The simplest is that the word is the name of something totally new to those who borrow it. English, for example, has borrowed *whisky* from Scots Gaelic, *yogurt* from Turkish, *tomato* from Nahuatl, *sauna* from Finnish, *ukulele* from Hawaiian and *kangaroo* from the Guugu-Yimidhirr language of Australia. The reason for this is that English-speakers had never seen whisky or yogurt or tomatoes or saunas or ukuleles or kangaroos before encountering these things overseas, and so they simply took over the local names for them.

Another important motivation is prestige. At any given time in any given place, some languages typically enjoy more prestige than others, and speakers of less prestigious languages are often eager to show off their command of a more prestigious language by introducing some of its words into their own speech. For example, after the Norman conquest of England, Norman French enjoyed far more prestige than English, and English-speakers reacted by borrowing huge numbers of Norman French words into English, such as *picture, courage, army, treasure, language, female* and even *face, fool* and *beef*; in many cases these fashionable words simply displaced their native English equivalents, which dropped out of use, as happened with native *here* 'army' and *andwlita* 'face'.

Loan words are often a good indication of social relations in history. For example, it is likely that the large numbers of Scandinavian words (including, unusually, *she* and *its*, since pronouns are rarely borrowed) which were borrowed by English indicate generally good neighbourly relations between the natives and Viking settlers in the east of Britain, instead of the pillaging raids depicted in literature and film.

See also: **language contact**

Further reading: Blake 1996; Fennell 2000; Hock and Joseph 1996; Katamba 1994; Trask 1996.

LOCALIZATION

The concentration of certain mental faculties in particular areas of the brain. We have long known that individual areas of the brain are responsible for handling specific tasks. For example, not only are there identifiable areas of the brain that process vision, there are even areas that process specific aspects of vision, such as colour vision and the perception of movement.

Language is no different: there are particular **language areas** in the brain that process specific aspects of language use. In the mid-nineteenth century, the French surgeon Paul Broca and the German neurologist Carl Wernicke identified the two most important of these: ***Broca's area*** provides the grammatical structure for utterances and sends instructions to the speech organs, while ***Wernicke's area*** handles comprehension of speech and access to vocabulary. Both of these areas are usually located on the left side of the brain.

Broca and Wernicke reached their conclusions by examining brain-damaged patients who exhibited specific disabilities of language, and then by performing post-mortem inspections to determine which parts of the brain had been damaged. In recent years, however, the development of brain-scanning devices like *PET* (positron emission tomography), *CT* (computerized tomography) or *MRI* (magnetic resonance imaging) *scanners* has allowed us to monitor the brain of a healthy, conscious person who is performing some linguistic task like speaking or reading; we can see directly which parts of the brain are active during each of these tasks, and as a result we now have a fairly detailed map of the language areas in the brain.

See also: **aphasia; language areas; neurolinguistics**

Further reading: Akmajian *et al.* 1995; Ingram 2007; O'Grady *et al.* 1996.

LOGONOMIC RULES

Very high-level rules governing discourse in a particular setting. In a given setting, there are a number of high-level rules governing the conduct of discourse: rules about who is allowed to speak and when, about who is allowed to interrupt or to change the subject, about who is allowed to make jokes, about what counts as a joke, about what is considered offensive, and so on. These are the *logonomic rules* governing that discourse, and they are so familiar to participants (at least, to participants with experience of that type of discourse) that they are virtually subconscious.

For example, the rules governing a seminar discussion in a university are very different from those governing a performance by a stand-up comedian in a night club. What is considered acceptable, funny or offensive among a group of conservative farmers drinking in a bar in South Africa or Montana will likely be very different from the norms accepted by a lesbian or gay organization planning a political campaign against discrimination.

Every normal speaker learns the rules appropriate to each type of discourse in which he or she regularly takes part, and every normal speaker can shift effortlessly from one set of rules to another as changing settings require: this is part of that **communicative competence** which we acquire along with the acquisition of our purely linguistic knowledge. And one of the most unpleasant experiences we are likely to have is to be thrust into a setting of which we have no experience and hence don't know the rules or, still worse, in which we disapprove of the rules.

An imperfect knowledge of the logonomic rules governing a setting in which you find yourself will lead to your being regarded as, at best, lacking in charm and social graces and, at worst, ignorant, antisocial, stupid and offensive. Speaking out of turn, interrupting when you're not entitled to, using a frostily formal tone in an informal setting (or vice versa), attempting jokes which offend the others – all these are failures to observe the logonomic rules and evidence of your inadequate communicative competence.

See also: **communicative competence; ethnography of communication**

Further reading: Bonvillain 1993; Foley 1997; Harris 1993; Matthews 1979; Newmeyer 1983.

MANNER OF ARTICULATION

The action of the speech organs involved in producing a particular **consonant**. A **consonant** is produced by narrowing the **vocal tract** at some point along its length. The particular speech organs chosen to make the *constriction* represent the **place of articulation**, but, even at a single place, it is usually possible to make several different kinds of constriction. The type of constriction made in a particular instance is the *manner of articulation*.

There are several types of manner. In a *plosive* (like [b] or [k]), a complete closure is made, blocking off the airflow, and the closure is released suddenly. In an **affricate** (like [tʃ] or [ts]), a complete closure is made and then released gradually, with friction noise. In a *fricative* (like [f] or [z]), there is no complete closure, but air is forced through a tiny opening, producing friction noise. These three types are collectively called *obstruents*, because the airflow is strongly obstructed.

The remaining types are collectively called *sonorants*. In a *nasal* (like [m] or [n]), a complete closure is made in the mouth, but the velum is lowered, so that air flows out through the nose. In an *approximant* (like [w] or most types of English /r/), the air is allowed to flow through a relatively large opening, and no friction noise is produced. (At the phonetic level, such consonants are strictly **vowels**, but they pattern in languages like consonants.) In a *flap* (like the [ɽ] of many languages of India), the tongue is 'flipped' rapidly from one place to another, briefly striking something else as it moves. A *tap* (like Spanish [ɾ] in *pero* 'but') is similar except that the tongue finishes where it started. (Some books do not distinguish between flaps and taps, but it is preferable to do so.) In a *trill* (like Spanish [r] in *perro* 'dog'), the air forced through a smallish opening forces the tongue to vibrate. All these are examples of *median* consonants, in which all airflow is through the centre-line of the mouth. However, it is also possible to block off the centre-line and force the air to flow through one or both sides of the mouth; such a consonant is *lateral*. We can produce a *lateral affricate* (like the [tɬ] in Nahuatl, the Aztec language of Mexico), a *lateral fricative* (like the [ɬ] of Welsh *Llanelli*), or a *lateral approximant* (commonly just called a *lateral*) (like English [l]).

See also: **consonant**; **phonetics**; **place of articulation**

Further reading: Ashby 1995; Ball and Rahilly 1999; Ladefoged and Maddieson 1996; Laver 1994.

MARKEDNESS

The property which distinguishes less neutral linguistic forms from competing ones which are more neutral. Though the concept is older, the term *markedness* was introduced by the European linguists of the *Prague School* in the 1920s, and it is now regarded as linguistically central.

Markedness is a very broad notion applying at all levels of analysis. Generally speaking, a *marked form* is any linguistic form which is less usual or less neutral than some other form – the *unmarked form* – from any of a number of points of view. (Note that no linguistic item is absolutely neutral; neutrality is a relative concept.) A marked form may be distinguished from an unmarked one by the presence of additional linguistic material, by the presence of additional nuances of meaning, by greater rarity in a particular language or in languages generally, or in several other ways.

For example, voiceless vowels and voiceless laterals are marked with respect to voiced ones, since the voiceless ones are far rarer than the voiced ones in the world's languages and since the voiceless ones are generally found only in languages that also have voiced ones, while most languages have only the voiced ones. The affricate [pf], as in German *Pflaume* 'plum', is marked with respect to both [p] and [f], since the last two are very frequent in languages, while [pf] is exceedingly rare.

English *lioness* is marked with respect to *lion*, since it contains additional morphological material and since it is of less general applicability. English *brethren* is marked with respect to *brothers*, since the first (historically, simply the plural form of *brother*) is restricted to certain special contexts, and *bunny* is marked with respect to *rabbit*, since the first carries additional emotive meaning absent from the second. A passive sentence like *Janet was arrested by the police* is marked with respect to the active *The police arrested Janet*, since the passive contains more material, has a more complex structure, and is rarer than the active.

The several criteria for markedness may not always coincide. For example, in some Pacific languages, passive sentences are far commoner than active ones; hence the passive ones, although marked from the point of view of grammar, are unmarked from the point of view of discourse. Markedness values can also change over time: the formal Latinate phrase *prior to* was once highly marked with respect to native English *before*, but for very many speakers *prior to* has now become the ordinary, and hence unmarked, form, as in *prior to the war*.

See also: **phonology**; **sociolinguistics**

Further reading: Hawkins 1984.

MARKER

In **sociolinguistics**, a ***marker*** is one of those features of a language variety which are likely to be perceived by its speakers as having social significance. For example, northern English speakers are highly aware that their **accents** differ from southern English speakers particularly in the pronunciation of the vowels in *bus* (N. /bʊs/, S. /bʌs/), *grass* (N. /græs/, S. /grɑːs/) or *boat* (N. /bɔːt/ or /boːt/ or /bøt/, S. /bəʊt/). Since they are usually above the level of conscious awareness, markers are useful in sociolinguistic research where speakers with different accents are observed ***accommodating*** (i.e., moving their accents towards each other).

In grammar, a marker is the affixed morpheme that indicates the grammatical function of the word: such as the plural *-s* or past *-ed* in English.

See also: **accent**; **indicators**; **sociolinguistics**; **stereotypes**

Further reading: Llamas *et al.* 2007; Stockwell 2002a.

MEANING

The characteristic of a linguistic form which allows it to be used to pick out some aspect of the non-linguistic world. The study of meaning has a long history in a number of disciplines, notably philosophy, but the linguistic study of meaning, **semantics**, largely dates only from the late nineteenth century, and it has become generally regarded as a central part of linguistics only since the 1960s. Linguists are chiefly interested in the meanings of linguistic forms in everyday speech. More particularly, linguists are interested in the way some meanings relate to other meanings – that is, it is the *system* of meanings which is seen as important, rather than the meanings of individual items.

Like philosophers, linguists carefully distinguish different types of meaning. The central and intrinsic meaning of a linguistic form is its **denotation** or **sense**, while the fuzzy and sometimes variable associations of that form constitute its **connotations**. The relation between a form and the non-linguistic thing it picks out in a given context is its **reference**. An extended and non-literal meaning is a **metaphor**.

Debates in linguistics around meaningfulness have been conducted, with *formalist linguistics* emphasizing the arbitrariness of reference, **cognitive linguists** emphasizing its embodied and experiential construal, **psycholinguists** stressing its dynamically constructed nature, and **sociolinguists** and **discourse analysts** pointing to the performed and socially negotiated politics of the setting in meaning construal.

See also: **connotation**; **denotation**; **metaphor**; **reference**; **selection restriction**; **semantics**; **sense**

Further reading: Allan 1986; Frawley 1992; Hofmann 1993; Hudson 1995; Hurford and Heasley 1983; Leech 1974; Palmer 1976.

MEDIUM

Any one of several signalling systems within which a language may be embedded. A *primary* medium for language is one which is not derived from any other medium and which may be the medium in which a child acquires its first language. The most familiar and most widely used primary medium is **speech**, in which linguistic information is encoded within sounds which are produced by the vocal tract acting upon a stream of air. Speech has been used as a medium since our remote ancestors first evolved language, and it was probably the first medium we ever used (though some scholars query this). The other primary medium is **sign language**, in which linguistic information is encoded within signs made chiefly with the hands, arms, shoulders, head and face. This is the medium used today by the majority of deaf people, at least in places in which they have a chance to learn it. Signing is of unknown antiquity; it has become steadily more prominent since the eighteenth century, but sign languages have very likely been constructed and used for a very long time, whenever circumstances permitted. It is important to realize that a true sign language is autonomous and in no way derived from a spoken language.

A *secondary* medium is one which is derived from a primary medium. The most familiar secondary medium is *writing*, which usually consists of an attempt at converting speech into permanent marks. Writing is a recent invention in human affairs, being little more than 5,000 years old, and until very recently knowledge of writing (and reading) was confined to a tiny minority of the world's population. True sign languages can also be converted into writing, though systems for doing this are still in their infancy and mostly used only by specialists; most signers find it more convenient to learn to read ordinary writing. Also secondary are systems like *Signed English* (or *Manually Coded English*), in which a spoken language (like English) is transferred into the medium of hand-gestures.

A *tertiary* medium is one derived from a secondary medium. The slow and cumbersome system called *finger-spelling* is a tertiary system, since it is derived from writing, with each letter of the alphabet being rendered by a finger-sign. Morse code bleeps in electronic form are tertiary. Early systems of *shorthand* were often tertiary, being derived from writing, but modern shorthand systems are all secondary, being derived directly from speech.

See also: **literacy**; **sign language**; **speech**; **writing system**

Further reading: Coulmas 1996; Crystal 1997; Trask 1995.

MENTAL SPACE

A conceptual representation of a semantic domain in **cognitive linguistics**. In the *mental space theory* of French linguist Gilles Fauconnier, the conceptual representation of the meaning of a sentence is held in an idealized form. Further referential tokens in the discourse connect to the mental space and it is used to interpret the utterance. The theory has been combined with conceptual **metaphor** theory to explain metaphoric discourse in terms of several input mental spaces producing a *blended space*. This new mental representation is able to develop its own logic beyond the range of its inputs. The theory of blending thus claims to account for the transformative experience of metaphor.

See also: **cognitive linguistics; metaphor; possible worlds theory; text world theory**

Further reading: Fauconnier 1994, 1997; Fauconnier and Turner 2002; Hickmann and Robert 2006.

MENTALISM

The doctrine that the mind can be invoked in scientific investigation and even be made the object of study itself. In the late nineteenth century, psychology had become obscurantist and almost metaphysical. The new doctrine of **behaviourism** attempted to sweep this away by focusing only on what could be directly observed and preferably measured. But the behaviourists themselves often went so far as not only to deny the possibility of appealing to unobservable things like minds, but even to reject the very existence of minds.

More recently, the pendulum has swung the other way again, and today most psychologists, philosophers and linguists are perfectly happy to invoke invisible things like minds and purposes and even to make mind itself the object of study. This approach is called *mentalism*, and it is now the dominant point of view in all three disciplines, which themselves are now partly united within the new discipline of **cognitive** science.

See also: **behaviourism; cognitive linguistics**

Further reading: Malmkjær 2004; Ungerer and Schmid 1996.

METALANGUAGE

A language used to talk about another language. Linguists, philosophers and many others often need to talk about particular languages, or about languages in general. Naturally, the discussion itself has to be couched in a language of some sort, and this fact can quickly lead to hopeless confusion if we are not careful. We must therefore distinguish carefully between the *object language* (the language which we are talking about) and the *metalanguage* (the language we are using to talk about the object language).

It is perfectly possible to use, say, English as a metalanguage in order to talk about English as an object language, and indeed we do this all the time, but it is precisely here that confusion can most quickly arise: if we fail to distinguish between the English we are talking about and the English we are using to talk about it, we can easily become lost.

Consider the following example. Using English as a metalanguage to talk about English, we may assert the following: a grammatical English sentence may not contain two consecutive instances of the preposition *of*. This is true. But beginning students often challenge this by pointing to examples like this very sentence: the grammatical functions of *of* in English are numerous. Is the sentence itself a counterexample?

No, it is not. It appears to be a counterexample only if we confuse the metalanguage with the object language. The statement above is a statement in the metalanguage, and the first occurrence of *of* in it is part of that statement. But the second occurrence of *of* is different: this is merely a piece of the object language, one which we happen to be talking about here. That is, the first *of* is doing what *of* normally does, while the second *of* is doing nothing at all: it is merely being talked about. If this is not obvious, observe what happens when the object language is French: the grammatical functions of *de* in French are numerous. Here it should be easy to see that the French preposition *de* is doing nothing in this English sentence except being talked about.

The two instances of *of* are an example of what philosophers call the *use-mention distinction*: the first *of* is being used normally, while the second is merely being mentioned (talked about): the latter could appear in italics or in 'scare quotes' to signal this graphically.

At the very least, when we use English as a metalanguage to talk about languages, we need to invoke a battery of technical terms and concepts, just as a specialist studying physics, music or psychology needs to invoke technical terms and concepts. In fact, we sometimes go further, and invent a special artificial language to use as our metalanguage. The various types of *formal logic* used by logicians, philosophers and linguists for describing English and other languages are just this: specially invented metalanguages.

See also: **linguistics**; **philosophy of language**

Further reading: Chapman 2000, 2006; Lyons 1995; Robson and Stockwell 2005.

METAPHOR

The non-literal use of a linguistic form, designed to draw attention to a perceived resemblance. The literary use of metaphors is ancient and well studied, and the fields of rhetoric and literary criticism have developed a formidable battery of Greek terms for naming many different kinds of metaphor. But metaphors are in fact commonplace in ordinary speech and writing: we speak of the *foot* of a mountain or the *eye* of a needle, we refer to Saussure as the *father* of linguistics, and we speak of a failing business enterprise as a *lame duck*. Like every language, English is stuffed with thousands of such metaphors, and most of them are so familiar that we no longer even regard them as metaphorical in nature. Indeed, linguists have realized for some generations now that metaphors are a commonplace way of extending the expressive resources of a language. And essentially, of course, all referential linguistic tokens are metaphorical because of **arbitrariness**.

Since the early 1980s, however, those linguists developing the new discipline of **cognitive linguistics** have been drawing attention to the pervasive influence in languages of *cognitive metaphors*, large-scale metaphors which condition a broad range of expressions and which appear to be related to the way we perceive the world. An example is the underlying metaphor LIFE IS A JOURNEY, which appears in any number of locutions: *I'll cross that bridge when I come to it*; *She knows where she's going*; *There were two paths open to him*; *The baby has arrived*; *Their paths crossed*; *She has finally arrived* (succeeded); *He is gone* (dead); *It's been a long road*; and many others. A *cognitive* or *conceptual metaphor* is thus seen as a mental mapping between two domains: a source domain of familiar meanings and a target domain of the new meaning in focus. Many of the *tropes* of classical rhetoric express in various stylistic forms (such as *synecdoche*, *litotes*, *hyperbole*, *metonymy*, and stylistic *metaphor* itself) aspects of an underlying cognitive metaphor;

169

though it has been suggested that conceptual *metonymy* is a different sort of mapping.

See also: **cognitive linguistics; meaning**

Further reading: Carter 1997; Cruse 1986; Giora 2003; Goatly 1997; Hiraga 2005; Lakoff and Johnson 1980; Kövecses 2005; Saeed 1997; Ungerer and Schmid 1996.

MINIMAL PAIR

A pair of words in a language which have different meanings but which have identical forms except at one single point. The English words *pet* and *bet* have different meanings, but they consist of identical sequences of sounds in all positions except one: in this case, initial position. Here the first word has [p], while the second has [b]. Consequently, the difference in meaning must derive entirely from the contrast between [p] and [b]; we must therefore assign English [p] and [b] to different **phonemes** /p/ and /b/, and *pet* and *bet* constitute a *minimal pair* for the phonemes /p/ and /b/. Other minimal pairs for English /p/ and /b/ include *planned* and *bland*, *nipple* and *nibble*, and *rip* and *rib*.

Finding a minimal pair for two sounds constitutes certain proof that the two sounds in question must belong to different phonemes. Sometimes this is fairly easy, as with English [s] and [ʃ]: *sun* and *shun*, *puss* and *push*, *lass* and *lash*. Sometimes it is not so easy, as with English [ʃ] and [ʒ], for which we can only find minimal pairs by invoking proper names (*Aleutian* versus *allusion*) or made-up words (*mesher* versus *measure*). Larger minimal sets can be found. For example, the set *sum*, *sun*, *sung* constitutes a minimal triplet for the English phonemes /m/, /n/ and /ŋ/.

In **sociolinguistics** and in a slightly different sense, minimal pairs of words are given to informants to test their accent features, especially when the informants are acutely aware that their speech is under examination: *moon/moan*; *which/witch*; *blew/blue*; *law/lore*.

See also: **distribution; phoneme; phonotactics**

Further reading: Carr 1993; Fromkin and Rodman 1998; Stockwell 2002a.

MINIMALIST PROGRAM(ME)

A version of generative grammar proposed by Noam Chomsky in the mid-1990s. The emphasis in developing transformational and representative rules should be on making them as economical as possible. In other words, no rules should be redundant, and every rule should be *interpretable* in the sense here of rendering a final linguistic form. The **deep structure** and **surface structure** levels of traditional generative grammar and in **Government-and-Binding Theory** are removed to leave only the *logical form* and the *phonetic form*.

Transformational-generative grammar in the hands of Chomsky can be seen either as a unified and principled theory developing with substantial shifts from the 1960s to the present, with *Minimalism* as its latest version, or as a set of radically different revisions that each amount to an abandonment of the previous system. Several features remain consistent, however, to do with the emphasis on syntax and phonology, the emphasis on generative rules, and the delineation away from the sociolinguistic or performative context.

See also: **Government-and-Binding Theory**; **transformational grammar**

Further reading: Antony and Hornstein 2003; Chomsky 1995; Hendrick 2003; Hornstein, Nuñes and Grohmann 2005; Lasnik 2003; Lasnik *et al.* 2005; Radford 1997, 2004.

MINORITY LANGUAGE

A long-established language spoken as a mother tongue by people in some part of a country in which the national or official language is something else. We commonly tend to assume that everybody in, say, France speaks French. In fact, virtually all adults in France *do* speak French – but not always as their first language. In various regions of the country, the first language of all or most local people is Alsatian German, Dutch, Breton, Basque, Catalan, Occitan or Corsican. Each of these is the mother tongue in its region, and people who learn one of these as their first language in early childhood may not even begin learning French until later in life, especially after beginning formal education.

Such languages are called *minority languages*, and minority languages are not confined to France. Alongside Spanish, Spain has

Galician, Basque and Catalan; alongside German, Germany has Frisian and Wendish (the second is a Slavic language); alongside English, Britain has Welsh and Scots Gaelic; alongside English, the USA has Navaho, Hopi, Lakota, and dozens of other indigenous languages, as well as other immigrant languages. Russia and China each have over 100 minority languages, and countries with no significant minority languages are in fact a rarity – though Iceland and Portugal may be two cases.

In every case, a minority language has been spoken in its area for centuries, sometimes even for millennia, but its speakers have simply found themselves incorporated into a nation-state in which the principal language is something else. In some cases, most speakers of a minority language may live and die without ever acquiring an adequate command of the prestige language; in others, all speakers normally become fluent in the prestige language, or at least acquire an adequate working knowledge of it. Even in Britain, Spain and France, monoglot speakers of Welsh, Basque and Corsican were numerous only a few generations ago (and Basque, at least, still has a handful of elderly monoglot speakers today), but, because of dramatic advances in communications, transport and education, almost all European adults are today fluent in the national language of the country they find themselves living in.

This very fact, of course, places great pressure on minority languages. In the not-too-distant past, speakers of minority languages like Welsh and Basque were often openly persecuted by centralist governments, which were inclined to see the use of regional languages as unpatriotic, subversive, even dangerous. Today open persecution is less usual in Europe (though not always elsewhere, and it has not disappeared entirely in Europe: for example, Greece has recently been ferociously persecuting its Macedonian-speaking minority). However, minority languages are nevertheless often in grave danger of dying out. A good knowledge of the national language is absolutely required for living in a modern nation-state – to get an education, to find a job, to deal with tax returns and innumerable other official documents, to travel round the country, to understand newspapers, television and films. Further, knowledge of a major language like English or French opens the door to opportunities, not just throughout the country, but throughout the world. Consequently, speakers of minority languages find themselves using the prestige language ever more regularly, while the role of their mother tongue decreases correspondingly. In some cases, parents may actually strive to have their children learn the prestige language, rather than their own mother tongue, in the hope that these children will have a better life as a result.

Such pressures have already led to the disappearance of countless minority languages, including Cornish and Manx in Britain and hundreds of indigenous languages in North America and Australia. Today these pressures are greater than ever, but in many cases speakers of minority languages are waking up to the threat and becoming increasingly militant in their demands for greater official recognition and encouragement of their languages. In a few cases, as with the Swedish-speakers of Finland and the Basque-speakers of Spain, a greater or lesser degree of protection has already been achieved, but in most cases protection is limited or non-existent, and it seems inevitable that hundreds or thousands of minority languages will disappear in the next two or three generations.

See also: **language death**

Further reading: Crystal 1997; Holmes 1992; Romaine 1994; Wardhaugh 1987.

MIRROR NEURONS

It was discovered in the 1990s that the same brain neurons 'fired' both when a person performs an action and when that person observes someone else performing the action. Most suggestively for linguistics, these neurons are located in *Broca's area*, a region associated with language. The phenomenon of mirror neurons has lent support to the *gestural hypothesis* of language evolution, which proposes that language developed as a communication system out of physical imitation in a community.

Furthermore, the *mirror neuron* effect occurs more strongly when the observed action is tending towards an instrumental goal rather than an apparently unmotivated action. For example, more neurons 'fire' when the action involves picking up an apple and eating it than when simply picking up an apple and moving it. By extension, this seems to suggest that language evolved primarily as a goal-driven mechanism (which would give support to **schema** theory), and communication towards a purpose was a primary function of language origin. As with most theories of language evolution, conclusive evidence is hard to come by.

See also: **cognitive linguistics; origin and evolution of language**

Further reading: Goldstein 2002.

MODALITY

The **grammatical category** associated with the expression of obligation, permission, prohibition, necessity, possibility and ability. It is by no means easy to separate *modality* from the more traditional category of **mood**, which expresses degree or kind of reality. But for some decades now linguists have preferred to apply the label modality to the linguistic expression of the six categories named above. This term is particularly convenient in discussing a language, such as English, which contains a specific set of *modal auxiliaries* for expressing these concepts.

The English modals include *can, could, may, might, will, would, shall, should, must* and *ought (to)*, together with their negated forms. Familiar examples like *You can do it, You could do it, You may do it, You should do it, You must do it, You can't do it* and *You mustn't do it* all express aspects or degrees of one (or more) of the six named categories.

In practice, modality shades off imperceptibly into several other categories: *evidentiality* (the amount and nature of the evidence which you have for saying something), *modalization* (the probability or regularity of an occurrence), *modularity* (the degree of commitment or willingness involved on somebody's part), *hedging* (reducing your own commitment to what you are saying) and *vague language*. These extensions of modality have been particularly investigated within **Systemic Linguistics**.

See also: **mood**

Further reading: Coates 1983; Frawley 2006; Hurford 1994; Palmer 1974, 1979, 2001.

MODIFIER

A linguistic element in a sentence which is grammatically linked to a second element and adds information about that second element.

A sentence is typically made up of smaller grammatical units called **phrases**, and a phrase typically consists of a grammatically central word, its **head**, accompanied by some *modifiers*, each of which provides some information about whatever is denoted by the head.

Consider the sentence *The little girl in the pond was shrieking delightedly*. Here the **noun phrase** *the little girl in the pond* has the head *girl* (the whole phrase denotes some kind of girl), and *girl* has two modifiers: *little* and *in the pond*. Each of these modifiers provides further information about the girl in question: among girls generally, this particular one is both little and in the pond. The word *the*, in contrast, is not a modifier but a *specifier*: it provides no information about the girl (it would make no sense to say that this girl is *the* compared to other girls), but rather it provides information about how the entire noun phrase fits into the whole discourse (in this case, it indicates that the girl in question has already been mentioned earlier and is familiar to the listener).

Similarly, the **verb phrase** *shrieking excitedly* consists of the head *shrieking* and the modifier *excitedly* – that is, of all the possible ways of shrieking, this particular shrieking was done in an excited manner.

Modifiers can be quite large and complex, and they need not occur immediately next to their heads. In the sentence *The women who had volunteered for the beauty contest climbed giggling onto the stage*, the head *women* is modified both by the relative clause *who had volunteered for the beauty contest* and by the adjective *giggling*, the second of which is separated from its head by the verb *climbed*.

The relation between a modifier and its head is *modification*.

See also: **head**; **phrase**

Further reading: Hurford 1994; Jackson 2002.

MOOD

The **grammatical category** which expresses the degree or kind of reality attached to an utterance. *Mood* is not well developed as a grammatical category in English, and we mostly use words and constructions to express mood distinctions. In this way, we can assign varying degrees of certainty to an utterance: *Susie smokes, I hear that Susie smokes, It appears that Susie smokes, Surely Susie* *smokes, Susie probably smokes, Maybe Susie smokes, I wonder if Susie smokes, It's unlikely that Susie smokes.* We can also assign different degrees of reality within conditions: *If Susie smokes, then* ... (an open condition: maybe she smokes) is different from *If Susie smoked, then* ... (a counterfactual condition: she doesn't smoke). American English (but not British English) makes an overt mood distinction between *I insist that Susie smokes* (I'm telling you: she definitely does) and *I insist that Susie smoke* (I demand to see her smoking – perhaps in a film role).

Questions may be regarded as expressing another kind of mood: *Does Susie smoke?* And so can commands: *Susie, smoke that cigarette!* (perhaps our tyrannical film director again, to a reluctant actress).

In some other languages, there are more or less elaborate distinctions of mood built into the grammar and frequently expressed either by variation in verb-forms or by particles.

Mood shades off imperceptibly into **modality**, and no sharp line can be drawn between them.

See also: **modality**

Further reading: Coates 1983; Hurford 1994; Palmer 2001.

MORPHEME

The smallest identifiable grammatical unit. We sometimes think of *words* as the smallest units of grammar, but words in fact are not the smallest grammatical units. For example, the word *unhappiness* is clearly built up from three smaller pieces: the prefix *un-*, the stem *happy* and the suffix *-ness*. Each of these pieces is a *morpheme* of English, and not one of them can be broken down any further in grammatical terms: all of them are minimal units (there is no word *hap* to go with *-y* for example). Each of these morphemes is used to build other English words. For example, the *prefix un-* occurs also in *unhappy, unclear, unwilling, uninteresting* and *unsatisfied*; the **stem** *happy* occurs also in *unhappy, happiness, happier* and *happily*, and also, of course, in the word *happy* itself; and the *suffix -ness* occurs also in *quickness, sadness, lewdness, childishness* and *unpreparedness*.

Morphemes are of different types. We say that *happy* is a *lexical morpheme*, meaning that it has dictionary meaning: we can provide a definition for it. But the *-ly* of *happily* is different: this is a **grammatical morpheme**, which performs a strictly grammatical function – in this case, that of turning an adjective into an adverb. Quite independently, we can say that *happy* is also a **free morpheme**: it can stand alone to make a word, as it does in the word *happy*. But the prefix *un-* and the suffixes *-ness* and *-ly* are **bound morphemes**: they can never stand alone, but must always be attached to at least one other morpheme within a word. In this example, *-y* is not a morpheme within *happy*, though it is a morpheme in *shaky*.

In the ideal case, a single morpheme has a single constant form and a single constant meaning or function but, in practice, many morphemes vary in form, depending on where they occur. For example, the morpheme *sane* has one form when it occurs in the words *sane* and *insane*, but a different form when it occurs in the word *sanity* (listen to the pronunciation, since the English spelling is not very helpful here). Likewise, the negative prefix *in-* exhibits several different forms in the words *insincere*, *impossible* and *illegal*. We call these variant forms the **allomorphs** of the morpheme.

In the case above, it is a trivial matter to divide a word into the morphemes of which it is built, but sometimes such division is not so easy. Clearly the past-tense form *loved* (as in *She loved him*) consists of two morphemes, the verb-stem *love* and a grammatical morpheme which we can call *Past*, and it's not too hard to draw a line between them. But the past-tense form *took* must likewise consist of two morphemes, the verb-stem *take* and the morpheme *Past*, yet this time we can't draw a neat line at all: the two morphemes are just wrapped up in a single bundle, and we have to appeal to a more abstract level of representation to show that *took* is really *take* plus *Past*.

The term morpheme was coined in the late nineteenth century by the Polish linguist Jan Baudouin de Courtenay, but it was not always used in the modern sense. That modern sense was established by the American linguist Leonard Bloomfield in the 1930s, and it was Bloomfield and his American successors who made the study of morphemes a central part of linguistics.

See also: **affix**; **derivation**; **inflection**; **morphology**; **stem**; **word-formation**

Further reading: Bauer 1988; Brown and Miller 1991; Jeffries 2006; Katamba 1994.

MORPHOLOGY

Word structure, or the branch of linguistics which studies this. Words typically have internal structure, and in particular they consist of smaller units called **morphemes**. For example, the verb-form *taking* consists of two morphemes: the verb-stem *take* and the grammatical ending *-ing*. Similarly, the noun *textbook* consists of the morphemes *text* and *book*, and the the adverb *slowly* consists of the morphemes *slow* and *-ly*.

Morphology is conventionally divided into two main areas. These are **inflection** – the variation in form of a single word for grammatical purposes, as with *take, takes, took, taken, taking* – and **word-formation** – the construction of new words from existing words, as with *textbook* from *text* and *book* and with *slowly* from *slow* and *-ly*. A particularly important type of word-formation is **derivation**, as in *slowly*, *rewrite* and *unhappiness*.

See also: **affix; derivation; inflection; morpheme; stem; word-formation**

Further reading: Bauer 1988; Brown and Miller 1991; Katamba 1989, 2006; Matthews 1991.

MOTHERESE

The distinctive style of speech used in addressing young children. Adults looking after very young children, and above all mothers doing this, typically talk to those children using a highly distinctive type of language. They use special words like *choo-choo*, including many diminutives like *horsie* and *doggie*; they confine themselves to the simplest grammatical forms and constructions; they use exaggerated intonation patterns; they frequently repeat themselves; and they often expand the child's utterances into longer adult utterances by responding, for example, to the child's 'Daddy sock' with 'Yes, Daddy is putting his socks on'.

This special type of speech is popularly known as 'baby-talk', but this term is never used in linguistics; instead, it is variously known as *caregiver speech*, *caretaker speech* or *motherese*. Linguists are still debating the importance of care-giver speech in allowing acquisition to occur. There is no question, however, that many of the sociolinguistic norms for speakers are established by the person who is most responsible for modelling their **vernacular,** or *mother-tongue.*

See also: **origin and evolution of language; vernacular**

Further reading: Aitchison 1989.

MOVEMENT

Any of various processes or structures in which an element of a sentence appears in a position other than its canonical position. Grammarians have long realized that some particular sentences depart from the usual norms in the order of their elements, but it was only in the 1950s, originally within the formalism of **transformational grammar,** that linguists began to speak, metaphorically but conveniently, of the movement of elements out of their ordinary position.

Movement phenomena are numerous and diverse. One familiar example in English involves question-words (WH-words) like *who* and *what*: we say *Susie was talking to Mike*, but we also say *Who was Susie talking to?* and *The guy who Susie was talking to is Mike*, in both of which the question-word *who*, which is logically the object of the preposition *to*, fails to appear after *to* and instead appears earlier in the sentence. This kind of movement is called *WH-movement* or *extraction.*

A second type of movement is *extraposition*, in which a complex element is shifted to the end of its sentence. So, instead of *That Susie is drunk is obvious*, we prefer to say *It is obvious that Susie is drunk*, in which the *that*-clause has been extraposed. Similarly, instead of *A student who speaks Basque turned up this morning*, we can say *A student turned up this morning who speaks Basque*, in which the *who*-clause is extraposed.

A third type is *fronting*, in which an element is moved to the beginning of its sentence. So, instead of *She inherited her brains from her mother*, we can say *From her mother she inherited her brains*, in which the phrase *from her mother* has been fronted. Likewise, instead of *I can't cope with this* we can say *This I can't cope with*, with fronting of *this*. When, as is often the case, an element is fronted to make it an explicit topic, we speak of *topicalization.*

Finally, there is a rather unusual type of movement called **raising;** see that entry for information.

See also: **raising**; **topic**

Further reading: Kroeger 2004, van Valin 2001.

NAME

A linguistic form which serves to pick out a unique person, place or thing. Grammatically speaking, a name is a **noun phrase**, but one with the highly distinctive function of pointing at some individual entity: *Abraham Lincoln, Paris, the Golden Gate Bridge*. (Traditionally these have rather confusingly been called *proper nouns*.)

Probably every person in every society receives a *personal name* (or *given name*), typically shortly after birth, though in some societies an adult name is conferred later in life. In some societies, there is a conventional list of personal names, one of which is selected; in others, completely original names may be constructed and bestowed. In the first case, it may be necessary to distinguish individuals bearing the same name by adding something to the name. This can be done in several ways. A descriptive word may be used to indicate something about the individual, such as personal characteristics (size, complexion [*Little, White*]), profession (*Miller, Smith*), location of dwelling (*Atwater, Woods*), place of origin (*Bristol, Welsh*), memorable incident; this is an *epithet* (or, if humorous, a *sobriquet*). Or a *patronymic* may be added, identifying the name-bearer's father (*Johnson, Prichard*).

When such a second name ceases to be the property of a particular individual, and comes to be handed down to the name-bearer's descendants, it has become a *surname* (or *family name*). As can be seen, many English surnames derive from epithets and patronymics. Surnames in Europe are mostly of medieval origin, and even today they are not in use in Iceland and are little used in Turkish Cyprus.

Place names, or *toponyms*, are conferred everywhere upon every kind of significant location: settlements, rivers, lakes, seas, valleys, forests, fields, mountains and hills, roads and streets, bridges, city gates, houses, places of worship, office buildings, sports stadiums ... the list is endless. Names are also conferred upon ships, trains, planes, railway lines, festivals, holy days, books, newspapers ... , upon virtually everything that human beings consider important.

Name-giving practices differ considerably from society to society, and anthropological linguists are often interested in studying these practices.

Names exhibit some unusual linguistic properties, and their study is a specialist subdiscipline within linguistics. The study of names, and particularly of the origins and histories of names, is **onomastics**.

See also: **onomastics**

Further reading: Crystal 1995, 1997; Dunkling 1995.

NARRATIVE

A **text** which tells a story. A *narrative* differs from most other types of text in that it relates a connected series of events, either real or fictional, in a more or less orderly manner. In addition to familiar kinds of written narratives, such as history books and novels, there are oral narratives, that is, stories told in conversation.

Narratives are of interest to linguists from various social, anthropological and structural points of view. In the early 1970s, the American linguist William Labov examined natural oral narratives and proposed a general six-part structure for them:

1 an *abstract* – indicating that a story is about to begin
2 an *orientation* – setting the scene and introducing the main characters
3 the *complicating action* – the main events
4 a *resolution* – the outcome
5 an *evaluation* – explaining the point of the story, and
6 a *coda* – signalling that the story is over.

It seems that this is the **prototype** form for narratives: deviations from this form generate certain effects in the audience.

More recently, a number of linguists have devoted themselves to the study of narratives of various types, and some of them have attempted to develop *story grammars*, general structural outlines to which particular types of narrative tend to conform. Naturally, practitioners of **anthropological linguistics** are interested in examining the rules for constructing narratives in different languages and cultures. The field of *narratology* has developed as an interdiscipline crossing linguistics with literary criticism and theory.

See also: **genre**; **text**

181

Further reading: Carter *et al*. 1997; Fabb 1997; Labov 1972; Palmer 1996; Polanyi 1985; Propp 1968; Ryan 1991; Toolan 1988, 1994a, 1994b.

NATIONAL LANGUAGE

The single principal language of a country. By and large, we expect citizens of France to speak French, even if their mother tongue is something else. We expect to hear French spoken in the steeets, on television and in films. We expect books and newspapers to be printed in French. We expect signs and advertisements to be in French, and we expect to be able to conduct all our business in French, from buying a loaf of bread to making a will. In other words, French is the *national language* of France – the single language that is used by pretty much everyone for pretty much everything.

In the same way, English is the national language in Britain, in Australia, in the USA and elsewhere, as German is in Germany and Dutch in the Netherlands. But not every country has a national language. Belgium is about equally divided between Dutch-speakers (Flemish) and French-speakers (Walloon), and neither language can be used throughout the country. The same is true of Canada, divided into English-speaking and French-speaking parts, and of Switzerland, divided into regions speaking four different languages; the same was true of Czechoslovakia and Yugoslavia before they broke up, partly as a result of these very linguistic divisions. The perception and encouragement of a single national language is often a manifestation of a **standard language** ideology, where other **minority languages** are suppressed, neglected or stigmatized.

The position of a national language may be enshrined in law (as in France) or not (as in the USA). But every country, whether it has a national language or not, is obliged to recognize one or more **official languages** in which official business may be conducted.

See also: **minority language**; **official language**; **standard language**

Further reading: Holmes 1992; Wardhaugh 1987, 2005.

NATURAL CLASS

A class of linguistic objects all of which behave in much the same way in a language and which therefore often need to be referred to in a description of the language. Every language contains a large number of linguistic elements of various kinds: phonemes, morphemes, words, and so on. Now, if every word in a language behaved completely differently from every other word, and similarly for the other kinds of objects, then the language would be virtually chaotic, and no organized description would be possible: we would have nothing but a collection of miscellaneous observations.

But, of course, languages are not built like this at all. Instead, almost all of these linguistic objects fall rather naturally into just a few types, or classes, and all the items in one class exhibit very similar behaviour. These classes are the **natural classes** of the language.

For example, almost all the words of English (or of any other language) fall naturally into just a few classes: the **parts of speech**, such as **nouns**, **verbs** and **adjectives**. Every noun behaves in much the same way as every other noun, and so on for the other parts of speech. Consequently, when we describe English, we can make a number of important statements about the behaviour of the entire class of nouns, and we do not have to concern ourselves with every noun individually.

The same goes for morphemes, phonemes and other classes of objects. For example, the English phonemes /p t k/, as in *pip*, *tit*, *kick*, form a natural class, since what is true of one of them is nearly always true of the others as well, and so, by giving this class a suitable name, the class of *voiceless plosives*, we can make all the required statements about all of them at once.

There are two complications. First, it may be the case that, while the members of a class behave identically in some respects, they behave somewhat differently in other respects; this is the problem of **subcategorization**, which is most prominent with parts of speech. Second, our natural classes may sometimes overlap, so that a larger natural class may contain within it several smaller natural classes whose memberships are partly identical. This problem is most familiar with phonemes, and it is the reason we prefer to work with **distinctive features**.

One of the first goals in any description of a language is to identify the natural classes that it contains and to provide suitable labels for those classes, so that the description can then take advantage of these classes whenever required. Failure to do this leads inevitably to the endless unprincipled labelling of things, a feature of **traditional grammar** widely regarded as one of its failings: though the traditional grammarians certainly identified some natural classes, they failed to recognize others that were just as important. A large part of descriptive and theoretical linguistics in the twentieth century has been devoted to the development of efficient and principled ways of identifying, labelling and manipulating natural classes.

See also: **distinctive feature; morpheme; part of speech; subcategorization**

Further reading: Lakoff 1987; O'Grady *et al.* 1996.

NATURAL-LANGUAGE PROCESSING

The use of computer programs to process large quantities of language data. *Natural-language processing*, or NLP, began to emerge in the 1950s when high-speed computers first became available. The original goal was *machine translation* (MT), constructing programs that could translate a text from one language into another with a minimum of human intervention. MT is still an active area today, but most work in NLP is now concerned with a much broader range of applications.

Workers in NLP are concerned to devise computational techniques for analysing substantial bodies of material in a *natural language* in order to obtain results comparable to those a human being might obtain, but of course to do it very much faster and more accurately. The central task is the construction of efficient and robust *parsers*. A parser is a program which can take a sentence in a natural language, work out its grammatical structure, and assign a meaning to it, so that the resulting meaning can then be manipulated by other parts of the system.

Modern NLP systems are increasingly ambitious: they try to deal not merely with single sentences but with sizable texts, often including pragmatic and discourse factors. No system as yet comes anywhere near the vast flexibility of language processing by humans, but in particular domains NLP systems can be highly successful. A familiar if simple example is the system used by travel agents for booking airline flights, but more elaborate systems are also in regular use; for example, for extracting information from a huge *corpus* of language data when preparing a dictionary, or in internet search engines. NLP is now a central part of the enterprise of constructing *artificial intelligence*, computer programs which can mimic the behaviour of human beings in a range of areas.

(Note that the acronym NLP also stands for *neuro-linguistic programming*, a form of fairground quackery in which trauma victims, addicts, depressives and others with serious mental disorders are 'cured' by repeating certain linguistic representations of their behaviour: it is based on an extreme form of the *Sapir-Whorf hypothesis*.)

See also: **computational linguistics**

Further reading: Dale *et al*. 2000; Jurafsky and Martin 2000.

NEUROLINGUISTICS

The study of the connections between language and brain. The study of the relation between language and brain was begun in the mid-nineteenth century by the Frenchman Paul Broca and the German Carl Wernicke. What they did was to study and characterize the **aphasia** (disturbed language) of people who had suffered brain damage, and then, after the sufferers' deaths, to conduct post-mortem examinations in order to find out which areas of the brain had been damaged.

In this way, they succeeded in identifying two specific areas of the brain, today called *Broca's area* and *Wernicke's area*, each of which is responsible for specific aspects of language use. These findings confirmed the reality of the **localization** of language in the brain; moreover, since these areas are nearly always located on the left side of the brain, they also confirmed the **lateralization** of the brain.

In the mid-twentieth century, the American neurologist Norman Geschwind elaborated the view of the brain as consisting of a number of specialized components with connections between them, and he also provided the basis of our modern classification of the several **language areas** in the brain and of the types of aphasia resulting from damage to each.

More recently, the introduction of sophisticated brain scanners has allowed specialists to examine the activity in the brains of healthy, conscious subjects who are performing specific linguistic tasks like reading, speaking and listening. The new data have both confirmed and extended our understanding of the location and functions of the several language areas.

See also: **language areas; lateralization; localization**

Further reading: Ingram 2007; O'Grady *et al*. 1996; Steinberg 1993.

NEUTRALIZATION

The disappearance of a phonological contrast in a particular position. It is clear that English has, among others, the two **phonemes** /p/ and /b/. These two distinguish a number of **minimal pairs**, such as *pie* and *buy*, *pike* and *bike*, *pray* and *bray*, *nipple* and *nibble*, *rip* and *rib*, and *slap* and *slab*. However, there is at least one position in which they do not contrast at all: after an /s/ in the same syllable. In English, we cannot possibly make a difference between two different words such as *spit* and *sbit*, or *spade* and *sbade*.

In this position, therefore, we say that the contrast between /p/ and /b/ is **neutralized**: it no longer exists here and, in this position, /p/ and /b/ can no longer be used to distinguish pairs of words.

The concept of neutralization was introduced and developed chiefly by the East European linguists of the **Prague School** in the 1930s, and especially by the Russian linguist Nikolai Trubetzkoy. The existence of neutralization is a powerful reminder that the **phonology** of a language is a matter of the **behaviour** and **patterning** of sounds, and not of their absolute phonetic value.

See also: **minimal pair**; **phoneme**; **phonology**

Further reading: Carr 1993; Clark and Yallop 1995; Gussmann 2002; Hawkins 1984; Katamba 1989; Lass 1984; Odden 2005.

NOMINALIZATION

Any grammatical unit which behaves like a **noun** or a **noun phrase** but which is built up from something very different. The English word *arrive* is a verb, as in *She arrived at ten o'clock*, but the word *arrival* is a noun, as in *Her sudden arrival surprised us*. Clearly the noun *arrival* is built up from the verb *arrive*, and so we say that *arrival* is a **nominalization** of *arrive*.

This is an example of the simplest kind of nominalization, but much more complex and elaborate types are possible. For example, in *Tom and Sally Perkins study volcanoes*, the sequence *study volcanoes* is a **verb phrase**, but in *Studying volcanoes is dangerous work*, this verb phrase has been nominalized into a noun phrase (it is the subject of the sentence).

Yet another type of nominalization can be built up from *Susie smokes*, which is a complete sentence. This entire sentence can be nominalized into a noun phrase, as in *That Susie smokes surprises me*, in which the nominalization *that Susie smokes* is again the subject of its sentence.

English allows **adjectives** to be nominalized only in limited circumstances, as in *The poor are always with us*, in which the adjective *poor* has been nominalized into a noun. But Spanish allows any adjective at all to be nominalized, as in *el rojo* 'the red one', in which the adjective *rojo* 'red' has been nominalized.

The use of nominalizations for various communicative purposes has been particularly investigated within **Systemic Linguistics**, within which nominalizations are treated as a kind of grammatical **metaphor**.

See also: **critical discourse analysis**; **noun phrase**

Further reading: Jackson 2002; Jeffries 2006.

NON-VERBAL COMMUNICATION

Any aspect of communication which does not involve words. When you talk to somebody else, you stand or sit a certain distance away, you adopt particular postures, you wear particular expressions, you make particular gestures, and your choices often communicate things that your words do not express directly: whether you are interested or bored, whether you are nervous or confident, whether you are attracted to the other person or not, and so on. All of these are aspects of non-verbal communication, and many of them are culture-bound, so that, when trying to speak a foreign language, you may inadvertently convey something you don't intend.

The various non-verbal aspects of speaking are treated chiefly under two rubrics: **paralanguage** for vocal but non-verbal behaviour and the **ethnography of communication** for non-vocal behaviour. With the easier use of portable video-recording equipment, the field of *kinesics* has grown up to investigate the communicative effects of body movement, especially accompanying verbal communication.

(Note carefully that, in language studies, the term *verbal* means 'expressed in words, either spoken or written'; the everyday sense of this term to mean 'spoken, oral' is never used in linguistics.)

See also: **ethnography of communication**; **paralanguage**

Further reading: Poyatos 1993, 2002.

NOTATIONAL CONVENTION

Any recognized shorthand for stating a linguistic **rule** briefly. Linguistics makes heavy use of notational conventions, some of them universal, others confined to particular theoretical frameworks. In **phonology**, the rule 'The consonant /n/ is lost between vowels' may be written as follows: n → ø/V____V. In **syntax**, the rule VP → V NP (PP) means 'a verb phrase may consist of a verb plus a following noun phrase, with an optional prepositional phrase at the end'. Mastery of these conventions is essential for work in descriptive and theoretical linguistics; they not only provide a systematic and standard disciplinary language, they also allow general rules to be stated precisely without interference from the surface words themselves.

See also: **formal grammars**; **International Phonetic Alphabet**; **metalanguage**; **rule**

Further reading: Aarts and McMahon 2006.

NOUN

The **part of speech** which includes words like *girl*, *tree* and *happiness*. Traditional grammarians often tried to define a noun as 'the name of a person, place or thing', but this doesn't work. Clearly, for example, *red* is the name of a colour, and so, by this definition, it should be a noun – and yet it is most usually an **adjective**, as in *Susie is wearing her red skirt*.

Like any part of speech, nouns can be adequately defined only in terms of their grammatical behaviour. In English, an obvious grammatical characteristic of nouns is that most of them can appear in two different grammatical forms, called *singular* and *plural*. Most English nouns form their plural by adding -*s*, as in *girl/girls* and *tree/trees*, but some have irregular plurals deriving from historically fossilized forms, as in *child/children*, *goose/geese*, *sheep/sheep* or from other languages by **borrowing**: *radius/radii*. However, not all nouns do this: some have only a singular form (like *wheat*, *furniture* and the anglicized form of the Italian plural *spaghetti*), while others have only a plural form (like *scissors*, *police* and *pants* – though some retailers will engage in a bit of ***back-formation*** to try to sell you their new *pant*).

A better way of identifying nouns is to use a suitable grammatical *frame*. Consider the two frames *The – was nice* and *The – were nice.* If you can put a single word into one of these blanks to make a good sentence, then that word must be a noun, because the grammar of English allows nouns, and only nouns, to appear in these positions. The first frame accepts singular forms of nouns, like *girl, spaghetti* and *furniture*, while the second accepts plural forms, like *trees, pants* and *police.* (Of course, there is no guarantee that the result will be sensible: *The torture was nice* doesn't sound very normal, but it's clearly grammatical, and so *torture* is a noun.)

See also: **noun phrase**; **part of speech**

Further reading: Hurford 1994; Jackson 2002; Jeffries 2006; Mahlberg 2005.

NOUN PHRASE

A syntactic unit which can act as a subject or an object. Consider the following unremarkable sentence: *A small party of Spanish adventurers managed to capture the Aztec capital.* A traditional view of sentence structure holds that the **subject** and the **direct object** of the sentence are the nouns *party* and *capital*, respectively. But this is not strictly correct. The true subject or object are the phrases *a small party of Spanish adventurers* and *the Aztec capital.* These are **noun phrases** (or **NPs** for short), and noun phrases are the only things that can act as subjects or objects in English sentences. A noun phrase is a syntactic unit – a constituent – and a noun phrase may be identified in two different ways. First, it must occupy one of only a few possible slots in a sentence structure. Second, it must have one of only a few possible types of internal structure.

With only a couple of exceptions, an English noun phrase is always built up around a single **noun**, and that noun is the **head** of the noun phrase, the item which is chiefly responsible for the nature of the NP. In my examples, *party* and *capital* are the heads of the two NPs. The first NP denotes a particular party, and the second a particular capital, and the other words in the NP serve only to provide further identification.

The most obvious exception is a noun phrase consisting of a **pronoun**. In the sentence *They managed to capture it*, the pronouns *they* and *it* make up complete NPs all by themselves, one serving as

189

the subject, the other as the object. This is what a pronoun typically does: it makes up a noun phrase all by itself, and a pronominal NP is the most familiar kind of NP (in English) which is not built around a head noun (the facts are different in some other languages).

A noun phrase, then, is so called because it is (usually) built around a noun and because it constitutes a complete syntactic unit, a **phrase**. A noun phrase is one kind of **syntactic category**.

A simple but convenient way of testing whether some phrase is a noun phrase is to try inserting it into a suitable *frame* to see if the result is a grammatical sentence. Here's an example of a frame: – *am/is/are nice.* Any syntactic unit which can fit into the blank successfully must be a noun phrase, because it will have to be the subject of the sentence. (The reason we need several possible verb-forms is that an English verb shows **agreement** with its subject.) So, all of the following are NPs (or at least they *can* be NPs): *she, spaghetti, this little book, most of the other students in my class, the woman I was talking to, Rome and Paris.*

The reason for the qualification – 'or at least they *can* be NPs' – here is the following. In *Spaghetti is nice, spaghetti* forms an NP all by itself, but in *This spaghetti is nice,* the subject NP is *this spaghetti,* and this time *spaghetti* is not a noun phrase, but only a part of a noun phrase.

As happens with any kind of phrase, a noun phrase may contain within itself a smaller noun phrase. In my example *a small party of Spanish adventurers,* this big NP contains within it the smaller NP *Spanish adventurers* (try this in the frame). This NP is doing another typical NP job: it is serving as the object of the **preposition** *of,* and the resulting prepositional phrase has been incorporated into the bigger NP.

Among the several possible structures for an NP, by far the most frequent is a combination of a **determiner** with a certain other syntactic category; this other category is called an *N-bar* (or sometimes a *nominal group*). Examples (in each case, the first bracketed item is the determiner and the second is an N-bar): [*that*] [*girl*]; [*two*] [*little puppies*]; [*the*] [*woman in the blue skirt*]; [*a*] [*book* (*which*) *I'm reading*]. Note that *girl* in the first example is both a noun and an N-bar, and note that the other examples definitely have the structure shown; for example, the structure *[the woman]* [*in the blue skirt*] is quite wrong for the third example, as shown by the asterisk.

Introductory textbooks often decline to recognize N-bars when drawing structures for NPs, in the hope of making life simpler for the reader: however, N-bars are essential for all serious work on

English sentence structure. Note also that, within the **Government-and-Binding Theory**, noun phrases have recently been re-named *determiner phrases* (DPs), for theory-internal reasons.

See also: **determiner**; **noun**; **phrase**; **pronoun**

Further reading: Greenbaum and Quirk 1990; Jackson 2002; Jeffries 2006.

NUMBER

The **grammatical category** which relates most directly to the number of entities. For human beings, the number of people or objects under discussion is often of some importance, and our languages typically provide us with a rich vocabulary for making limitless distinctions along this dimension: *none, one, two, three, twenty-seven, one-half, 0.42, about a hundred, some, few, many, no more than four, a handful*, and so on. So far these distinctions have nothing to do with grammar. But it is perfectly possible for a language to build some of these distinctions into its grammar – not all of them, of course – and a language which does so has the grammatical category of *number*.

English, like most European languages, has the category of number, but English has only a very simple contrast between a *singular* (representing one entity) and a *plural* (representing two or more entities). Hence **nouns** denoting things which can be counted typically have two forms: *dog/dogs, child/children, cactus/cacti*. Nouns denoting things that cannot be counted typically have only one form, most often one which is treated grammatically as a singular: *water, happiness, disgrace, wheat* (but note that *oats* has only a plural form). A few words, though, are idiosyncratic and exceptional, such as *furniture*, which has only a singular form, and *pants*, which has only a plural, even though both nouns appear to denote things we could reasonably count.

Observe that the English number system makes no explicit provision for zero or for fractions, and here we must arbitrarily choose either a singular or a plural form: we say *nobody is ready*, with a singular form, but we agonize in other cases: should we say *none of the students is ready* or *none of the students are ready*?

Some other languages make more elaborate distinctions of number than does English. In Arabic, for example, a noun typically

191

has three forms: *malikun* 'king', *malikani* 'two kings', *malikuna* 'three or more kings'; the second form is called the **dual**. (The English comparative-superlative system has something of this in distinguishing the *latter* or the *worse* from the *last* or the *worst* in a list). The Pacific language Larike has four forms for pronouns: *mane* 'he' or 'she', *matua* 'they two', *matidu* 'they three', *mati* 'they (four or more)'; the third form is the **trial**. The East African language Tigre has a different system: *färäs* 'horse', *ʔäfras* 'a few horses', *ʔäfresam* 'horses'; the second form is the **paucal**.

In still other languages, the category of number is absent altogether, at least for nouns. Mandarin Chinese is one such. The Chinese word *shū* 'book', like every noun, has only the one unvarying form, and there is nothing in Chinese corresponding to the English *book/books* distinction. When distinctions of number are important, they must be expressed in words: 'one book', 'two book', 'many book'. Some English nouns, especially in dialectal variation or fossilized forms, are similarly invariant: *two foot* (as a measurement of length), *ten-year-old*, *threepenny*.

Even though we give the name number to the grammatical category, it is important to realize that grammatical number is something quite different from real-world number: it represents no more than an (always imperfect) attempt to map certain real-world distinctions into the grammar.

See also: **grammatical category**; **person**; **tense**

Further reading: Hurford 1994; Jackson 2002.

NUMBER OF LANGUAGES

A count of the total number of distinct languages spoken as mother tongues. It is by no means a simple matter to count the world's living languages. To start with, of course, we suffer from incomplete information. Until very recently, large parts of the planet were poorly investigated, and we simply had little or no information about the languages spoken there. This was particularly true of New Guinea, Australia, south-east Asia, many parts of Africa and, above all, the Amazon basin. Today, thanks to the dogged efforts of hundreds of linguists, we are much better off than we were a generation ago, but, even so, a previously unknown language still turns up occasionally: one was discovered in Brazil in 1995.

But there is a much bigger problem. Our familiar picture of Europe, in which a single language is spoken over hundreds of miles and shows rather sharp boundaries with neighbouring and quite distinct languages, is a recent development in human affairs and is still today not typical of most of the globe (and even parts of Europe are not like this). Far more typically, what we find is a *dialect continuum*. That is, as we travel across the terrain, the local speech just changes gradually, and we appear to be looking at nothing more than regional dialects of a single language. But, over a sufficient distance, we find that the differences in the local varieties are so great that speakers of these distant varieties cannot understand one another at all. That is, all speakers can talk easily to their near neighbours, and with more difficulty to more distant neighbours, but not at all to those still farther away.

The question then arises: how many languages are we looking at? And where should we draw the lines between them? There is no principled answer to such questions, and, in practice, linguists just have to do the best they can. Naturally, different linguists looking at the same part of the world do not always come to the same conclusions; furthermore, when better information becomes available, all of the earlier decisions may have to be revised, and linguists may not agree about what revisions to make, either. Hence, we will get different assessments of the number of languages spoken in the area depending on whose work we are reading.

What makes Europe different is the rise, in the past few centuries, of nation-states with central governments and well-defined boundaries. These political boundaries have largely imposed upon the dialect continua of Europe a substantial degree of order: in practice, today, what language you speak depends largely on no more than what side of a boundary you live on.

Consider Dutch and German. For centuries, a single Germanic dialect continuum has covered much of northern and central Europe. The local varieties spoken on both sides of what is now the Dutch–German frontier were not significantly different, but local varieties spoken farther apart were often very different indeed: even today, two speakers from, say, Berlin and Heidelberg cannot understand each other at all if they use their own local varieties. The greatest differences, in fact, have always been north–south: the Netherlands, Belgium and northern Germany on the one hand versus southern Germany, Switzerland and Austria on the other.

But the political frontiers have been drawn, and today two speakers born a kilometre apart, but finding the Dutch–German frontier separating them, consider that they speak two different languages: Dutch in one case, German in the other. And mass education, of course, reinforces this perception: one speaker learns standard Dutch in school, the other standard German, the same standard German being learned by other speakers hundreds of kilometres away whose mother tongue is incomprehensibly different. Hence the 'official' decision is that we are looking at just two languages, and the enormous regional variation is quietly ignored.

The local varieties spoken in Belgium, Luxembourg, Alsace, Switzerland and Austria are, again, all incomprehensibly different from all the other varieties and from one another. And again the decisions are political. The Swiss and the Austrians have decided that they too speak German. The Luxembourgers, after much vacillation, are now seemingly concluding that they do not, and they are making efforts to establish their **Letzebuergesch** as a distinct language. The Belgians have long insisted that they spoke a distinct language called **Flemish**, but they have now changed their minds and agreed that they speak Dutch – but note that the local speech of western Belgium is incomprehensible to speakers in Antwerp and in Amsterdam. The Alsatians, with long-standing political grievances against the Germans, also consider that they speak a separate language – though, if Germany had succeeded in its repeated attempts to annex the territory, the outcome might be very different.

Similar political decisions are important elsewhere. Varieties of Finnish, Romanian and Persian are spoken in sizable areas of the former Soviet Union, but, for political purposes, the Soviet authorities always insisted that the varieties on their territory were entirely separate languages, called Karelian, Moldavian and Tadjik respectively. If, as most linguists do, we follow the Soviet line, then we get three additional languages that we would not have got if Soviet policy had been different.

So how many languages are there? Most estimates have ranged between 5,000 and 6,000, or occasionally as low as 4,000 or even 3,000. The most authoritative source we have at present, the *Ethnologue* volume (Grimes 2000), currently recognizes just over 6,500 mother tongues, though a more recent study based in Wales and associated with UNESCO has reported the astounding total of just over 10,000 languages. However, because of accelerating **language death**, this total is declining rapidly, and more than half of these languages may be gone within a century.

Globalization of travel and communication is to blame: even though this apparently offers more opportunities for language contact (which could lead to **pidginization** and thence **creoles**), in practice the dominance of English as a **lingua franca** seems to be having the opposite effect.

See also: **language death**; **national language**; **standard language**

Further reading: Crystal 1997, 2003; Grimes 2000; Krauss 1992.

OBSERVER'S PARADOX

The problem for data collection in linguistic fieldwork when the presence of the researcher affects the form of language being used by the informants. People being recorded are often likely to be self-conscious and this can have an effect on their linguistic performance. Interactants in an extended setting usually *accommodate* towards each other's language patterns, so the researcher's language variety is likely to influence the speech under investigation. Even an artificial test situation in itself can skew results without the creator of the test being present in the room.

Various methods in **sociolinguistics** have been developed to minimize the effects of the *observer's paradox*. Misleading informants into thinking that their knowledge is being tested rather than the way they express themselves, or surreptitious recordings have been used, though these are increasingly ethically questionable. Reducing the formality of the setting by using relaxed seating, casual dress, informal interviews or conversations has been successful. Matching the researcher with the informants in terms of age, gender or ethnicity has also been used. Using protocols that engage the informants in emotionally involving responses (the 'danger-of-death' question: tell me about a time when you feared for your life), spending an extended period living amongst the informants (*participant observation*), recording events which are already public and being recorded (such as media broadcasts, court proceedings or political debates) – all these have been used to minimize the potential interference of the research process itself.

The question of **ethics** in linguistic fieldwork research is raised by the issue. Some have argued that the desire to minimize or even eradicate the observer's paradox represents a desire to write out the messiness of human informants in the research process, and sociolinguists ought to be more humane and sensitive to linguistic performance. Others argue that the phenomenon means that only extended **qualitative** research can be valid, rather than the sort of empirical and artificial setting which tends to be the hallmark of **quantitative** work.

See also: **sociolinguistics**

Further reading: Labov 1994; Llamas *et al.* 2007; Milroy 1987b.

OFFICIAL LANGUAGE

A language which can be used for conducting official business in a particular country. In a modern nation-state, every one of us is constantly obliged to engage in some kind of official business with the authorities. We have to get driving licences and passports, fill in income-tax returns, obtain birth certificates for our children, fill in forms both when we obtain jobs and when we become unemployed, make out wills, get our children into school, buy and sell houses, and so on. Some of us have to participate in local or national government, or to appear in court. For these purposes, every government specifies one or more languages in which such business may legally be conducted, and a language singled out in this way is an *official language* within the territory of that government. But which language or languages should be official in a given country?

In some cases the choice is easy. Since Swedish is the first language of practically all native-born Swedes, Swedish is the only reasonable choice for the official language. In other cases, the choice is more difficult. Belgium is about equally divided between Dutch-speakers and French-speakers, and the Belgian government has been obliged to draw up complicated laws about which languages can be used officially in which parts of the country. Spain has long recognized nothing but Spanish – the majority language – as official, but constant objections from the millions of Spanish citizens whose first language is Catalan, Galician or Basque have now persuaded Madrid to set up autonomous regions with their own regional governments, several of which recognize the local language as co-official with Spanish. Nigeria is inhabited by speakers of dozens of different languages, and the government has reacted by choosing English – the language of the former colonial power – as the official language, to avoid antagonizing any part of the population.

Attempts at making Hindi the sole official language in India have encountered fierce resistance from the hundreds of millions of Indians who speak other languages. After independence from Britain in 1948, English was supposed to be phased out, but it has proven a useful 'neutral' language as it does not privilege any native ethnic group; so in practice English remains the official language there too.

See also: **minority language; national language**

Further reading: Holmes 1992; Llamas *et al*. 2007; Stockwell 2002a; Wardhaugh 2005.

ONOMASTICS

The study of names. Onomastics is a branch of **philology**, and its pursuit requires the same painstaking scrutiny of historical documents as any other branch of philology, especially since names have a habit of changing more dramatically and more irregularly than ordinary words. For example, until the documents are consulted, it is far from obvious that the name of the English village of *Bridgwater* originally meant 'bridge [at a place owned by a man named] Walter', that the name of the American river the *Picketwire* continues an earlier French *Purgatoire* 'Purgatory', or that the district of London called *Pimlico* derives its name in a complex fashion from the North Carolina river now called the *Tar-Pamlico*.

Onomasticians study both **anthroponyms** (personal names, especially surnames, but also given names) and **toponyms** (place names); toponyms include **habitation names** (names of settlements), **hydronyms** (names of bodies of water), **oronyms** (mountain names), and the names of valleys, fields, roads, streets, houses, forests, and any other features that can be named.

See also: **name; philology**

Further reading: Crystal 1995; Trask 1996.

OPEN-ENDEDNESS

The ability to use language to say new things, without limit. A non-human species typically has no more than a handful of messages, or *calls*, available to it – perhaps one meaning 'This is my territory', another meaning 'danger in the air', and so on. Every time a non-human creature opens its mouth, it can do no more than to choose one message from this short list, and that's it. A monkey may be able to say 'Snake!', if that message is available in the system, but that same monkey cannot possibly produce an unprecedented 'Look out – two hunters with rifles!' or, still less, on spotting its first Land Rover, 'Hey, everybody – what do you suppose that is?'

Human languages are utterly different. We have not the slightest difficulty in producing and comprehending totally new utterances that we have never used or heard before, and indeed we do this almost every moment: most of the utterances you produce and hear every day have very likely never before been produced by anybody. Consider a few examples: *A large tear rolled down the little pink dragon's nose*; *Peanut butter is a poor substitute for putty*; *Luxembourg has declared war on New Zealand*; *Shakespeare wrote his plays in Swahili, and they were translated into English by his African bodyguards.* You have no difficulty in understanding these – even if you don't believe all of them.

But even your most routine utterances may never before have been uttered by anybody: *I ran into Susie's ex-husband at the match last night*; *Does anybody know what language the word 'shampoo' comes from?*; *Aunt Bea has sent us some photos of her granddaughter's christening.*

This limitless ability to produce and understand totally new utterances is called **open-endedness**, and it should be perfectly clear to you that, without it, our languages and indeed our lives would be unrecognizably different from what they are. Perhaps no other feature of language so dramatically illustrates the vast, unbridgeable gulf separating human language from the signalling systems of all other creatures.

The importance of open-endedness has been realized by linguists for decades; the term was coined by the American linguist Charles Hockett in 1960, though others have sometimes preferred the labels **productivity** or **creativity**.

See also: **design features**; **displacement**; **stimulus-freedom**

Further reading: Carter 2004; Maybin and Swann 2006.

OPTIMALITY THEORY

A development of generative grammar formulated by Alan Prince and Paul Smolensky in the 1990s. The theory holds that all languages have a set of constraints which produce the basic phonological and grammatical patterns of that particular language. In many cases, an actual utterance violates one or more of these constraints, so a sense of well-formedness applies to that utterance which violates the least number or least important constraints. Constraints can be classified in two types: faithfulness and markedness. The faithfulness principle constrains a word to match the underlying morphological form (such as plural *tram* +-*s* in *trams*). But words like *buses* or *dogs* do not follow this constraint (the first falls foul of the constraint that prevents the pronunciation of two consecutive /s/ sounds and the second places a /z/ instead of an /s/). These two examples, though, follow markedness constraints, and in these cases the particular markedness 'scores' higher than the faithfulness constraint, so the alternate forms are allowed. Differences between languages, then, are a matter of the relative importance given to particular constraints, and a description of these constitutes a description of the language.

See also: **minimalist programme; phonology**

Further reading: Archangeli and Langendoen 1997; Blutner and Zeevat 2003; Dekkers *et al.* 1999; Kager 1999; Kuhn 2003; McCarthy 2001, 2004; McMahon 2000.

ORACY

Skill in speaking and listening. We have long had the term **literacy** to denote skill in reading and writing, but recently a number of educationalists and academics have been drawing attention to the importance of skill in speaking and listening. To this notion the somewhat unfortunate label *oracy* has been applied, though a few people, disliking this term, use *oralcy* or *orality* instead.

Sociolinguists and anthropological linguists have discovered that oral skills can be deeply important: oral skills are highly valued in any number of societies and may confer great prestige. In American inner-city ghettos, gang members can acquire status by their ability to hurl biting insults; in small African and Asian communities, the most effective speakers are likely to be the headmen and chiefs.

In English, the evaluation of oral skills is complicated by the powerful tendency to judge speakers entirely in terms of their use of standard English: so, very often, a piece of pompous, turgid and disorganized standard English is rated more highly than a sharp and effective piece of speaking delivered in a conspicuously non-standard variety.

See also: **literacy**

Further reading: Halliday 1989; Ong 1982; Tarleton 1988.

ORIGIN AND EVOLUTION OF LANGUAGE

The series of steps by which human language came into existence. Very little is known about how human language came into existence, though there is no shortage of speculation by specialists in a dozen different disciplines.

The members of most non-human species have some way of communicating with their fellows, and mammals in particular typically use a combination of *calls* (vocal signals) with postures, gestures and expressions. Proponents of the *continuity hypothesis* see language as deriving directly from such systems by simple elaboration. But most linguists and many others see these signals as more akin to such non-linguistic activities as sobbing, laughing and screaming, and they prefer to invoke *discontinuity hypotheses*, by which language has an entirely different origin, one not detectable in living non-human species.

Specialists differ in the date they assign to the rise of language. The most popular view sees language as arising with our own species, *Homo sapiens*, a little over 100,000 years ago. But some anthropologists believe they can detect evidence for language areas in the brains of our hominid ancestors of 1 million or 2 million years ago, while, on the other hand, some archaeologists argue that full-blown language can only have arisen around 40,000–50,000 years ago, a time when they see evidence for a spectacular flowering of art, culture and material goods.

There is no question that language has given humans a huge evolutionary advantage. Much of the physical evidence is in the form of feedback circularity: standing up on two legs raised our sensory organs for more input and freed our hands up; having fingers in front of our eyes allowed us to iconically represent numbers (up to 10) which developed our memories and abstract reasoning and grew our brains; increasingly subtle dexterity promoted brain growth; balancing a head on shoulders allowed the head to be bigger; the head grew in size because the jaw, forehead and vocal tract enlarged; having children with large heads while two-legged mothers had smaller pelvises meant that babies had to be born before their 'full' term development was complete; so babies are helpless in comparison with other mammals, and language gives us a means of passing on childcare knowledge and increases the individual's chances of surviving infanthood; and so on.

While specialists in some other disciplines often like to portray language as something not very different from what vervet monkeys do, and hence as requiring a minimum of explanation, almost all linguists are satisfied that human language is in fact dramatically, utterly different from everything else we can see, that language, more than anything else, is what makes us human, and that the origin of language is therefore a major problem which we are not close to solving. Most linguists further believe that our language faculty is genetic in nature, that our remote ancestors simply evolved it, and hence that we are born to use language in the way that birds are born to fly.

See also: **animal communication**; **bioprogram hypothesis**; **genetic hypothesis of language**; **innateness hypothesis**; **protolanguage hypothesis**

Further reading: Aitchison 1996; Crystal 1997; Foley 1997; Malmkjær 2004.

ORTHOGRAPHY

A standardized system for writing a particular language. A given orthography consists of a particular version of a particular **writing system** (in the case of English, a version of the Roman alphabet employing both small letters and capital letters), a standardized system of **spelling**, often a system of word-division (in English, by white spaces), and (in almost all cases today) a particular system of **punctuation**. Often there are additional devices, such as (in English) the use of the arabic numerals (1, 2, 3, . . .) for writing numbers, the specialized use of certain *symbols* (such as +, = , &, %, $, @), the presence of certain *abbreviations* (such as *Dr*, *St*, *etc*., *e.g*.), and the use of distinctive typefaces like italic and boldface; these devices may or may not be regarded as strictly a part of the orthography, but more commonly are not.

There are numerous orthographic systems in use around the world. Various *alphabetic* systems such as the Roman, Arabic and

Cyrillic use graphemes to represent (roughly) phonemes. *Logographic* systems use pictures or symbols to represent entire words as well as the sounds occurring in those words: as in Egyptian hieroglyphics or modern Chinese. *Syllabary* systems use a single symbol to represent a syllable (typically a consonant plus a vowel), such as Mayan, Cherokee and much Japanese. The last of these is more complex, since Japanese writers can use logograms borrowed from China called *kanji*, as well as two syllabic systems *katakana* and *hiragana*, and also some adapted Roman symbols called *romaji*.

The orthography of English has developed gradually over the centuries. The English spelling system was largely fossilized by printing around 600 years ago, so much modern English orthography actually represents medieval pronunciation (*through, knight, folk*): this is quite useful as it means modern spelling does not privilege any single accent, and English writing can be used to write any pronunciation. However, written texts from King Alfred's time to the present nevertheless show numerous orthographic changes. Letters have been added to or removed from the alphabet: early printing presses did not have the Anglo-Saxon <þ> so a <Y> was used with a point ground out of the block at the top, leading to spellings such as 'Ye old shop', which was always pronounced as 'the' and never /ji/. The forms of certain letters (notably <s> as <ſ> or <f>) have often varied, and the spellings of individual words have changed (*sunne* to *sun*, *coude* to *could* by mistaken analogy with *would* and *should*). Punctuation practices have varied enormously; the use of capital letters has varied; roman numerals have mostly given way to arabic numerals; individual abbreviations have come and gone; and so on. Consequently, if you want to read texts in Old English or Middle English, you must master not only the language but the orthography as well.

See also: **punctuation**; **spelling**; **writing system**

Further reading: Crystal 1995, 1997; Joshi and Aaron 2006; Malmkjær 2004; Robinson 1995; Sampson 1985.

PARADIGM

A complete set of the *inflected* forms of a single word, especially as an example. In foreign-language teaching of a traditional kind, it is commonplace to present a full set of the various grammatical forms assumed by a single word, with the understanding that this set constitutes a model for the behaviour of a whole set of words belonging to a single grammatical class. Such a set of forms is a single *paradigm*. So, for example, a textbook of Latin might provide the paradigm for the noun *amicus* 'friend', as follows; the various functions of the named case-forms must be learned separately, of course:

	Singular	Plural
Nominative	*amicus*	*amici*
Vocative	*amice*	*amici*
Genitive	*amici*	*amicorum*
Dative	*amico*	*amicis*
Accusative	*amicum*	*amicos*
Ablative	*amico*	*amicis*

(This is the American order; British tradition puts the accusative straight after the vocative.) The point of this is that all the other Latin nouns belonging to this class, the class of 'masculine second-declension nouns' or 'masculine *o*-stems', behave in exactly the same way, so that, once you know the forms of *amicus*, you automatically know how to make all the forms of all these other nouns (apart from any which are irregular and must be learned separately).

Note that paradigms are not confined to nouns: verbs, adjectives and other **parts of speech** may also exhibit paradigms, sometimes very elaborate ones.

In modern language-teaching, paradigms are less prominent than formerly, but they are still routinely provided for reference. In descriptive work in linguistics, however, paradigms can still be an illuminating and economical way of presenting the morphological facts of a language in which words vary their forms substantially for grammatical purposes.

The branch of morphology that deals with paradigms is called *morphosyntax* to signal that there is a strong relationship with **syntax**.

See also: **inflection**; **morphology**; **paradigmatic relation**

Further reading: Blake 2001; Culler 1986.

203

PARADIGMATIC RELATION

The relation between a set of linguistic items which, in some sense, constitute choices, so that only one of them may be present at a time in a given position. The notion of a *paradigmatic relation* was introduced by the Swiss linguist Ferdinand de Saussure in the early twentieth century as a generalization of the traditional concept of a **paradigm**. If you look at the several forms of the Latin noun *amicus* listed under **paradigm**, you will realize that, in any given position in a Latin sentence in which the word *amicus* is present, one, and only one, of the several forms will occur, the choice being determined by the grammatical context.

What Saussure did was to point out that the relation among the several forms in a traditional paradigm is essentially the same as the relation among other sets of linguistic elements. So, for example, the English **determiners**, like *a(n)*, *some*, *the*, *this/these* and *that/those*, all stand in a paradigmatic relation, because, in a single **noun phrase**, there will be one and only one of them at the beginning (as a rule: there are exceptions): *a book*, *some books*, *the book*, *this book*, *those books*, and so on. It is for this reason that all these words are assigned to a single **part of speech**. In large measure, all the members of any part of speech are assigned to that part of speech because they are related in the same way: they all occur in the same positions, but only one of them can occur at a time.

The concept of a paradigmatic relation is closely related to that of a **system**, a set of competing choices and the rules for choosing among them, and the term paradigmatic relation contrasts most obviously with **syntagmatic relation**.

Note that, in **psycholinguistics**, the term paradigmatic relation is used in a somewhat different sense, to denote the mental associations between words which form part of a set of mutually exclusive items, as when a subject given *black* responds with *white*.

See also: **paradigm**; **syntagmatic relation**

Further reading: Culler 1986.

PARALANGUAGE

The non-linguistic aspects of speaking. When we speak, of course, we communicate a good deal of purely linguistic information to our listeners. In addition, however, we make use of strictly non-linguistic variables like pitch, loudness, tempo, timbre and voice quality. Our use of these things conveys information about our mood and attitude: about whether we are angry, amused, nervous, excited, impatient, tired or whatever. These aspects of speaking are collectively called *paralanguage* or, informally, *tone of voice*.

Such paralinguistic features as high pitch, falsetto, creaky voice, a 'gravelly' voice, breathy or whispery voice, nasalization, and loud or soft speech are variously used in many languages to indicate respect, submission, mockery, boredom, romantic or sexual feelings, impatience and many other things; the details differ greatly from language to language.

Note that the term paralanguage is sometimes used more narrowly, to include only voice quality, and sometimes more broadly, to include most or even all aspects of **non-verbal communication**. The sense given here is recommended, since suitable terms are already available for the narrower and broader senses.

The equivalent of paralanguage can also be observed in **sign language**: signers may produce signs rapidly or slowly, more deliberately or more casually, using large movements or small ones.

See also: **ethnography of communication; non-verbal communication**

Further reading: Poyatos 1993, 2002.

PAROLE

The real utterances produced by real people in real situations. The term *parole* was introduced by the Swiss linguist Ferdinand de Saussure in the early twentieth century; in Saussure's treatment, this term contrasts specifically with **langue**, the abstract system of a language. Saussure's parole represents essentially the same thing as Chomsky's **performance**, though his **langue** is significantly different from Chomsky's **competence**.

See also: **langue; performance**

Further reading: Culler 1986.

PARSING

Traditionally, parsing was an exercise in the language classroom for labelling the parts of speech in a sentence (**noun, verb, adjective**, or *nominative, accusative, dative,* and so on). In modern linguistics, it is associated with the attempt towards **natural-language processing** in **computational linguistics.** A *parser* program depends on a rule-driven model of grammar to be able to tag an input sentence with its constituent structure. **Phrase-structure grammars** are popular as the basis for computer parsers.The result turns the natural language string into a hiererchically and systemically organized set of data, which is then available for interrogation by, for example, *concordance programs* or further software that aims to 'understand' and 'interpret' the sequence in order to generate a 'reply'. The numerous 'scare quotes' here are to signal the fact that, although this aspect of artificial intelligence research has progressed to the point at which voice-operated computers are commonplace, there is still a long way to go before a computer program passes the *Turing test.* (This is a simple test devised by the British mathemetician and crypto-grapher Alan Turing in the 1950s aimed to replace the question of whether a machine could ever think by the more measurable question of whether a machine can appear to have natural language. If a person conversed with two entities in another room, one a human and the other a computer, and could not tell the difference, then the machine would have passed the Turing test. Several people have noted that this is not quite the same as 'intelligence', but it remains an as yet-unreached landmark in natural-language processing research.)

See also: **case**; **computational linguistics**; **phrase-structure grammar**

Further reading: Heil 1998; Nivre 2006; Turing 1950.

PART OF SPEECH

Any one of the grammatically characterized classes into which the **words** of a language are grouped. Every language contains many thousands of words. If all these words behaved differently for grammatical purposes, the language would be unmanageable; but they don't. Instead, they are grouped into a small number of clas-ses, variously called *parts of speech* or *word classes* or *lexical cate-gories*; the words in each class behave in much the same way, while words in different classes behave differently. Not all languages have the same classes: some classes, such as **noun** and **verb**, appear to be universal, while others, such as **adjective** and **preposition**, are found in some languages but not in others.

English has over a dozen parts of speech; the precise number varies according to the analysis, since some linguists prefer to draw finer distinctions than others. The meaning of a word is an unreliable guide to its part of speech. Membership is determined by grammatical criteria, and there are at least three types of criteria to which we can appeal.

The first criterion is **distribution**, the positions in which a word can occur. For example, consider the following 'frames': *This – is good*; *These – are good*. If we try to put words into the blanks to produce good sentences, we find that **nouns**, and only nouns, will work, because English grammar allows only nouns in this position. Hence *spaghetti, dogs* and *arrangement* are nouns, while *happy, from* and *deliver* are not. (The reason we need two frames is that English nouns occur in two forms: singular and plural; see **number**.)

The second criterion is **inflection**. In English, a typical noun has exactly two grammatical forms: singular and plural: *dog/dogs, box/boxes, child/children, radius/radii*. (A few, though, have only one or the other, such as *happiness, furniture, oats* and *police*.) An **adjective** may have three forms: *big/bigger/biggest*. A verb usually has four or more: *love/loves/loved/loving; take/takes/took/taken/taking*. A **preposition** has only a single form: *to, under, without*.

The third criterion is **derivation**. A noun may take the suffix *-ful* or *-ous* to form an adjective: *joy/joyful, power/powerful, glory/glorious, mountain/mountainous*. An adjective may take the suffix *-ness* or *-ity* to form a noun: *great/greatness, topical/topicality*. A verb may take the prefix *re-* or *un-* to form a different verb: *write/rewrite, do/undo*. In each case, only a member of the appropriate class can take that prefix or suffix successfully.

These tests are not infallible, and they must be used with care. For example, you might think that the frame *This is a – dress* would pick out adjectives, and it's true that adjectives will go in here: *red, short, pretty*. But nouns will equally go into this position: *cotton, maternity, cocktail*. A better frame here would be *This is a very – dress*, which does indeed pick out only adjectives.

A feature of English and of some other languages is that a word can belong to two or more different classes without changing its form. For example, *brown* is a noun in *a nice shade of brown*, an adjective in *a brown skirt*, and a verb in *Please brown the meat*. Likewise, *straight* is a noun in *Schumacher accelerated down the straight*, an adjective in *a straight line*, and an adverb in *She hit the ball straight*. There are many of these, but note that a word can only belong to one part of speech at a time. Some other languages do not tolerate this and require *each* word to belong only to one part of speech.

As a rule, the words in a single class do not all show absolutely identical behaviour; instead, they are further divided into several subclasses, often overlapping, which show somewhat different behaviour. This is **subcategorization**.

Some word classes are large and can readily accept new members: these are called *open classes*. Others are small and accept new members only with difficulty: these are *closed classes*. In English, noun, verb and adjective are open classes, while pronoun and preposition are closed classes. Languages may differ here: in some languages, the class of adjectives is small and closed.

See also: **adjective**; **adverb**; **conjunction**; **determiner**; **noun**; **preposition**; **pronoun**; **verb**

Further reading: Crystal 1995; Givón 1993; Hurford 1994.

PERCEPTUAL STRATEGY

Any of several rough principles which listeners may use in interpreting utterances. A *perceptual strategy* is essentially a kind of principled guess about how the words we are hearing fit into a syntactic structure. In the past several decades, practitioners of **psycholinguistics** have proposed a number of such strategies, and the reality of these strategies is supported by varying amounts of experimental evidence.

One of these is the *principle of late closure*, which says 'if possible, put the next word into the phrase you are currently processing'. By this principle, if you hear *Susie decided gradually to get rid of her teddy-bears*, you will associate *gradually* with *decided*, and not with *to get rid of her teddy-bears*.

Another proposed strategy is the *canonical sentoid strategy*, by which the first string of words that could possibly be a sentence is assumed to be a sentence. It is this strategy which makes **garden-path sentences** so difficult to interpret: when you hear *The horse shot from the stable fell down*, you naturally take *The horse shot from the stable* as a complete sentence and are left floundering by the continuation, even though the whole utterance has a perfectly straightforward interpretation.

Perceptual strategies have attracted a great deal of attention, and they have enjoyed some success in accounting for the comprehension of short utterances. With long and complex utterances, however, it becomes very difficult to identify any useful strategies, and some workers are now questioning the utility of perceptual strategies as a tool for investigation.

See also: **language processing; performance; psycholinguistics**

Further reading: Aitchison 1989.

PERFORMANCE

Real utterances produced by real people. When we speak, our utterances are frequently disturbed in various ways. We make slips of the tongue; we forget things; we pause to consider our words; we start an utterance and then break it off; we may even lose track of what we are saying altogether. Likewise, when we listen, we may fail to catch something, or we may mishear it or misunderstand it. Linguists have long realized that these disturbances to our linguistic behaviour largely result from non-linguistic causes, and hence that they should not be treated on the same footing as the linguistic behaviour itself. Consequently, we make a fundamental distinction between our (somewhat idealized) capacity to use language, called **langue** by Saussure and **competence** by Chomsky, and our actual linguistic behaviour, called **parole** by Saussure and *performance* by Chomsky.

Linguists with a theoretical orientation are usually interested in competence, and so they disregard what they see as the irrelevant 'noise' of speech errors. But there are other linguists, especially those interested in **language processing**, who are deeply interested in speech errors, and these may be fairly said to be engaged in the study of performance.

See also: **competence; language processing; langue**

Further reading: Steinberg 1993.

PERFORMATIVE

An utterance which is itself an act of doing something. A typical utterance, such as *I'm going to a film*, cannot readily be regarded as doing something: saying this does not constitute going to a film. But some utterances are different. Saying *I promise to buy you a teddy-bear*, all by itself, constitutes making a promise to buy a teddy-bear, and nothing further is required to complete (as opposed to fulfil) the promise. An utterance of this sort is called an (*explicit*) **performative utterance**, and a verb which can be so used, in this case *promise*, is a **performative verb**.

Further examples of performative utterances are *I now pronounce you husband and wife* and *I hereby name this ship HMS Pooty*. In these cases, clearly, the utterances will have no effect unless a number of obvious conditions are met (the speakers are a minister of religion or a governmental representative on one hand, and a person with some prestige status on the other; the settings are a wedding and a shipyard, and so on). These are the *felicity conditions* for that utterance. If the felicity conditions are not satisfied, then the resulting utterance is not really false or wrong: it is merely infelicitous, and it has no effect (or at least not the intended effect).

The existence of explicit performative utterances was first pointed out by the British philosopher J.L. Austin in the 1960s. Austin's work has been continued by several linguists and philosophers, and it has led to the development of the theory of **speech acts**.

See also: **speech act**

Further reading: Austin 1962; Saeed 1997; Thomas 1995; Yule 1996.

PERSON

The **grammatical category** relating to differing roles in speech. The (personal) **pronouns** of English make a three-way distinction: the pronoun *I* means 'the speaker', *you* means 'the addressee', and *he, she* and *it* all mean 'somebody or something else'. We say that these forms distinguish *persons*: *first person* for *I*, *second person* for *you*, and *third person* for the others. The category represented is also called person, and this three-way person contrast appears to be universal in languages.

Observe that the third-person forms express further distinctions of animacy and sex, but these other distinctions have nothing to do with person. Finnish *hän* and Turkish *o* mean 'he' or 'she' indifferently; these languages lack the English sex-distinction. Other languages, though, make sex-distinctions in their word for 'you' and sometimes also for 'I'.

The plural forms of the personal pronouns are more complicated. The first-person plural *we* does not normally mean 'the speakers'; instead, it means 'the speaker and one or more others associated with the speaker', and something similar is often true when *you* is used as a plural. (Among the world's languages, modern English is unusual in not formally distinguishing a singular *you* from a plural *you*, though of course in older and modern dialectal forms there are distinctions between *thou* and *you*, or *you* and *y'all*.)

Some North American and Pacific languages distinguish two sets of third-person forms, one (the *proximate*) serving to indicate the individual who is currently the centre of attention and the other (the *obviative*) indicating all individuals who are not currently the centre of attention. The obviative has sometimes been labelled the 'fourth person', but this term is not obviously appropriate.

See also: **grammatical category**; **number**; **tense**

Further reading: Hurford 1994; Jackson 2002.

PHILOLOGY

The branch of **historical linguistics** concerned with the histories of individual words and names. Historical linguists exhibit a range of interests. Some are chiefly interested in determining which languages are connected in **genetic relationships** and in working out the structures of particular **language families**; others are concerned with identifying the particular changes which have affected individual languages; still others are looking for general principles of **language change**. But some are mainly interested in identifying the origins of particular words or names and in tracing the histories of these items through time. We give the name *philology* to this pursuit, and we divide philology into **etymology** – the study of the origins of ordinary words – and **onomastics** – the study of the origins of names.

Philology has been around a long time and, until not so long ago, this term was often applied to historical linguistics generally – though no longer. Philological work is exacting, and it requires a mastery of detail perhaps greater than in any other branch of linguistics. Few other areas of the subject offer so many ways for the unwary practitioner to go astray: overlooking a single crucial datum may lead to catastrophe, and that datum may lie buried in an obscure publication or manuscript in a library hundreds of miles away. Nevertheless, philologists have achieved prodigious success in their undertakings, and the great etymological dictionaries of English, Spanish, Latin and other languages are among the treasures of linguistics – though all of them contain errors which remain to be corrected by later scholars.

See also: **etymology**; **historical linguistics**; **language change**; **onomastics**

Further reading: Trask 1996.

PHILOSOPHY OF LANGUAGE

The branch of philosophy which studies the properties of human languages. There are many aspects of language which are of equal interest to linguists and to philosophers, particularly (though not exclusively) in the domain of **semantics** (the study of meaning). Philosophers of language are often interested in such questions as how a piece of language can refer to the real or conceptual world, how the truth or falsehood of a statement can be determined, how the meaning of an utterance depends upon its context, and what the relation is between language and mind.

Though philosophers have pondered problems of language since ancient times, the subject was particularly stressed in the late nineteenth century by the German philosopher Gottlob Frege, who is consequently often regarded as the father of the discipline. Among the most prominent philosophers of language in the twentieth century are the Britons Bertrand Russell, Peter Strawson, Donald Davidson, J.L. Austin, Paul Grice and John Searle, the Pole Alfred Tarski, and the Americans Willard van Orman Quine, Richard Montague, Jerrold Katz, Jerry Fodor and Saul Kripke, but there are many others who also deserve mention.

(Special note: there is a school of philosophy called *linguistic philosophy*, so named because its proponents maintain that many philosophical problems arise from insufficient attention to language; this has nothing to do with the philosophy of language and should not be confused with it.)

See also: **semantics**

Further reading: Chapman 2000, 2006; Martin 1987; Robson and Stockwell 2005; Stainton 1996.

PHONATION TYPE

Any one of the several different ways the vocal folds may behave in producing speech. The vocal folds (or vocal cords) are two moveable masses of tissue in the larynx between which air from the lungs must flow during speech. The vocal folds can behave in a number of different ways, sometimes with different parts of them doing different things. Most familiarly, they can be brought close enough together to vibrate along their entire length, producing **voicing**, or they can be moved far apart, preventing vibration and producing *voicelessness*, or, more precisely, *breath*. They can also be pressed tightly together, blocking all air flow and producing a different type of voicelessness.

We can also close the vocal cords except for an opening at the back through which air flows noisily; this is *whisper*. Or we can close them apart from an opening at the front which vibrates very slowly; this is *creak*. Or we can stretch them tightly along their entire length so that they vibrate very rapidly; this is *falsetto*. Various combinations of these are possible, such as *whispery voice*, *creaky voice*, *whispery falsetto* and *whispery creaky voice* ('whisky voice').

Not all of these possibilities are used for linguistic purposes, but several of them are. English contrasts only voicing and voicelessness, but many other languages have a third possibility, most often creaky voice or whispery voice.

See also: **airstream mechanism**; **International Phonetic Alphabet**; **voicing**

Further reading: Ball and Rahilly 1999; Ladefoged 1993, 1971; Ladefoged and Maddieson 1996.

PHONEME

One of the basic sound units of a language. Every spoken language, or more precisely every distinguishable **accent** of a language, possesses a smallish set of basic *abstract* sound units, both **consonants** and **vowels**, and every word in that language must consist of a permitted sequence of those basic sound units, which are called **phonemes**. The number of phonemes in particular languages varies considerably, from a known minimum of ten in the Brazilian language Pirahã to a known maximum of 141 in the African language !Xũ. The average number seems to be about twenty-five to thirty.

The several accents of English vary noticeably in their set of phonemes, from as many as forty-five in some accents of England to as few as thirty-six in some accents of North America. These differences lie mostly in the vowels, with most varieties having exactly twenty-four consonant phonemes, though a few varieties differ even here.

Phoneme symbols are always enclosed within slashes, and the symbol chosen for each phoneme is usually a phonetic symbol intended to suggest how that phoneme is most typically realized phonetically. So, for example, the phoneme that occurs at the beginning of *thin* is commonly realized as a voiceless dental fricative [θ], and so the phoneme is represented as /θ/. Likewise, the entire word *thin* is represented as /θɪn/, with three phoneme symbols for the three phonemes present in it, while *think* is /θɪŋk/, and *this* is /ðɪs/.

A crucial point is that a single phoneme need not always get the same phonetic realization. English /p/, for example, is phonetically an aspirated plosive [pʰ] in *pin*, but an unaspirated plosive [p] in *spin*. Phonetically, then, we have [pʰɪn] and [spɪn], but phonemically we have merely /pʰɪn/ and /spɪn/: the phonetic difference is predictable, and it 'does not count' in English. There is only one phoneme /p/ here, and English-speakers typically do not even notice the phonetic difference; we say that [pʰ] and [p] are **allophones** of the phoneme /p/. In contrast, Mandarin Chinese has pairs of words like [pʰā] 'crouch' and [pā] 'eight', and so [pʰ] and [p] clearly belong to two different phonemes, /pʰ/ and /p/, and these words are phonemically /pʰā/ and /pā/ (the diacritic is a tone mark).

English has pairs of words like [dɛn] *den* and [ðɛn] *then*, and so [d] and [ð] clearly belong to two different phonemes, /d/ and /ð/, and these two words are phonemically /dɛn/ and /ðɛn/. In Spanish, however, things are different. Spanish has a single phoneme /d/, which phonetically is [d] after pause but [ð] between vowels. Thus, *dedo* 'finger' is phonemic /dedo/ but phonetic [deðo]; *dama* 'lady' is phonemic /dama/ and phonetic [dama]; but *la dama* 'the lady' is phonemic /la dama/ but phonetic [la ðama].

The phoneme concept was worked out only slowly in the nineteenth century; the two Polish linguists Jan Baudouin de Courtenay and Mikołaj Kruszewski are usually credited with being the first to understand it fully. The concept was carried to the west, where it was championed by Daniel Jones in England and by Edward Sapir in the USA; by the 1930s it was almost universally understood and used in linguistics.

In the 1960s, American linguists, led by Noam Chomsky and Morris Halle, began to develop and defend a much more abstract conception of the phoneme than had formerly been normal, within the new framework called *generative phonology*; their new conception was dubbed the *systematic phoneme*, as opposed to the traditional *autonomous* (or *classical*) *phoneme*. Moreover, the phoneme, which had previously been regarded as an indivisible minimal unit, was now decomposed into a matrix of smaller units, the **distinctive features**, which were increasingly regarded as the true fundamental units of phonology. Since the 1980s, this trend has continued to the point at which many phonologists now work exclusively with features and ignore phonemes altogether – though an understanding of phonemes is still considered essential in most introductory linguistics courses.

See also: **distribution; minimal pair; neutralization; phonology; phonotactics; transcription**

Further reading: Gussmann 2002; Lass 1984; Odden 2005; Sommerstein 1977.

PHONETICS

The study of **speech sounds**. Phoneticians (practitioners of phonetics) investigate such topics as the anatomical, physiological and neurological basis of speech (this is *physiological phonetics*), the actions of the speech organs in producing speech sounds (*articulatory phonetics*), the acoustic nature of the sound waves which transmit speech (*acoustic phonetics*), and the manner in which the ears and brain interpret speech (*auditory* and *perceptual phonetics*). Phoneticians have long used various mechanical devices in their investigations; today they more commonly use a battery of electronic instruments backed up by computers, and most phonetics today is therefore *instrumental phonetics*. Those phoneticians who prefer to work entirely by ear, without instruments, are said to be doing *impressionistic phonetics*.

A modern phonetician is expected to be at home in a laboratory full of instruments, but is nevertheless also expected to undergo a good deal of *ear training*, acquiring the ability to recognize and characterize speech sounds entirely by ear. Also necessary is a mastery of the **International Phonetic Alphabet**, the standard system for transcribing speech sounds.

Phoneticians may choose to investigate either the total range of speech sounds which can be produced by human beings (this is *general phonetics* or *anthropophonics*), or the manner in which speech sounds are used in real human languages (this is *linguistic phonetics*, and it overlaps with **phonology**).

Phonetics was substantially developed by the ancient Indians and by the medieval Arabs, but the modern tradition began in the sixteenth century in England, and it was in nineteenth- and twentieth-century Britain that such figures as Alexander Melville Bell, Henry Sweet and Daniel Jones chiefly created modern phonetics, though most of the instrumental techniques are far more recent. Phonetics lies at the heart of *dialectology*.

See also: **consonant; International Phonetic Alphabet; phonology; sociolinguistics; speech sound; transcription; vowel**

Further reading: Ashby 1995; Ball and Rahilly 1999; Collins and Mees 2003; Johnson 1997; Ladefoged 1993, 1971; Ladefoged and Maddieson 1996; Laver 1994.

PHONOLOGY

The sound systems of languages, or the branch of linguistics which studies these. Whereas **phonetics** is chiefly concerned with the physical nature of **speech sounds**, *phonology* deals with the ways in which sounds behave in languages.

It took a long time for linguists to understand the difference between phonetics and phonology, but, by the late nineteenth century, the Polish linguists Mikołaj Kruszewski and Jan Baudouin de Courtenay had laid the foundations of phonology as a discipline. The new phonological ideas spread out gradually cross Europe in the early twentieth century; meanwhile, American linguists were making similar progress somewhat independently.

The central concept in the new phonological approach was the **phoneme** principle, an understanding of which permitted great advances in the analysis of the sound systems of languages. This principle at last allowed linguists to understand the sounds of a language as constituting an orderly *system*, instead of being a mere collection of individual sounds; this insight was one of the early successes of the general approach to language study called **structuralism**.

Important contributions to phonology were made by the European linguists of the *Prague School* in the 1930s and by the *American structuralists* in the 1940s and 1950s. In the late 1950s, phonology was transformed by the introduction of **distinctive features** (phonological units smaller than phonemes); these features were combined with certain ideas taken from Noam Chomsky's new theory of **transformational grammar** to produce a dramatically new approach named *generative phonology*, which focused on the phonological process occurring in languages. Since the 1980s, generative phonology has broken up into a variety of more elaborate and competing approaches, the majority of which are collectively known as *non-linear phonology*; the two most prominent of these are *metrical phonology* and *autosegmental phonology*, but several others exist.

See also: **minimal pair**; **neutralization**; **phoneme**; **phonetics**; **phonotactics**

Further reading: Carr 1993; Collins and Mees 2003; Gussenhoven and Jacobs 1989; Gussmann 2002; Hawkins 1984; Lass 1984; McCarthy 2004, Shockey 2003, Sommerstein 1977.

PHONOTACTICS

The rules for combining **phonemes** into words in a language. Every variety of every language possesses a larger or smaller set of phonemes, and every legitimate word in that language must consist of a permitted sequence of those phonemes. But the key word here is 'permitted': no language allows its phonemes to occur in just any sequence at all. Instead, each language imposes strict limits on the sequences of phonemes which are allowed to occur in a word, and those restrictions are its *phonotactics*.

For example, English allows a word to begin with /b/ (as in *bed*), with /r/ (as in *red*), with /l/ (as in *led*), with /n/ (as in *net*), with the cluster /br/ (as in *bread*), and with the cluster /bl/ (as in *bled*). But it does not permit a word to begin with the cluster /bn/: no such word as *bned is even conceivable in English (the asterisk indicates this). Moreover, if a word begins with /br/ or /bl/, then the next phoneme must be a vowel: nothing like *blsed or *brved is possible either (but such a combination may be possible in another language).

Phonotactic constraints may differ widely from one language to another, even when the sets of phonemes are somewhat similar. For example, Hawaiian allows no consonant clusters at all, and every syllable must end in a vowel, and so *kanaka* 'man' is a legal word, but something like *kanak or *kanka is not. Japanese has a similar rule, so when words are borrowed from English that would be illegitimate phonotactically, they are nipponized: *biru* 'beer', *sunugurasu* 'sunglasses', *gurufurendu* 'girlfriend'. The Caucasian language Georgian permits astounding consonant clusters, as in *mts'vrtneli* 'trainer' and *vprtskvni* 'I'm peeling it'. The Canadian language Bella Coola, unusually, permits words containing no vowels at all, like *łkʷtχʷ* 'make it big'!

See also: **phoneme**; **phonology**

Further reading: Hawkins 1984; Kreidler 1989.

PHRASE

A grammatical unit which is smaller than a **clause**. The term *phrase* is an ancient one, and it has long been used to denote a grammatical unit which typically (though not invariably) consists of two or more words, but which does not contain all of the things found in a clause. For example, a *prepositional phrase* consists of a **preposition** with its object, as in *under the bed, with her girlfriend* and *of the wine*.

Especially since the 1940s, linguists have recognized a much larger variety of phrases than was formerly the case; among the more important are the **noun phrase** (such as *the little girl*), the **verb phrase** (such as *was singing in the bath*) and the **adjective phrase** (such as *pretty as a picture*). Each of these types of phrase represents a single *phrasal category*, and a phrasal category is one type of **syntactic category** – that is, it represents one of the basic building blocks used in constructing sentences. Generally speaking, at any point in a sentence in which, say, a noun phrase can occur, *any* noun phrase can be used, subject only to the (non-grammatical) requirement of making sense.

The precise set of phrasal categories recognized varies somewhat according to the particular grammatical framework being used; in particular, **Government-and-Binding Theory** recognizes a number of phrasal categories not recognized by most other frameworks.

Observe that a phrase may consist of only a single word; for example, the sentence *Susie smiled* consists of the noun phrase *Susie* and the verb phrase *smiled*. These units are phrases because they occupy the positions of phrases and behave like phrases; strictly speaking, therefore, we have here a verb phrase *smiled* which happens to consist only of the verb *smiled*. This double layer of structure is routinely displayed in a **tree** diagram, and failure to make it leads quickly to confusion.

Every phrase is built up from a **head**, an item (usually a single word) which itself determines what kind of phrase the whole thing is. A one-word phrase consists of a head with no other material at all.

Occasionally, in modern linguistics, the term phrase is generalized to denote *any* syntactic unit in a sentence (any *constituent*), of whatever size or nature; this is the sense of the term in names like **phrase-structure grammar**. So, for example, in the sentence *Susie discovered that she was pregnant*, the unit *she was pregnant* is a complete clause, and hence it is not a phrase in the narrower sense of the term, but it *is* a phrase in this extended sense.

See also: **head**; **modifier**

Further reading: Hurford 1994; Jackson 2002; Jeffries 2006.

PHRASE-STRUCTURE GRAMMAR

A type of **generative grammar** which represents **constituent structure** directly. We normally regard the structure of any sentence as an instance of **constituent structure**, in which smaller syntactic units are combined into larger units, which are then combined into still larger units, and so on. This kind of structure can be readily handled by a *phrase-structure grammar* (PSG) (the full form of the name is *context-free phrase-structure grammar*, or CF-PSG).

The idea of a PSG is simple. We first note what syntactic categories appear to exist in a given language, and what different internal structures each of these can have. Then, for each such structure, we write a **rule** that displays that structure. So, for example, an English sentence typically consists of a **noun phrase** followed by a **verb phrase** (as in *My sister bought a car*), and we therefore write a *phrase-structure rule* as follows: S → NP VP. This says that a sentence may consist of a noun phrase followed by a verb phrase. Further, an English NP may consist of a **determiner** (like *the* or *my*) followed by an *N-bar* (like *little girl* or *box of chocolates*), and so we write another rule: NP → Det N'. We continue in this way until we have a rule for every structure in the language.

Now the set of rules can be used to *generate* sentences. Starting with S (for 'sentence'), we apply some suitable rule to tell us what units the sentence consists of, and then to each of those units we apply a further rule to tell us what units *it* consists of, and so on, until we reach the level of individual words, at which point we simply insert words belonging to the appropriate **parts of speech**. The result is usually displayed graphically in a **tree**.

PSGs are the most appropriate type of grammar for teaching elementary syntax, and moreover they are powerful enough to describe successfully almost every construction occurring in any language, though there exist one or two rare and unusual constructions which they cannot handle.

PSGs were introduced by the American linguist Noam Chomsky in the 1950s, but Chomsky had little interest in them, and they were not really explored seriously until the British linguist Gerald Gazdar began developing a sophisticated version around 1980; his version was dubbed *Generalized Phrase-Structure Grammar* (GPSG). More recently, the Americans Carl Pollard and Ivan Sag have constructed a very different-looking version called *Head-Driven Phrase-Structure Grammar* (HPSG), which is both linguistically interesting and convenient for computational purposes. HPSG bases its formal rules on a richly organized and structured lexicon. A lexical item (a word) is made of two features: its sound and its syntactic-semantic information, which are in turn divided into further sub-features. An example would be the verb 'set in' which almost always has a semantics of negativity and adversity (*bad weather set in*, *financial problems set in*) and cannot be used with human agents. To describe the grammar of the verb fully we need to have a lexico-semantic information module built in to the description. HPSG is an early example of the fact that grammar and lexis are interdependent.

See also: **constituent structure**; **generative grammar**; **tree**

Further reading: Bennett 1995; Borsley 1996; Brown and Miller 1991; Lyons 1991; Pollard and Sag 1994.

PIDGIN

An auxiliary language created by people with no language in common. Very many times in human history, people with no language in common have found themselves thrown together and obliged to deal with one another. Sometimes the language of just one group will be learned by the others and used as a **lingua franca**, but often something quite different happens: words from one or more of the languages of the people involved will be taken and stitched together into a kind of crude way of communicating. This is a *pidgin*. A pidgin is nobody's mother tongue, and it is not a real language at all: it has no eleborate grammar, it is very limited in what it can convey, and different people speak it differently. Still, for simple purposes, it does work, and often everybody in the area learns to handle it.

Pidgins can and do arise whenever the conditions are favourable, and very many have been created just in the past few hundred years. Several were created along the east and west coasts of Africa, to facilitate trading among Africans, Europeans and Arabs. Many others were constructed in North America and the Caribbean, particularly to enable African slaves to talk to one another and to their European masters. And still others were constructed in the Far East, mainly for trading purposes. The sugar plantations of Hawaii attracted workers from a dozen countries in Asia and the Pacific, and this led to the creation of yet another pidgin. Many pidgins arise temporarily and disappear when the situation around them changes: for example, during the USA–Korean War (1950–3).

There are several possible fates for a pidgin. First, it may eventually drop out of use. This has happened to Hawaiian pidgin, now almost entirely displaced by English, the prestige language of Hawaii. Second, it can remain in use for generations, or even centuries, as has happened with some west African pidgins. Third, and most dramatically, it can be turned into a mother tongue. This happens when the children in a community have nothing but a pidgin to use with other children, in which case the children take the pidgin and turn it into a real language, by fixing and elaborating the grammar and greatly expanding the vocabulary. The result is a **creole**, and the children who create it are the first native speakers of the creole.

See also: **bioprogram hypothesis**; **creole**; **natural-language processing**

Further reading: Chaudenson 2001; Holm 1988–9; Holmes 1992; Kouwenberg and Singler 2005; Romaine 1994, 1988; Sebba 1997.

PLACE OF ARTICULATION

A label for the speech organs most directly involved in producing a **consonant**. By definition, the production of a consonant involves a **constriction** (narrowing or closure) somewhere in the vocal tract between the glottis and the lips. We have a standard terminology for labelling the particular parts of the vocal tract directly involved in making that constriction, and each such label denotes a particular *place of articulation*.

Toward the bottom end of the vocal tract, we can safely use simple labels like *glottal* and *pharyngeal*. Farther up, we need in principle to identify both the lower articulator and the upper one (in that order), and for this purpose we use a compound label with the first identifier ending in -*o* and the second in -*al* (or -*ar*). Examples:

- *dorso-velar* – back (dorsum) of tongue plus velum; e.g., [k]
- *lamino-alveolar* – blade (lamina) of tongue plus alveolar ridge; e.g., English [n] for most speakers
- *apico-dental* – tip (apex) of tongue plus upper teeth; e.g., French [t]
- *sublamino-prepalatal* – underside of tongue plus front of palate; e.g., [ɖ] in many Australian languages.

If the lower articulator is obvious or unimportant, we can omit it from the label; hence we can say *velar* instead of *dorso-velar*, or *alveolar* for any consonant involving the alveolar ridge.

A few traditional terms are unsystematic, such as *retroflex* for any consonant in which the tip of the tongue is curled up, *palato-alveolar* for a consonant involving a long constriction from the alveolar ridge to the palate, and *bilabial* in place of the expected *labio-labial*. Note also *coronal* for any consonant during which the blade of the tongue is raised, whether or not the blade is involved in the articulation.

For a consonant involving two simultaneous constrictions, we use the *-al* ending twice, so that [w], for example, is **labial-velar** (though the unsystematic **labio-velar** is also found).

See also: **consonant; manner of articulation**

Further reading: Ashby 1995; Ball and Rahilly 1999; Collins and Mees 2003; Ladefoged 1971.

POLITENESS

The linguistic expression of courtesy and social position. While *politeness* has non-linguistic aspects, we are here concerned only with its linguistic expression. Except when we are deliberately looking for a confrontation, we normally take care to ensure that what we say (and what we don't say) is chosen appropriately so as to avoid embarrassing or offending anyone.

Sociolinguists often discuss politeness phenomena in terms of *face*. Face is what you lose when you are embarrassed or humiliated in public. We may distinguish your *positive face* (your need to maintain and demonstrate your membership in a social group) from your *negative face* (your need to be individual and independent, to get what you want without offending anyone). A *face-threatening act* is any piece of behaviour which can easily make another person lose face; a *face-saving act* is any piece of behaviour which lessens or removes the threat of losing face.

The linguistic aspects of politeness have been much studied in recent years, and a number of important variables have been identified: tone of voice, markers of status, terms of address, degrees of certainty or confidence, discourse markers (like English *please*), the choice between speaking and remaining silent, acceptability of direct questions, and others. The rules of politeness vary considerably from society to society, and it is very easy to give inadvertent offence when talking to speakers of another language.

For example, speakers of Malagasy (in Madagascar) consider it impolite to give direct answers to questions or to make predictions that might turn out to be wrong. Speakers of Navaho (in the USA) consider it impolite to speak at all in the presence of a higher-ranking person, or to provide their own names. Both Javanese and Japanese have rich and complex systems for the overt linguistic marking of status among speaker, listener and person talked about, including both different vocabulary and different grammatical forms, and failing to mark status appropriately is a grave breach of decorum. Note that it is inappropriate to say that *X language is more polite than Y language*. Different languages simply encode their normal level of politeness with different features.

See also: **communicative competence; ethnography of communication**

Further reading: Bonvillain 1993; Brown and Levinson 1987; Eelen 2001; Holmes 1992; Mills 2003; Watts *et al.* 2005.

POLYSYNTHESIS

The phenomenon in which a single word consists of more than one morpheme. Languages which tend towards a 1:1 word to morpheme ratio (such as Thai, Vietnamese and Bulgarian) are known by contrast as *analytic* languages. The term *polysynthetic* is usually reserved for those languages at the other extreme end of the scale, which employ many morphemes (over 5:1) in word-formation. Native North American and Arctic languages are particularly well known for their polysynthetic aspects. For example, the Siberian Yupik language can express 'He wants to get a big boat' as *angya-rla-ng-yoocle-tuk* ('boat-big-get-wants-he'), where every morpheme after *angya* 'boat' is a bound affix, and each of these bears no relation to the full lexical word that could have been used in its place. English has a few examples of long polysynthesis, mainly technical terms from various fields and none in colloquial usage: *diaminoethanetetraacetic acid, antidisestablishmentarianism, deoxyribonucleic acid (DNA)*.

Polysynthesis is sometimes also used broadly to include examples of *incorporation*, where compounding is made not from bound morphemes but from full lexical items. Again, this too is common in Native North American languages (which may account for the confusion in usage of the term). English has an element of this: *breastfeed, dog-walk, self-harm, pub-crawl, overrun*. Even more widely, *incorporation* is sometimes used to include the process of creating compound verbs.

See also: **derivation; morpheme**

Further reading: Baker 1996; van Valin and LaPolla 1997.

POSSIBLE WORLDS THEORY

Originally developed in the **philosophy of language**, this was a means of determining the truth or falsity of propositions. A sentence could be judged either true, false or lacking a truth-value only when it was considered to be uttered in relation to a set of states of affairs that constituted the world surrounding the sentence. Our own reality is the *actual possible world* which could be considered alongside other counterfactual possible worlds, in which sentences would have different truth values. For example, *This book is open about two-thirds of the way through* contains a proposition that is true if you are reading the paper version of this book. However, if you are reading this as an e-book, then it is arguably either false or lacking in truth-value.

Possible worlds theory, in this original sense, was a logical theory and the *worlds* involved were simply reduced semantic sets. However, more recently, principles in possible worlds theory have been developed in **cognitive linguistics** to be able to consider the sorts of rich worlds that exist in mental representations. Work in **schema** theory and **text world theory**, in particular, owes much to possible worlds theory. These appraoches have all proven fruitful in the field of *cognitive poetics*, a development of **stylistics** which uses **cognitive linguistics** in the exploration of literary works.

See also: **cognitive linguistics**; **schema**; **stylistics**; **text world theory**

Further reading: Ronen 1994; Ryan 1991; Semino 1997; Stockwell 2002b.

POWER

The relation between the type of language used by an individual and that individual's access to positions of power and influence. In almost every society of any size or complexity, there are notable differences in the type of language used by different sectors of society, and, furthermore, associated differences in the access enjoyed by the different groups to powerful and well-paid positions. For example, in the English-speaking world, the contrast is primarily between standard English and the various non-standard forms of English, and it is obvious that speakers of standard English typically enjoy more power, more prestige and more money than the others, who are far more likely to be confined to positions of low prestige, with comparatively little money or influence and often with little chance for advancement. What, if anything, should we do about this state of affairs?

Broadly speaking, there have been two answers proposed to this question. Some people emphasize the importance of teaching prestige forms of language to speakers of non-prestige forms in order to empower them, while others object to the imposition of prestige forms on the ground that it effectively denies power to speakers of other varieties. In the English case, the first group are essentially arguing that it is the very command of standard English which itself confers access to power and prestige and, hence, that it is our social duty to extend this command to as many people as possible, since otherwise non-standard speakers will remain marginalized and unable to play a full part in society. The second group, in great contrast, argue that standard English is nothing more than the identifying badge of a particular and maximally powerful group, a mere sign of class membership and, hence, that stressing the imposition of standard English denies the value of non-standard forms, so that non-standard speakers are implicitly dismissed as inadequate and unworthy of power. Many members of the second group go so far as to demand that non-standard varieties of English should be formally recognized as the equal of standard English, and that non-standard English should become the vehicle of education for its speakers, a position which appals the members of the first group.

Much commentary on language by journalists, politicians and other non-linguist observers is primarily concerned with power and authority in language, even where this is not explicit.

See also: **standard language**

Further reading: Crowley 1989; Fairclough 2001; Honey 1997.

PRAGMATICS

The branch of linguistics which studies how utterances communicate meaning in context. The study of **meaning**, commonly known as **semantics**, has long been one of the most daunting and difficult areas of language study. In the 1950s and 1960s, however, linguists and philosophers slowly began to realize that part of the difficulty lay in their failure to distinguish two quite different aspects of meaning.

The first type of meaning is *intrinsic* to a linguistic expression containing it, and it cannot be separated from that expression. The study of this kind of meaning is the domain of semantics, as we now understand the term. But there is a second kind of meaning, one which is not intrinsic to the linguistic expression carrying it, but which rather results from the interaction of the linguistic expression with the *context* in which is it used. And to the study of this kind of meaning we give a new name: *pragmatics*.

Consider the sentence *Susie is a heavy smoker*. In all circumstances, this sentence carries with it its intrinsic meaning: Susie smokes a large quantity of tobacco every day. This meaning is intrinsic and inseparable. But now consider what happens when this sentence is uttered as a response to three different utterances produced by Jessica in three different contexts.

1 [Jessica is trying to have smoking banned in offices]: *Can you ask Susie to sign this petition?*
2 [Jessica is trying to arrange a blind date for Dave, a non-smoker who hates cigarette smoke]: *Would Susie like to go out with Dave?*
3 [Jessica, a medical researcher, is looking for smokers to take part in some medical tests]: *Do you know of anybody I could ask?*

In each case, you will agree, something very different is being communicated. In the first case: Susie is unlikely to sign the petition, so there's no point in asking her. In the second: Dave and Susie won't get on, so there's no point in fixing them up. Third: Susie will be a suitable person for your study.

Now, it is not possible to maintain that this single unvarying sentence actually *means* all of these different things. Rather, these three meanings have been communicated as a consequence of the interaction between what was said and the *context* in which it was said. Every time the context changes, what is communicated changes as well. And it is this variable, context-bound relation between what is said and what is communicated that is the subject-matter of pragmatics.

It should be noted that, outside the USA, the term pragmatics is often used in a much broader sense, so as to include a great number of phenomena that American linguists would regard as belonging strictly to **sociolinguistics**: such as **politeness**, **narrativity**, and the signalling of **power** relations.

227

See also: **conversational implicature**; **cooperative principle**; **meaning**; **relevance**; **semantics**; **speech act**

Further reading: Blutner and Zeevat 2003; Grundy 1995; Schiffrin 1994; Thomas 1995; Verschueren 1999; Yule 1996.

PREDICATE

That part of a sentence other than its subject. It was the Greek philosopher Aristotle who first divided sentences into subjects and predicates. Given a fixed subject *Susie*, we can construct sentences by adding to this subject any number of different predicates: *smokes, is clever, has been promoted, wants to buy a new car, believes that astrology is garbage*. In each case (in English), the predicate role is filled by a **verb phrase**; this is typically so in most languages, though some languages permit predicates belonging to other **syntactic categories**.

It is important to realize that logicians use the term *predicate* in a very different way, one which is now prominent in linguistics, especially in **semantics**. In the system of formal logic called *predicate logic*, the sentence *Bruce is bald* would typically be represented as *Bald (Bruce)*. Here *Bald* is a (logical) predicate corresponding to English *is bald*, and it is a *one-place predicate* requiring only one **argument** (noun phrase) in order to be satisfied. The sentence *Bruce loves Kathy* might be similarly represented with a one-place predicate as *Love-Kathy (Bruce)*, but more commonly we would represent it as with a *two-place predicate*, as follows: *Love (Bruce, Kathy)*. This time the predicate *Love* requires two arguments in order to be satisfied.

Since both of these conflicting usages are widespread in linguistics, you must take care that you understand which sense is intended when you encounter the term.

See also: **verb phrase**

Further reading: Hurford 1994; Jackson 2002.

PREPOSITION

The **part of speech** which includes words like *to*, *with* and *of*. Like many other languages, English possesses a smallish class of words called *prepositions*. A preposition has only one major property: it combines with a following **noun phrase** – its *object* – to form a larger syntactic unit – a *prepositional phrase*. Typical prepositions include *of, to, in, for, with, under, about, inside, after, in front of* and *in spite of*. (Note that some of these can also belong to other parts of speech.) Here are some typical prepositional phrase: *to the car, for a while, with Susie, after the war, in spite of the weather*. Some prepositions, like *under* and *after*, express identifiable meanings. Others, such as *of*, have a purely grammatical function: in the noun phrase *the end of the year*, the preposition *of* serves merely to connect the smaller noun phrase *the year* to the rest of the bigger one, but *of the year* is still a prepositional phrase.

Prepositions are analysed in **cognitive linguistics** as the realization of *image schemas*: basic representations of the physical and spatial movement involved in *through, over, under, into, from, beside* and so on.

In some languages, such as Japanese and Basque, the items that do the job of prepositions follow their object instead of preceding it, and we therefore call them *postpositions*. Japanese examples: *Tokyo ni* 'to Tokyo'; *Tokyo de* 'in Tokyo'. Prepositions and postpositions together are collectively called *adpositions*.

Some languages, such as the Australian languages, lack adpositions altogether, and use entirely different grammatical devices to do the same job.

See also: **landmark**; **syntax**; **trajector**

Further reading: Collins Cobuild 1990; Hurford 1994.

PRESCRIPTIVISM

The imposition of arbitrary norms upon a language, often in defiance of normal usage. Every language exhibits a good deal of regional and social **variation**. If very many people want to use a language for a number of different purposes, then it is convenient and even necessary to have a single agreed form of the language – a **standard language** – known and used by everybody, or at least by all educated speakers. Otherwise, if people insist on using their own particular varieties, the result will be confusion and misunderstanding. But, since languages are always changing, there will always be doubts and disagreements over which forms and usages should be recognized as part of the standard language.

Prescriptivism consists of the attempts, largely by teachers and writers, to settle these disagreements by insisting upon the use of those particular forms and usages which they personally prefer and by condemning those others which they personally dislike. Of course, some degree of prescriptivism is necessary, particularly in education: people who naturally use forms which are blatantly not accepted as standard by the community as a whole must learn to use the standard forms, at least in those circumstances which call for the standard language, or else they will be severely disadvantaged.

But the problem is that many prescriptivists go much further than this convenient *codification*, and try to condemn usages which are in fact perfectly normal for even educated speakers, and to insist instead upon usages which were current generations or centuries ago but which are now effectively dead, or even upon usages which have never been normal for anybody.

A famous example concerns the so-called *split infinitive*. For generations, virtually all English-speakers have spontaneously said things like *She decided to gradually get rid of the teddy-bears she had spent twenty years collecting.* Here the sequence *to gradually get rid of* is the 'split infinitive'. Many prescriptivists have condemned this usage, on the supposed ground that *to get* is a single verb-form, the 'infinitive', and therefore 'logically' cannot be split up. Such people typically insist instead on something like *She decided gradually to get rid of* . . .. But this is all wrong.

First, the proposed 'correction' is badly misleading: it suggests that it is the decision which is gradual, rather than the disposal. Second, the sequence *to get* is not an infinitive, nor is it a verb-form, nor is it even a grammatical unit at all. The true infinitive here is *get*, while *to* is nothing but a linking particle. The adverb *gradually* logically belongs next to *get rid of*, and that's where speakers normally put it. That *to get* is not a grammatical unit can be shown in a number of ways, not least of which is the observation that speakers regularly break it up. (Another test is the construction illustrated by *She has asked me to change my hairstyle, but I don't want to*, in which the understood *change* is deleted while *to* is obliged to remain – hardly possible if *to change* were really a unit.) Hence the prescriptivists' position is ignorant and wrong-headed: it represents an attempt to replace normal and elegant usage by something which is silly, unnatural and hard to understand, and which is used by nobody except some prescriptivists and those few who take them seriously.

Many prescriptivists also object to the familiar English practice of ending a sentence with a preposition, apparently on the bizarre ground that this construction is not possible in Latin. They take exception to ordinary English utterances like *Who were you talking to?*, *What's this gadget for?* and *That's something I just can't put up with*, demanding instead unnatural things like *To whom were you talking?*, *For what is this gadget?*, and I have no idea what they would do about the last one.

Prescriptivists also reject such ordinary utterances as *Who do you trust?*, demanding instead *Whom do you trust?*, a form which was current hundreds of years ago but is now dead, except in frostily formal styles of speech and writing. Other examples of feeble-mindedness include the aversion to multiple negation (double negatives for emphasis); prejudice against *ain't*; insisting on *fewer* for count-nouns instead of *less* (*Five items or less* at the super-market check-out); distaste for the impersonal *you* for *one* (*one doesn't do such things*); and hang-ups over spellings and apos-trophes when there is no communicative problem at all. It is deeply unfortunate that so many commentators have seen fit to lose touch with reality and to pursue their own absurd little bugbears at such length and with such passion.

See also: **descriptivism**; **purism**

Further reading: Crystal 1997; Edwards 1994; Milroy and Milroy 1997; Pinker 1994.

PRESTIGE

A feature identified in **sociolinguistics** as the high esteem and social value which speakers attach to certain language varieties. For example, in Britain the *received pronunciation (RP)* accent is regarded as prestigious even though it is spoken by less than 5 per cent of the UK population: it is seen as an indicator of education, wealth, trustworthiness, attractive looks and honesty! The opposite of *prestige* is *stigma*, which attaches to other varieties depending on the viewpoint of the stigmatizer. Some varieties display *covert pres-tige*, where speakers will share a sense of value for the standard language, but will unconsciously accentuate their own stigmatized variety in certain contexts. For example, middle-class men in var-ious parts of England have been observed switching away from RP and towards the local working-class accent when the setting is perceived as being casual, colloquial and male-oriented. They will often **hypercorrect** (i.e., overdo) the working-class accent in this situation. The effects of prestige, *stigmatization* and *hypercorrection* are important factors in **language change**.

See also: **accent**; **sociolinguistics**

Further reading: Bex and Watts 1999; Llamas *et al.* 2007; Trudgill 1995.

PRESUPPOSITION

A particular sort of inference. Consider the sentence *John's wife runs a boutique*. Now, when we hear this, we are immediately entitled to draw the following inference: *John is married*. This is an example of a ***presupposition***: we say that the first sentence ***presupposes*** the second.

A presupposition differs from other types of inference, such as an **entailment** or a **conversational implicature**, in several ways. Most obviously, a presupposition survives negation. If I negate the original sentence, the result is *John's wife doesn't run a boutique* – and this still presupposes that *John is married*. Both the original sentence and its negation have the interesting property that they are bizarre and uncooperative things to say if John is in fact a bachelor. Very informally, then, a presupposition of statement P is something which has to be true before P can possibly be a plausible thing to say.

In a widespread view, introduced by the British philosopher Peter Strawson around 1950, we can say that P presupposes Q if and only if Q has to be true before P can be *either* true or false. That is, if Q is false, then P can be neither true nor false: it simply has no truth value at all. So, if John is a bachelor, then *John's wife runs a boutique* is not false, nor is it true; it is simply devoid of truth value. But not everyone agrees with this interpretation, and some linguists, following the British philosopher Bertrand Russell, would prefer to conclude that the statement really is false. This disagreement is bound up in a larger controversy over whether presuppositions properly belong to the domain of **semantics** or to that of **pragmatics**.

Note that questions and commands can have presuppositions. The question *Do you still drink a bottle of vodka every night?* is bizarre and unanswerable if you have never drunk vodka on that scale (this is what is informally known as a 'loaded question'), and the command *Take your hat off!* is bizarre and impossible to obey if you aren't wearing a hat.

See also: **conversational implicature; entailment**

Further reading: Grundy 1995; Levinson 1983; Saeed 1997; Verschueren 1999.

PRODUCTIVITY

The degree of freedom with which a particular grammatical pattern can be extended to new cases. We most often speak of productivity in connection with patterns of **word-formation**. The noun-forming suffix -*ness* is highly productive: *happiness, preparedness, salaciousness, user-friendliness*. The same is true of the verbal prefix *re-*: *rewrite, reconsider, reappoint, renegotiate, reboot* (a computer).

But the noun-forming suffix -*th* is totally unproductive: we have existing cases like *warmth* and *depth*, but we cannot form any new ones: **happyth, *bigth, *sexyth* (the asterisk indicates forms that are unacceptable). The noun-forming suffix -*dom* is weakly productive: to established cases like *kingdom* and *martyrdom* we occasionally add new ones like *gangsterdom, tigerdom* and *stardom*, but we can't do this freely: **policedom, *universitydom, *childdom*.

The adverb-forming suffix -*wise* was formerly unproductive and confined to a few cases like *clockwise* and *otherwise*, but today we freely coin new formations like *healthwise, moneywise, clotheswise* and *fitnesswise*. The noun-prefix *mini-* didn't even exist before 1960, but today it is prodigiously productive: *miniskirt, minicomputer, mini-microphone, minibus*, even *mini-war*.

See also: **word-formation**

Further reading: Bauer 1988; Katamba 1994; Matthews 1991.

PRONOUN

The **part of speech** which includes words like *she, them* and *something*. Pronouns have been recognized as a distinct part of speech since ancient times. Essentially, a pronoun is a single word (or rarely a longer form), with little or no meaning of its own, which functions as a complete **noun phrase**.

Pronouns are classified into several types. A *personal pronoun* points at some participant in a speech situation: *I, you, we, she, they*. A *demonstrative pronoun* points in space or time, like the *this* in *This is a good book*. An *interrogative pronoun* asks a question, like *who* in *Who's there?* An *indefinite pronoun*, such as *somebody* or *anything*, fills a slot in a sentence without providing much specific meaning, as in *Do you need anything?* A *relative pronoun* introduces a relative clause, like the *who* in *The students who streaked the graduation ceremony are in trouble*. Finally, a *reflexive pronoun* like *herself* and a *reciprocal pronoun* like *each other* refer to other noun phrases in the sentence in specific ways, as in *She cursed herself* and *They are seeing a lot of each other*.

As a rule, a pronoun cannot take a **modifier**, but there are a few exceptions: *little me, poor you, something interesting*.

See also: **anaphor**; **noun phrase**

Further reading: Collins Cobuild 1990; Hurford 1994; Jackson 2002; Jeffries 2006.

PROSODY

Variations in pitch, loudness, rhythm and tempo (rate of speaking) during speech. The term *prosody* is an ancient one, but it was originally applied only to the analysis of verse structure. Linguists in the twentieth century have taken over the term and applied it specifically to the several variations in the behaviour of the voice cited above.

These prosodic features may or may not be expressly linguistic in nature. **Tone languages** and languages with *pitch* or *stress* accents make specific linguistic use of pitch and/or loudness, but utterances in all languages are characterized by noticeable variations in all four of these features. Particularly important is the use of pitch variations in **intonation**, which is universal in languages.

Prosodic phenomena are notoriously difficult to study, but some considerable progress has been made in examining at least some of them. Nevertheless, elementary textbooks of **phonetics** and of **phonology** only rarely discuss prosodic features in any detail.

It should be noted that the terms prosody and prosodic also have some rather special uses. In the theory of phonology called *prosodic phonology*, the term prosody is given a highly distinctive technical sense which is peculiar to that theory. In some contemporary theories of phonology and of **morphology**, the adjective *prosodic* is likewise given some rather distinctive senses for labelling things which are important in those theories. Finally, note that in some quarters prosody is used merely as a synonym for **suprasegmental**, a usage which is not recommended.

See also: **intonation**; **stress**; **suprasegmental**; **tone language**

Further reading: Ball and Rahilly 1999; Laver 1994; Shockey 2003.

PROTO-LANGUAGE

The hypothetical ancestor of a **language family**. When we find some languages which are clearly connected in a **genetic relationship**, and which therefore form a language family, it follows by definition that all are descended from a single ancestral language; that is, that they all started off long ago as no more than regional dialects of that ancestral language. Given enough data, historical linguists can apply **comparative reconstruction** to obtain substantial information about what that ancestral language was like, even though in most cases it was never itself recorded. The **reconstruction** which they obtain in this way is a reasonably accurate picture of the ancestral language, which is called the *proto-language* for the whole family.

A proto-language is named by prefixing *Proto-* to the name of the family. For example, the ancestor of the *Germanic* languages (English, German, Swedish and others) is *Proto-Germanic*; the ancestor of the *Romance* languages (Spanish, French, Italian and others) is *Proto-Romance*; and the ancestor of the vast **Indo-European** family is *Proto-Indo-European*.

See also: **Indo-European**; **language family**; **reconstruction**

Further reading: Hock 1986; Trask 1996.

PROTO-LANGUAGE HYPOTHESIS

The hypothesis that human language arose rather abruptly from a vastly simpler precursor. The proto-language hypothesis was developed in the 1980s by the British-born American linguist Derek Bickerton. A keen student of **pidgins** and **creoles**, Bickerton was impressed by the rapidity with which a pidgin (which is not a full language) can be converted into a creole (which is) when the conditions are right. He therefore developed the argument that some of our remote ancestors must have had only **proto-language**, a crude and limited system somewhat resembling a pidgin, and that this must have developed, probably very suddenly, into true language when certain critical conditions were in place in the brain.

Bickerton argues that proto-language can still be observed today in certain circumstances: in pidgins, in the speech of individuals suffering from certain kinds of disability, in the speech of very young children, and in the severely limited linguistic accomplishments of laboratory animals instructed in something resembling a human language. The hypothesis is deeply controversial.

See also: **animal communication; origin and evolution of language**

Further reading: Bickerton 1981, 1990, 1996.

PROTOTYPE

An important feature of the way that semantic knowledge is held in memory, and therefore an important concept in **semantics, psycholinguistics** and **cognitive linguistics**. Human categories have been found to display *prototype* effects, so, for example, most people have a sense of the 'best example' of a *bird*: sparrow, pigeon, crow, perhaps, rather than emu, ostrich, penguin or *dromas ardeola* (crab plover). Similar ranges of examples can be applied to categories such as *furniture, fruit, linguists* and in fact every conceivable category, including provisional categories such as *things to do on a Friday night, what to wear to a family party*, and so on. Categorization is thus not an 'either-or' matter but a matter of *radiality*, with central examples of a thing and peripheral or poor examples of a thing. Thus a potato is not simply a 'non-fruit'; it is just a very bad example of a fruit. You can test this by noting that it is a better example of a fruit than a television set.

Note that prototypical organization is culture specific. The crab plover might be a very prominent example of a bird if you live around the Indian Ocean. Prototypes are also malleable: a screwdriver can be recategorized as a good example of an envelope-opener if it is all that you have to hand. Prototypicality seems to be the cognitive mechanism underlying the notion of *basic level concepts* which tend to be the most neutrally lexicalized (*bird, dog, computer,* rather than *starling, terrier* or *IBM*).

See also: **cognitive linguistics**; **semantics**

Further reading: Lakoff 1987; Taylor 2003; Ungerer and Schmid 1996.

PSYCHOLINGUISTICS

The study of the connections between language and mind. Psycholinguistics began to emerge as a distinct discipline in the 1950s. To some extent, its emergence was promoted by the insistence at the time of the linguist Noam Chomsky that **linguistics** should be regarded as a part of cognitive psychology, but there were other factors as well, notably the growing interest in the question of **language acquisition** by children.

There is no doubt that the study of acquisition has so far been the most prominent and successful area of psycholinguistics. But a number of other topics have also been explored, with varying degrees of success. Many of these are aspects of **language processing**, the steps involved in producing and comprehending speech. Others include the links between language use and memory, the linguistic examination of reading, and more recently possible links with perception and cognition.

We now possess a great deal of data in most of these areas, but progress in developing theoretical interpretations has been slow. The enthusiastic early attempts at understanding mental processing of language in terms of **transformational grammar** proved a failure, and contemporary theorizing tends to be less ambitious: grand schemes are out, and psycholinguists now content themselves with trying to provide accounts of specific aspects of language behaviour.

Psycholinguists would also like to link their findings to those of **neurolinguistics**, the study of language and brain, but this has not proved at all easy. Some psycholinguists are also contributing to the development of **cognitive linguistics** and of **cognitive science** generally.

See also: **language acquisition**; **language processing**; **neurolinguistics**

Further reading: Aitchison 1989, 1994; Field 2003; Garman 1990; Garnham 1985; Steinberg 1993.

PUNCTUATION

A conventional system of marks representing information about the structure of a written text. The earliest **writing systems** used no punctuation, and often they didn't even separate words. The Greeks introduced the earliest known punctuation during the classical period, but it was very different from ours. In those days, and for long after, silent reading was unknown, and the reader of a text spoke the words out loud, even when reading alone.

Greek orators who were preparing speeches for delivery found it helpful to add marks to their texts to remind them where to pause briefly, where to make a dramatic pause, where to raise the voice, and so on. And these marks, added purely for rhetorical purposes, were the first punctuation.

The Romans and the medieval Carolingians gradually elaborated the set of punctuation marks, and these marks began to be used to indicate structural aspects of texts, rather than breathing places. With the eventual development of silent reading, this structural function entirely displaced the old oratorical one, and today our punctuation systems express mainly structural information.

All other widely used writing systems have also developed systems of punctuation, though it is notable that a standard punctuation system is generally the very last aspect of a writing system to become established. Even in Europe, languages like English, French and German, all written in the roman alphabet, all use slightly different punctuation and, moreover, American punctuation differs in a few respects from British. Punctuation can also change: modern English punctuation is very different from that used in the eighteenth century.

See also: **writing system**; **orthography**

Further reading: Foley 1993; Sampson 1985.

PURISM

The belief that words (and other linguistic features) of foreign origin are a kind of contamination sullying the purity of a language. Almost all languages are in contact with other languages, and all languages **borrow** words (and sometimes other features) from those neighbouring languages. Sometimes speakers of the receiving language take exception to the presence in their language of these 'foreign' elements, which they see as 'impurities', and agitate to have them removed and replaced by native elements. This attitude is called *purism*, and it is widespread.

For example, the French authorities, dismayed by the hundreds of English words pouring into French every year, have made strenuous efforts to eradicate some of these English words from their language and to replace them with novel French creations, and their recommendations have the force of law in certain domains. Thus, *computer* has been officially replaced by *ordinateur*, *software* by *logiciel*, *light pen* by *crayon optique*, *floppy disc* by *disquette*, *pie chart* by *camembert*, *videoclip* by *bande promo*, *bookmobile* first by *bibliothèque circulante* but now by *bibliobus*, and *bulldozer* by *bouledozeur* (!) (this last was a failure and has been abandoned). The English word *debugging* was at first rendered as *débogage*, but more recently the amusing *déverminage* has been coined. Often such coinages fail under pressure from popular usage.

Purism has almost never been a force among speakers of English, but speakers of French, German, Icelandic, Turkish and Basque (just to name a few) have at times engaged in large-scale purges of foreign elements, with varying degrees of success.

See also: **prescriptivism**

Further reading: Milroy and Milroy 1997.

QUALITATIVE APPROACH

A trend towards the description and explanation of language use within naturally occurring social and cultural settings. The various strands of what we now call the **qualitative approach** have been visible within sociology since the 1920s, but only since the 1980s has this approach become prominent in the study of language.

This label is applied to a particular methodology, or set of methodologies, particularly within **sociolinguistics** and **conversation analysis**, in which *authenticity* is regarded as crucial, and in which authenticity is achieved through the detailed description of the social settings and social practices which yield language data. A qualitative approach typically focuses on the study of small numbers of speakers or texts, since an abundance of data and statistical studies are seen as less important than revealing the social meanings which speakers and writers attach to their linguistic activities. Consequently, this approach contrasts rather vividly with the **quantitative approach**. (Moreover, the depth of detailed data collected in qualitative research renders it almost impossible to deal with more than a few informants.)

Qualitative research employs observation, textual analysis, interviews, and the recording and transcribing of speech. While these may also be used in quantitative work, in qualitative research they are given a different status. For example, in quantitative investigations, observation is limited to the initial exploratory stages, essentially to the stages at which the topic of research is being identified, since observation alone is here considered to be too unreliable to yield usable data. In qualitative research, however, the observation of participants is considered fundamental in revealing the social and political factors which underpin language use. Thus, disciplines which regularly employ qualitative methodology, such as ethnography, social anthropology and cognitive anthropology, often rely solely upon observation and other 'open-ended' research procedures.

See also: **conversation analysis; ethnography of communication; quantitative approach**

Further reading: Johnstone 2000; Milroy 1987b; Milroy and Gordon 2003; Silverman 1993; Wengraf 2001.

QUANTITATIVE APPROACH

A statistical approach to the study of **variation** in language. Variation in the way people use their language is very prominent, but for generations linguists could see no way of making any sense of it: instead, variation was typically seen as an irrelevant nuisance and ignored. In the 1960s, however, the American sociolinguist William Labov pioneered a wholly new approach to language study, one which made variation itself a prime object of examination. The key to this approach was the introduction of statistics: Labov collected statistical data on the frequency of competing forms used by different speakers and then looked for correlations with non-linguistic factors. This is the *quantitative approach*, and it has proved outstandingly successful.

What Labov and his successors found is this. If we merely observe a speaker, or a group of speakers, all we can notice is that speakers sometimes use this form and sometimes that one, in a seemingly haphazard manner. However, if we tabulate the *frequency* of each competing form, we often find first that one individual differs notably from another and second that the frequency of a particular form correlates strongly with some non-linguistic variable. Most often, the non-linguistic variables are obvious ones like sex, age, social class and degree of formality, but sometimes we find more unexpected correlations.

What these studies have shown is that variation is not haphazard at all. Instead, variation is highly structured: statistically speaking, each individual behaves in a highly consistent way, with some individuals behaving differently from others, depending on some of the variables just mentioned, and, moreover, the behaviour of each individual changes in a predictable way when the context of speaking becomes more or less formal.

The quantitative approach has revolutionized the study of language by demonstrating that linguistic behaviour is even more highly structured than we had previously suspected; it has contributed enormously to the study of **language change**, and it has provided a resolution of the **Saussurean paradox**.

See also: **language change**; **social stratification of language**; **sociolinguistics**; **variation**

Further reading: Hudson 1996; Labov 1972; Milroy 1992.

RAISING

Any of various phenomena in which a linguistic element appears in a higher clause than is semantically appropriate. Consider the sentence *It appears that Susie is falling asleep*. Here *Susie* is, both logically and grammatically, the subject of the verb phrase *is falling asleep* within the lower (subordinate) clause. But the same information can be expressed differently: *Susie appears to be falling asleep*. This time *Susie*, still the logical subject of *be falling asleep*, appears as the grammatical subject of *appears*. In this case, we say that *Susie* has been **raised** out of the lower clause into the higher one, and, since the item undergoing raising is the subject of the lower clause, we call this phenomenon **subject-raising**, or sometimes more specifically **subject-to-subject raising**, since the raised element ends up being the subject of the higher clause.

This is not the only kind of raising. Consider the example *I believe that she is happy*. Here *she* is again the subject of the lower clause. But we can express this as *I believe her to be happy*, in which *her* is apparently now the object of the verb *believe* in the higher clause, as shown by its form. This is **subject-to-object raising**. (A note: a minority of linguists would prefer to analyse this last example as having the structure *I believe [her to be happy]*, with *her* still being the subject of *to be happy*; proponents of this unusual analysis sometimes refer to the bracketed sequence as a **small clause**.)

Now consider the example. *It is difficult to please Susie*, in which *Susie* is the object of the verb *please*. This can equally be expressed as *Susie is difficult to please*, in which *Susie* has been raised to become the subject of *is difficult*. This last construction was therefore formerly called **object-to-subject raising**, though today it is more usually known by the quaint name **tough-movement**, since it is most frequent with verb phrases expressing degrees of difficulty.

Finally, consider the example *It seems that I never meet the right women*. This is more idiomatically expressed as *I never seem to meet the right women*, in which the negative item *never* has been raised out of the lower clause, where it logically belongs, into the higher clause. This is **negative raising**, and it is illustrated also by cases like *I can't seem to find my keys*, equivalent to *It seems that I can't find my keys*.

Raising phenomena are complex and intricate, and they have received a good deal of attention from syntacticians in recent years.

See also: **control, movement**

Further reading: Borsley 1991.

RANK SCALE

In **systemic linguistics** but also commonly in language description, language is divided into several levels from the largest units down to the smallest, roughly as follows:

discourse
text
sentence
clause

phrase
lexeme
morpheme
phoneme

Each level corresponds roughly with a sub-discipline within linguistics: **discourse analysis, text linguistics, syntax and semantics,** *lexicology,* **morphology,** and **phonology.** In **Systemic Linguistics,** the rank scale is hierarchical, with each level above encompassing the levels below. So, for example, syntactic embeddedness can be described in terms of elements from one level being *rank-shifted* to another level: *The man who wrote this book also wrote that book* contains a clause that is rank-shifted into the noun-phrase.

See also: **Systemic Linguistics**

Further reading: Halliday 2004; Thompson 2004.

RECONSTRUCTION

Working out features of dead and unrecorded languages, or of unrecorded earlier stages of single languages. In the vast majority of cases, a given language can be clearly seen to share a common ancestry with at least some other languages – that is, the languages in question all started out long ago as no more than **dialects** of a single ancestral language, which itself is almost never recorded. In such cases, practitioners of **historical linguistics** are naturally interested in trying to work out as much as they can about the nature of that unrecorded ancestral language.

Moreover, even a single language is only ever recorded since some particular point in time, often a rather recent one, and historical linguists are also interested in obtaining information about the prehistory of that language.

Since the end of the eighteenth century, historical linguists have been painstakingly constructing effective and reliable methods of performing these tasks, and we now know a great deal about how to go about them. The business of obtaining information about unrecorded languages is *reconstruction*, and there are two main types.

In **comparative reconstruction**, a linguist compares several languages which are known to be related; each of these languages normally preserves some features of their common ancestor, but has lost others. Since different languages preserve different ancestral features, it is often possible to determine in some detail what the ancestral language was like, and hence what changes have occurred in each of the daughter languages. Key to this is the identification of *cognates*: words, phrases or grammatical patterns in two languages that have a common root.

In **internal reconstruction**, the linguist works with only a single language and tries to determine what an earlier unrecorded stage of that language was like, and hence what changes occurred to produce the earliest recorded form.

Both types of reconstruction are most commonly performed upon recorded languages, but, once we have managed to reconstruct some unrecorded languages in reasonable detail, it is perfectly possible to apply the same methods to these and to reconstruct even further back in time. Naturally, though, a reconstruction based upon reconstructions is generally less secure than one based upon attested languages, and in practice there are limits on how far back we can go.

See also: **comparative reconstruction**; **historical linguistics**; **Indo-European**; **internal reconstruction**; **language change**

Further reading: Fox 1995; Hock 1986; Hock and Joseph 1996; Trask 1996.

RECURSION

The occurrence in a sentence of a **syntactic category** containing within it a smaller instance of the same category. Recursion is pervasive in the grammars of the languages of the world, and its presence is the chief reason we are able to produce a limitless variety of sentences of unbounded length just by combining the same few building blocks.

For example, a **noun phrase** (NP) in English may contain within it a **prepositional phrase** (PP), and a prepositional phrase always contains a noun phrase. Hence we can build up an NP containing a PP containing an NP containing a PP ... and so on, as far as we like. In the sentence *I've bought a book about the history of the debate between defenders of different theories of education*, everything after *bought* is a single large NP beginning with *a book*; this NP contains a single large PP beginning with *about*, which in turn contains another NP beginning with *the history*, which contains a smaller PP beginning with *of*, and so on, until the final NP *education* contains no further PP. Here both the NPs and the PPs illustrate recursion. Similarly, the well-known verse containing the line *This is the dog that chased the cat that killed the rat that ate the malt that lay in the house that Jack built* illustrates the recursion of relative clauses, with each *that* introducing a new relative clause embedded within the one already begun, so that everything after *dog* is one huge relative clause containing a series of smaller relative clauses, each one embedded within another.

See also: **constituent structure**; **phrase**; **syntax**

Further reading: Brown and Miller 1991; Keyser and Postal 1976.

REFERENCE

The relation between a linguistic expression and something which it picks out in the real or conceptual world. A linguistic expression which *refers* to (points at) something in the non-linguistic world is a *referring expression*, and the most familar such expressions are **noun phrases**.

A simple **noun** like *dog* does not itself refer to anything: it merely denotes the entire class of dogs. But, when it is embedded in a suitable noun phrase, the whole phrase may succeed in referring to something specific in the world: *this dog, the little dog with the floppy ears, that dog that Aunt Sophie used to have*, and so on. And the relation between such an expression and the thing it picks out is one of *reference*.

Proper names may also refer and, indeed, they hardly do anything else: *Abraham Lincoln, the Golden Gate Bridge, Spain* – these really have no intrinsic meaning at all, and they merely point to particular entities.

Reference is entirely in the mind of the speaker, and the same linguistic expression may be a referring expression sometimes but not at other times. If I say *Janet wants to marry a Norwegian*, and I have in mind a *particular* Norwegian who Janet wants to marry – say, Olaf Thorqvist the Olympic skier – then *a Norwegian* is clearly a referring expression (here a *specific indefinite*). But, if I say the same thing, meaning only that Janet has a curious desire to acquire a Norwegian husband, *any* Norwegian husband, then *a Norwegian* is not a referring expression in this strict sense (it is a *non-specific indefinite*), since I have nobody in mind for the linguistic expression to point at.

There is a further complication with expressions like *the fastest runner in Brazil*. I can use this quite happily without having the faintest idea who that fastest runner in Brazil might be. Here I am merely assuming that the expression must, in principle, pick out someone or other, even though I don't know who. Such an expression is an *attributive expression*, and it is not usually counted as a referring expression.

See also: **deictic category**; **meaning**; **sense**

Further reading: Hofmann 1993; Hurford and Heasley 1983; Saeed 1997.

RELEVANCE

A major determinant of meaningfulness. In **pragmatics**, the British philosopher Paul Grice developed his notion of **conversational implicature** based on the *maxims* of quality, quantity, relevance and manner. The British linguist Deirdre Wilson and the French philosopher Dan Sperber developed *relevance* into a 'super-maxim' in their 1980s *relevance theory*. This holds that the interpretation of an utterance depends on resolving the context of the utterance to produce the optimum level of information with the least processing effort. *Relevance theory* produces a scale of interpretations of an utterance from *strong* relevance to *weak* relevance. The theory is useful for dealing with non-asserted meanings, where interlocutors make inferences about each other's intentions. The assumption of relevance in communicativeness can explain the *implicatures* conveyed when all the Gricean maxims are flouted.

See also: **conversational implicature**; **cooperative principle**; **pragmatics**

Further reading: MacKenzie 2002; Sperber and Wilson 1995.

RHETORIC

Perhaps the oldest branch of linguistic study, the term *rhetoric* has altered its meaning over its 3,000-year old history, but at heart refers to the study of language and its effects. Originally part of the classical Greek education 'trivium' with **grammar** and *dialectic* (reasoning), rhetoric was concerned with the art of persuasion and oratorical authority. Aristotle divided rhetoric into *ethos* (the status and authority of the speaker), *pathos* (his empathetic and emotional disposition) and *logos* (rationality and logical organization of language). Later Roman and Renaissance revisions established the five 'canons' of rhetoric as *inventio* (invention), *memoria* (memory), *pronuntiatio* (delivery), *dispositio* (the organization of ideas) and *elocutio* (style and register). The last of these transforms into **stylistics** in the modern era.

Rhetoric has again become popular as an umbrella term for a socially situated and ideologically aware form of language study. In the USA, it has particularly been used to refer to college composition courses. Elsewhere in the world, it has been used in connection with creative-writing courses which aspire to something more rigorous than impressionistic mutual congratulation.

See also: **stylistics**

Further reading: Sloane 2001.

ROOT

The minimal common form, or **morpheme**, which appears in all the different forms of a single word. In Spanish, the *root* of the verb meaning 'sing' is *cant-*, and this appears in all forms of the verb, such as *canto* 'I sing', *cantábamos* 'we were singing', *cantó* 's/he sang', *cantarás* 'you will sing', *cantarían* 'they would sing', *cantemos* 'we might sing', *cantando* 'singing', and so on. Likewise, in Arabic, the root of the verb meaning 'write' is *ktb*, which appears in all forms of the verb, including derivatives: *katab* 'he wrote', *yiktib* 'he will write', *maktuub* 'written', *kaatib* 'writer', *kitaab* 'book', *kutub* 'books', and so on.

A root must be carefully distinguished from a **stem**, which consists of a root plus some additional material. In English, though, this difference is rarely significant.

See also: **morphology**; **stem**

Further reading: Jackson 2002; Katamba and Stonham 2006.

RULE

A statement expressing a generalization about the facts of a language. Since ancient times, descriptions of languages have featured rules of one sort or another, but, before the rise of modern linguistics, these rules were usually expressed very informally, in ordinary language. Linguists, in contrast, have usually been at pains to state their rules with maximal explicitness; to this end, they have devised various **notational conventions**, which allow rules to be stated in a manner that is at once fully explicit, maximally economical and embedded within a particular theoretical framework. This drive towards explicitness was promoted by the *American structuralists* during the 1940s, but these linguists were more interested in **distribution**, and rules only became fully prominent with the rise of **generative grammar** in the 1950s.

Rules can be stated at every level of linguistic description, from phonology to pragmatics. A rule need not be exceptionless. For example, the rule of English that says that a noun forms its plural by adding <-s> is genuine, and it applies to most new nouns entering the language, but there are some well-known historical or borrowed exceptions, like *feet*, *children* and *radii*.

It is important to realize that rules in linguistics are statements about actual linguistic behaviour. Earlier grammarians, with their devotion to **prescriptivism**, often stated 'rules' which were not rules at all, but only their opinions about what should be considered good usage, such as 'Don't end a sentence with a preposition'. Linguistically unsophisticated people often assume even today that this is what rules are, but such a conception has no place in serious linguistic work, which is embedded firmly within **descriptivism**.

See also: **descriptivism**; **notational convention**; **prescriptivism**

Further reading: Sampson 1975.

SAUSSUREAN PARADOX

How can speakers continue to use a language effectively when that language is constantly changing? The Swiss linguist Ferdinand de Saussure was the first to demonstrate that a language is not just a collection of linguistic objects like speech sounds and words; instead, it is a highly structured system in which each element is largely defined by the way it is related to other elements. This **structuralist** view of language has dominated linguistic thinking ever since. But it immediately leads to a puzzle. We know that every language is constantly changing. So: how can a language continue to be a structured system of speech sounds, words, grammatical forms and sentence structures when all of these are, at any given moment, in the middle of any number of changes currently in progress? This paradox greatly puzzled linguists for generations. Today, though, we are well on the way to resolving it at last. The key insight has come from the study of **variation** in language. Though variation was formerly dismissed as peripheral and insignificant, we now realize that variation in fact forms a large part of the very structure of any language, that speakers make use of that variation just as they make use of other aspects of language structure, and that variation is the vehicle of change, as speakers simply shift the frequencies of competing variant forms over time.

See also: **language change**; **quantitative approach**; **structuralism**; **variation**

Further reading: Milroy 1992; Trask 1996; Weinreich *et al.* 1968.

SCHEMA

A set of knowledge that is idealized from experience. Though the notion of idealized mental knowledge appears in the nineteenth century, it was developed in the 1970s specifically in relation to language problems in *artificial intelligence* research. It became apparent that machine language needed more than a semantic and even pragmatic module in order to be able to pass as natural human language. Giving the computer a restricted 'experience' would provide the rich knowledge set that humans use to 'fill out' the underdeterminacy of language. The classic example is the 'restaurant schema', which explains how people can negotiate and understand objects and utterances even in restaurants that they have never been in previously, on the basis of their idealized mental respresentation.

Various problems with schema theory have led to its adaptation in a range of *world*-based approaches. For example, a schema is not a rich world so it is not clear how far inferencing is valid; it is not really a social world, so it does not explain how interlocutors can communicate with a shared schema; the boundaries of a schema are not well defined, so a 'restaurant schema' might be an 'eating out schema', or it might be a general collection of café schema, pub schema, dinner-party schema, and so on. The ambiguities in schema theory have, however, led to it being used in literary settings in **stylistics**.

See also: **cognitive linguistics; frame; possible worlds theory; stylistics; text world theory**

Further reading: Cook 1994; Schank 1982, 1986; Schank and and Abelson 1977; Stockwell 2003.

SEGMENT

Any one of the discrete units which occur in sequence in speech. In **phonetics**, a segment is a **speech sound**; in **phonology**, it is a **phoneme**. But both levels of analysis recognize that a single word or a longer piece of speech consists of a sequence of discrete units, occurring one after the other. The word *pat*, for example, may be represented at the phonetic level as [pʰæt], and at the phonological level as /pæt/, with a sequence of three segments in either case.

All those aspects of phonology which pertain to segments and their behaviour are collectively known as *segmental* phonology, in contrast to the study of *suprasegmental* phenomena, which must be described with reference to phonological units larger than a single segment.

As a general rule, a given piece of speech will contain the same number of segments at both levels, but there are exceptions. For example, in many American accents, the word *can't* contains four segments at the phonemic level, /kænt/, but only three at the phonetic level, [kʰæ̃t]. Here the phonemic segment /n/ loses its segmental nature at the phonetic level and is realized only as a feature of nasalization occurring on the vowel [æ].

See also: **phoneme; speech sound; suprasegmental**

Further reading: Ball and Rahilly 1999; Catford 1977.

SELECTION RESTRICTION

A restriction on the combining of words in a sentence resulting from their meanings. It is easy to construct apparently grammatical sentences which are senseless because the meanings of the words in those sentences cannot be combined in a comprehensible way: *You have deceived my watermelon*; *The square root of seven is green and squishy*; *She dropped her shyness into the pond with a splash*. The restrictions which are violated here are **selection restrictions**, or **selectional restrictions**. For example, the verb *deceived* here can be regarded as requiring the selectional component [+human] as a direct object, and *watermelon* is [–human].

In the early 1960s, there was an attempt by Noam Chomsky to treat such restrictions as part of the grammar, and hence to regard my examples as ungrammatical, but this idea was quickly dropped as unworkable, and today such restrictions are universally regarded as belonging to **semantics** or (more usually) **pragmatics**. In the semantic view, we regard my examples as impossible to interpret at all; in the pragmatic view, we consider merely that it is difficult or impossible to find a context in which one of these would be a plausible thing to say.

See also: **meaning**; **well-formedness**

Further reading: Allan 1986; Leech 1974; Radford 1988.

SEMANTIC ROLE

Any one of several ways in which a person or thing may be involved in an action or a state of affairs. The notion of *semantic roles* (also called *participant roles* or *deep cases* or *thematic roles* or *theta roles*) is important in many approaches to linguistic description, particularly in those approaches which embrace **functionalism**. The idea is that a given entity which is involved in some event must play some identifiable part in that event. For example, in the sentence *Susie tightened the nut with a spanner*, *Susie* is an Agent (she is the instigator of the action), *the nut* is a Patient (something is happening to it), and *a spanner* is an Instrument (it is being used to accomplish some purpose). In contrast, in *Susie received a letter*, *Susie* is a Recipient (something is arriving at her), while *a letter* is a Theme (nothing is happening to it except that it is being moved).

Analysis of sentences or texts in terms of semantic roles may be illuminating, but analysts often do not agree as to which semantic roles should be recognized, and it is frequently very difficult to assign roles in a principled manner. For example, in *Susie filled the bucket with water*, it is clear that *Susie* is an Agent, but what are *the bucket* and *water?* Location? Goal? Patient? Theme? Instrument? Because of the difficulty of answering such questions, many linguists have preferred to reject semantic roles altogether in constructing their descriptions, but many others are convinced that semantic roles are of fundamental importance in spite of the difficulties.

See also: **semantics**

Further reading: Frawley 1992; Halliday 2004; Hurford and Heasley 1983; Palmer 1994; Radford 1988; Saeed 1997; Thompson 2004.

SEMANTICS

The branch of linguistics which studies **meaning**. The study of meaning has something of a chequered history in linguistics. People have since ancient times been interested in questions of meaning, but very little progress was made before the late nineteenth century, and semantics did not really exist as a distinct field. Around that time, however, the French linguist Michel Bréal, who coined the term *semantics*, made a serious and largely successful attempt to introduce semantics into European linguistic work. And, once the Swiss linguist Ferdinand de Saussure had made the **linguistic sign** the cornerstone of his influential theories, semantics was here to stay in European linguistics.

Oddly, some of the most important work in semantics was being done from the late nineteenth century onwards by philosophers, but it was a long time before linguists became aware of this work and began to join forces with the philosophers.

American linguists were comparatively reluctant to consider semantic questions. The two principal figures in the early twentieth century, Edward Sapir and Leonard Bloomfield, did not entirely neglect the matter, but they had little to say about it, and Bloomfield's successors, the *American structuralists* of the 1940s and 1950s, were so pessimistic about the chances of applying linguistic techniques successfully to the seeming swamp of meaning that they effectively defined linguistics as a field excluding semantics.

In the 1960s, however, shortly after the Chomskyan revolution, a few American linguists began to be interested in semantic questions. They were ignorant of the vast philosophical literature, and their first attempts were fumbling, but before long they had caught up and were beginning to join forces with the philosophers. The work of the American philosopher Richard Montague had an enormous effect upon the linguists, and Montague's ideas have since become the basis of a great deal of important work in linguistic semantics.

One of the most important advances was made gradually during the 1960s, when it was realized that there were two fundamentally different types of linguistic meaning. One type of meaning is intrinsic to the linguistic form containing it, and is always present in that form, while the second type of meaning results from the interaction between the linguistic form of an utterance and the context in which it is uttered. Today we understand semantics as properly the study of the first type, while to the study of the second type we give a new name: **pragmatics** (a term actually coined by the American philosopher C.S. Peirce in the nineteenth century). Failure to make this distinction had earlier proved a severe obstacle to progress.

In recent years approaches to semantics have proliferated, and the subject is now one of the liveliest areas in linguistics. The majority of the current approaches represent versions of *formal semantics*: attempts at elucidating meaning by developing particular versions of *formal logic* that can capture aspects of meaning. Among the most influential threads of investigation have been *truth-conditional semantics*, which attempts to reduce meaning to questions of truth and falsehood, *model-theoretic semantics*, which operates in terms of miniature artificial universes called *models*, and *situation semantics*, which embeds the study of meaning within miniature contexts called *situations*.

Most of the activity just mentioned is concerned with the semantic interpretation of sentences, but the study of word meaning, called *lexical semantics*, has also been extensively developed.

See also: **meaning**; **pragmatics**; **selection restriction**; **sense relation**

Further reading: Cruse 1986; Frawley 1992; Hofmann 1993; Hudson 1995; Hurford and Heasley 1983; Kreidler 1998; Saeed 1997.

SEMIOTICS

The study of the social production of meaning from sign systems. Semiotics, also called semiology, traces its origins to the work of the

Swiss linguist Ferdinand de Saussure in the early twentieth century, and particularly to Saussure's idea of the **linguistic sign**. Nevertheless, semiotics has never been regarded as part of linguistics, and it has been developed almost exclusively by non-linguists, particularly in France, where it is often considered an important discipline. In the English-speaking world, it enjoys almost no institutional recognition.

Though language itself is taken to be the paradigm case of a sign system, in practice most semiotic work has concentrated upon the analysis of such varied domains as advertising, cinema and myths. The influence of the central linguistic concept of **structuralism** (another of Saussure's contributions) has led semioticists to attempt structuralist interpretations of a wide range of phenomena. An object of study, such as a film or a cycle of myths, is viewed as a **text** which communicates meaning, and that meaning is assumed to derive from the orderly interaction of meaning-bearing elements, the *signs*, which themselves are embedded in a structured system, somewhat analogously to the meaning-bearing elements in a language.

In spite of its deliberate emphasis upon the social nature of the sign systems examined, semiotics tends to be highly abstract and at times seemingly impenetrable. In recent years, however, semioticists have increasingly turned to the study of popular culture, and semiotic treatments of soap operas and pop music are now commonplace. Under the new guise of *social semiotics*, the field has joined forces with **critical discourse analysis** and cultural studies to investigate the interactions between visual and verbal in the modern world.

See also: **linguistic sign**; **symbolic system**

Further reading: Cobley 2001; Eco 1976; Leeds-Hurwitz 1993; Sebeok 1984, 1994; Tobin 1990.

SENSE

The central meaning of a linguistic form, regarded from the point of view of the way it relates to other linguistic items. The central meaning of a linguistic form, such as *cat*, can be approached from at least two different points of view. One way is to consider all the things in the world and decide to which ones the form *cat* can reasonably be applied; this approach leads to what we call the **denotation** of *cat*. The other is to compare the meaning of *cat* with the meanings of other linguistic forms, such as *lion* and *dog*, and to decide what semantic characteristics the form *cat* has which allow it to be applied to some things but not to others. This leads to what we call the *sense* of the form.

A very crude interpretation of the sense of *cat* might look something like this: carnivorous mammal, has four legs and a long tail, has fangs and sharp retractable claws, has excellent eyesight even in dim light, ... You can easily see some shortcomings here: Manx cats have no tail, cheetahs cannot retract their claws, and so on. What we are describing here is really a *stereotype* of a cat, a maximally typical (but hypothetical) cat, and a real animal qualifies as a cat if it matches the stereotype sufficiently well, even if not perfectly. (Note: a stereotype is different from a **prototype**. A prototype of a cat would be a single real cat which was regarded as so eminently typical of cats generally that we might like to hold it up as a model of perfect cathood, and cats encountered in real life would be determined as good or bad examples of catness on that basis. But note that not everyone uses the terms *stereotype* and **prototype** in exactly the manner described here.)

In formal versions of semantics, the sense of a linguistic form is often formalized as its **intension** – that is, as the *set* (in the formal mathematical sense) of all the properties which an object must have before the form can be properly applied to it.

Sense is most commonly contrasted with **reference**, but it is essentially just a different way of looking at the same kind of meaning singled out as **denotation** in a different approach.

See also: **denotation**; **prototype**; **reference**; **stereotype**

Further reading: Allan 1986; Hurford and Heasley 1983; Ungerer and Schmid 1996.

SENSE RELATION

Any of several ways in which the meanings of words may be related. Words do not have meanings in isolation; instead, the meaning of a word is usually related in important ways to the meanings of other words. Some of the most prominent of these relations in meaning are known collectively as *sense relations*, and there are several kinds.

In *synonymy*, two words have identical or nearly identical meanings: *cat* and *feline*, *pail* and *bucket*, *violin* and *fiddle*, *fruitful* and *productive*. Such pairs of *synonyms* are not always completely interchangeable: the words may differ in degree of formality, as with *felon* and *crook*, or they may differ in their **connotations** (associations), as with *rabbit* and *bunny*. However, if both words can be applied in principle to exactly the same things, they are *cognitively synonymous*.

In *antonymy*, two words have opposite meanings. Some pairs of *antonyms* are **gradable antonyms**, representing extremes along a continuum, as with *hot* and *cold* or *big* and *small*. Other pairs are **binary antonyms**, which are mutually exclusive and which between them exhaust the possibilities, as with *alive* and *dead*.

Somewhat different are **converse pairs**, such as *wife* and *husband* or *above* and *below*: if I am your husband, then you are my wife; if the table is below the clock, then the clock is above the table.

In *meronymy*, one word denotes a part of another. For example, *hand* is a meronym of *arm*, and both words are meronyms of *body*.

In *hyponymy*, one word denotes a special case of what is denoted by the other. For example, *spaniel* is a **hyponym** of *dog*, which in turn is a hyponym of *animal*, while *dog* is a **superordinate** of *spaniel*. In *plesionymy*, a word which is a rough approximation or specification of another word can be stated along with it: *it's not raining, more drizzling*; *my father is a shopkeeper, a greengrocer*.

Words which relate semantically in appropriate ways (*little girl, children play football*) are **philonyms**; words which clash semantically (*the trees looked on*; *mean streets*) are **xenonyms**.

In all cases, rhetorical effects are generated where one item is selected in place of another similar sense relation: insult (*That woman is a mammal*), metaphor (*I poured myself home*), formality (*He composed an epistle*), euphemism (*Washington ordered the bombing*), and so on.

See also: **meaning**; **semantics**

Further reading: Cruse 1986; Hurford and Heasley 1983.

SENTENCE

The largest purely grammatical unit in a language. Of course, there are larger linguistic units than sentences: individual paragraphs (in writing), individual turns (in conversation) and individual discourses. But these larger units are no more than very weakly linked by purely grammatical means. The largest linguistic unit which is held together by rigid grammatical rules is the *sentence*. We need to clarify this term a little, since it is frequently misunderstood. For most linguists, in most circumstances, a sentence is an abstract linguistic object: specifically, it is a linguistic object put together entirely in accordance with the rules for constructing sentences in a language, rules which have to be identified (in a linguistic description) by patient and painstaking investigation. More particularly, a sentence does not have to be something which somebody might reasonably say, and not everything that we might reasonably say is a sentence.

Consider this exchange. *Mike*: *Where's Susie? Alice*: *In the library.* Here Mike's utterance represents a sentence, but Alice's response does not: even though it is a perfectly normal and unremarkable thing to say, *In the library* is not a sentence of English (the asterisk indicates this fact), because it is not constructed according to the rules for making English sentences. Instead, it is only a *fragment* of a sentence: we do not always speak in complete sentences, and we very often use fragments like this one.

Now consider Noam Chomsky's famous example sentence: *Colourless green ideas sleep furiously.* Chomsky's point is that, even though this thing makes no sense at all, it is constructed in accordance with all the rules for making sentences in English, and hence it is a grammatical (well-formed) sentence of English.

A further point is that a sentence is not just a string of words; rather, it is a string of words with a grammatical (syntactic) structure assigned to it. Consequently, an ambiguous string of words like *Visiting relatives can be a nuisance* or *I saw her duck* represents two (or more) quite different sentences, each with its own structure. We often take advantage of this possibility of assigning different structures to identical or similar strings of words for humorous effect, as in the old gag *Time flies like an arrow; fruit flies like a banana* and in the punchline of a certain cat-food commercial: *Cats like Felix like Felix.* **Pragmatics** makes the useful distinction between the abstract sentence and the actual spoken or written **utterance**.

See also: **ambiguity**; **clause**; **syntax**; **utterance**; **well-formedness**

Further reading: Brown and Miller 1991; Lyons 1968; Matthews 1981.

SEX DIFFERENCES IN LANGUAGE

Differences between the speech of men and women. In some languages, there are very conspicuous differences between men's and women's speech: men and women may use different words for the same thing, they may use different grammatical endings, they may even use different sets of consonants and vowels in their pronunciation.

English has nothing quite so dramatic as this, but several decades of research have turned up some interesting differences even in English – though not all of the early claims have been substantiated by later work. For example, it has been suggested that women use more *tag questions* than men – as in *It's nice, isn't it?* – as if to seek approval for their opinions, but this has not been borne out by investigation. It has also been suggested that men swear more than women, but this too appears not to be so, at least among younger speakers.

On the other hand, it does appear to be true that certain words are more typical of women, including terms of approval like *cute*, *divine* and *adorable* and specific colour terms like *beige*, *burgundy* and *ecru*. Women have also been observed providing more back-channel (*hmm*, *yeah*, *ah-ha*), asking more questions, inviting approval and agreement, and generally being more socially supportive in conversation than men. The British sociolinguist Jennifer Coates and the American sociolinguist Deborah Tannen have discovered that men and women organize their conversations very differently. Men tend to be rather competitive; women engage in highly cooperative conversations. Men engage in floor-holding; women *latch* on to topics, completing the speaker's turn, or interject approval or disagreement. That is, a conversation among women is a collaborative enterprise, with all the women pulling together to construct a satisfactory discourse which is the product of all of them, while a conversation among men is rather a sequence of individual efforts.

These differences can lead to serious misunderstanding in mixed conversations. While her husband or boyfriend is speaking, a woman may constantly contribute supporting remarks in the normal female fashion, but the man may well interpret these remarks as interruptions (which they are not) and become very annoyed. In fact, it is quite clear that, in mixed conversations, men interrupt women far more than the reverse.

It is clear that such differences in behaviour are indexes not directly of **gender** but of **power**. Men in subservient job situations and women in powerful settings have been observed using the power-marked pattern of discourse, regardless of gender.

See also: **gender**; **power**; **turn-taking**

Further reading: Cameron and Kulick 2003; Coates 1996, 1998, 2004; Connell 1995; Holmes 1992; Holmes and Meyerhoff 2003; Romaine 1994; Tannen 1991.

SEXIST LANGUAGE

Language which, deliberately or unconsciously, is patronizing or contemptuous towards one sex, usually women. Sexism, of course, is not specifically a linguistic issue, but it shows up in languages in various ways, some of them rather deeply embedded. Almost without exception, sexist usages are patronizing of women. Here are a few examples.

As is well known, English has only the sex-marked singular pronouns *he* and *she*, and hence a speaker addressing or talking about a mixed group has a problem: *Somebody has forgotten his umbrella* is sexist, while *Somebody has forgotten his or her umbrella* is almost unbearably clumsy. In this case, popular speech usually solves the problem by using *their*: *Somebody has forgotten their umbrella*. But some people find this distasteful, and it doesn't really work very well in cases like *Any student who considers themself adequately prepared is requested to present themself for their oral examination.*

Many pairs of sex-marked words have developed very differently. A *master* is a powerful or skilful man; a *mistress* is a woman kept for sexual purposes. A *courtier* is a polished man of high social status; a *courtesan* is just an upmarket whore. There is nothing wrong with calling a man a *bachelor*, but calling a woman a *spinster* is contemptuous. Even a single word may behave differently: in American English, at least, when you call a man a *pro*, you mean that he is experienced, competent and reliable; when you call a woman a *pro*, you mean she's a prostitute.

The female suffixes *-ess, -ette, -ienne, -ine, -ix,* and *-euse* cause particular problems: consider the sense of diminutiveness or secondariness in *actress, poetess, jewess, authoress, sculptress, stewardess, waitress, governess, comedienne, heroine, masseuse, usherette, brunette, aviatrix* and the marked forms for *confidante, blonde, divorcee* and *starlet*. But there are many other such cases. Men play *golf* and *tennis,* while women play *women's golf* and (worse) *ladies' tennis.* Many people still qualify professional names with *lady doctor, female professor* or *male nurse.* Among the most blatant examples of all are the following, both genuine: *The assailant attacked his next-door neighbour's wife* (the woman was not his neighbour?); *The pioneers trekked across the prairies with their cattle, their seed-corn and their wives* (the wives were only there to cook, clean, sew and raise the children while their husbands were busy pioneering?). Many of these forms are beginning to pass into archaism, but they can still be found.

Once rarely remarked on, sexist language has been drawing the fire of feminists for several decades now, and a number of linguists have turned their attention to the issue. Attempts at stamping out sexist usages have enjoyed some success, and terms like *fireman, postman* and *chairman* are now commonly replaced by *firefighter, letter carrier* and *chairperson* (or simply *chair*); similarly, the use of *man* or *men* to denote human beings in general is slowly giving way to *human beings* or *humans.* Here is a rare example of **prescriptivism** being used for a socially useful purpose. However, other prescriptions such as *mistress copy* (for the *master copy* of a document), and attempts to avoid *manhole* and *man-eating tiger* have been more questionable and less successful.

See also: **language planning**

Further reading: Cameron and Kulick 2003; Coates 2004; Hofstadter 1985.

SIGN LANGUAGE

A language whose medium is signs made with the hands and head. **Speech** is the most familiar medium of language, but it is not the only one possible. Deaf people cannot hear speech, and many deaf people learn and use a *sign language* as their primary language, often as their first language. Many different sign languages exist, including *British Sign Language* (BSL) in the UK and *American Sign Language* (ASL) in the USA; these two are not related to each other, and neither is related in any way to English.

A true sign language is not a crude approximation to a spoken language; it is a genuine natural language with a large vocabulary and a rich and complex grammar, and it is every bit as flexible and expressive as a spoken language. The basic units are *signs* made chiefly with the hands and the head; in ASL and BSL, these signs can be modified in various ways to express shades of meaning like 'many', 'often', 'slightly', 'quickly', 'very' and 'repeatedly', notions which would require separate words in English. An example: in ASL, touching the middle finger to the forehead means 'be sick'; by modifying the distance, direction, and speed of movement, and the number of touches, the signer can explicitly express (at least) any of 'get sick', 'get sick easily', 'often sick', 'never stops being sick', 'sickly', 'slightly sick', 'very sick', and 'sick for a long time'. Indeed, it has been remarked that the grammars of ASL and BSL are more similar to the grammars of certain Native American languages, such as Hopi, than to the grammar of English.

Just like **creoles**, sign languages emerge spontaneously whenever deaf children are brought together. A recent example is Nicaraguan Sign Language, created and used by the deaf children who were brought together to receive an education after the Nicaraguan revolution of 1979. ASL and BSL, in fact, were deliberately invented by hearing people in the nineteenth century, but the modern versions are vastly more elaborate than the original ones, as native signers have expanded the vocabulary and elaborated the grammar to meet their needs. And, just like spoken languages, sign languages change over time: already ASL is showing evidence of developing regional dialects.

So strong is the **language instinct** that a deaf child will eagerly begin babbling with its hands, and it will seize upon any gestures it sees and do its best to turn them into a sign language, even without reinforcement; such a system is called *home sign*.

Linguists were at first slow to appreciate that sign languages were true languages, but, since the pioneering work of the American linguist Ursula Bellugi in the 1970s, sign languages have come to be treated on a par with spoken languages, though most introductory textbooks of linguistics provide regrettably little coverage of the topic.

See also: **language**; **language instinct**; **natural-language processing**

Further reading: Deuchar 1984; Klima and Bellugi 1979; Miles 1988; Morgan and Woll 2002; Padden 1988; Smith 1990; Steinberg 1993; Valli and Lucas 2001.

SLANG

Informal and often ephemeral linguistic forms. We all use our language in different ways, depending on the circumstances. Most obviously, we speak differently in formal contexts and in informal contexts. Especially when speaking informally, we often take pleasure in resorting to *slang*: informal but colourful words and expressions.

Slang expressions are usually introduced by the members of a particular social group; they may remain the property of that group and serve as a badge of group identity, or they may instead become much more widely known and used. The majority of slang forms are transient: they are used for a few months or a few years, and then they pass out of use, to be replaced by even newer slang terms.

Just in the past fifty years in English, something really excellent has been described at times, by certain groups of speakers at least, as *groovy, fab, brill, tremendous, wicked, ace, spiffing, smart, outstanding, cool, far out, awesome, sweet, triff, def,* and countless other terms. One or two of these are perhaps still in use, but the rest are already quaint anachronisms. We have variously said of a man who is drunk that he is *loaded, soused, fried, pickled, sozzled, pissed, blitzed, bombed, smashed* or *tired and emotional,* or that he *has had a skinful* or is *three sheets to the wind.* Slang terms tend to be **over-lexicalized** areas of life which are or have been taboo: sex, death, excrement, drunkenness and intoxication, racism, sexism, homophobia and so on.

An unusual case of a long-lived slang term is *booze* for alcoholic drinks; this has been in the language for centuries, but it is still used, and it is still regarded as slang. On occasion, a slang term may lose its slang status altogether; this has happened with *mob*, an old slang word (short for *mobile*) which is now unquestionably standard English. Slang is often playful and creative, and its presence is evidence of the vitality of a language.

See also: **prescriptivism**; **vernacular**

Further reading: Crystal 1995; Partridge 1970, 2002.

SOCIAL HISTORY OF LANGUAGE

The study of the history of language as a social institution. Traditionally, **historical linguistics**, and in particular the study of **language change**, has focused upon internal structural changes: changes in pronunciation, grammar and vocabulary. In the 1960s, however, linguists began to turn their attention to the social context of language change, to the ways in which changes are introduced and propagated by speakers, and to the social forces accompanying these changes, and this type of investigation has proved very illuminating. More recently still, a few scholars have begun to turn their attention to broader issues in the history of language. Among these issues are the choice between languages or language varieties in particular communities at particular times, the social pressures associated with these choices, the rules governing conversation among various social groups in the past, the connections between language and both individual and national identity, and the reasons for changes in all these things over time. To this new discipline we give the name *social history of language.*

The social history of language is perhaps more obviously a branch of social history than of linguistics, but it complements the more familiar concerns of linguists by providing an overview of the circumstances in which particular languages were used in particular communities at various times in the past. Socially situated and ideological explanations for language change are often persuasive.

See also: **language planning**

Further reading: Burke 1993; Crowley 1989, 1996; Crowley 1997; Fennell 2000; Honey 1997; Leith 1997; Lodge 1993; McCrum *et al.* 1992.

SOCIAL NETWORK

A means of measuring the degree of linguistic influence exerted at a local level on and by individuals. A social network can be 'scored' on the basis of how many people are intimately connected within it (its *density*) and on the extent to which the connections between people are not one-dimensional – so, for example, people are related as friends, neighbours, colleagues, football team-mates, churchgoers, and so on (the *multiplexity* of the network). In a **sociolinguistic** study in Belfast, Northern Ireland, the linguist Lesley Milroy discovered that a dense and multiplex social network operated as a strong linguistic norm reinforcement mechanism. Accent features (and innovations) within strong social networks were maintained and diffused through the wider community.

See also: **language change**; **prestige**; **sociolinguistics**; **speech community**

Further reading: Milroy 1987a; Llamas *et al.* 2007.

SOCIAL STRATIFICATION OF LANGUAGE

Marked differences in the speech of people belonging to different social classes in a community. In most communities of any size, there are conspicuous differences in the social status of people, and these social classes are usually hierarchically ordered in overt **prestige**, from highest to lowest.

It has long been realized that members of different social classes tend to speak differently, but it is only since the 1960s that sociolinguists, such as the American William Labov and the Briton Peter Trudgill, have begun to undertake systematic studies of these differences. Such studies often reveal a great deal of information about the differing linguistic behaviour of the several social classes. For example, in London, *t*-glottaling (the pronunciation of the /t/ in words like *water* as a glottal stop) is maximally prominent amongst lower working-class speakers, less prominent among middle-working-class speakers, still less prominent among upper-working-class speakers, and virtually absent amongst middle-class speakers of all types. On the other hand, the *respectively* construction, as in *Esther and Larry drank whisky and brandy, respectively*, is maximally prominent among higher-class speakers but absent altogether in working-class speech.

These are examples of the *social stratification of language*: a steady rise or fall in the frequency of particular linguistic forms as we move through the social classes. And note that word 'frequency': only sometimes is a particular form either categorically present or totally absent in the speech of a particular class. Very often, it is present in the speech of all or nearly all classes, but it differs in frequency, and 'correct' behaviour for a member of a class involves getting the frequency right: using a form too frequently or too rarely will make an individual's speech sound anomalous to the other members of his or her class.

See also: **sociolinguistics**; **variation**

Further reading: Labov 1972; Trudgill 1995; Llamas *et al.* 2007.

SOCIOLINGUISTICS

The branch of linguistics which studies the relation between language and society. Though the social aspect of language attracted early attention, notably from the great Swiss linguist Ferdinand de Saussure at the beginning of the twentieth century, it was perhaps only in the 1950s that serious investigation began. Pioneers like Uriel Weinreich, Charles Ferguson and Joshua Fishman drew attention to a range of fascinating phenomena, such as **diglossia** and the effects of **language contact**. But the key figure here is arguably the American William Labov, who in the 1960s began a series of investigations of **variation** in language, investigations which have revolutionized our understanding of how speakers use their languages and which have finally resolved the **Saussurean paradox**.

Sociolinguistics may be usefully defined as the study of variation in language, or more precisely of variation within speech communities, since the purely geographical aspects of variation had been studies for generations by the students of *dialect geography* and *dialectology*, the study of regional **dialects**. In a speech community of any size, there is considerable variation among individuals: stockbrokers do not speak like plumbers, women do not speak like men, young people do not speak like old people, and so on. Moreover, even a single individual is not confined to a single variety of the language: you do not use the language in the same way when you are chatting to friends in a bar, when you are being interviewed for a job, when you are writing an essay, and when you are being introduced to royalty. Earlier linguists had, of course, noticed this variation, but they were inclined to dismiss it as peripheral, as inconsequential, even as a nuisance getting in the way of good descriptions. Today, however, we recognize that variation is an integral and essential part of language, and that absence of variation is almost pathological.

Sociolinguistics in the USA is strongly focused on language variation and change; elsewhere in the world, other matters that shade into **pragmatics** and the sociology of language are also regarded as part of the discipline.

See also: **sex differences in language**; **social stratification of language**; **variation**

Further reading: Bratt-Paulston and Tucker 2003; Cameron and Kulick 2003; Chambers 2003; Chambers and Trudgill 1998; Chambers *et al.* 2002; Coulmas 2005; Eckert and Rickford 2001; Fennell 2000; Harris 2006; Holmes 1992; Hudson 1996; Llamas *et al.* 2007; Milroy and Gordon 2003; Romaine 1994; Stockwell 2002a; Trudgill 1995; Wardhaugh 2005.

SOUND SYMBOLISM

An attempt at constructing a word whose sound directly conveys (some aspect of) its meaning. The most familiar type of sound symbolism is *onomatopoeia*, in which the meaning of a word is a real-world sound and the form of the word attempts to mimic the sound. Examples: *bang, boom, murmur, hiss, quack, meow, clink, ding-dong, thud*. But other types exist.

English has a group of words with initial /sl-/, all with meanings in the general area of 'slippery, slimy, gooey': *slurp, slip, slide, slink, slush, slop, slosh, sludge, slurry, slime, slug* (the creature), *slaver*, and so on. The sequence /sl-/ in these cases is a *phonaestheme*, and this kind of sound symbolism is *phonaesthesia*.

Yet another type of sound symbolism is represented by two Basque words for 'butterfly', *tximeleta* and *pinpilinpauxa* (<tx> = English <ch> , <x> = English <sh>). Here the fluttery sound of the words seems designed to mimic the fluttery appearance of the creature.

One more rather frequent type is represented by the *ideophones* of many languages, which attempt to mimic types of motion. Examples from the Carib language Apalai: *seky seky* 'creep up', *ty ty ty* 'person walking', *wywywywy* 'hammock swinging', *ururururo* 'trees falling', *tutututu* 'fast approach', and so on.

Sound symbolism constitutes a partial exception to the more usual **arbitrariness** of linguistic forms.

See also: **arbitrariness**; **iconicity**

Further reading: Crystal 1988, 1995, 1997; Palmer 1996.

SPEECH

Spoken language, either in general or in particular instances. The term *speech* is used in linguistics in three rather different ways, which sometimes need to be distinguished.

First, speech is a **medium** for language; in this sense, the term contrasts with **writing** and with **sign language**.

Second, speech is the overall linguistic behaviour of people who speak, including any patterns visible in that behaviour. This is the sense of the term in compound terms like **speech community** and **speech act**.

Third, speech is the real utterances produced by real people on real occasions. This is the sense of the term in *speech error*, and it is exactly equivalent to the terms **parole** and **performance**.

See also: **medium; performance**

Further reading: Biber 2006; Knowles 1987; Shockey 2003.

SPEECH ACT

An attempt at doing something purely by speaking. There are very many things that we can do, or attempt to do, simply by speaking. We can make a promise, ask a question, order or request somebody to do something, make a threat, name a ship, pronounce somebody husband and wife, and so on. Each one of these is a particular *speech act*.

In the majority of cases, it makes no sense to ask whether an utterance constituting a speech act is true or false. Utterances like *Clean up your room!; Can you lend me a pen?*; *I promise to buy you a teddy bear*; and *I dub thee knight, Sir Clarence* have no truth value, but they may be more or less appropriate to the circumstances, or, as we say, more or less *felicitous*. An utterance like *Clean up your room!* is infelicitous if I have no authority over you, and *I now pronounce you husband and wife* fails unless a number of obvious conditions are met. The conditions required for a speech act to be successful are accordingly often called *felicity conditions*.

Speech acts belong to the domain of **pragmatics**, and their study, called *speech-act theory*, is a prominent part of that discipline. The study of speech acts was introduced by the British philosopher J.L. Austin in the 1960s, and it has been developed by a number of others, notably the philosopher John Searle. Austin originally distinguished three aspects of a speech act: the *locutionary act* (the act of saying something and its basic content), the *illocutionary act* (what you're trying to do by speaking), and the *perlocutionary act* (the effect of what you say). Today, however, the term speech act is often used to denote specifically an illocutionary act (promising, threatening, informing, persuading, defending, blaming, and so on), and the intended effect of a speech act is its *illocutionary force*.

See also: **performative; pragmatics**

Further reading: Grundy 1995; Levinson 1983; Mey 1993; Saeed 1997; Schiffrin 1994; Thomas 1995; Verschueren 1999; Yule 1996.

SPEECH COMMUNITY

A group of people who regularly interact by speaking. A speech community may be large or small, and it may be highly homogeneous or decidedly heterogeneous. What matters is that everybody in it should regularly speak to at least some of the other people in it, and that the community should not be broken up by sharp boundaries across which speaking rarely or never takes place.

Not infrequently, an individual may belong to several speech communities of different sizes. For example, a rural American in the Midwest belongs to a small local community with whom he interacts intensely, a much larger surrounding community with whose members he interacts less frequently, and, less centrally, to the entire community of English-speakers in the world. In the majority of cases, though, when we speak of a speech community, we have a smaller community in mind, not a larger one.

It is not necessary for everybody in a community to speak the same variety of a language. For example, London and New York include English-speakers speaking a striking range of different varieties of English. And it is not even necessary for everybody in the community to speak the same language at all. For example, Singapore has large numbers of native speakers of Malay, Cantonese, Tamil and English; few people can speak all four, but almost everybody can speak at least two, and Singapore does not consist of several isolated communities having little to do with one another.

See also: **bilingualism**; **community of practice**; **diglossia**; **social network**; **social stratification of language**

Further reading: Chambers 2003; Edwards 1994; Holmes 1992; Llamas *et al.* 2007.

SPEECH EVENT

A significant piece of speaking conducted according to rules. All **speech** possesses structure of some kind, but there are certain pieces of speaking which are rather special. Each one has a recognizable beginning and end and is constructed according to certain rules known to both speakers and listeners. Examples include a university lecture, a sermon, an after-dinner speech, a debate and a job interview. Such a highly structured piece of speech is a *speech event*.

A speech event involves *participants* who assume clearly defined *roles*, and it takes place in a well-defined *setting*. The *rules* governing the event are clearly defined and known to all participants; violating these rules is a serious lapse. Naturally, linguists are often interested in identifying the rules governing particular sorts of speech events.

(Note: a few people apply the term speech event more broadly, to include ordinary conversations, brief exchanges and even *speech situations* [such as cocktail parties], but these extended usages are not usual in linguistics.)

See also: **discourse**

Further reading: Duranti 1997.

SPEECH SOUND

One of the individual sounds produced in sequence during speech. When we speak, the several speech organs are all in constant motion: the lips, the jaw, the velum, the glottis and the several parts of the tongue are all moving about at their own pace, with only the occasional moment of motionlessness. Nevertheless, we hear the result as a linear sequence of individual sounds, each following the last, and each having its own distinguishing characteristics. Each one of these perceived sounds is a *speech sound*.

For example, a typical pronunciation of the English word *cleaned* can be represented in phonetic **transcription**, with an absolute minimum of phonetic detail, as [klind]. Here the transcription shows that we hear this word as a sequence of five speech sounds, namely [k], [l], [i], [n] and [d]. In purely phonetic terms, this is an oversimplification: the voicelessness of the [k] is extended into the [l], the nasality of the [n] begins during the [i], and there are many other phonetic details not represented in this very simple transcription – and yet what we hear is something reasonably represented as [klind].

It is important to realize this perceptual nature of speech sounds. For example, a typical American pronunciation of *can't* differs from *cat* only in that the first has a nasalized vowel: [kãt] versus [kæt]. Yet American speakers perceive the first as consisting of four speech sounds, [kænt], but the second as only three, [kæt]. Speakers hear the speech sounds that are 'supposed' to be there, rather than objective physical reality.

Speech sounds are classified into two types: **consonants**, which involve a significant obstruction to the flow of air, and **vowels**, which don't.

See also: **consonant**; **phoneme**; **segment**; **vowel**

Further reading: Ashby 1995; Ball and Rahilly 1999; Ladefoged 1993; Ladefoged and Maddieson 1996.

SPEECH THERAPY

Also called *language pathology*, this is the application of linguistic knowledge to assist speakers with speech disabilities. These can range from the major **aphasic** effects of brain trauma such as strokes and physical features such as cleft palates, to temporary disfluencies such as *stammering* (*stuttering* in the USA), *lisping* and others. Many of these are features of child language acquisition, and much progress can often be made without surgical or physical intervention by the application of training techniques both for the sufferer and parents or carers. For example, about 5 per cent of children under five years of age experience some significant disfluency, often related to periods of rapid language-acquisition progress. This can present itself as repetition of initial syllables, repetition of single words – especially connectors (*but*, *and*, *so*) – or 'blocks' like an unreleased phonetic *stop*. Most children develop fluency again without any intervention, but typical ways of treating stammering include: paying attention to the child; slowing the pace of life down, including speed of language; avoiding over-complicated syntax or vocabulary; and encouraging rather than focusing on the problem.

See also: **aphasia**; **applied linguistics**

Further reading: Fabbro and Asher 1999.

SPELLING

A conventional way of writing the words of a language using an alphabetic writing system. Most languages are not normally written at all, and a few more, like Chinese and Japanese, are usually written in non-alphabetic writing systems. The rest of the world's languages are regularly written using some alphabet or other (there are dozens in use), and, in each language, its conventional system for representing particular words in writing is its *spelling* system.

In a particular type of ideal spelling system, called *phonemic spelling* (or, informally but inaccurately, 'phonetic spelling'), each single **phoneme** is always spelled in the same way, and different phonemes are always spelled differently. Most spelling systems do not approach this ideal, though a few, such as the Finnish and Italian systems, come moderately close.

The reasons for departing from this ideal are numerous, important and often intractable. The notoriously messy and irregular spelling of English illustrates all of them.

First, once a spelling is established, it becomes part of ordinary education, and speakers are reluctant to change it, even when the pronunciation of the language changes, as it frequently does. This is the reason for such odd spellings as *knee, night, of, write, steak, iron, sugar* and *lamb*: once they represented the pronunciation perfectly, but the pronunciations of these words have changed substantially, while the spellings have not been changed.

Second, it is convenient to use similar spellings for related words even when those words are pronounced very differently. If we spelled *photograph* and *photography* just as we pronounce them, the obvious relation between them would no longer be visible.

Third, when words are taken from foreign languages, it seems natural to people who know those languages to retain the foreign spelling, even when this doesn't match the English pronunciation. This is the reason for spellings like *machine, Zeitgeist, concerto, lasagne* and *chic*, and, with complications, for *photograph, xylophone* and *psychology*.

Fourth, spellings are sometimes contaminated by the spellings of other words. So, for example, *isle* is taken from Old French and retains its Old French spelling, while the native English word *island*, which was formerly spelled *iland*, has acquired its *s* by contamination (and so has *aisle*).

Fifth, and most importantly, we do not all pronounce our words in the same way. So, for example, some people pronounce *caught* and *court* identically, while others pronounce them very differently, and so what would be a perfect spelling system for one group would be hopeless for the other – and the same is true of *caught* and *cot*, *horse* and *hoarse*, *pull* and *pool*, *marry* and *merry* (and also *Mary*), *dew* and *do*, *poor* and *pour*, *father* and *farther*, and countless other such pairs. On top of this, many individual words are pronounced in very different ways by different people: *either*, *economics*, *tomato*, *grass*, *suggest*, *library*, *sterile*, *contribute* and many, many others. There are, in fact, many advantages in having a spelling system that does not privilege a single accent; this, and natural conservative inertia, has defeated just about every attempt at **prescriptivist** spelling reform ever proposed, at least for English.

See also: **orthography**; **writing system**

Further reading: Coulmas 1996; Crystal 1997; Robinson 1995; Sampson 1985.

STANDARD LANGUAGE

That variety of a language considered by its speakers to be most appropriate in formal and educational contexts. Consider the case of English. English is spoken as a mother tongue by some 400 million people, as an everyday second language by tens of millions more, and as a fluent foreign language by further millions. Many of these people also write in English.

The English used by all these people is far from uniform: there are both regional differences and differences among social groups within a single community, and today sociolinguists often speak of *Englishes* to denote this whole range of varieties. But one of these varieties has a very special status: this is the variety called *standard English*.

Standard English is the form of English acquired through education; indeed, acquisition of standard English is a large part of what we understand as education in the English-speaking world. Most broadcasting, and almost all publication, is couched in standard English.

Standard English may be spoken in any of a large range of regional **accents**; no particular accent is associated with standard English, though in particular countries there are some accents often regarded as more appropriate to standard English than others. And standard English itself is not quite uniform: for example, there are detectable differences in vocabulary and grammar between standard American and standard British English, though these are not large. Further, of course, standard English is not immutable: it changes from generation to generation, and the standard English of the eighteenth century already sounds quaint and distant to us. Finally, standard spoken English is not always identical to standard written English: we write *Many students are ill*, but we don't say this; instead, we say *Lots of students are ill*.

No such thing as standard English existed 500 years ago; instead, there were only innumerable regional and social varieties. But, since then, a range of social and political pressures have combined to give rise to a single variety of English accepted as the standard everywhere.

Standard English arose largely out of a series of countless historical accidents: certain words, forms and usages happened to be accepted by educated people in positions of prestige, while others were not accepted. The single most important factor was the political, economic and cultural influence of the city of London and the surrounding region: it was largely the forms used in this area that became the basis of standard English.

In recent years, there has been a vigorous and surprising debate among academics and educators about the place of standard English in education: one group sees a command of standard English as an enormous benefit and as the right of every pupil; the other sees standard English as the elitist possession of a privileged class and interprets attempts at teaching standard English, together with the associated dismissal of non-standard forms of English, as hostile attempts at oppressing working-class speakers and denying them power.

Almost every other language which is used in education likewise has a recognized standard form: French, German, Finnish, Basque, Arabic, and so on. A few languages even have *two* standard forms: Norway recognizes two standard forms of Norwegian, and the standard Mandarin Chinese of Taiwan is somewhat different from that of China. For many years the Dutch-speakers of Belgium attempted to maintain a different standard form of Dutch from that used in the Netherlands, but they have now abandoned this policy.

See also: **Black English**; **dialect**; **national language**; **official language**; **vernacular**

273

Further reading: Bex and Watts 1999; Blake 1996; Crystal 1995; Holmes 1992; Honey 1997; Leith 1997; Milroy and Milroy 1993, 1997.

STEM

A linguistic form which cannot stand alone but which serves as a basis for constructing word-forms which can stand alone. In a number of European languages, the grammatical forms of a single word are constructed in a very orderly way; this is particularly noticeable with verbs.

Consider Spanish. The simplest possible form of a Spanish verb is its **root**, a form which cannot stand alone but which is always present in every form of that verb. In order to construct a verb-form, we must first add one of several possible suffixes to the root; the result, which still cannot stand alone, is one of the several *stems* of that verb. Finally, to the stem is added one of several possible *endings*, to produce a complete verb-form.

The root of the verb meaning 'sing' is *cant-*. To this we can add any of several tense or mood suffixes. The present-tense suffix happens to be *-a-*, and so the present stem is *canta-*. To this we can add any of several endings to get forms like *canta* 's/he sings' with a zero-suffix, *cantamos* 'we sing' and *cantan* 'they sing'. For the imperfect, the suffix is *-aba-*, and so the imperfect stem is *cantaba-*, leading to such forms as *cantaba* 's/he was singing', *cantábamos* 'we were singing' and *cantaban* 'they were singing'. The future suffix is *-ar-*, and so the future stem is *cantar-*, producing *cantará* 's/he will sing', *cantaremos* 'we will sing' and *cantarán* 'they will sing'. Likewise, the conditional suffix *-arí-* leads to a stem *cantarí-* and forms like *cantaría* 's/he would sing', *cantaríamos* 'we would sing' and *cantarían* 'they would sing', and present subjunctive *-e-* yields forms like *cante* 's/he might sing', *cantemos* 'we might sing' and *canten* 'they might sing'.

Not all languages exhibit this kind of structure (English doesn't), but, for those that do, recognizing roots and stems provides an elegant account of much of their **morphology**.

See also: **morphology**; **root**

Further reading: Bauer 1988; Katamba and Stonham 2006; Matthews 1991.

STEREOTYPE

In **sociolinguistics**, a *stereotype* is a linguistic feature which speakers are so aware of as a distinctive feature that it has taken on an iconic status for them. In other words, it is a **marker** which is highly salient for the speech community as a sign of identity. Stereotypes often have the appearance of caricatures and are in fact often historically outdated features which a speech community has not in fact used for a while.

In **grammar**, a stereotype is a sequence of words which appears to be made up of separate lexemes but in fact is treated as a *formulaic sequence*. As such, it is unproductive of further variation. Proverbs, quotations, aphorisms and other idioms might be seen as stereotypes in this sense.

See also: **indicator**; **marker**

Further reading: Chambers 2003; Llamas *et al.* 2007.

STIMULUS-FREEDOM

Our ability to say anything at all, including nothing, in any situation. The signals used by non-human species are overwhelmingly *stimulus-bound*: each signal is produced always and only when a particular stimulus is received. For example, a vervet monkey always gives an eagle warning call upon spotting an eagle, and it never does this at any other time.

Human language is utterly different. Save only for our (non-linguistic) cries of pain and fear, we are perfectly free to choose what we are going to say in every context. In other words, our speech is *stimulus-free*. If your friend Julia asks *What do you think of my new skirt?*, you may reply *It's too short*, or *It doesn't go with your pink blouse*, or even *If that doesn't get Mike's attention, nothing will*. You can even decline to answer, and change the subject. Of course, there are all sorts of social pressures that make some replies more likely than others. If you value Julia's friendship, you probably won't reply *God, Julia – with your fat legs, you should stick to kaftans*. But there's nothing about English that prevents you from saying this, and you could say it, if you wanted to.

275

Though he was not the first to notice it, the American linguist Charles Hockett drew particular attention to stimulus-freedom in 1960.

See also: **design features**; **displacement**; **open-endedness**

Further reading: Trask 1995.

STRESS

Strong prominence on a particular syllable. In English, almost every word has at least one syllable which is noticeably more prominent than the other syllables; this is the *stressed* syllable, and the position of the stress is usually easy to identify. All of us agree without hesitation that the stress falls upon the first syllable of *victim* and *terrify*, on the second syllable of *linguistics* and *invention*, on the third syllable of *kangaroo* and *circulation*, and on the only syllable of *cat* and *smile*. There is some variation among speakers: some people stress the first syllable of *exquisite, controversy, harass* and *vagaries*, while others stress the second.

A word of several syllables often has, in addition to its **main stress** (or **primary stress**), a **secondary stress** (a lesser degree of stress) on another syllable. For example, *education* has its main stress on the third syllable but a secondary stress on the first syllable. Even short words may bear secondary stress: the words *baseball, borax, textbook, croquet* and *ice cream* all bear main stress on one syllable and secondary stress on the other, though with the last two examples speakers vary as to which is which.

Stress differences may distinguish pairs of words otherwise identical, as with the nouns 'subject and 'record and the verbs sub'ject and re'cord. For some (not all) speakers, the same stress difference is all that distinguishes *billow* from *below*.

Stress on a syllable in English is produced by a complex interaction of several phonetic factors: a stressed syllable is louder than an unstressed one, it has a higher pitch, and it is longer.

Quite apart from the ordinary **word-stress** just described, English also allows **sentence-stress**: strong stress placed on a particular word to emphasize it within an utterance, as in *I will NEVER give in to these threats*. A sentence-stress is always placed on a syllable which bears the main stress normally. But very different is **contrastive stress**, in which any syllable at all, even one which is normally unstressed, may be stressed in order to highlight a contrast with something else: *I said ACcept, not EXcept.*

Many other languages also have word-stress, such as Spanish, German and Russian (and are thus termed *stress-timed* languages). Others (*syllable-timed*), however, do not: French and Japanese, for example, lack word-stress. Some varieties of English, like Indian English and Jamaican English, are relatively syllable-timed rather than stress-timed like British English or Australian English.

See also: **suprasegmental**

Further reading: Ball and Rahilly 1999; Collins and Mees 2003; Giegerich 1992; Gussmann 2002; Knowles 1987; Kreidler 1989; Laver 1994; Lehiste 1970; Roach 1991.

STRUCTURALISM

An approach to the study of language which sees a language as a structured system. Before the twentieth century, linguists took an *atomistic* view of language: they saw a language as essentially a collection of individual elements, such as speech sounds, words and grammatical endings. At the beginning of the twentieth century, the Swiss linguist Ferdinand de Saussure put forward a very different view: he argued that a language is best viewed as a structured system, with each element in it defined chiefly by how it is related to other elements. In this view, which has come to be called *structuralism*, it is the system which is the primary object of study, and not the individual elements present in that system.

Saussure's influence helped to make structuralism the dominant approach in European linguistics. In the USA, structuralist ideas were somewhat independently developed by Edward Sapir and more especially by Leonard Bloomfield. Bloomfield's successors in the 1940s and 1950s took his ideas to extremes in developing *American structuralism*, a vigorous but excessively dogmatic approach to linguistic description which attached great importance to **distribution**. In the 1960s, Noam Chomsky and his followers rebelled against the excesses of their predecessors, and they came to use *structuralism* as a swear word to denote everything they disliked about the earlier work, but in fact Chomsky's **generative grammar** is no less structuralist than other approaches, in the original sense of the term. Indeed, virtually all serious work in linguistics in the twentieth century has been structuralist in outlook, though many contemporary linguistists continue to regard structuralism as a term of abuse and would not apply the term to their own work.

Structuralist ideas were eventually picked up, largely from the influential Russian linguist Roman Jakobson, by the French anthropologist Claude Lévi-Strauss, who introduced them into anthropology, from where they spread into the social sciences generally, and even into such fields as literary criticism. Quite independently, Saussure's structuralist approach was deeply influential in the development of **semiotics**.

See also: **cognitive linguistics**; **generative grammar**; **linguistics**

Further reading: Lepschy 1970; Malmkjær 2004; Sampson 1980; Sturrock 1993.

STRUCTURE

A particular pattern which is available in a language for constructing a linguistic unit, or an instance of this. Structures can be recognized in languages at every level of analysis: phonemes combine to build morphemes, morphemes combine to build words, words combine to build phrases, phrases combine to build clauses and sentences, sentences combine to build texts, and so on. At every one of these levels, the smaller units must be combined into larger ones in particular orderly ways determined by the rules of the language, and we therefore say in each case that we are looking at an instance of a particular *structure*.

For example, the morpheme *bad* is built up from the three phonemes /b/, /æ/ and /d/, and many analysts would argue that, in fact, this is done by first combining /æ/ and /d/ into /æd/, and then adding /b/ to produce /bæd/. The adjective *happy* can take the prefix *un-* to produce the adjective *unhappy*, and this in turn can take the suffix *-ness* to produce the noun *unhappiness*. (We cannot analyse *unhappiness* as consisting instead of *un-* plus *happiness*, because *happiness* is a noun, and the rules of English word-structure do not permit *un-* to be added to a noun.) The words *little* and *girl* can be combined to construct the ***N-bar*** *little girl*, which can then take a determiner like *the* to build the noun phrase *the little girl*.

Most usually today, we apply the term structure both to a general pattern and to any individual instance of it, but the general pattern is sometimes called a *construction*, while an individual instance has sometimes been called a *syntagm*. The relation between the elements in a structure is a **syntagmatic relation**.

The approach to language study called **structuralism** gets its name because it emphasizes the importance of recognizing units of structure at every level, though in fact the recognition of **systems** in languages is no less important in the structuralist approach.

See also: **structuralism**; **syntagmatic relation**; **system**

Further reading: Jeffries 2006.

STRUCTURE-DEPENDENCE

The property of languages by which grammatical statements must be made in terms of structural units. When we describe the **syntax** of a language, we find that we never need to make any statements involving such notions as 'the second word in the sentence', 'a word ending in a vowel', 'a word of three or more syllables' or 'the first six words in the sentence'. Grammars simply do not function in terms of such notions; instead, they function in terms of purely structural units like **verb**, **noun phrase** and **auxiliary**, and we call this phenomenon *structure-dependence*.

Consider the way in which yes–no questions are constructed in English. If we mentally start with a statement, then, in order to convert it to a yes–no question, we must move the finite auxiliary out of its verb phrase and to the left of the subject noun phrase. This is so regardless of what the finite auxiliary is and regardless of whether the noun phrase and the verb phrase are small and simple or large and complex:

[*She*] [[*is*] [*dancing*]].
[*Is*] [*she*] [*dancing*]?

[*Most of our students*] [[*can*] [*do this*]].
[*Can*] [*most of our students*] [*do this*]?

[*The selection of the remaining members of the team*] [[*can't*]
    [*wait until our captain gets back*]].
[*Can't*] [*the selection of the remaining members of the team*]
    [*wait until our captain gets back*]?

279

In short, yes–no questions are constructed in terms of structural units, not in terms of words, and every other syntactic process in English and in other languages works in the same way,

It is because of this structure-dependence that descriptions of the syntax of a language are commonly presented in terms of **constituent structure** and in terms of **syntactic categories**.

See also: **constituent structure**; **recursion**; **structure**; **syntactic category**

Further reading: Jeffries 2006; Radford 1988.

STYLISTICS

The study of the aesthetic uses of languages, particularly the use of language in literature. On the whole, the European linguistic tradition has almost always seen the study of the purely structural aspects of language as bound up with the study of its aesthetic aspects; for example, in the middle of the twentieth century, the great Russian linguist Roman Jakobson contributed equally to theoretical linguistics and to the critical examination of literary works.

In the English-speaking world, however, there was long a seemingly unbridgeable gulf between linguistics and literary criticism, and neither discipline paid any attention to the other. In the past several decades, however, this has changed, and a number of scholars have been applying the analytical techniques of theoretical linguistics to the elucidation of literary works and to the examination of the aesthetic aspects of language generally. To this discipline we now give the name *stylistics*. A practitioner of stylistics may choose to pursue such topics as the ironic use of language in the novels of V.S. Naipaul, the sound structure of a poem by Dylan Thomas, the use of regional and social varieties of English for comic effect in Shakespeare's *Henry V*, or the use of archaisms to achieve stateliness in religious language. What sets all this apart from ordinary literary criticism is the explicit use of the concepts and analytical techniques of linguistic theory. As linguistics (and psychology, social theory and the philosophy of language) has developed, so stylistics has borrowed its insights in order to augment its analytical toolkit. For example, early stylistics in the 1960s and 1970s focused on semantic and syntactic aspects of poetry, largely; the 1980s saw an expansion drawing on pragmatics and discourse analysis into extended prose fiction and drama; the 1990s and recent work has drawn heavily on cognitive science to produce a *cognitive poetics* and on computational linguistics to produce a *corpus stylistics*. In the past few years, the label *literary linguistics* (once used in the 1920s in Russia) has begun to be applied again to the linguistic analysis of literature.

See also: **cognitive linguistics**; **structuralism**

Further reading: Bradford 1997; Fabb 1997; Fowler 1996; Simpson 1996, 2004; Stockwell 2002b; Thornborrow and Wareing 1998; Wales 2001.

SUBCATEGORIZATION

Differences in syntactic behaviour among the words in a single **part of speech**. English has a class of **verbs**, almost all of which are united by sharing certain important properties, such as being marked for **tense** and taking the ending *-ing* for certain grammatical purposes. If we didn't recognize a class of verbs, we would be unable to state a number of important generalizations. Nevertheless, not all verbs behave identically.

Consider the following frames:

1 *Susie will –*.
2 *Susie will – Mike.*
3 *Susie will – me a letter.*
4 *Susie will – to come.*
5 *Susie will – that she's ready.*
6 *Susie will – me that she's ready.*

Now try to fit the following verbs into each blank: *decide, tell, want, send, speak, show*. You will find that each verb fits successfully into some blanks to produce a grammatical sentence, but not into others. For example, *decide* fits only into (1), (4) and (5).

This is an instance of *subcategorization*. Even though all these words are verbs, they exhibit important differences in the structures in which they can appear, and we say that verbs are *subcategorized* accordingly. Note that the necessary subcategories all overlap considerably, and hence we cannot simply subcategorize verbs into type (1), type (2), and so on.

Subcategorization is most prominent with verbs, but other parts of speech show the same phenomenon.

See also: **part of speech**; **syntactic category**; **syntax**

Further reading: Radford 1988.

SUBJECT

The *subject* is the primary **argument** of a sentence. Traditionally, the subject is the nominated actor or 'doer' of the verb, though many **grammars** distinguish the grammatical subject from the logical or 'real' subject: in *The baby was kissed by the politician*, the grammatical subject is different from the logical subject. And there are examples where the subject is plainly not the active agent: *the lake shimmered in the wind*, *The wine drinks well*. The identification of subject is thus relatively straightforward at the surface level, but more difficult when function is considered. It should be said, though, that all languages have subjects, though they encode the nomination of the primary argument in various different ways.

A subject is prototypically a **noun phrase**, though it is possible for other **parts of speech** and categories to act as subjects: **verb phrases** can be nominalized or *rank-shifted* to operate as subjects (*Running up the hill is tiring*, *To finish this book is his main aim*). Some languages allow a *dummy subject* or *expletive* (in the grammatical sense) where the syntax requires a subject-slot to be filled but the pronoun used has no semantic referential value. Typical in English are existential statements (*There are ten boys here*), statements that introduce modal forms (*It is true that there are no bananas*) or assertions about the weather (*It is raining*).

See also: **argument**; **direct object**; **noun**; **noun phrase**

Further reading: Hurford 1994; Jackson 2002; Jeffries 2006.

SUBORDINATION

Any type of sentence structure in which one **clause** forms part of a larger clause. The recognition of subordination is ancient in our grammatical tradition, and any clause which is part of a larger one is a **subordinate clause**. Subordinate clauses are of several types; in the examples below, each subordinate clause is bracketed.

A **complement clause** is attached to a preceding word: *Janet suspects* [*that she is pregnant*] (a **verb-complement clause**); *Susie's announcement* [*that she was a lesbian*] *startled her parents* (a **noun-complement clause**); *Susie is happy* [*that Natalie can move in with her*] (an **adjective-complement clause**).

A **relative clause** is attached to a preceding noun, which it modifies, and always contains a **gap** (*e*) somewhere inside it: *The job* [*that Susie wants* e] *involves a lot of travelling*.

An **embedded question** (or **indirect question**) is a question which is not being asked directly: *I asked them* [*if they had seen Susie*]; *Janet doesn't know* [*what she wants*].

An **adverbial clause** behaves like an **adverb** within its sentence and must be introduced by a suitable marker of subordination: [*When Susie gets here*], *we'll have dinner*; [*If you need any help*], *give me a ring*; *Susie is upset* [*because she has quarrelled with Natalie*].

Earlier grammarians took the view that a subordinate clause was not part of the clause containing it (its **matrix clause**), but today we always regard a subordinate clause as forming an integral part of its matrix clause.

See also: **clause**; **sentence**

Further reading: Collins Cobuild 1990; Greenbaum and Quirk 1990; Hurford 1994.

SUPRASEGMENTAL

An aspect of pronunciation whose description requires a longer sequence than a single consonant or vowel. Though phoneticians and linguists had earlier been aware of the importance of suprasegmental phenomena in speech, the term **suprasegmental** was coined by the **American structuralists** in the 1940s. It covers several rather diverse phenomena.

A very obvious suprasegmental is **intonation**, since an intonation pattern by definition extends over a whole utterance or a sizable piece of an utterance. Also clearly suprasegmental is the kind of word-accent called **pitch accent**, as in Japanese and Basque, in which an accentual pitch pattern extends over an entire word. Less obvious is **stress**, but not only is stress a property of a whole **syllable** but the stress level of a syllable can only be determined by comparing it with neighbouring syllables which have greater or lesser degrees of stress.

The tones of **tone languages** are also suprasegmental, since not only does a tone fall on a whole syllable but tonal differences like 'high' and 'low' can only be identified by comparing syllables with neighbouring syllables.

The American structuralists also treated *juncture* phenomena as suprasegmental. Differences in juncture are the reason that *night rate* does not sound like *nitrate*, or *why choose* like *white shoes*, and why the consonants in the middle of *pen-knife* and *lamp-post* are the way they are. Since these items contain essentially the same sequences of **segments**, the junctural differences have to be described in terms of different juncture placement within sequences of segments.

In most of these cases, the phonetic realization of the suprasegmental actually extends over more than one segment, but the key point is that, in all of them, the *description* of the suprasegmental must involve reference to more than one segment.

Some people use **prosody** as a synonym for suprasegmental, but phonologists prefer the latter term.

See also: **intonation**; **segment**; **stress**; **tone language**

Further reading: Ball and Rahilly 1999; Clark and Yallop 1995; Ladefoged 1993; Laver 1994; Lehiste 1970; Shockey 2003.

SURFACE STRUCTURE

The syntactic structure which is most obviously assignable to a particular sentence. Every sentence in every language has some kind of syntactic structure. Consider the following English example: *Susie is hard to please*. Now, while the structure assigned to this sentence may vary somewhat, depending upon the analyst and the framework used, the majority view would probably analyse it as follows: it consists of a subject noun phrase *Susie* and a predicate verb phrase *is hard to please*; the latter in turn consists of a copular verb *is* and an adjective phrase *hard to please*; the adjective phrase in turn consists of an adjective *hard* and a verb phrase *to please*. We can represent this structure schematically as follows: [*Susie*] [*is*] [*hard*] [*to please*], or even better, given more space, as a **tree** diagram.

Now this structure is the *surface structure* of the sentence: that is, it is the syntactic structure which we would most naturally assign to this sentence, and, in many theories of grammar, this is the *only* syntactic structure that would be assigned. However, it is obvious that the meaning of the sentence relates to this structure in a very curious way: this is really a statement about pleasing Susie, and hence, in some semantic or logical sense, *Susie* appears to be, not the subject of *is*, but rather the object of *please*.

Most frameworks would treat this fact in a strictly semantic way, but **transformational grammar** and its various descendants take a different line: they assign a **deep structure** to the sentence, a structure which is very different from the surface structure and much closer to the meaning – something along the following lines: [[NP] [*please*] [*Susie*] [*is*] [*hard*], where 'NP' represents an unidentified subject for *please*. A good deal of grammatical machinery is then required to convert this deep structure into the required surface structure. These rules are *transformations*, and it is the set of transformations that define languages as being different from each other, producing different apparent surface structures.

See also: **deep structure; tree**

Further reading: Lyons 1991.

SYLLABLE

A fundamental but elusive unit in **phonology**. Every word consists of a sequence of some number of *syllables*, and even speakers with no knowledge of phonetics or of linguistics usually find it easy to agree on how many syllables a word contains. For example, we all agree that *girl* and *salt* contain one syllable, that *butter* and *behind* contain two, that *linguistics* and *kangaroo* contain three, that *education* and *development* contain four, and so on.

Differences in judgement usually reflect genuine differences in pronunciation. For example, *police* and *collapse* are pronounced as one syllable by some speakers but as two by others, *library* and *medicine* are pronounced as two syllables by some but as three by others, *February* is often uttered with two syllables and can be read out with four, and *temporarily* has five syllables for most Americans but only three for many Britons.

In spite of the conspicuous prominence of syllables, however, it has proved exceedingly difficult to provide an objective definition of the syllable. Attempts have been made at defining the syllable in terms of everything from muscular contractions to perceived peaks of loudness, but so far no definition has proved satisfactory.

Nevertheless, the syllable appears to be a genuinely fundamental unit in **phonology**, and many important generalizations about the sound systems of languages can be stated in terms of syllables more readily than in any other way. As a consequence, the most influential theories of phonology developed since the 1980s have generally attached great importance to syllables, and in some of them the syllable is taken as the most fundamental unit of all, in terms of which everything else is defined. (In contrast, earlier theories of phonology generally took either **phonemes** or **distinctive features** as the fundamental units).

See also: **phonology**; **segment**

Further reading: Gussmann 2002; Hogg and McCully 1987; Katamba 1989; Lass 1984; Odden 2005.

SYMBOLIC SYSTEM

An integrated set of signs, each with a conventional meaning. The notion of a *symbolic system* lies at the heart of the discipline called **semiotics**. A very simple symbolic system is the set of colours exhibited by a traffic light, each of which has a conventional but agreed significance. Only slightly more complex is the set of signals used by a cricket umpire or an American football referee to announce what has happened on the field. Yet another example is the system of stripes, bars, stars and other items worn on a military uniform to indicate rank and affiliation.

Language is often viewed as a paradigm case of a symbolic system, though one that is vastly more complex than these simple examples. Much of the driving force of semiotics is the belief that such socially constructed objects as myths and films can also be usefully viewed as symbolic systems, and interpreted as such in illuminating ways.

See also: **linguistic sign**; **semiotics**

Further reading: Cobley 2001; Eco 1976; Leeds-Hurwitz 1993; Peirce 1992; Sebeok 1984, 1994; Tobin 1990.

SYNCHRONY

The absence of a time element in linguistic description. In the early twentieth century, the Swiss linguist Ferdinand de Saussure introduced his celebrated distinction between *synchrony* and **diachrony**. In a synchronic approach to describing a language, we focus on that language at one moment in time and describe it as we find it at that moment (a sort of 'snapshot' of the state of the language). This need not be the present moment: we can equally construct a description of present-day English or of Shakespeare's English. In either case, we take no interest in how the language of that moment differs from the same language at any earlier or later moment; as soon as we start paying attention to that, we are taking a diachronic approach. In linguistic research, synchronic studies are obviously much more directly evidential than diachronic studies, which tend to require complex methodologies and inferencing.

See also: **descriptivism**; **diachrony**

Further reading: Nevalainen *et al*. 2006.

SYNTACTIC CATEGORY

Any one of the several types of grammatical unit from which the sentences of a language are constructed. The structure of a sentence is **constituent structure**, and a constituent structure is built up by combining smaller units into larger ones. These units, the *syntactic categories*, are of several types, and they are also of different sizes.

The smallest syntactic categories are the *lexical categories*, commonly called the **parts of speech**, such as **noun**, **verb**, **preposition** and **determiner**; there are about fifteen of these in English. Each member of a lexical category is a single word.

Much larger are *phrasal categories*, representing the several different types of **phrase** existing in the languages, such as **noun phrase** and **verb phrase**. A typical instance of a phrasal category consists of several words, but a particular phrase may contain only one word or dozens. Most grammarians recognize only five different phrasal categories in English, though some prefer to acknowledge a larger number.

In between these two sizes are the *intermediate categories*. The need for these is debated among grammarians, but one kind is essential: the *N-bar*. A noun phrase like *the little girl* unquestionably consists of a determiner *the* and an N-bar *little girl*, which itself consists of the adjective *little* and the noun *girl*.

Of course, we also need the unique syntactic category **sentence**. Subordinate clauses present a few difficulties. In the sentence *Susie decided that she would go home*, the complement clause *that she would go home* is often assigned to another special syntactic category called *S-bar*; an S-bar consists of a *complementizer* (here *that*; *complementizer* is another part of speech) plus the sentence *she would go home*.

The recognition of a suitable set of syntactic categories allows us to analyse all the sentences of a language as being built up, by means of a fairly small set of rules allowing **recursion**, from just these few categories.

See also: **head**; **part of speech**; **phrase**; **recursion**; **subcategorization**; **X-bar**

Further reading: Brown and Miller 1991; Kroeger 2004; van Valin 2001.

SYNTAGMATIC RELATION

The relation between any linguistic elements which are simultaneously present in a **structure**. The concept of a *syntagmatic relation* was introduced in the early twentieth century by the Swiss linguist Ferdinand de Saussure. In Saussure's terminology, any kind of structural unit in a language at any level is a *syntagm* or *syntagma*, a word constructed on the analogy of **paradigm**, and a syntagm consists of some set of smaller structural units, all combined according to the appropriate rules and all standing in syntagmatic relation to one another.

For example, the English phonemes /t/, /k/ and /æ/ are syntagmatically related in one way in the word /tæk/ *tack*, in a second way in /kæt/ *cat*, in a third way in /ækt/ *act*, and in a fourth way in /tækt/ *tact*. Similarly, the morphemes {*un-*}, {*happy*} and {*-ness*} are syntagmatically related in a particular way in the word *unhappiness*, and the words *the*, *little* and *girl* are syntagmatically related in the noun phrase *the little girl*. In every case, the larger unit which is composed of smaller ones is a syntagm.

A particular pattern into which a large number of individual syntagms fit is a **structure**. So, for example, the structure illustrated by *the little girl* recurs in other, similar, syntagms like *these old clothes, my new car* and *some dirty books*. (Today, however, we more usually apply the term **structure** to each particular instance of a general pattern, and avoid the word *syntagm*).

Syntagmatic relations contrast most obviously with **paradigmatic relations**, and this pair of terms constitutes one of Saussure's famous dichotomies.

Note that, in psycholinguistics, the term syntagmatic relation is used in a somewhat different sense, to denote the mental association between words which frequently occur together, as when a subject given *black* responds with *magic, tie* or *sheep*.

See also: **distribution**; **paradigmatic relation**; **structure**

Further reading: Kroeger 2004; van Valin 2001.

SYNTAX

Sentence structure, or the branch of linguistics which studies this. The first European steps in the examination of syntax were taken by the ancient Greeks, beginning with Aristotle, who first divided sentences into **subjects** and **predicates**. Thereafter, progress was slow, and toward the middle of the twentieth century syntax was lagging far behind **phonology** and **morphology**.

In the 1940s, the American linguist Zellig Harris began developing an interesting new way of looking at syntax. A decade later, his student Noam Chomsky presented a greatly modified version of Harris's ideas, involving the introduction of **generative grammar** and of the particular variety of generative grammar called **transformational grammar**. Chomsky argued that syntax was not only tractable but the very heart of serious linguistic investigation, and he persuaded a generation of linguists that he was correct. As a result, the study of syntax became vastly more prominent than formerly; still today, many linguists of a Chomskyan persuasion see syntax as the very core of language structure, though non-Chomskyan linguists, thanks to the dramatic advances in other areas of investigation, would now see syntax as only one important area among many.

In the 1960s, the American linguist Joseph Greenberg published his pioneering work in syntactic **typology**, as a result of which another tradition of syntactic investigation, independent of Chomsky's, has grown up and flourished. Often closely linked to this typological work, but partly independent of it, is the kind of syntactic work favoured by the proponents of **functionalism**.

This recent concentration of effort upon syntactic problems has uncovered a wealth of fascinating data and led to innumerable theoretical interpretations. Here are just two examples of the many striking phenomena discovered in English.

First, consider the following four virtually identical-looking sentences:

1 *After Lisa got up, she had a shower.*
2 *After she got up, Lisa had a shower.*
3 *Lisa had a shower after she got up.*
4 *She had a shower after Lisa got up.*

In the first three of these, *she* can possibly refer to *Lisa*, but, in the fourth, it cannot.

Second, the sentence *It is easy to annoy Janet* can be readily recast as *Janet is easy to annoy*, but the similar-looking *It is inadvisable to annoy Janet* cannot be recast as **Janet is inadvisable to annoy* (*indicates ungrammaticality).

Facts like these, previously unnoticed and largely unsuspected, have provided the grist for decades of syntactic investigation and theorizing, and quite a number of different *theories of grammar* have been put forward and developed.

See also: **recursion**; **structure-dependence**; **syntactic category**

Further reading: Brown and Miller 1991; Givón 2001; Hendrick 2003; Hudson 1998; Jeffries 2006; Kroeger 2004, 2005; Kuhn 2003; Lasnik *et al*. 2005; Lyons 1968; Matthews 1981; O'Grady *et al*. 1996; Poole 2002; van Valin 2001.

SYSTEM

A set of competing possibilities in a language, together with the rules for choosing among them. The single greatest insight of the approach to language study called **structuralism** was the recognition that a language is best viewed as a *system* of elements, with each element being chiefly defined by its place within the system, by the way it is related to other elements. Further, the overall system of a language consists of a number of subsystems and sub-subsystems, all of which overlap in various ways.

A simple example of a system in English is our (personal) pronoun system, which consists of the items *I/me*, *we/us*, *you*, *he/him*, *she/her*, *it* and *they/them*. Whenever we need to use a pronoun, we must choose exactly one item from this system, and in many cases we must choose one of the two forms that exist. Naturally, the choice is not free: it is dependent upon other choices which are being made at the same time. This whole set of forms, together with the rules determining which one is appropriate in a given instance, constitutes our pronoun system.

Among the other systems present in English are the consonant system, the verb system, and the system of word-forming prefixes. All the items forming part of a single system stand in a **paradigmatic relation** to one another, meaning that they represent mutually exclusive choices.

See also: **paradigmatic relation**; **structuralism**; **structure**

Further reading: Thompson 2004.

SYSTEMATIC CORRESPONDENCE

A certain type of pattern linking words in different languages. The members of a **language family** share a common ancestor – that is, they all started off long ago as nothing more than regional dialects of that ancestral language, but have diverged over time into distinct languages. One type of change is change in pronunciation, and it is characteristic of change in pronunciation that it is often highly regular: a particular sound in a particular environment tends strongly to change in the same way in a given language in every word containing it.

As a result of this, the words of related languages often exhibit a set of conspicuous patterns, each of the following general form: if word W1 in language L1 contains a sound S1 in a particular position, then word W2 of the same meaning in language L2 will contain the sound S2 in the same position. Such a pattern is a *systematic correspondence*.

Here is a simple example, from the two New Guinean languages Sinaugoro and Motu (data from Terry Crowley 1997); these data are only a sample of some patterns which in fact apply to a much larger set of words:

We can easily see several systematic correspondences here which apply in all positions: Sinaugoro /m/ : Motu /m/; Sinaugoro /n/:

Sinaugoro	Motu	
Tama	tama	'father'
Tina	sina	'mother'
Tai	tai	'cry'
Tui	tui	'elbow, knee'
ɣita	ita	'see'
ɣate	ase	'liver'
Mate	mase	'die'
Natu	natu	'child'
Toi	toi	'three'

Motu /n/; Sinaugoro /a/ : Motu /a/; Sinaugoro /ɣ/ : Motu zero; and so on. Whenever a Sinaugoro word contains one of the sounds in a correspondence, the Motu word of the same meaning contains the other one in the same position.

But Sinaugoro /t/ is more complicated: some words show the correspondence Sinaugoro /t/ : Motu /t/, while others show Sinaugoro /t/ : Motu /s/. Further examination, though, reveals that there is a clear basis for the difference: the second correspondence applies always and only when the consonant is followed by a front vowel /i/ or /e/, while the first applies in all other circumstances.

The existence of such correspondences demonstrates that the languages in question share a common ancestor (in this case, of course, a rather recent one), and these correspondences are the material to which we apply **comparative reconstruction** in order to work out the properties of the unrecorded ancestral language.

See also: **comparative reconstruction; historical linguistics; language family**

Further reading: Crowley 1997; Trask 1996.

SYSTEMIC LINGUISTICS

An important version of **functionalism**. In the 1930s and 1940s, the British linguist J.R. Firth began laying the groundwork for a somewhat novel social approach to language. His student Michael Halliday greatly developed Firth's ideas in distinctive directions of his own. Beginning in the 1960s with a new approach to grammatical analysis which he called **Scale-and-Category Grammar**, Halliday went on to construct an elaborate and ambitious framework which eventually came to be called **Systemic Linguistics**, or SL.

SL is an avowedly functionalist approach to language, and it is arguably the functionalist approach which has been most highly developed. In contrast to most other approaches, SL explicitly attempts to combine purely structural information with overtly social factors in a single integrated description. Like other functionalist frameworks, SL is deeply concerned with the *purposes* of language use. Systemicists constantly ask the following questions: What is this writer (or speaker) trying to do? What linguistic devices are available to help them to do it, and on what basis do they make their choices?

Halliday distinguishes among three distinctive **functions of language** (or *metafunctions*). The *ideational* (or *experiential*) *function* is the conveying of semantic content representing information about our experience of the external world (including our own minds). The *textual function* is the linking of linguistic elements to other linguistic elements, so that the various parts of a **text** can be integrated into a coherent and cohesive whole and related to the wider context of our speech or writing. The *interpersonal function* is the establishment and maintenance of social relations, including persuading other people to do things or to believe things.

Systemicists stress the utility of their framework in the analysis of **texts**, an area beyond the scope of many other approaches, and they accordingly devote more attention to the treatment of texts than to the analysis of isolated sentences. Because of this preoccupation with texts, the concepts of *coherence* and **cohesion** play a central role in the framework. And SL has proven useful especially in the fields of **stylistics** and **critical discourse analysis**.

Halliday and his followers have recently been applying the name **Functional Grammar** to the more explicitly grammatical aspects of SL, and the term *systemic functional linguistics* has also been used.

See also: **cohesion**; **functionalism**; **text**

Further reading: Bloor and Bloor 2004; Butler 1985; Eggins 2004; Halliday 2004; Thompson 2004.

TAGMEMICS

A grammar developed by the American linguist Kenneth Pike in the 1950s. In tagmemic theory there are three main levels or systems: **phonology**, *lexis* and **grammar** and within each level there are sub-levels. So in tagmemic grammar there are **morpheme, word, phrase, sentence** and *paragraph* levels. Tagmemics maps the same distinction between the abstract phoneme and the concrete phonetic sound onto higher levels of language. So a set of synonyms (*letter, note, line, epistle, message, missive, correspondence*) can be regarded as different realizations of the single conceptual *tagmeme* underlying them. At a syntactic level, for example, subject, object and predicate tagmemes are realized by surface words. Pike was the first to make this *emicletic* distinction (derived from *phonemic/phonetic*), where an *emic* analysis refers to the significant concept that the researcher is interested in, and the *etic* aspect is the actual realization that would be familiar to the language users.

See also: **grammar**

Further reading: Pike 1967, 1982.

TENSE

The **grammatical category** which relates to time. Every language is capable of expressing limitless distinctions of time: *soon, tomorrow, next Wednesday at 2.00, 137 years ago, 138 years from now*. It is possible for a language to build a few of these time distinctions into its grammar, and a language which does so has the category of *tense*. Tense is thus the grammaticalization of time. In most tense languages, tense is marked on **verbs**, but there are exceptions.

Some languages lack tense entirely; an example is Chinese, which has nothing corresponding to the *I go/I went* contrast of English. Some tense languages distinguish only two tenses, while others have three, four, five or more; the African language Bamileke-Dschang distinguishes eleven tenses. Other possibilities for tenses include distinguishing near-future tense (today, or soon after today) from distant future events, hypothetical or desired events, and events which are still in the process of happening, as well as several other possible time signatures. A useful way of describing tense and **aspect** in **discourse** is to compare the relative positions of the *coding* *time* (the moment of utterance or composition) with the *reference time* (the explicit moment being referred to) and the *event time* (the event's duration or status). Combining all possibilities of sequencing of these before or after each other produces a scheme of twenty-two possible forms, without constraints of particular languages.

English has only two tenses: a *non-past* ('present') tense, mostly used for talking about present and future time, and a *past* tense, mostly used for talking about past time. English verb-forms therefore generally come in pairs, one for each tense:

She lives in London/She lived in London.
She is living in London/She was living in London.
She has lived in London/She had lived in London.
She has been living in London/She had been living in London.
She is going to live in London/She was going to live in London.
She will live in London/She would live in London.
She can live in London/She could live in London.

Unlike some other languages, English has no distinct future tense. Instead, we use a variety of non-past ('present') forms for expressing a range of attitudes towards future events: *I go to London tomorrow*; *I'm going to London tomorrow*; *I'm going to go to London tomorrow*; *I'll go to London tomorrow*; *I'll be going to London tomorrow*; *I must go to London tomorrow*; *I may go to London tomorrow*. Observe that all these examples illustrate some further distinctions of importance in English grammar, but these others are not distinctions of tense. Instead, they are distinctions of **aspect** or of **modality**.

See also: **aspect, modality**

Further reading: Bybee *et al.* 1994; Comrie 1985; Hornstein 1990; Hurford 1994.

TEXT

A continuous piece of spoken or written language, especially one with a recognizable beginning and ending. Linguists have long used the word *text* very informally to denote any stretch of language they happened to be interested in. Especially since the 1960s, however, the notion of a text has acquired a theoretical status in several quarters, and the analysis of texts is now seen as a major goal of linguistic investigation. However, the conception of what constitutes a text is not everywhere the same.

For some linguists, a text is no different from a **discourse**. For others, a text is a more or less physical product, the *result* of a discourse, which itself is then seen as a more abstract process leading to the construction of a text. For still others, a text is primarily defined by its possession of an identifiable purpose, an approach which leads quickly to the classification of texts into a number of kinds (*text-types*) differing in purpose – and, consequently, often also in their linguistic characteristics. Yet others see a text as an abstraction, with a discourse being the physical realization of a text. Finally, some linguists merely consider that a text is written while a discourse is spoken.

The analysis of texts is a prominent feature of several types of **functionalism**, and above all of **Systemic Linguistics**, in which the analysis of texts is often seen as the primary goal of linguistic investigation, with the analysis of smaller units like sentences being interpreted largely in terms of their contribution to a text. Quite independently, the approach to teaching English called *language in use* focuses strongly upon the analysis of texts, particularly those which are familiar and meaningful to students. In Europe, a particular approach called **text linguistics** has become prominent in recent decades; this lays particular emphasis on **textuality**, the defining characteristics of different types of texts.

Particularly associated with Systemic Linguistics, but also prominent in other approaches, are the two concepts of *coherence* and **cohesion**. Some linguistic approaches have recently incorporated the originally literary concept of **intertextuality**. Some philosophers of language take the widest possible view that anything you can represent to yourself (that is, any thoughts you can consciously have) is a text, and so in effect everything is a text.

See also: **cohesion**; **intertextuality**; **Systemic Linguistics**; **text linguistics**; **textuality**

Further reading: Crystal 1997; Gramley and Pätzold 1992; Schiffrin 1994; Thompson 2004; van Peer 1994.

TEXT LINGUISTICS

A particular approach to the analysis of **texts**. *Text linguistics* is primarily a European creation, and it is especially prominent in

Germany and the Netherlands. The approach focuses upon the varying purposes of different texts and upon the explicit identification of the formal linguistic properties which distinguish one type of text from another; these properties are taken to define the **textuality** of a text. In the 1970s, a pioneering project at the University of Konstanz in Germany attempted to construct an explicit text grammar; the project was not seen as a success, and more recent investigations have been characterized by greater elaboration and sophistication.

Text linguistics makes heavy use of familiar linguistic concepts and terminology, and much work in the field consists of attempts at extending familiar types of linguistic analysis to units larger than a single sentence. Consequently, it has a great deal in common with the approach called **discourse analysis** in the English-speaking world, and some outsiders see little difference between the two. The functionalist approach called **Systemic Linguistics** shares important ideas with text linguistics, but is rather distinct in nature.

See also: **discourse analysis**; **Systemic Linguistics**; **text**; **textuality**

Further reading: de Beaugrande 1994; de Beaugrande and Dressler 1981; Malmkjær 2004.

TEXT WORLD THEORY

An approach to human discourse processing developed initially by the British linguist Paul Werth in the 1990s. *Text world theory* addresses the main problem for *worlds* theories which concerns how the knowledge **frame** is used to select only that textual and contextual information which is needed for the interpretation at hand and disregard the rest. Text world theory places *text-drivenness* at the heart of the process and provides a range of semantic processes (assertion, entailment, presupposition, inferencing, and so on) to explain which knowledge is nominated and brought to bear upon the discourse situation.

A key useful feature of the theory is its *fractal structure*. The top level of the *discourse world* corresponds with reality, and is built with objects and participants. The next level, the *text world*, has a different ontological status but is also built with objects, participants and a spatiotemporal signature. Further embedded levels (*sub-worlds* in the early theory) are the products of *world switches* that are effected by, for example, modalization, metaphor, negation or **deictic** shifts 'backwards' or 'forwards' – they too have the same organizational structure. Text world theory draws on other *worlds* theories in its use of *counterparts* of elements operating across worlds. The theory has proven most useful in relation to literary discourse in **stylistics** and *cognitive poetics*.

See also: **cognitive linguistics**; **possible worlds theory**; **schema**; **stylistics**

Further reading: Werth 1999; Gavins 2007; Stockwell 2002b.

TEXTUALITY

The characteristics of a **text** which make clear what sort of text it is intended to be. A newspaper story does not resemble a scholarly monograph, and a poem is quite dissimilar to a television commercial. Each particular type of text has its own typical characteristics; when we encounter a text, we expect to see the appropriate characteristics, and recognizing those characteristics allows us to recognize quickly what sort of text we are looking at.

The identifying properties of each type of text constitute its *textuality*, or *texture* (though the latter term is also used in *cognitive poetics* to refer to the aesthetic experience of reading). One of the principal goals of **text linguistics** is to identify, as explicitly as possible, the distinguishing features of each type of text.

See also: **genre**; **intertextuality**

Further reading: Halliday 2004; Halliday and Hasan 1976; Stockwell 2007; Thompson 2004.

TONE LANGUAGE

A language in which words can be distinguished purely by the pitch of the voice used on individual syllables. In a tone language, words consisting of identical sequences of consonants and vowels can be distinguished in pronunciation (and meaning) by the differing ways in which the pitch of the voice behaves on each syllable; these different pitch patterns are called *tones*. A tone language may have between two and eight (or, rarely, more) different tones.

Mandarin Chinese is a tone language with four tones. In Mandarin, a syllable like *shu* means nothing until it receives a tone. We thus have *shū* 'write' (with a high-level tone), *shú* 'sorghum' (with a rising tone), *shù* 'technique' (with a falling tone), and *shǔ* 'category' (with a falling-rising tone). Most Chinese words are one syllable long, but not all tone languages are like this. Margi (spoken in Nigeria) has contrasts like these: *yíná* 'to dye' (two high tones), *yìnà* 'to rinse' (two low tones), *ámà* 'husband's mother' (high-low), *àmá* 'but' (low-high). Tones can be used for grammatical purposes. Many African languages use tones to inflect verbs, as does Kanuri (spoken in Nigeria): *lezè* 'he goes' (falling tone), *lezé* 'he is to go' (high tone); *tussè* 'he rests', *tussé* 'he is to rest'.

In a true tone language, every syllable has its own tone, which is independent of the tones on other syllables. Rather different is a language with a **pitch accent**, in which a single pitch contour is superimposed upon an entire word, and the pitch of one syllable is not independent of the pitch of other syllables. In Japanese, for example, which has two possible pitches, high (H) and low (L), all that can ever happen in a word is that the pitch may go up once and then (later) go down once. Examples: *hana* (LL) 'nose', *hana* (LH) 'flower'; *shiro* (LH) 'castle', *shiro* (HL) 'white'; *sakura* (LHH) 'cherry', *zakuro* (HLL) 'pomegranate', *kokoro* (LHL) 'heart'. Patterns like HLH, HLLH and LHLH are prohibited, and so also are HH and HHH.

See also: **intonation**; **suprasegmental**

Further reading: Hyman 1975; Katamba 1989; Ladefoged 1971; Lehiste 1970; Yip 2002.

TOPIC

That part of a sentence or utterance which the whole thing is 'about'. The division of a sentence, from the point of view of its information content, into a **topic** and a **comment** is essentially the same as the **given/new** distinction, but the notion of a topic has some further linguistic uses.

The topic of a sentence is that part of it which the whole sentence is about. For example, if I am advising my students as to which books they should read to learn about a particular subject, I might hold up a particular book and say *I can't recommend this book.* Here the topic is clearly *this book*: this noun phrase identifies what I'm talking about, and the rest of my utterance constitutes the comment, what I'm saying about it.

English provides us with some more explicit ways of marking something as a topic. One is ***topicalization***, in which the topic is simply moved to the front of the sentence: *This book I can't recommend.* Here *this book* has been explicitly topicalized. Another device is the *as for* construction: *As for* this *book, I can't recommend it.*

The notion of a topic must be clearly distinguished from that of **focus**; even some professional linguists confuse these two.

See also: **focus**; **given/new**

Further reading: Brown and Miller 1991; Greenbaum and Quirk 1990; Thompson 2004.

TRADITIONAL GRAMMAR

The entire body of grammatical work done in Europe and America before the rise of modern **linguistics** in the twentieth century. The European grammatical tradition began with the Greeks and was continued by the Romans, both of whom were chiefly interested in describing their own languages. The descriptive procedures and terminology they developed eventually came to be applied to modern languages like French and English, and the resulting Latin-based descriptions of English were taught in what for 400 years were called 'grammar schools' until at least the 1960s, since when many schools in English-speaking countries have ceased teaching any English grammar at all.

The work of the traditional grammarians still forms the foundation of modern grammatical work, but we have introduced very many changes and extensions. We reject their insistence on **prescriptivism** as the basis of description; we recognize many more **parts of speech** than they did; we assign **constituent structure** to sentences; we have identified a large number of grammatical phenomena which they overlooked; we try to construct **generative grammars**; and we deny that there is anything special about the grammar of Latin, which is now seen as just one possible grammatical system among many.

Some contemporary work, such as the series of English grammars prepared by Randolph Quirk and his colleagues, is still noticeably traditional in orientation, but it is nonetheless strongly influenced by the advances in grammatical study achieved during the twentieth century.

See also: **descriptivism**; **linguistics**; **prescriptivism**

Further reading: Lepschy 1994; Malmkjær 2004; Palmer 1971; Robins 1997.

TRAJECTOR

A term from *cognitive grammar* to explain how prepositions are conceptualized. Prepositions like *over*, *through*, *into*, *from*, *against*, *about* and so on are metaphorically derived from an idealized spatial concept which is called an *image-schema*. The notion of *over*, for example, involves one object in the focus of attention (the *figure*) describing a motion path over the top of an object that receives less attention (the *ground*). Figure and ground in image-schemas are termed trajectors and **landmarks** respectively. Trajectors take the focus of attention at a cognitive level, and their realization in linguistic form is an example of the **cognitive linguistic** principle that sees cognitive and perceptual processes as the basis for language.

See also: **cognitive linguistics**; **foregrounding**; **landmark**

Further reading: Langacker 1987–91, Ungerer and Schmid 1996.

TRANSCRIPTION

A representation of speech in written form, using conventional symbols. Since conventional writing systems are almost never adequate for representing pronunciation in a fully explicit and consistent manner, phoneticians and linguists have found it necessary to invent their own systems of symbols for transcribing speech sounds, individual words and connected speech.

There are two types of transcription that indicate pronunciation, and the difference is very important, though both types commonly use the **International Phonetic Alphabet**. In a *phonetic transcription*, the object is to record the physical and objectively real speech sounds in as much detail as is required for the current purpose, and two transcriptions of the same utterance may differ in the amount of detail they include. A phonetic transcription is always enclosed in square brackets. So, for example, if we take a typical pronunciation of the English word *please*, the phonetic transcription [pliz] presents only the bare minimum of phonetic information. For many purposes, we would prefer the more detailed transcription [pʰliːz], which explicitly records both the aspiration (puff of breath) following the [p] and the length of the vowel [iː]. A still more detailed version would be [pʰl̥iːz], which notes that the [l] is voiceless, because of the presence of the aspiration. If the speaker is American, we might write [pʰłiːz], where the symbol [ł] explicitly indicates the typical American 'dark l' (an [l] pronounced with the back of the tongue raised). The amount of phonetic detail that might be included in a phonetic transcription is almost unlimited, but we normally content ourselves with recording only the information that seems relevant to our purpose. The more detail we include, the *narrower* is the transcription; the less detail we include, the *broader* is the transcription.

It is important to note that a phonetic transcription records physical reality. Hence a trained phonetician can successfully transcribe *any* piece of speech, even one in a language unknown to her (or him). She does not need to know anything about the language she is listening to; she only needs to be able to hear the speech sounds being produced and to identify them.

A *phonemic transcription* is very different. In a phonemic transcription, we do not transcribe any physical speech sounds at all. Instead, we transcribe the **phonemes** of the language we are listening to, the basic sound units of that language. But this is only possible after we have first carried out a complete phonological analysis of the language and decided what phonemes exist, which speech sounds belong to which phonemes, and what symbols we will use to represent the phonemes. It is therefore not possible to produce a phonemic transcription of a totally unfamiliar language.

A phonemic transcription is always enclosed in phoneme slashes. Since we already have a complete phonemic analysis of English, we are therefore able to provide a phonemic transcription of *please*, as soon as we agree on the phoneme symbols to be used. Naturally enough, we all prefer /p/ for the first consonant phoneme, /l/ for the second consonant phoneme, and /z/ for the last one, but there is some disagreement about the vowel: some linguists prefer to represent the vowel phoneme as /i/, but others prefer the lengthened form /iː/, and so *please* is phonemically either /pliz/ or /pliːz/, depending on which symbol we prefer for the vowel phoneme. (We must be consistent, of course.)

Transcripts are also used in **sociolinguistics, discourse analysis** and **computational linguistics** to indicate the written record of speech. Here, the transcript is often written in conventional spelling, perhaps simply with the obvious features of writing omitted or used differently: for example, capital letters for names and the beginnings of sentences are not used, full-stops and dashes indicate short pauses rather than grammatical markers, square brackets are used to show where speakers overlap, and so on. The form of the transcript is a matter of the degree of detail required in the analysis: if you are interested in syntactic expressions, for example, there is no need for the detail of a phonetic transcription.

See also: **International Phonetic Alphabet**; **phonetics**; **phonology**

Further reading: Ball and Rahilly 1999; Ladefoged 1993.

TRANSFORMATIONAL GRAMMAR

A particular type of **generative grammar**. In the 1950s, Noam Chomsky introduced into linguistics the notion of a **generative grammar**, which has proved to be very influential. Now there are very many different types of generative grammar which can be conceived of, and Chomsky himself defined and discussed several quite different types in his early work. But, from the beginning, he himself favoured a particular type, to which he gave the name *transformational grammar*, or TG; TG has sometimes also been called *transformational generative grammar*.

Most types of generative grammar in which anybody has ever been interested can be usefully viewed as working like this: starting with nothing, the rules of the grammar build up the structure of a sentence piece by piece, adding something at each step, until the sentence structure is complete. Crucially, once something has been added to a sentence structure, it must remain: it cannot be changed, deleted or moved to a different location.

TG is hugely different. In TG, the structure of a sentence is first built up in the manner just described, using only *context-free rules*, which are a simple type of rule widely used in other types of generative grammar. The structure which results is called the **deep structure** of the sentence. But, after this, some further rules apply. These rules are called *transformations*, and they are different in nature. Transformations have the power to change the structure which is already present in a number of ways: not only can they add new material to the structure (though only in the early versions), but they can also change material which is already present in various ways, they can move material to a different location, and they can even delete material from the structure altogether. When all the relevant transformations have finished applying, the resulting structure is the **surface structure** of the sentence. Because of the vast power of transformations, the surface structure may look extremely different from the deep structure.

TG is thus a theory of grammar which holds that a sentence typically has more than one level of structure. Apart from the structure which it obviously has on the surface, it also has an abstract underlying structure (the deep structure) which may be substantially different. The point of all this, in Chomsky's view, is that certain important generalizations about the structures of the sentences in a language may be stated far more easily in terms of abstract deep structures than otherwise; in addition, the meaning of a sentence can often be determined much more straightforwardly from its deep structure.

TG has developed through a number of versions, each succeeding the other. In his 1957 book *Syntactic Structures*, Chomsky provided only a partial sketch of a very simple type of transformational grammar. This proved to be inadequate, and, in his 1965 book *Aspects of the Theory of Syntax*, Chomsky proposed a very different, and much more complete, version. This version is variously known as the *Aspects model* or as the *Standard Theory*. All textbooks of TG published before 1980 (and a few of those published more recently) present what is essentially the Standard Theory, sometimes with a few additions from later work.

Around 1968 the Standard Theory came under attack from a group of younger linguists who hoped to equate deep structure, previously a purely syntactic level of representation, with the semantic structure of a sentence (its meaning). This programme, called *Generative Semantics*, led to the positing of ever more abstract underlying structures for sentences; it proved unworkable, and it finally collapsed. Around the same time, two mathematical linguists demonstrated that standard TG was so enormously powerful that it could, in principle, describe anything which could be described at all – a potentially catastrophic result, since the whole point of a theory of grammar is to tell us what is possible in languages and what is not possible. Yet these **Peters-Ritchie results** suggested that TG was placing no constraints at all on what the grammar of a human language could be like.

Chomsky responded to all this in the early 1970s by introducing a number of changes to his framework; the result became known as the **Extended Standard Theory**, or EST. By the late 1970s further changes had led to a radically different version dubbed the **Revised Extended Standard Theory**, or REST. Among the major innovations of the REST were the introduction of **traces**, invisible flags marking the former positions of elements which had been moved, a reduction in the number of distinct transformations from dozens to just two, and a switch of attention away from the transformations themselves to the **constraints** which applied to them.

But Chomsky continued to develop his ideas, and in 1981 he published *Lectures on Government and Binding*; this book swept away much of the apparatus of the earlier transformational theories in favour of a dramatically different, and far more complex, approach called **Government-and-Binding Theory**, or GB. GB retains exactly one transformation, and, in spite of the obvious continuity between the new framework and its predecessors, the name 'transformational grammar' is not usually applied to GB or to its even more recent successor, the **minimalist programme**. Hence, for purposes of linguistic research, transformational grammar may now be regarded as dead, though its influence has been enormous, and its successors are maximally prominent.

See also: **derivation; generative grammar; Government-and-Binding Theory**

Further reading: Antony and Hornstein 2003; Cook and Newson 1996; Grinder and Elgin 1973; Lyons 1991; Malmkjær 2004.

TRANSITIVITY

The manner in which a **verb** is related to the **noun phrases** in its clause. Grammarians have been aware of differences in transitivity since ancient times, though in the twentieth century we have become aware that transitivity is a more complex matter than had previously been thought.

We may begin by noting a fundamental difference between two types of clause (or sentence). In a prototypical *intransitive* construction, the (intransitive) verb has a subject but no object: *Susie smiled*; *Susie is vacationing in Bermuda*. Here it would make no sense to ask 'What did Susie smile?' or 'What is Susie vacationing?' In a prototypical *transitive* construction, the (transitive) verb has both a subject and an object; the subject represents an agent instigating the action, and the object represents a patient affected by the action: *Susie slapped Dave*; *Susie is ironing a skirt*.

However, in English and in other languages, these two constructions are also used to express states of affairs which are less than prototypical. For example, *Susie smokes* and *Susie is eating* are clearly intransitive, and yet here it *does* make sense to ask 'What does Susie smoke?' or 'What is Susie eating?' In some sense, the verbs *smoke* and *eat* are really transitive, but we do not bother here to identify the object (what is smoked or eaten), because it is obvious or unimportant. Such an apparently intransitive construction is sometimes called an *absolute transitive* construction.

Consider the following sentences, all of which are transitive in form: *Susie bought a car*; *Susie speaks French*; *Susie understands our problem*; *Susie weighs 110 pounds*. These illustrate steadily decreasing levels of prototypical transitivity: *Susie* is less and less of an agent, and the object is less and less affected by the action – indeed, the last two don't really involve any action at all. In short, the world provides a very wide range of possible relations between entities, but English, like many other languages, provides only two grammatical constructions, and every possibility must be squeezed into one or the other of the two constructions.

Unlike some other languages, English exhibits a special type of transitive construction in which the verb takes *two* objects. Examples of this *ditransitive* construction are *Susie gave Natalie a kiss* and *Susie showed me her new skirt*. And, like many other languages, English also has a special type of intransitive construction in which the verb is followed by a noun phrase which does not behave like an object, as in *Susie is our regional manager* and *Susie has become a mother*.

Within **Systemic Linguistics**, the notion of transitivity has been greatly extended and generalized; here the term is understood as denoting the kind of activity or process expressed by a sentence, the number of participants involved and the manner in which they are involved.

See also: **verb**

Further reading: Collins Cobuild 1990; Halliday 2004; Kilby 1984; Thompson 2004.

TREE

A particular type of graphical representation of the structure of a sentence. Most linguists believe that the structure of any sentence is typically a **constituent structure**, in which the sentence consists of some pieces, and each piece consists of some smaller pieces, and so on, down to the smallest pieces; moreover, each piece belongs to some particular **syntactic category**. This kind of structure can be vividly illustrated by a graphical device called a *tree*.

Consider the sentence *The little girl washed her doll*. The tree below illustrates its structure.

Every *branch* of the tree represents a single *constituent* of the sentence, and every constituent, or *node*, is labelled with a *node*

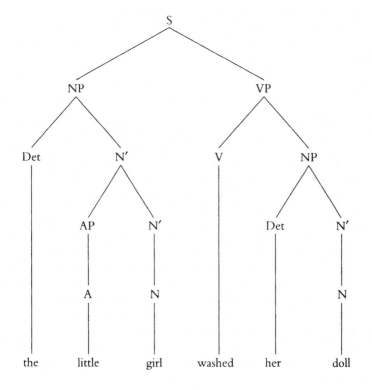

label explaining to which syntactic category it belongs. These standard abbreviations have the following meanings: S = Sentence; NP = Noun Phrase; VP = Verb Phrase; Det = Determiner; N' = N-bar; V = Verb; AP = Adjective Phrase; A = Adjective; N = Noun. A tree of this sort may also be called a *tree structure*, a *tree diagram* or a *phrase marker*.

The precise nature of the tree drawn depends to some extent on the particular grammatical framework being used. The tree shown above would be more or less the tree preferred by most linguists, but the proponents of certain frameworks, most notably the Chomskyan framework called **Government-and-Binding Theory**, would draw a much more elaborate tree involving a number of abstract nodes containing no overt material; the Chomskyans would also regard the tree as strictly representing only the **surface structure** of the sentence, which might have a significantly different **deep structure**, also representable as a tree.

See also: **constituent structure**; **phrase-structure grammar**; **surface structure**

Further reading: Kroeger 2004.

TROPE

In **rhetoric**, the *tropes* were figures of speech that were supposed to express certain emotional and persuasive effects. The main tropes are **metaphor**, *analogy*, *simile*, *metonymy*, *synecdoche*, *litotes*, *hyperbole*, *irony* and so on. Traditionally these were largely defined in terms of their stylistic realization rather than their conceptual content. The difference between metaphor and simile, for example, was simply seen as the difference between an assertion (A is B) and a comparison (A is like B). However, it has been argued in modern **cognitive linguistics** that most of these are surface realizations of an underlying *conceptual metaphor*, in the sense that they all replace the lexical expression of the literal referent with an alternative. Conceptually, the only difference between a metaphor and a simile is in the degree of stylistic commitment to the meaning. Conceptual metaphor is presented as a *mapping* between a *source* domain and a *target* domain. The only difference is in the recent work which has seen a metonymy as being a mapping within a single domain. The fields of **stylistics** and *cognitive poetics* have again become interested in the linguistic texture of tropes.

See also: **metaphor**; **rhetoric**; **stylistics**

Further reading: Stockwell 2002b; Goatly 1987.

TURN-TAKING

That aspect of conversational structure by which the identity of the speaker changes from time to time. In our idealized notion of a conversation, we expect the *floor* to pass from one individual to another in an orderly manner: one person speaks while the others remain silent, and then the speaker falls silent and another person takes the floor. What is interesting about this is that there appear to be clear rules determining when and how the floor is handed over from one person to another: if there were not, a conversation would be merely a noisy jumble of several people trying to speak at once.

It was the American sociologist Harvey Sacks and his colleagues who first drew attention, in the 1970s, to the importance of turn-taking and the rules governing it. However, these rules are by no means easy to discover, and sociolinguists have in recent years devoted a good deal of study to trying to elucidate them. Moreover, it seems clear that very young children do not understand the concept of turn-taking, and specialists in **language acquisition** are therefore curious to find out how an understanding of turn-taking is acquired. Similarly, the operation of turn-taking and the different ways in which keeping a turn, giving up a turn and interrupting indicate power dynamics have generated interest from **discourse analysts** and **sociolinguists**, especially with reference to the way that men, women and mixed groups conduct conversations.

See also: **adjacency pair**; **communicative competence**; **ethnography of communication**; **sex differences in language**

Further reading: Coates 1996; Duranti 1997.

TYPOLOGY

The classification of languages according to their structural features. One way of classifying languages is according to the **genetic**

relationships among them; that is, according to their historical origin. However, we can also classify languages according to the kinds of structures they exhibit. Such a classification is *typological*, and a typological classification is, in principle, entirely independent of the histories of the languages involved – though languages which are genetically rather closely related, naturally, are often also very similar typologically.

In principle, we might pick on virtually any structural feature and use it as the basis of a classification. For example, we could divide languages into those in which the word for a canine animal is [dɔg] and those in which it isn't. (The first group here would contain exactly two known languages: English and the Australian language Mbabaram.) But such a classification would be pointless, since it wouldn't lead anywhere.

The only typological classifications which are of interest are those which are *fruitful*. By this we mean that the languages in each category should turn out to have other features in common, features which were not used to set up the classification in the first place.

For example, we might classify languages into those which have *tones* (like Chinese and Yoruba) and those which don't (like English and Japanese). But this isn't very fruitful, since neither the tone languages nor the non-tone languages turn out to have much of anything else in common, apart perhaps from an interesting geographical distribution, with tone languages concentrated in east Asia and west Africa.

Another possibility is to classify languages according to their **morphology**, or word-structure. In the early nineteenth century, Wilhelm von Humboldt tried this. He classified languages into three types: *isolating* (a word typically consists only of a single morpheme, as in Vietnamese or classical Chinese), *agglutinating* (a word typically consists of a neat linear sequence of morphemes, all clearly recognizable, as in Turkish or Swahili), and *inflecting* (a word typically consists of several morphemes which are tangled up together in a messy way and cannot easily be separated, as in Latin or Russian). While famous, and possibly descriptively useful, this classification too has failed to be very fruitful, though it was later developed further by Edward Sapir, who proposed several numerical indices for characterizing word structure in some detail.

But the most celebrated and fruitful of all typological classifications has proved to be one in terms of **basic word order**. Proposed by Joseph Greenberg in 1963 and more recently developed by John

Hawkins and others, word-order typology has revealed a number of striking and previously unsuspected correlations. For example, a language with SOV order is highly likely to have modifiers that precede their head nouns, auxiliaries that follow their main verbs, postpositions instead of prepositions, and a rich case system for nouns. A VSO language, in contrast, usually has modifiers that follows their nouns, auxiliaries that precede their verbs, prepositions, and no cases.

See also: **basic word order**; **morphology**; **universal**

Further reading: Comrie 1989; Croft 2002; Crystal 1997; Hawkins 1983; Horne 1966; Nevalainen *et al.* 2006; Whaley 1997.

UNIVERSAL

A statement which is true of all languages. Investigators of the past, such as the eighteenth-century German philosopher Wilhelm von Humboldt, were sometimes interested in searching for universal properties of language. But the modern interest in the subject really begins with the American linguist Joseph Greenberg in the 1960s. Since Greenberg's pioneering work, which led to a major project based at Stanford University, a number of other linguists have thrown themselves into the search for universals of language.

A separate strand of investigation was opened up around the same time by the American linguist Noam Chomsky, who proposed a search for **universal grammar**. As a result, we now distinguish between *formal universals* – universal constraints upon the form the grammar of any language can take, and usually stated at a high level of abstraction within some particular theory of grammar – and *substantive universals* – statements about the linguistic objects which can or cannot be present in languages and about their behaviour.

Here are a few substantive universals which have so far stood up well: every language distinguishes nouns and verbs; every language distinguishes three persons; every language has at least three vowels (the Caucasian language Kabardian is a possible exception to this last one, with perhaps only two vowels).

A *near-universal* is a statement which has only a very few exceptions. Here is an example: every language has at least one nasal consonant. This is almost true, but there are a couple of exceptions, which therefore become intriguing.

311

A particularly rewarding approach has been the identification of *implicational universals*, which have the form 'if a language has property P, then it must also have property Q'. Pioneered by Greenberg, this approach has been particularly developed by John Hawkins. An example: if a language has front rounded vowels, then it also has back rounded vowels.

The search for universals may sometimes lead to a **typology**. If we contemplate a conceivably universal property P, and we then find that a number of languages lack P, we may be able to set up a typological classification of P-languages versus non-P-languages. Of course, like any typology, this one will only be interesting if it turns out that the languages in each group fairly consistently have *other* properties in common besides P or not-P.

See also: **typology**; **universal grammar**

Further reading: Comrie 1989; Croft 1990; Crystal 1997; Greenberg 1963; Hawkins 1983.

UNIVERSAL GRAMMAR

The grammatical properties shared by all human languages. When the American linguist Noam Chomsky introduced his **innateness hypothesis** in the 1960s, he was arguing that important parts of the structure of human languages are built into our brains at birth. Since about 1980, Chomsky has been elaborating his position and arguing that certain fundamental principles for constructing sentences can be found in all languages and must be part of our genetic endowment, present from birth. These principles he collectively terms *universal grammar*.

Naturally, Chomsky attempts to formulate these principles within his own theoretical framework, although that framework has changed dramatically over the years. The principles are necessarily rather abstract, having to do with things like how far apart two linguistic elements can be within a sentence when they are linked in some way.

Chomsky and his followers are convinced that such principles genuinely exist, and much of their work has been devoted to uncovering them. But this has proved to be difficult: proposed principles are endlessly reformulated to cope with recalcitrant data, and a number of apparent counterexamples are dealt with by appealing to various theoretical gadgets which allow the principles to be violated in certain circumstances. Critics are often deeply suspicious of these seemingly ad-hoc manoeuvres, and some of them doubt whether the principles of universal grammar are really there at all.

See also: **Government-and-Binding Theory**

Further reading: Antony and Hornstein 2003; Cook and Newson 1996.

USAGE

The collective speaking and writing habits of a particular group of people, or a particular one of these habits. English, like any language, is far from being completely uniform. In particular, certain words, spellings, pronunciations, meanings and grammatical forms are not commonly found everywhere, but are typical only of certain places, certain professions or certain styles. Consequently, a careful description of English must provide this information, and good dictionaries of English regularly do this. Dictionaries routinely label certain forms with annotations such as (for geography) *Australian, Scots, chiefly American*, (for technical terms in various professions) *mathematics, botany, nautical, grammar*, and (for style) *slang, taboo, archaic, informal*. Such **usage labels** indicate that a particular usage is only appropriate in some particular context, and would be unexpected or out of place elsewhere.

It should be stressed that most items marked with such usage labels are no less a part of English than other items, and it is a misunderstanding to conclude that, say, slang terms or swear words are not 'real English'. But archaic words are something of a special case. These are words which have dropped out of use and no longer form a part of the modern language, except perhaps in deliberately archaic contexts like religious language, and dictionaries sometimes include them purely as a convenience to users who are trying to read texts written centuries ago. For example, because of the importance we attach to the works of Shakespeare, some dictionaries make a point of including every single word and word-meaning found in Shakespeare, even if these are found nowhere else at all.

The application of usage labels is a natural part of the approach we call **descriptivism**: describing the facts of a language as they appear to exist.

See also: **descriptivism**

Further reading: Crystal 1995.

UTTERANCE

A particular piece of **speech** produced by a particular individual on a particular occasion. In linguistics, a **sentence** is an abstract linguistic object forming one part of the total expressive resources of a given language. When we speak, therefore, we do not strictly produce sentences: instead, we produce ***utterances***. An utterance is a single piece of speech marked off as a unit in some way; for example, by pauses and **intonation**.

There is only one English sentence of the form *What's for dinner?* But, every time you say *What's for dinner?*, you are producing a different utterance. Each one of these utterances may differ noticeably from others: it may be faster or slower, louder or softer; one may be cheerful or eager, while another may be bored or suspicious, and the particular social context in which it is uttered will vary. But every one of these utterances corresponds to the same English sentence.

Moreover, an utterance need not correspond to a sentence at all. Consider the following exchange. Mike: *Where's Susie?* Sarah: *In the library.*

Here Mike's utterance corresponds to an English sentence, but Sarah's response does not: there is no English sentence of the form *In the library* (as the asterisk indicates). Of course, Sarah's response is perfectly normal: it's just that not all of our utterances correspond to sentences. Instead, some of them correspond only to ***fragments*** of sentences.

Even more dramatically, we frequently produce utterances which are interrupted or broken off. Examples: *Mike, would you get me … oh, never mind; I'll get it myself; I was just looking for the … um …* [tails off into silence]. These are still utterances, but obviously they do not correspond directly to any sentences.

See also: **sentence, speech**

Further reading: Cutting 2002; Grundy 1995; Verschueren 1999.

VARIABLE

A key element in **sociolinguistics**, the notion of the variable is based on the premise that a linguistic feature can have different realizations and that these are distributed in correspondence with a social factor. The ***linguistic variable*** is a language feature (most usually a phonetic feature of a particular **accent**, though lexical and grammatical variables have also been used) which has at least two distinguishable **variants**. The distribution of these variants can be shown not to be random but to have a correlation with a *social variable* such as age, class, gender, geography, politics, education, and so on. Mapping the nature and frequencies of these correlations is a major explanatory method in **variationist sociolinguistics**. In statistical terms, the linguistic variable is the **dependent variable**, and the social variable is the **independent variable**.

For example, in the most famous small-scale study in sociolinguistics, the American linguist William Labov explored the pronunciation of the linguistic variable of rhoticity (pronunciation of non-prevocalic /r/) in the phrase 'fourth floor'. By asking a question to which he knew this was the answer, and then pretending to mishear so that the informant repeated it, he was able to observe four occurrences of /r/: word-medial non-prevocalic; word-final non-prevocalic; emphatic word-medial non-prevocalic; and emphatic word-final non-prevocalic. By asking these in three different New York department stores of hierarchical status, he was able to demonstrate a prestige value for rhoticity in New York accents. Many sociolinguistic studies have applied this basic principle since.

See also: **accent**; **sociolinguistics**

Further reading: Llamas *et al.* 2007; Stockwell 2002a; Wardhaugh 2005.

VARIATION

The existence of observable differences in the way a language is used in a speech community. It is a commonplace observation that a single language is not used in a totally homogeneous manner within a single community. Stockbrokers do not speak like plumbers; men do not speak like women; older people do not speak like younger people. Moreover, even the speech of a single person is not homogeneous: you don't speak in the same way when you're chatting to friends in a bar and when you're being interviewed for a job, and even in a single context you might say *telephone* or *I got cheated* one moment but *phone* or *I got ripped off* the next.

This **variation** was long regarded by most linguists as no more than a collection of tiresome details getting in the way of good descriptions, as something to be swept under the carpet and forgotten about. But times have changed. In the 1960s, the **socio-linguists**, led by the American William Labov, began to make variation a central object of investigation, and the result has been a revolution in linguistics: we now realize that variation, far from being peripheral and inconsequential, is a vital part of ordinary linguistic behaviour.

To begin with, variation often shows strong correlations with social variables like social class and sex, and the **social stratification of language** is now a prominent feature of sociolinguistic investigations. Further, the introduction of the **quantitative approach** to language description has revealed important patterns of linguistic behaviour which were previously invisible. The concept of a sociolinguistic **variable** has become central to the description of speech. A variable is some point of usage for which two or more competing forms are available in a community, with speakers showing interesting and significant differences in the frequency with which they use one or another of these competing forms.

Furthermore, it has been discovered that variation is typically the vehicle of **language change**, and as a result a satisfactory resolution has finally been obtained for the **Saussurean paradox**.

See also: **quantitative method**; **Saussurean paradox**; **social stratification of language**; **sociolinguistics**

Further reading: Chambers 2003; Chambers *et al.* 2002; Foulkes and Docherty 1999; Holmes 1992; Hudson 1996; Llamas *et al.* 2007.

VERB

The **part of speech** which includes words like *go, see, understand* and *seem*. The class of **verbs** is universal: no language has ever been discovered which lacked a distinct class of verbs. The most proto-typical verbs denote actions performed by an agent, such as *run, sing, throw, hit* and *give*. But many other items are verbs even though they have less typical meanings, such as *die, sleep, believe, understand, elapse, ensue, become, seem, have* and *be*. The English **auxiliaries**, like *must* and *should*, are also usually classed as verbs, though a few linguists disagree here.

What unites the class of verbs is their grammatical behaviour. For example, verbs in English and in many other languages are marked for **tense**: *Susie drinks brandy* versus *Susie drank brandy.*

Verbs also frequently exhibit **agreement**, though English has only a tiny amount of this, as in *Susie smokes* versus *Susie and Janet smoke.*

But the most central characteristic of a verb is the requirement that it must be accompained by one or more **noun phrases**, its **arguments**, in a grammatical sentence. For example, *smile* and *smoke* take only one argument (*Susie smiled*; *Susie smokes*); *buy* and *kiss* require two (*Susie bought a car*; *Susie kissed Natalie*); and *give* and *show* require three (*Susie gave me this book*; *Susie showed Mike her new car*). A very few verbs, though, are unusual, such as *rain* and *seem*: *It's raining*; *It seems that Susie is away.*

These differences in grammatical behaviour illustrate **sub-categorization**, and they involve differences in **transitivity**.

See also: **subcategorization**; **tense**; **transitivity**

Further reading: Greenbaum and Quirk 1990; Hurford 1994; Jackson 2002.

VERB PHRASE

A unit of sentence structure consisting of a **verb** and the other elements closely linked to it. Traditional grammarians divided a typical sentence into two parts: a **subject** and a **predicate**. In our modern elaboration of this, the **syntactic category** which acts as a subject is a **noun phrase**, while the category acting as a predicate is a *verb phrase*. A verb phrase always contains a verb, and it usually contains some other material closely linked to that verb.

Here are some examples, with the verb phrases serving as predicates bracketed: *Susie [smokes]*; *Susie's sister [has a new girlfriend]*; *The rest of us [strolled down to the pub for a drink]*.

A verb phrase need not serve as a predicate. In the following examples, the bracketed verb phrases are doing something different: *[Smoking forty cigarettes a day] is bad for your health*; *[Needing some legal advice], Susie rang her lawyer*; *Susie has decided [to buy a new car]*.

When a sentence contains an **auxiliary**, linguists differ in their analyses. For most linguists, the sentence *Susie has finished her dinner* contains two verb phrases, a smaller one inside a larger one, as follows: *Susie [has [finished her dinner]]*. Others, though, would recognize only one verb phrase: either *Susie [has finished her dinner]* or *Susie has [finished her dinner]*, with the auxiliary excluded from the verb phrase in this last analysis.

317

With multiple auxiliaries, things become more complicated. Most linguists would analyse *Susie* [*has* [*been* [*smoking a lot*]]] as containing three verb phrases, as shown. The first dissenting view would again recognize only one, as in *Susie* [*has been smoking a lot*], while the other has a serious problem, possibly to be resolved as *Susie* [*has been*] [*smoking a lot*].

See also: **predicate**; **syntactic category**; **verb**

Further reading: Gramley and Pätzold 1992; Greenbaum and Quirk 1990; Jackson 2002.

VERNACULAR

The ordinary, everyday speech of a particular community, sometimes informally called its **mother tongue**. The term **vernacular** is most commonly contrasted with **standard language**. The vernacular speech of a particular community is the ordinary speech used by the people in a particular community, such as Chicago, Liverpool or Sydney, when this is noticeably different from the standard form of the language.

Especially where European languages were concerned, the linguists of the past normally concentrated on the standard forms of languages. Non-standard vernacular forms were silently ignored, except only in the study of regional **dialects**, for which the speech of elderly rural speakers was considered most appropriate; at the same time, the speech of younger speakers or of urban speakers was similarly ignored.

Interest in vernacular forms developed only slowly during the twentieth century, but it became increasingly prominent with the rise of **sociolinguistics** in the 1960s. Today, there is intense interest in vernacular forms of speech, which are now seen as every bit as worthy of study as standard varieties of languages. Most prominent so far is the study of vernacular forms of English, for which the British sociolinguists Jim and Lesley Milroy have recently coined the slightly facetious term *real English*, partly in recognition of the observation that certain forms and usages absent from standard English, such as *he don't*, are extremely widespread in vernacular forms of English almost everywhere.

See also: **standard language**

Further reading: Cheshire and Stein 1997; Milroy and Milroy 1993, 1997.

VOCAL TRACT

The part of our body through which air passes during speech. The vocal tract runs from the lungs up through the trachea (or wind-pipe), through the pharynx (the space at the back of the mouth), and there it divides into the oral cavity (the space inside the mouth) and the nasal cavity; it reaches the outside world at the lips and at the nostrils. As a general rule, during speech, air flows upwards and outwards through the vocal tract, though in certain less usual **air-stream mechanisms** something different happens.

In the throat, the vocal tract passes through a complex structure called the *larynx*; within the larynx is an opening called the *glottis*, which can be opened wide to allow air to pass through freely, closed tight to block the flow of air, or closed loosely. In this last case, two bands of tissue called the *vocal folds* – between which the glottis is located – undergo vibration, and this produces **voicing**.

Between the oral cavity and the nasal cavity is a hinged flap of tissue called the *velum* (or 'soft palate'); when the velum is raised, the nasal cavity is closed off, and no air can flow through it, but, when the velum is lowered, air can flow out through the nose.

Within the oral cavity, the size and shape of the vocal tract can be greatly varied, by raising or lowering the jaw, by moving the tongue around, and by altering the position of the lips. Whenever these movements are such as to greatly obstruct the flow of air, the resulting sound is a **consonant**; when the obstruction is minimal, the result is a **vowel**.

See also: **airstream mechanism; phonetics; voicing**

Further reading: Ashby 1995; Ball and Rahilly 1999; Clark and Yallop 1995; Collins and Mees 2003; Denes and Pinson 1993.

VOICE

The **grammatical category** governing the way the subject of a sentence is related to the action of the verb. English has only a two-way distinction of voice. In the *active voice*, the subject of the sentence is typically the entity performing the action, as in *Tamerlane imprisoned Sultan Bayezit*. In the *passive voice*, the subject is instead the entity undergoing the action, as in *Sultan Bayezit was imprisoned by Tamerlane*, or in *Sultan Bayezit was imprisoned*. The first is called the *long passive*, or *passive-with-agent*; the second is the *short passive*.

In English, the active voice is *unmarked* (see **markedness**): it is grammatically simpler and far more frequent in speech. The passive voice is *marked*, and it is most typically used either to make the entity undergoing the action the centre of attention, or to remove the entity performing the action (the *agent*) from the centre of attention, and possibly to remove it from the sentence altogether. For example, we write *Uranium was discovered in 1789, but its importance was not recognized before the middle of the twentieth century*. Here the dates are far more important than the name of the discoverer, and identifying the people who failed to recognize the importance of uranium would be pointless, since these people included everybody.

Not all languages have a contrast between active and passive voices. But some other languages have additional voices, allowing the subject of the sentence to be not only the performer of the action or the recipient of the action, but also the instrument with which the action is performed, or the place in which the action is done.

See also: **verb**

Further reading: Greenbaum and Quirk 1990; Hurford 1994; Jackson 2002; Klaiman 1991; Palmer 1971.

VOICING

Vibration of the vocal folds. The vocal folds (or vocal cords) are two movable masses of tissue in the larynx (the voice box). They can be brought close together so that they vibrate all along their length as air flows up from the lungs and into the pharynx, mouth and nose. This vibration is *voicing*, and any speech sound which is produced with such vibration is *voiced*. Examples of voiced sounds are [a], [w], [n], [l], [z], [b] and [dʒ]. If you put your fingers to your throat while pronouncing one of these, you can feel the vibration.

If the vocal folds are moved farther apart, they cannot vibrate. A speech sound produced without vibration is *voiceless*. Examples of voiceless sounds are [f], [s], [p], [k], [h] and [tʃ]. The glottal stop, [ʔ], is also voiceless, but for a different reason: here the vocal folds are pressed so tightly together that no air can flow through them and hence no vibration occurs.

The vocal folds can also behave in more complicated ways, producing several complex **phonation types** in addition to voicing and voicelessness.

Note that the term **voicing** is also applied to something else: to a change in pronunciation in which a formerly voiceless sound becomes voiced. For example, the Spanish phoneme /s/ is normally a voiceless sound [s], but in certain circumstances it becomes a voiced sound [z], as in *mismo* 'same' (in standard European pronunciation, however, not all speakers do this).

See also: **consonant**; **phonation type**

Further reading: Ball and Rahilly 1999; Catford 1988; Collins and Mees 2003; Laver 1994.

VOWEL

A **speech sound** produced with no obstruction of the airstream. From the point of view of **phonetics**, speech sounds may be conveniently divided into two types: those which are produced with a substantial obstruction of the airstream and those which are not. The first are **consonants**, the second *vowels*.

If you pronounce a few vowels, such as [a], [i] and [u], you will find that the flow of air through your **vocal tract** is nowhere impeded. What makes one vowel sound different from another is the size and shape of the space within your mouth: the jaw is higher or lower, the tongue is higher or lower, either the front or the back of the tongue may be raised, and the lips may be rounded or spread. These variations affect the way in which the air in the mouth resonates, and they are responsible for the different qualities of the vowels.

Certain speech sounds which are strictly vowels are commonly treated as consonants, for a reason to be explained below. For example, the English *y*-sound, as in *yes* and *yard*, whose phonetic symbol is [j], is really nothing but a very brief version of the vowel

[i], as in *see*, and the [w] of *weed* and *war* is likewise only a brief version of the vowel [u], as in *moon*. Moreover, for most (not all) English-speakers, the /r/ at the beginning of *red* is really only a slightly odd vowel pronounced with some part of the tongue raised. Yet all of these are generally classed as consonants.

The reason for this is that there is a second way of defining vowels and consonants, one which gives different results from the first. This second approach is the one preferred in **phonology**, in which we are more concerned with the way sounds behave than with their phonetic nature. And the point is that the sounds just mentioned, even though they are phonetically vowels, *behave* like consonants in English.

A **syllable** always contains a *peak of sonority*, a part which is louder and more sonorous than the rest, and in most languages (including English), this peak must be a vowel. In the majority of syllables, this vowel is preceded and/or followed by some number of consonants. Usually these consonants are consonants by any definition, as in *key* /kiː/, *eat* /iːt/, *sat* /sæt/, *slap* /slæp/ and *fleeced* /fliːst/. However, the sounds /j/, /w/ and /r/ pattern like consonants, not like vowels, as in *yes* /jes/, *wet* /wet/ and *red* /red/, and consequently they are classed as consonants, in spite of their phonetic nature.

When you come across the word vowel, therefore, you must check to see if it is being used in the phonetic sense or in the phonological sense.

See also: **consonant**; **speech sound**; **syllable**

Further reading: Ball and Rahilly 1999; Collins and Mees 2003; Ladefoged 1993; Ladefoged and Maddieson 1996; Laver 1994.

WELL-FORMEDNESS

The status of a linguistic form in a language which conforms to the rules of that language. Well-formedness is a central concept in the analytical study of language, and it can be recognized at several different levels of analysis.

At the level of **phonology**, it is clear that *brick* is a well-formed English word, consisting of a permissible sequence of English consonants and vowels. So is *blick*, even though no such word happens to exist: this word *could* exist, since it obeys all the rules. But *bnick* is not well formed, since the rules of English do not permit a word to begin with the sequence /bn-/. Even a real word may be ill formed: the French word *genre* is well formed in French, but not in English, and English-speakers must either struggle to give it a French-style pronunciation, or simply change the pronunciation to conform to the rules of English, producing something that sounds like *jonra* or *jonner*. Even *sphere* is arguably not well formed, since English does not normally allow a word to begin with the sequence /sf-/: nobody would name a new detergent *Sfizz*.

At the level of **morphology**, words like *unhappiness* and *existentialism* are well formed, since they obey all the rules for combining **morphemes** into words, but things like *happy-un-ness* and *exist-al-ism-ence* are not, since they violate these same rules. Even though they follow the regular rules for making plurals, the forms *womans* and *childs* are not well formed, since *woman* and *child* happen to be subject to special rules that require their plurals to be *women* and *children*.

At the level of **syntax**, *There's a spider on the bed* is well formed, but *Bed the on spider a there's* is anything but well formed, since it violates the rules of English word-order. Similarly, *Susie has written a letter* is well formed, but *Susie has writing a letter* is not, since it violates a rule of English syntax. Syntactic well-formedness is often called **grammaticality**.

At the level of **semantics**, there are also rules for combining meanings. For example, the phrase *a tall woman* is semantically well formed, while *a female woman* is somewhat anomalous, since the meaning of *female* is already present in the meaning of *woman*, and *a valid woman* is virtually impossible to interpret sensibly. *Jezebel killed Ahab, but Ahab didn't die* is semantically anomalous, assuming only one Ahab is involved, since *Ahab died* is an integral part of the meaning of *killed Ahab*. Making these make sense often involves imagining different **possible worlds** in which physical laws or social attitudes are at odds with our own.

At the level of **pragmatics** and **discourse**, some utterances and exchanges are well formed while others are not. In reply to the question *Is Susie coming to Mike's party on Saturday?*, the response *I don't think so* is obviously well formed, and the response *Natalie wants to go to a concert* might be well formed in certain circumstances (for example, if Natalie is Susie's girlfriend), but the response *Susie used to be that little girl in the pizza commercial* would probably not be well formed in any circumstances.

Anything which is not well formed is ***ill-formed***, or sometimes ***anomalous***. A very great deal of work in linguistics consists of identifying the rules governing well-formedness at all levels of analysis.

See also: **rule**; **structure**

Further reading: Jeffries 2006.

WORD

A linguistic unit typically larger than a **morpheme** but smaller than a **phrase**. The term *word* might seem familiar and straightforward enough, but in fact words can be defined in at least four different ways, and these ways are not equivalent at all.

- An *orthographic word* is something written with white spaces at both ends but no white space in the middle. Orthographic words are of minimal linguistic interest.
- A *phonological word* is something pronounced as a single unit.
- A *lexical item*, or **lexeme**, is a dictionary word, an item which you would expect to find having its own entry in a dictionary.
- A *grammatical word-form* (GWF) (or *morphosyntactic word*) is any one of the several forms which a lexical item may assume for grammatical purposes.

Let's look at some examples. The item *ice cream* is two orthographic words, but a single phonological word (it's pronounced as a unit), a single lexical item (it's entered in the dictionary), and a single GWF (indeed, it hardly has another form, unless you think the plural *ices cream* is good English).

The singular *dog* and the plural *dogs* are each a single orthographic word, a single phonological word, and a single GWF, but they both represent the same lexical item (they would only get one entry in the dictionary). The same is true of *take, takes, took, taken* and *taking*: five orthographic words, five phonological words, five GWFs (at least), but only one lexical item. The two lexical items here would be entered in the dictionary as *dog* and *take*; these are the *citation forms*, or the **lemma** form, of these lexical items, the forms we use in naming them or talking about them.

The contraction *hasn't* is a single orthographic word and a single phonological word, but it's two lexical items (*have* and *not*), and two GWFs (*has* and *not*). The phrasal verb *make up* (as in *She made up her face*) is two orthographic words, two phonological words, but only one lexical item (because of its unpredictable meaning, it must be entered separately in the dictionary). And it has several GWFs: *make up, makes up, made up, making up.* The very different sense of *make up* illustrated by *She made up a story* would be regarded by most linguists as a different lexical item from the preceding one (a separate dictionary entry is required), but this lexical item exhibits the same orthographic, phonological and grammatical forms as the first.

Consequently, when you are talking about words, it is essential to specify exactly which sense you have in mind, and it may be preferable to use one of the more specific labels.

The study of words is **lexicology**.

See also: **lemma**; **part of speech**

Further reading: Hoey 2005; Jackson 2000; Katamba 1994; Matthews 1991.

WORD-FORMATION

The process of constructing new words from existing materials. There are many ways of constructing new words, and English uses almost all of them.

In *compounding*, two (or more) existing words are simply combined. There are several different patterns available for doing this, as in *blackboard, redneck, overthrow, olive green, scarecrow* and *forget-me-not*. Sometimes an **affix** is also present, as in *blue-eyed* and *flat-earther*.

In **derivation**, affixes are added to an existing word, as in *prehistory, rewrite, unsafe, washable, prohibition* and *finalize*. Multiple affixes are possible, as in *misdirection, illegitimacy, transformational* and *existentialism*.

In *clipping*, a piece is removed from a longer word, as with *bra, gym, flu, phone* and *cello*. In *blending*, pieces of two words are combined, as in *smog* (*smoke* plus *fog*). In *back-formation*, a new word is extracted from a longer word that appears to contain an affix but historically does not, as with *pea* from earlier *pease*, *edit* from earlier *editor*, and *burgle* from the earlier *burglar*.

Reanalysis involves changing the structure assigned to a word and extracting a piece that formerly was not a part of it, as when *hamburger* (*Hamburg* +*-er*) was reanalysed as *ham* +*-burger*, yielding the *-burger* now used in *cheeseburger* and *vegeburger*.

Combining the initial letters of a phrase into a single word yields an **acronym** if the result can be pronounced as a word (as with *laser*, from *light amplification by the stimulated emission of radiation*), but an **initialism** if it must be spelled out letter by letter, as with *FBI* and *BBC*.

Most of our technical terms are constructed by gluing together Greek and Latin **combining forms** of appropriate meaning: so, for example, the recently discovered creatures which flourish at or above the temperature of boiling water have been named *hyperthermophiles*, from three Greek elements meaning 'high-heat-lover'.

See also: **affix**; **derivation**; **morphology**

Further reading: Adams 1973; Bauer 1983; Katamba 1994.

WRITING SYSTEM

A conventional system for representing a language with permanent marks. Though human beings have been able to speak for many tens of thousands of years, writing systems were invented only a little more than 5,000 years ago, in Asia Minor. True writing was preceded by **precursors** which were adequate for recording only certain types of information, such as taxes due and paid. In a true writing system, however, any utterance of the language can be adequately written down.

There are several conceivable ways of constructing a writing system. We might attempt to provide a separate symbol for every different word-form of a language. This would mean, for example, that separate symbols would have to be provided for all of *drive*, *drives*, *driving*, *drove*, *driven*, *driver*, *drivers*, *driveway*, and so on. But the number of symbols required would be astronomical, and every new word or word-form entering the language would require a new symbol, and so such a system is completely unworkable.

Or we could provide a separate symbol for each **morpheme** in the language. Thus *drive* would have its own symbol, but *drives* would be written with the symbol for *drive* plus the symbol for present-tense *-s*, and *driver* with the symbol for *drive* plus that for *-er*, and so on. This is called a **logographic** system (though it might better be called a **morphemographic** system), and it actually works fairly well with a language whose words show little or no variation in form for grammatical purposes. Chinese is such a language, and still today Chinese is written in a logographic script – though naturally the number of different characters required still runs into many thousands. But note that Chinese does not provide a separate character for every word. There is a character for the word *hŭo* 'fire' and another for the word *chē* 'vehicle', but the word for 'train', *hŭochē*, literally 'fire-vehicle', is simply written with a combination of these two characters.

A third possibility is to provide a separate symbol for every distinct syllable in the language. Japanese does this. So, the Japanese word *ikura* 'how many?' is written with one symbol for /i/, a second for /ku/, and a third for /ra/, and similarly for every other word (except that Japanese uses Chinese characters to write many words). This kind of writing system is a *syllabary*, and it really only works well with a language which has only a small number of distinct syllables – no more than a few dozen. When a language permits very many different syllables, then either the number of symbols required becomes huge, or the system must be *defective* in some way – for example, a single symbol may be used to represent a number of distinct but somewhat similar syllables. The *Linear B* syllabary used to write Mycenaean Greek was like this: for example, the same symbol was used to write *to, tho, tos, thon*, and other syllables.

Finally, we can provide a separate symbol for each **phoneme** in the language – that is, for each distinctive consonant and vowel. Such a writing system is an *alphabet*, and alphabetic writing, the last type to be invented, is now by far the world's most frequent type of writing. The first alphabets, invented by speakers of Semitic languages thousands of years ago, were in fact defective, in that they provided *letters* (as alphabetic symbols are called) only for consonants; it was the Greeks who constructed the first complete alphabet by adding letters for vowels. In an ideal alphabetic writing system, every consonant and vowel in the language has its own consistent letter, and the spelling of a word is completely predictable from its pronunciation, but in practice few alphabetic scripts approach this ideal. In English, with its exceptionally complex and irregular spelling system, the spelling of a word typically exhibits only a modest correlation with its pronunciation (note the spellings of *rite, write, right* and *wright*, the verb *lead* and the name of the metal *lead*, and curiosities like *debt, knight, buy, pharaoh* and *autumn*), and our supposedly alphabetic system has become more similar to the Chinese logographic script, in which the representation of each simple word has to be learned as a unit.

Mixed systems are possible. The enormously complex Japanese writing system mostly uses Chinese characters to represent the stems of words, but a Japanese syllabary to represent grammatical words and grammatical endings, and it uses a second syllabary for various special purposes, such as writing words of foreign origin. The ancient Egyptian hieroglyphic writing system was almost numbingly complex, using a mixture of characters of various types to provide clues about both pronunciation and meaning.

In principle, any language can be written in any writing system, though not always with the same degree of success. Several central Asian languages have, during the past century, been successively written in the Arabic alphabet, in the Roman alphabet and in the Cyrillic (Russian) alphabet, depending on which way the political winds were blowing; Korean is sometimes written in Chinese characters but at other times in the local Han'gul alphabet; Chinese and Japanese are both sometimes written in the Roman alphabet for special purposes, but both the Chinese and the Japanese have so far resisted pressures to change over completely to the Roman alphabet. Turkish, in contrast, abandoned the Arabic alphabet in the 1920s in favour of the Roman alphabet, at least officially.

Note carefully that every writing system ever used represents an attempt at recording utterances in a particular language. There has never been a real writing system which attempted to represent 'ideas' or 'thoughts' directly, without the mediation of a particular language, and suggestions to the contrary are ignorant and fantastic. (A few philosophers have occasionally tried to invent such systems, but they don't work.)

The study of writing systems is sometimes called *graphology* (not to be confused with the 'psychological' interpretation of handwriting, a form of charlatanism of the same name).

See also: **orthography; punctuation; spelling**

Further reading: Biber 2006; Coulmas 1996; Crystal 1997; Daniels and Bright 1996; Fromkin and Rodman 1998; O'Grady *et al.* 1996; Robinson 1995; Sampson 1985.

X-BAR

A system of syntactic description based on the notion that every constituent has a **head** element. The X stands for any lexical head, such as N (**noun**), V (**verb**) or P (**preposition**), and the 'bar' refers to the notational symbol placed over the X-element to indicate the other elements of the construction: $\bar{N}$ or N^2, which can read as 'N-bar' and 'N-double-bar'. The system asserts that every syntactic category is complex. Even nouns with no other element count as noun-phrases by virtue of having a zero entry for the 'bar' element. This forces the analyst to treat every construction as having a head.

X-bar theory consists of three basic syntactic assembly rules, which allow an enormous number of permutations, since they are **recursive**. First, an X-bar consists of an X (a head) plus any number of complements. Second, an X-bar can consist of an X-bar and an adjunct, in any sequence (this gives the recursive property). Last, an X-Phrase consists of an optional specifier and an X-bar, in any sequence. To give an example involving the last of these rules, a simple noun phrase like *this fat book* consists of a N-bar (*fat book*) plus a specifier (*this*). The N-bar phrase itself consists of another N-Bar (the head *book* with a zero bar element) plus a specifier (*fat*). The system – especially when drawn as a **tree** – gives the rules for constituent structure. The other rules, and all of them applied to verb-phrases and prepositional phrases, can be used to generate the syntactic sequences of, it is claimed, all the languages of the world. Almost all current theories of grammar employ some variant on this system.

See also: **head**; **phrase-structure grammar**; **transformational grammar**; **tree**

Further reading: Borsley 1999; Cook and Newson 1996.

Bibliography

Aarts, Bas and McMahon, April (eds) (2006) *The Handbook of English Linguistics*, Oxford: Blackwell.

Adams, Valerie (1973) *An Introduction to Modern English Word-Formation*, London: Longman.

Adolphs, Svenja (2006) *Introducing Electronic Text Analysis*, London: Routledge.

Auer, Peter, Hinskens, F. and Kerswill, Paul (eds) (2005) *Dialect Change*, Cambridge: Cambridge University Press.

Aitchison, Jean (1994) *Words in the Mind* (2nd edn), Oxford: Blackwell.

—— (1996) *The Seeds of Speech*, Cambridge: Cambridge University Press.

—— (1998) *The Articulate Mammal* (4th edn), London: Routledge.

—— (2001) *Language Change: Progress or Decay?* (3rd edn), Cambridge: Cambridge University Press.

Akmajian, Adrian, Demers, Richard A., Farmer, Ann K. and Harnish, Robert M. (1995) *Linguistics: An Introduction to Language and Communication*, Cambridge, MA: MIT Press.

Allan, Keith (1986) *Linguistic Meaning* (2 vols), London: Routledge.

Allen, Donald E. and Guy, Rebecca F. (1974) *Conversation Analysis: The Sociology of Talk*, The Hague: Mouton.

Antony, Louise M. and Hornstein, Norbert (eds) (2003) *Chomsky and His Critics*, Oxford: Blackwell.

Anttila, Raimo (1988) *An Introduction to Historical and Comparative Linguistics* (2nd edn), London: Macmillan.

Archangeli, Diana and Langendoen, D. Terence (eds) (1997) *Optimality Theory: An Overview*, Oxford: Blackwell.

Ashby, Patricia (1995) *Speech Sounds*, London: Routledge.

Asher, R.E. and Simpson, J.M.Y. (eds) (1994) *Encyclopedia of Language and Linguistics* (10 vols), Oxford: Pergamon.

Auer, Peter (ed.) (1998) *Code-Switching in Conversation: Language, Interaction and Identity*, London: Routledge.

Austin, J.L. (1962) *How to Do Things with Words*, Oxford: Clarendon Press.

Bach, Emmon (1974) *Syntactic Theory*, New York: Holt, Rinehart & Winston.

Baker, Marc (1996) *The Polysynthesis Parameter*, Oxford: Oxford University Press.

Bakhtin, Mikhail (1968) *Rabelais and his World* (trans. Helene Iswolsky), Cambridge, MA: MIT Press.

—— (1984) *Problems of Dostoevsky's Poetics* (ed. and trans. Caryl Emerson, *Problemy Tvorchestva Dostoyevskogo*, 1929), Manchester: Manchester University Press.

Baldi, Philip (1983) *An Introduction to the Indo-European Languages*, Carbondale and Edwardsville, IL: Southern Illinois University Press.

Ball, Martin and Rahilly, Joan (1999) *Phonetics: The Science of Speech*, London: Arnold.

Barnbrook, Geoff (1996) *Language and Computers: A Practical Introduction to the Computer Analysis of Language*, Edinburgh: Edinburgh University Press.

Barss, Andrew (ed.) (2003) *Anaphora: A Reference Guide*, Oxford: Blackwell.

Bates, Elizabeth (1976) *Language and Context: The Acquisition of Progmatics*, New York: Academic Press.

Bates, Elizabeth, Benigni, L., Bretherton, Inge, Camaioni, L. and Volterra, V. (1979) *The Emergence of Symbols: Cognition and Communication in Infancy*, New York: Academic Press.

Bates, Elizabeth, Bretherton, Inge and Synder, Lynn (1988) *From First Words to Grammar*, Cambridge: Cambridge University Press.

Bauer, Laurie (1983) *English Word-Formation*, Cambridge: Cambridge University Press.

—— (1988) *Introducing Linguistic Morphology*, Edinburgh: Edinburgh University Press.

—— (1998) *Vocabulary*, London: Routledge.

Beekes, Robert S.P. (1995) *Comparative Indo-European Linguistics*, Amsterdam: Benjamins.

Bennett, Paul (1995) *A Course in Generalized Phrase Structure Grammar*, London: UCL Press.

Berko Gleason, Jean (1997) *The Development of Language* (4th edn), Boston, MA: Allyn & Bacon.

Berlin, Brent and Kay, Paul (1969) *Basic Color Terms: Their Universality and Evolution*, Berkeley, CA: University of California Press.

Bex, Tony and Watts, Richard (eds) (1999) *Standard English: The Widening Debate*, London: Routledge.

Bhatia, V.K. (1993) *Analysing Genre: Language Use in Professional Settings*, London: Longman.

Biber, Douglas (2006) *University Language: A Corpus-Based Study of Spoken and Written Registers*, Amsterdam: Benjamins.

Bickerton, Derek (1981) *Roots of Language*, Ann Arbor, MI: Karoma.

—— (1984) 'The Language Bioprogram Hypothesis', *Behavioral and Brain Sciences* 7: 173–221.

—— (1990) *Language and Species*, Chicago, IL: University of Chicago Press.

—— (1996) *Language and Human Behaviour*, London: UCL Press.

Binnick, R. I. (1991) *Time and the Verb: A Guide to Tense and Aspect*, Oxford: Oxford University Press.

Blake, Barry (2001) *Case* (2nd edn), Cambridge: Cambridge University Press.

Blake, N.F. (1996) *A History of the English Language*, London: Macmillan.

Blakemore, Diane (1992) *Understanding Utterances*, Oxford: Blackwell.

Bloomfield, Leonard (1933) *Language*, New York: Holt, Rinehart & Winston.

Bloor, Thomas and Bloor, Meriel (2004) *The Functional Analysis of English: A Hallidayan Approach* (2nd edn), London: Arnold.

Blutner, Remhard and Zeevat, Henk (2003) *Optimality Theory and Pragmatics*, Basingstoke: Palgrave Macmillan.

Bodmer, Frederick (1944) *The Loom of Language*, London: Allen & Unwin.

Bonvillain, Nancy (1993) *Language, Culture, and Communication: The Meaning of Messages*, Englewood Cliffs, NJ: Prentice-Hall.

Borsley, Robert (1991) *Syntactic Theory: A Unified Approach*, London: Arnold.

—— (1996) *Modern Phrase Structure Grammar*, Oxford: Blackwell.

—— (1999) *Syntactic Theory: A Unified Approach* (2nd edn), London: Arnold.

Bradford, Richard (1997) *Stylistics*, London: Routledge.

Bratt-Paulston, C. and Tucker R. (2003) *Sociolinguistics: The Essential Readings.* Oxford: Blackwell.

British Dyslexia Association (1996) *Getting the Message Across: Dyslexia: A Hundred Years of Progress?* Birmingham: Questions.

Brown, Gillian and Yule, George (1983) *Discourse Analysis*, Cambridge: Cambridge University Press.

Brown, Keith and Miller, Jim (1991) *Syntax: A Linguistic Introduction to Sentence Structure* (2nd edn), London: HarperCollins.

Brown, Penelope, and Levinson, Stephen (1987) *Politeness: Some Universals in Language Usage*, Cambridge: Cambridge University Press.

Brutt-Griffler, J. (2002) *World English: A Study of its Development*, Clevedon: Multilingual Matters.

Buckingham, Thomas and Yorkey, Richard (1984) *Cloze Encounters: ESL Exercises in a Cultural Context*, London: Prentice-Hall.

Burke, Peter (1993) *The Art of Conversation*, Cambridge: Polity Press.

Burton-Roberts, Noel (1986) *Analysing Sentences*, London: Longman.

Butler, Christopher S. (1985) *Systemic Linguistics: Theory and Applications*, London: Batsford.

Butt, Miriam and King, Tracy (2000) *Argument Realisation*, Stanford, CA: CSLI.

Bybee, Joan L., Perkins, Revere and Pagliuca, William (1994) *The Evolution of Grammar: Tense, Aspect, and Modality in the Languages of the World*, Chicago, IL: University of Chicago Press.

Cameron, Deborah (1995) *Verbal Hygiene*, London: Routledge.

Cameron, Deborah and Kulick, Don (2003) *Language and Sexuality*, Cambridge: Cambridge University Press.

Caplan, David (1992) *Language: Structure, Processing and Disorders*, Cambridge, MA: MIT Press.

Carr, Philip (1993) *Phonology*, London: Macmillan.

Carter, Ronald (1997) *Investigating English Discourse*, London: Routledge.

—— (2004) *Language and Creativity: The Art of Common Talk*, London: Routledge.

Carter, Ronald, Goddard, Angela, Reah, Danuta, Sanger, Keith and Bowring, Maggie (1997) *Working with Texts: A Core Book for Language Analysis*, London: Routledge.

Catford, J.C. (1977) *Fundamental Problems in Phonetics*, Edinburgh: Edinburgh University Press.

—— (1988) *A Practical Introduction to Phonetics*, Oxford: Oxford University Press.

Chafe, Wallace (1970) *Meaning and the Structure of Language*, Chicago, IL: University of Chicago Press.

—— (1994) *Discourse, Consciousness and Time*, Chicago, IL: University of Chicago Press.

Chambers, J.K. (2003) *Sociolinguistic Theory: Linguistic Variation and its Social Significance* (2nd edn), Oxford: Blackwell.

Chambers, J.K. and Trudgill, Peter (1998) *Dialectology* (2nd edn), Cambridge: Cambridge University Press.

Chambers, J.K., Trudgill, P. and Schilling-Estes, N. (eds) (2002) *The Handbook of Language Variation and Change*, Oxford: Blackwell, pp. 402–22.

Channell, Joanna (1994) *Vague Language*, Oxford: Oxford University Press.

Chapman, Siobhan (2000) *Philosophy for Linguists*, London: Routledge.

—— (2006) *Thinking about Language*, Basingstoke: Palgrave Macmillan.

Chaudenson, R. (2001) *Creolization of Language and Culture*, London: Routledge.

Cheshire, Jenny and Stein, Dieter (eds) (1997) *Taming the Vernacular: From Dialect to Written Standard Language*, London: Longman.

Chilton, Paul (2003) *Analysing Political Disocurse*, London: Routledge.

Chomsky, Noam (1977) *The Logical Structure of Linguistic Theory*, New York: Plenum Press.

—— (1995) *The Minimalist Program*, Cambridge, MA: MIT Press.

—— (2000) *The Architecture of Language*, Oxford: Oxford University Press.

Clark, John and Yallop, Colin (1995) *An Introduction to Phonetics and Phonology* (2nd edn), Oxford: Blackwell.

Coates, Jennifer (1983) *The Semantics of the Modal Auxiliaries*, London: Croom Helm.

—— (1996) *Women Talk*, Oxford: Blackwell.

—— (ed.) (1998) *Language and Gender: A Reader*, Oxford: Blackwell.

—— (2004) *Women, Men and Language* (3rd edn), London: Longman.

Cobley, Paul (ed.) (2001) *The Routledge Companion to Semiotics and Linguistics*, London: Routledge.

Collins Cobuild (1990) *English Grammar*: London: HarperCollins.

Collins, Beverley and Mees, Inger (2003) *Practical Phonetics and Phonology: A Resource Book for Students*, London: Routledge.

Comrie, Bernard (1976) *Aspect*, Cambridge: Cambridge University Press.

—— (1985) *Tense*, Cambridge: Cambridge University Press.

—— (1989) *Language Universals and Linguistic Typology*, Oxford: Blackwell.

Comrie, Bernard, Matthews, Stephen and Polinsky, Maria (1997) *The Atlas of Languages*, London: Bloomsbury.

Connell, R.W. (1995) *Masculinities*, Cambridge: Polity Press.

Cook, Guy (1994) *Discourse and Literature*, Oxford: Oxford University Press.

—— (2003) *Applied Linguistics*, Oxford: Oxford University Press.

Cook, Vivian and Newson, Mark (1996) *Chomsky's Universal Grammar: An Introduction* (2nd edn), Oxford: Blackwell.

Cooper, R. (1989) *Language Planning and Social Change*, Cambridge: Cambridge University Press.

Corbett, Greville (1991) *Gender*, Cambridge: Cambridge University Press.

—— (2006) *Agreement*, Cambridge: Cambridge University Press.

Corder, S. Pit (1975) *Introducing Applied Linguistics*, London: Penguin.

Cotterill, Janet (ed.) (2002) *Language in the Legal Process*, Basingstoke: Palgrave Macmillan.

Coulmas, Florian (1996) *The Blackwell Encyclopedia of Writing Systems*, Oxford: Blackwell.

—— (2005) *Sociolinguistics: The Study of Speakers' Choices*, Cambridge: Cambridge University Press.

Coulthard, Malcolm (1985) *Introduction to Discourse Analysis* (2nd edn), London: Longman.

Cowper, Elizabeth A. (1992) *A Concise Introduction to Syntactic Theory*, Chicago, IL: University of Chicago Press.

Croft, William (2002) *Typology and Universals* (2nd edn), Cambridge: Cambridge University Press.

Croft, William and Cruse, David Alan (2004) *Cognitive Linguistics*, Cambridge: Cambridge University Press.

Crowley, Terry (1997) *An Introduction to Historical Linguistics* (3rd edn), Oxford: Oxford University Press.

Crowley, Tony (1989) *The Politics of Discourse: The Standard Language Question and British Cultural Debates*, Basingstoke: Macmillan (published in the USA as *The Politics of Standard English*).

—— (1996) *Language in History*, London: Routledge.

Cruse, David Alan (1986) *Lexical Semantics*, Cambridge: Cambridge University Press.

Cruttenden, Alan (1986) *Intonation*, Cambridge: Cambridge University Press.

Crystal, David (1975) *The English Tone of Voice*, London: Arnold.

—— (1988) *The English Language*, London: Penguin.

—— (1995) *The Cambridge Encyclopedia of the English Language*, Cambridge: Cambridge University Press.

—— (1996) *Rediscover Grammar* (2nd edn), London: Longman.

—— (1997) *The Cambridge Encyclopedia of Language*, Cambridge: Cambridge University Press.

—— (2000) *Language Death*, Cambridge: Cambridge University Press.

—— (2003) *English as a Global Language* (2nd edn), Cambridge: Cambridge University Press.

Culicover, Peter (1997) *Principles and Parameters*, Oxford: Oxford University Press.

Culler, Jonathan (1986) *Ferdinand de Saussure* (2nd edn), Ithaca, NY: Cornell University Press.

Cutting, Joan (2002) *Pragmatics and Discourse: A Resource Book for Students*, London: Routledge.

Dahl, Östen (1985) *Tense and Aspect Systems*, Oxford: Blackwell.

Dalby, Andrew (2003) *Language in Danger*, London: Penguin.

Dale, Robert, Moisl, Hermann and Somers, Harold (eds) (2000) *Handbook of Natural Language Processing*, New York: Marcel Dekker.

Daniels, Peter T. and Bright, William (eds) (1996) *The World's Writing Systems*, Oxford: Oxford University Press.

Davies, Alan (1999) *An Introduction to Applied Linguistics: From Practice to Theory*, Edinburgh: Edinburgh University Press.

Davis, Hayley G. (2001) *Words: An Integrational Approach*, Richmond: Curzon.

de Beaugrande, Robert (1994) 'Text Linguistics', in R.E. Asher and J.M.Y. Simpson (eds) (1994) *Encyclopedia of Language and Linguistics*, Oxford: Pergamon, Vol. IX, pp. 4573–8.

de Beaugrande, Robert and Dressler, Wolfgang (1981) *An Introduction to Text Linguistics*, London: Longman.

de Fina, A. (2003) *Identity in Narrative: A Study of Immigrant Discourse,* Amsterdam: Benjamins.

Dekkers, Joost, van der Leeuw, Frank and van de Weijer, Jeroen (eds) (1999) *Optimality Theory: Phonology, Syntax, and Acquisition*, Oxford: Oxford University Press.

Denes, Peter B. and Pinson, Elliot N. (1993) *The Speech Chain: The Physics and Biology of Spoken Language* (2nd edn), New York: W.H. Freeman.

Deuchar, Margaret (1984) *British Sign Language*, London: Routledge.

Dixon, R.M.W. (1994) *Ergativity*, Cambridge: Cambridge University Press.

Duchan, Judith F. (2003) *Frame Work in Language and Literacy: How Theory Informs Practice*, London: Guilford.

Duchan, Judith F., Bruder, Gail A. and Hewitt, L.E. (eds) (1995) *Deixis in Narrative: A Cognitive Science Perspective*, Hillsdale, NJ: Lawrence Erlbaum.

Dunkling, Leslie (1995) *The Guinness Book of Names*, Enfield: Guinness.

Duranti, Alessandro (1997) *Linguistic Anthropology*, Cambridge: Cambridge University Press.

Eckert, Penelope and McConnell-Ginet, Sally (1992) 'Think Practically and Look Locally: Language and Gender as Community-Based Practice', *Annual Review of Anthropology* 21: 461–90.

—— (1995) 'Constructing Meaning, Constructing Selves: Snapshots of Language, Gender and Class from Belten High', in K. Hall and M. Bucholtz (eds) *Gender Articulated: Language and the Socially Constructed Self*, London: Routledge, pp. 469–507.

—— (1999) 'New Generalizations and Explanations in Language and Gender Research', *Language in Society* 28 (2): 185–201.

—— (2003) *Language and Gender*, Cambridge: Cambridge University Press.

Eckert, Penelope and Rickford, John R. (eds) (2001) *Style and Sociolinguistic Variation*, New York: Cambridge University Press.

Eco, Umberto (1976) *A Theory of Semiotics*, Bloomington, IN: Indiana University Press.

Edwards, John (1994) *Multilingualism*, London: Penguin.

Edwards, Viv (2004) *Multilingualism in the English-Speaking World*, Oxford: Blackwell.

Eelen, G. (2001) *A Critique of Politeness Theories*, Manchester: St Jerome.

Eggins, Suzanne (2004) *An Introduction to Systemic Functional Linguistics* (2nd edn), London: Continuum.

Eggins, Suzanne and Slade, Diana (2004) *Analysing Casual Conversation*, London: Equinox.

Elgin, Suzette Haden (1983) *What Is Linguistics?* Englewood Cliffs, NJ: Prentice-Hall.

Emmitt, Marie, Komesaroff, Linda and Pollock, John (2006) *Language and Learning: An Introduction for Teaching* (4th edn), Oxford: Oxford University Press.

Epstein, David and Seely, T. Daniel (eds) (2002) *Derivation and Explanation in the Minimalist Program*, Oxford: Blackwell.

Fabb, Nigel (1997) *Linguistics and Literature*, Oxford: Blackwell.

Fabbro, Franco and Asher, R.E. (eds) (1999) *A Concise Encylopedia of Language Pathology*, Amsterdam: Elsevier.

Fairclough, Norman (ed.) (1992) *Critical Language Awareness*, London: Longman.

—— (1995) *Critical Discourse Analysis: The Critical Study of Language*, London: Longman.

—— (2001) *Language and Power* (2nd edn), London: Longman.

—— (2003) *Analysing Discourse: Textual Analysis for Social Research*, London: Routledge.

Fauconnier, Gilles (1994) *Mental Spaces* (original in French as *Espaces Mentaux*, 1984, Paris: Editions de Minuit), Cambridge: Cambridge University Press.

—— (1997) *Mappings in Thought and Language*, Cambridge: Cambridge University Press.

Fauconnier, Gilles and Turner, Mark (2002) *The Way We Think: Conceptual Blending and the Mind's Hidden Complexities*, New York: Basic Books.

Fennell, Barbara (2000) *A History of English: A Sociolinguistic Approach,* Oxford: Blackwell.

Ferguson, Charles A. (1959) 'Diglossia', *Word* 15: 324–40. Reprinted in Pier Paolo Giglioli (ed.) (1972) *Language and Social Context*, London: Penguin, pp. 232–51.

Fernando, C. (1996) *Idiom and Idiomaticity*, Oxford: Oxford University Press.

Field, John (2003) *Psycholinguistics: A Resource Book for Students*, London: Routledge.

Fillmore, Charles (1987) *Fillmore's Case Grammar*, Heidelberg: Groos.

Fishman, Joshua (ed.) (1999) *Handbook of Language and Ethnic Identity*, Oxford: Oxford University Press.

Fletcher, Paul and Macwhinney, Brian (eds) (1995) *The Handbook of Child Language*, Oxford: Blackwell.

Fodor, Jerry A. (1983) *Modularity of Mind: An Essay on Faculty Psychology*, Cambridge, MA: MIT Press.

Foley, John (1993) *The Guinness Encyclopedia of Signs and Symbols*, Enfield: Guinness.

Foley, William A. (1997) *Anthropological Linguistics: An Introduction*, Oxford: Blackwell.

Fought, C. (2007) *Language and Ethnicity*, Cambridge: Cambridge University Press.

Foulkes, Paul and Docherty, Gerry (eds) (1999) *Urban Voices: Variation and Change in British Accents*, London: Arnold.

Fowler, Roger (1996) *Linguistic Criticism* (2nd edn), Oxford: Oxford University Press.

Fox, Anthony (1995) *Linguistic Reconstruction*, Oxford: Oxford University Press.

Frawley, William (1992) *Linguistic Semantics*, Hillsdale, NJ: Lawrence Erlbaum.

—— (ed.) (2006) *The Expression of Modality*, Berlin: Mouton de Gruyter.

Fromkin, Victoria and Rodman, Robert (1998) *An Introduction to Language* (6th edn), Fort Worth, TX: Harcourt Brace.

Garman, Mike (1990) *Psycholinguistics*, Cambridge: Cambridge University Press.

Garnham, Alan (1985) *Psycholinguistics: Central Topics*, London: Methuen.

Garside, R., Leech, G. and McEnery, A. (eds) (1997) *Corpus Annotation: Linguistic Information from Computer Text Corpora*, London: Longman.

Gavins, Joanna (2007) *Text World Theory*, Edinburgh: Edinburgh University Press.

Gibbons, John (2003) *Forensic Linguistics: An Introduction to Language in the Justice System*, Oxford: Blackwell.

Giegerich, Heinz J. (1992) *English Phonology: An Introduction*, Cambridge: Cambridge University Press.

Giora, Rachel (2003) *On Our Mind: Salience, Context, and Figurative Language*, Oxford: Oxford University Press.

Givón, Talmy (1993) *English Grammar: A Function-Based Introduction* (2 vols), Amsterdam: Benjamins.

—— (1995) *Functionalism and Grammar*, Amsterdam: Benjamins.

—— (2001) *Syntax: An Introduction* (rev. edn), Amsterdam: Benjamins.

Gleason, H.A. (1961) *An Introduction to Descriptive Linguistics* (2nd edn), New York: Holt, Rinehart & Winston.

Goatly, Andrew (1997) *The Language of Metaphors*, London: Routledge.
Goldberg, Adele (2006) *Constructions at Work: The Nature of Generalization in Language*, Oxford: Oxford University Press.
Goldstein, E. Bruce (2002) *Sensation and Perception* (6th edn), Pacific Grove, CA: Wadsworth.
Goodluck, Helen (1991) *Language Acquisition: A Linguistic Introduction*, Oxford: Blackwell.
Gramley, Stephan and Pätzold, Kurt-Michael (1992) *A Survey of Modern English*, London: Routledge.
Green, Jonathon (1996) *Chasing the Sun: Dictionary-Makers and the Dictionaries They Made*, London: Jonathan Cape.
Green, Keith (ed.) (1995) *New Essays in Deixis: Discourse, Narrative, Literature*, Amsterdam: Rodopi.
Greenbaum, Sidney and Quirk, Randolph (1990) *A Student's Grammar of the English Language*, London: Longman.
Greenberg, Joseph H. (1963) 'Some Universals of Grammar with Particular Reference to the Order of Meaningful Elements', in J.H. Greenberg (ed.) *Universals of Grammar*, Cambridge, MA: MIT Press, pp. 73–113.
Grimes, Barbara F. (ed.) (2000) *Ethnologue: Languages of the World* (14th edn), Dallas, TX: Summer Institute of Linguistics.
Grinder, John T. and Elgin, Suzette Haden (1973) *Guide to Transformational Grammar: History, Theory, Practice*, New York: Holt, Rinehart & Winston.
Grundy, Peter (1995) *Doing Pragmatics*, London: Arnold.
Gumperz, John J. and Levinson, Stephen C. (eds) (1996) *Rethinking Linguistic Relativity*, Cambridge: Cambridge University Press.
Gussenhoven, Carlos and Jacobs, Haike (1998) *Understanding Phonology*, London: Arnold.
Gussmann, Edmund (2002) *Phonology*, Cambridge: Cambridge University Press.
Haegeman, Liliane (1994) *Introduction to Government and Binding Theory* (2nd edn), Oxford: Blackwell.
Halliday, Michael A.K. (1989) *Spoken and Written Language*, Oxford: Oxford University Press.
—— (2004) *An Introduction to Functional Grammar* (3rd edn, revised by Christian M.I.M. Matthiessen), London: Arnold.
Halliday, Michael A.K. and Hasan, Ruqaiya (1976) *Cohesion in English*, London: Longman.
Harris, Randy Allen (1993) *The Linguistics Wars*, Oxford: Oxford University Press.
Harris, Roxy (2006) *New Ethnicities and Language Use*, Basingstoke: Palgrave Macmillan.
Harris, Roy (1998) *Introduction to Integrational Linguistics*, Oxford: Elsevier.
Harris, Roy and Wolf, George (eds) (1998) *Integrational Linguistics: A First Reader*, Oxford: Elsevier.
Hawkins, John A. (1983) *Word Order Universals*, New York: Academic Press.

Hawkins, Peter (1984) *Introducing Phonology*, London: Hutchinson.

Heggie, Lorie and Ordóñez, Fernando (eds) (2004) *Clitic and Affix Combinations: Theoretical Perspectives*, Amsterdam: Benjamins.

Heil, John (1998) *Philosophy of Mind: A Contemporary Introduction*, London: Routledge.

Hendrick, Randall (ed.) (2003) *Minimalist Syntax*, Oxford: Blackwell.

Hickmann, Maya and Robert, Stéphane (eds) (2006) *Space in Languages: Linguistic Systems and Cognitive Categories*, Amsterdam: Benjamins.

Hiraga, Masako (2005) *Metaphor and Iconicity: A Cognitive Approach to Analysing Texts*, Basingstoke: Palgrave Macmillan.

Hock, Hans Henrich (1986) *Principles of Historical Linguistics*, Berlin: Mouton de Gruyter.

Hock, Hans Henrich and Joseph, Brian D. (1996) *Language History, Language Change and Language Relationship: An Introduction to Historical and Comparative Linguistics*, Berlin: Mouton de Gruyter.

Hockett, Charles F. (1958) *A Course in Modern Linguistics*, New York: Macmillan.

—— (1960) 'The Origin of Speech', *Scientific American* 203 (September): 88–96.

Hoey, Michael (2005) *Lexical Priming: A New Theory of Words and Language*, London: Routledge.

Hofmann, Theo R. (1993) *Realms of Meaning*, London: Longman.

Hofstadter, Douglas R. (1979) *Gödel, Escher, Bach: An Eternal Golden Braid*, Hassocks: Harvester.

—— (1985) 'A Person Paper on Purity in Language', in D.R. Hofstadter, *Metamagical Themas*, New York: Basic Books, pp. 159–67. Reprinted in Deborah Cameron (ed.) (1990) *The Feminist Critique of Language: A Reader*, London: Routledge, pp. 187–96.

Hogg, Richard and McCully, C.B. (1987) *Metrical Phonology: A Coursebook*, Cambridge: Cambridge University Press.

Holm, John (1988–9) *Pidgins and Creoles* (2 vols), Cambridge: Cambridge University Press.

—— (2000) *An Introduction to Pidgins and Creoles*, Cambridge: Cambridge University Press.

Holmes, Janet (1992) *An Introduction to Sociolinguistics*, London: Longman.

Holmes, Janet and Meyerhoff, Miriam (eds) (2003) *The Handbook of Language and Gender*, Oxford: Blackwell.

Honey, John (1997) *Language Is Power: The Story of Standard English and Its Enemies*, London: Faber & Faber.

Horne, Kibbey M. (1966) *Language Typology: 19th and 20th Century Views*, Washington, DC: Georgetown University Press.

Hornstein, Norbert (1990) *As Time Goes By: Tense and Universal Grammar*, Cambridge, MA: MIT Press.

Hornstein, Norbert, Nuñes, Jairo and Grohmann, Kleanthes (2005) *Understanding Minimalism*, Cambridge: Cambridge University Press.

Horrocks, Geoffrey (1987) *Generative Grammar*, London: Longman.

Huddleston, Rodney (1984) *Introduction to the Grammar of English*, Cambridge: Cambridge University Press.

Hudson, Richard A. (1984) *Invitation to Linguistics*, Oxford: Blackwell.

—— (1995) *Word Meaning*, London: Routledge.

—— (1996) *Sociolinguistics* (2nd edn), Cambridge: Cambridge University Press.

—— (1998) *English Grammar*, London: Routledge.

Hughes, Arthur and Trudgill, Peter (1996) *English Accents and Dialects: An Introduction to Social and Regional Varieties of English in the British Isles* (3rd edn), London: Arnold.

Hurford, James R. (1994) *Grammar: A Student's Guide*, Cambridge: Cambridge University Press.

Hurford, James R. and Heasley, Brendan (1983) *Semantics: A Coursebook*, Cambridge: Cambridge University Press.

Hyman, Larry M. (1975) *Phonology: Theory and Analysis*, New York: Holt, Rinehart & Winston.

Ilson, Robert (ed.) (1986) *Lexicography: An Emerging International Profession*, Manchester: Manchester University Press.

Ingram, David (1989) *First Language Acquisition: Method, Description and Explanation*, Cambridge: Cambridge University Press.

Ingram, John (2007) *Neurolinguistics*, Cambridge: Cambridge University Press.

Jackendoff, Ray (1993) *Patterns in the Mind: Language and Human Nature*, New York: Harvester Wheatsheaf.

Jackson, Howard (2000) *Words, Meaning and Vocabulary: An Introduction to Modern English Lexicology*, London: Cassell.

—— (2002) *Grammar and Vocabulary: A Resource Book for Students*, London: Routledge.

Jeffries, Lesley (2006) *Discovering Language: The Structure of Modern English*, Basingstoke: Palgrave Macmillan.

Jenkins, J. (2003) *World Englishes: A Resource Book for Students*, London: Routledge.

Johnson, K. (1997) *Acoustic and Auditory Phonetics*, Oxford: Blackwell.

Johnson-Laird, Philip H. (1983) *Mental Models: Towards a Cognitive Science of Language, Inference and Consciousness*, Cambridge: Cambridge University Press.

—— (1993) *The Computer and the Mind: An Introduction to Cognitive Science* (2nd edn), London: Fontana.

Johnstone, Barbara (2000) *Qualitative Methods in Sociolinguistics*, New York: Oxford University Press.

Joseph, J. (2004) *Language and Identity*, Basingstoke: Palgrave.

Joshi, R. Malatesha and Aaron, P.G. (eds) (2006) *Handbook of Orthography and Literacy*, Mahwah, NJ: Lawrence Erlbaum.

Jurafsky, Dan and Martin, James (2000) *Speech and Language Processing: An Introduction to Natural Language Processing, Computational Linguistics, and Speech Recognition*, London: Prentice-Hall.

Kager, Reni (1999) *Optimality Theory*, Cambridge: Cambridge University Press.

Kaplan, Ronald and Bresnan, Joan (1982) 'Lexical-Functional Grammar: A Formal System for Grammatical Representation', in J. Bresnan (ed.), *The Mental Representation of Grammatical Relations*, Cambridge, MA: MIT Press, pp. 173–281.

Katamba, Francis (1989) *An Introduction to Phonology*, London: Longman.

—— (1994) *English Words*, London: Routledge.

Katamba, Francis and Stonham, John T. (2006) *Morphology*, Basingstoke: Palgrave Macmillan.

Kempson, Ruth M. (1977) *Semantic Theory*, Cambridge: Cambridge University Press.

Keyser, Samuel Jay and Postal, Paul M. (1976) *Beginning English Grammar*, New York: Harper & Row.

Kilby, David (1984) *Descriptive Syntax and the English Verb*, London: Croom Helm.

Klaiman, M.H. (1991) *Grammatical Voice*, Cambridge: Cambridge University Press.

Klima, Edward S. and Bellugi, Ursula, (1979) *The Signs of Language*, Cambridge, MA: Harvard University Press.

Knowles, Gerald (1987) *Patterns of Spoken English*, London: Longman.

Kouwenberg, S. and Singler, J.V. (eds) (2005) *The Handbook of Pidgin and Creole Studies*, Malden, MA: Blackwell.

Kövecses, Zoltán (2005) *Metaphor in Culture: Universality and Variation*, Cambridge: Cambridge University Press.

Krauss, Michael (1992) 'The World's Languages in Crisis', *Language* 68: 4–10.

Kreidler, Charles W. (1989) *The Pronunciation of English*, Oxford: Blackwell.

—— (1998) *Introducing English Semantics*, London: Routledge.

Kroeger, Paul (2004) *Analysing Syntax*, Cambridge: Cambridge University Press.

—— (2005) *Analyzing Grammar*, Cambridge: Cambridge University Press.

Kuhn, Jonas (2003) *Optimality-Theoretic Syntax: A Declarative Approach*, Stanford, CA: CSLI.

Labov, William (1972) *Sociolinguistic Patterns*, Philadelphia, PA: University of Pennsylvania Press.

—— (1975) *What Is a Linguistic Fact?* Lisse: Peter de Ridder Press.

—— (1994) *Principles of Linguistic Change*, Vol. I: *Internal Factors*, Oxford: Blackwell.

Ladefoged, Peter (1971) *Preliminaries to Linguistic Phonetics*, Chicago, IL: University of Chicago Press.

—— (1993) *A Course in Phonetics* (3rd edn), Fort Worth, TX: Harcourt Brace Jovanovich.

Ladefoged, Peter and Maddieson, Ian (1996) *The Sounds of the World's Languages*, Oxford: Blackwell.

Lakoff, George (1987) *Women, Fire, and Dangerous Things*, Chicago, IL: University of Chicago Press.

Lakoff, George and Johnson, Mark (1980) *Metaphors We Live By*, Chicago, IL: University of Chicago Press.

Landau, Sidney I. (1984) *Dictionaries: The Art and Craft of Lexicography*, New York: Charles Scribner's Sons.

Langacker, Ronald W. (1987–91) *Foundations of Cognitive Grammar*, Berlin: Mouton de Gruyter.

—— (1990) *Concept, Image and Symbol: The Cognitive Basis of Grammar*, Berlin: Mouton de Gruyter.

Langlotz, Andreas (2006) *Idiomatic Creativity: A Cognitive-Linguistic Model of Idiom Representation and Idiom Variation in English*, Amsterdam: Benjamins.

Large, Andrew (1985) *The Artificial Language Movement*, Oxford: Blackwell.

Lasnik, Howard (2003) *Minimalist Investigations in Linguistic Theory*, London: Routledge.

Lasnik, Howard, Uriagereka, Juan and Boeckx, Cedric (2005) *A Course in Minimalist Syntax: Foundations and Prospects*, Oxford: Blackwell.

Lass, Roger (1984) *Phonology*, Cambridge: Cambridge University Press.

Laver, John (1994) *Principles of Phonetics*, Cambridge: Cambridge University Press.

Leech, Geoffrey (1974) *Semantics*, London: Penguin.

Leeds-Hurwitz, Wendy (1993) *Semiotics and Communication: Signs, Codes, Culture*, Hillsdale, NJ: Lawrence Erlbaum.

Lehiste, Ilse (1970) *Suprasegmentals*, Cambridge, MA: MIT Press.

Lehmann, Winfred P. (1992) *Historical Linguistics* (3rd edn), London: Routledge.

—— (1993) *Theoretical Bases of Indo-European Linguistics*, London: Routledge.

—— (ed.) (1967) *A Reader in Nineteenth-Century Historical Indo-European Linguistics*, Bloomington, IN: University of Indiana Press.

Leith, Dick (1997) *A Social History of English* (2nd edn), London: Routledge.

Lepschy, Giulio (1970) *A Survey of Structural Linguistics*, London: Faber & Faber.

—— (ed.) (1994) *History of Linguistics*, Vol. II: *Classical and Medieval Linguistics*, London: Longman.

Levinson, Stephen (1983) *Pragmatics*, Cambridge: Cambridge University Press.

Li, Wei (ed.) (2000) *The Bilingualism Reader*, London: Routledge.

Llamas, Carmen, Mullany, Louise and Stockwell, Peter (eds) (2007) *The Routledge Companion to Sociolinguistics*, London: Routledge.

Lockwood, W.B. (1969) *Indo-European Philology*, London: Hutchinson.

—— (1972) *A Panorama of Indo-European Languages*, London: Hutchinson.

Lodge, R. Anthony (1993) *French: From Dialect to Standard*, London: Routledge.

Lucy, John (1968) *Introduction to Theoretical Linguistics*, Cambridge: Cambridge University Press.

—— (1991) *Chomsky* (3rd edn), London: Fontana.

—— (1992) *Grammatical Categories and Cognition: A Case Study of the Linguistic Relativity Hypothesis*, Cambridge: Cambridge University Press.

—— (1995) *Linguistic Semantics: An Introduction*, Cambridge: Cambridge University Press.

Lucy, John and Shweder, Richard (1979) 'Whorf and His Critics: Linguistic and Nonlinguistic Influences on Colour Memory', *American Anthropologist* 81: 581–615.

Lust, Barbara (2006) *Child Language*, Cambridge: Cambridge University Press.

Heller, H. (ed.) (2007) *Bilingualism*, London: Palgrave.

McArthur, Tom (1986) *Worlds of Reference: Lexicography, Learning and Language from the Clay Tablet to the Computer*, Cambridge: Cambridge University Press.

McCarthy, John (2001) *A Thematic Guide to Optimality Theory*, Cambridge: Cambridge University Press.

—— (ed.) (2004) *Optimality Theory in Phonology: A Reader*, Oxford: Blackwell.

McCarthy, Michael (1991) *Discourse Analysis for Language Teachers*, Cambridge: Cambridge University Press.

McCarthy, Michael and Carter, Ronald (1993) *Language as Discourse: Perspectives for Language Teaching*, London: Longman.

McCrum, Robert, Cran, William and MacNeil, Robert (1992) *The Story of English* (2nd edn), London: Faber & Faber/BBC Books.

McEnery, Tony and Wilson, Andrew, (2001) *Corpus Linguistics: An Introduction* (2nd edn), Edinburgh: Edinburgh University Press.

McEnery, Tony, Xiao, Richard and Tono, Yukio (2006) *Corpus-Based Language Studies: An Advanced Resource Book*, London: Routledge.

MacKenzie, Ian (2002) *Paradigms of Reading: Relevance Theory and Deconstruction*, Houndmills: Palgrave Macmillan.

McMahon, April (1994) *Understanding Language Change*, Cambridge: Cambridge University Press.

—— (2000) *Change, Chance, and Optimality*, Oxford: Oxford University Press.

McMenamin, Gerald R. (ed.) (2002) *Forensic Linguistics: Advances in Forensic Stylistics*, Boca Raton, FL: CRC Press.

Macwhinney, Brian and Bates, Elizabeth (eds) (1989) *The Crosslinguistic Study of Linguistic Processing*, Cambridge: Cambridge University Press.

Mahlberg, Michaela (2005) *English General Nouns: A Corpus Theoretical Approach*, Amsterdam: Benjamins.

Mallory, J.P. (1989) *In Search of the Indo-Europeans*, London: Thames & Hudson.

Malmkjær, Kirsten (ed.) (2004) *The Linguistics Encyclopedia* (2nd edn), London: Routledge.

Martin, Robert M. (1987) *The Meaning of Language*, Cambridge, MA: MIT Press.

Masterman, Margaret and Wilks, Yorick (eds) (2005) *Language, Cohesion and Form*, Cambridge: Cambridge University Press.

Matthews, Peter (1979) *Generative Grammar and Linguistic Competence*, London: Allen & Unwin.

—— (1981) *Syntax*, Cambridge: Cambridge University Press.

—— (1991) *Morphology* (2nd edn), Cambridge: Cambridge University Press.

Maybin, Janet and Mercer, Neil (1996) *Using English: From Conversation to Canon*, London: Routledge/Open University.

Maybin, Janet and Swann, Joan (eds) (2006) *The Art of English: Everyday Creativity*, Basingstoke: Palgrave Macmillan.

Mey, Jacob (1993) *Pragmatics*, Oxford: Blackwell.

Miles, Dorothy (1988) *British Sign Language: A Beginner's Guide*, London: BBC Books.

Mills, Sara (2003) *Gender and Politeness*, Cambridge: Cambridge University Press.

—— (2004) *Discourse*, New York: Routledge.

Milroy, James (1992) *Linguistic Variation and Change*, Oxford: Blackwell.

Milroy, James and Milroy, Lesley (eds) (1993) *Real English: The Grammar of English Dialects in the British Isles*, London: Longman.

—— (1997) *Authority in Language: Investigating Standard English,* (3rd edn), London: Routledge.

Milroy, Lesley (1987a) *Language and Social Networks* (2nd edn), Oxford: Blackwell.

—— (1987b) *Observing and Analysing Natural Language: A Critical Account of Sociolinguistic Method*, Oxford: Blackwell.

Milroy, Lesley and Gordon, Matthew (2003) *Sociolinguistics. Method and Interpretation*, Oxford: Blackwell.

Morgan, Gary and Woll, Bencie (2002) *Directions in Sign Language Acquisition*, Philadelphia, PA: Benjamins.

Nettle, D. and Romaine, Suzanne (2000) *Vanishing Voices: The Extinction of the World's Languages.* Oxford: Oxford University Press.

Nevalainen, Terttu, Klemola, Juhani and Laitinen, Mikko (eds) (2006) *Types of Variation: Diachronic, Dialectical and Typological Interfaces*, Amsterdam: Benjamins.

Newmeyer, Frederick J. (1983) *Grammatical Theory: Its Limits and Possibilities*, Chicago, IL: University of Chicago Press.

Nida, Eugene (1975) *Componential Analysis of Meaning*, The Hague: Mouton.

Nivre, Joakim (2006) *Inductive Dependency Parsing*, Dordrecht: Springer.

Nofsinger, Robert E. (1991) *Everyday Conversation*, Newbury Park, CA: Sage.

O'Grady, William, Dobrovolsky, Michael and Katamba, Francis (1996) *Contemporary Linguistics: An Introduction*, London: Longman.

Odden, David (2005) *Introducing Phonology*, Cambridge: Cambridge University Press.

Oller, John W. and Jonz, Jon (eds) (1994) *Cloze and Coherence*, London: Associated University Presses.

Ong, Walter (1982) *Orality and Literacy: The Technologising of the Word*, London: Methuen.

Ouhalla, Jamal (1994) *Introducing Transformational Grammar*, London: Arnold.

Owens, Robert E., Jr. (1996) *Language Development: An Introduction* (4th edn), Boston, MA: Allyn & Bacon.

Padden, Carol A. (1988) 'Grammatical Theory and Signed Languages', in Frederick J. Newmeyer (ed.) *Linguistics: The Cambridge Survey*, Vol. II: *Linguistic Theory: Extensions and Implications*, Cambridge: Cambridge University Press, pp. 250–66.

Palmer, Frank (1971) *Grammar*, London: Penguin.

—— (1974) *The English Verb*, London: Longman.

—— (1976) *Semantics: A New Outline*, Cambridge: Cambridge University Press.

—— (1979) *Modality and the English Modals*, London: Longman.

—— (1994) *Grammatical Roles and Relations*, Cambridge: Cambridge University Press.

—— (2001) *Mood and Modality* (2nd edn), Cambridge: Cambridge University Press.

Palmer, Gary B. (1996) *Toward a Theory of Cultural Linguistics*, Austin, TX: University of Texas Press.

Partridge, Eric (1970) *Slang To-Day and Yesterday*, London: Routledge.

—— (2002) *A Dictionary of Slang and Unconventional English* (6th edn, ed. by Paul Beale), London: Routledge.

Peirce, Charles Sanders (1991) *Peirce on Signs: Writings on Semiotics* (ed. by James Hoopes), Chapel Hill, NC: University of North Carolina Press.

Pennycook, Alastair (2001) *Critical Applied Linguistics: A Critical Introduction*, Mahwah, NJ: Lawrence Erlbaum.

Piattelli-Palmarini, Massimo (ed.) (1979) *Language and Learning: The Debate Between Jean Piaget and Noam Chomsky*, London: Routledge.

Pike, Kenneth Lee (1967) *Language in Relation to a Unified Theory of Structure of Human Behavior* (2nd edn), The Hague: Mouton.

—— (1982) *Linguistic Concepts: An Introduction to Tagmemics*. Lincoln, NE: University of Nebraska Press.

Pinker, Steven (1994) *The Language Instinct: The New Science of Language and Mind*, London: Allen Lane/Penguin.

Polanyi, Livia (1985) *Telling the American Story: A Structural and Cultural Analysis of Conversation*, Norwood, MA: Ablex.

Pollard, Carl and Sag, Ivan A. (1994) *Head-Driven Phrase Structure Grammar*, Chicago, IL: University of Chicago Press.

Poole, Geoffrey (2002) *Syntactic Theory*, Basingstoke: Palgrave.

Poyatos, Fernando (1993) *Paralanguage: A Linguistic and Interdisciplinary Approach to Interactive Speech and Sound*, Amsterdam: Benjamins.

—— (2002) *Paralanguage, Kinesics, Silence, Personal and Environmental Interaction*, Amsterdam: Benjamins.

Pridham, F (2001) *The Language of Conversation*, London: Routledge.

Propp, Vladimir (1968) *Morphology of the Folktale*, Austin, TX: University of Texas Press.

Pullum, Geoffrey K. (1991) *The Great Eskimo Vocabulary Hoax and Other Irreverent Essays on the Study of Language*, Chicago, IL: University of Chicago Press.

Pullum, Geoffrey K. and Ladusaw, William A. (1996) *Phonetic Symbol Guide* (2nd edn), Chicago, IL: University of Chicago Press.

Radford, Andrew (1988) *Transformational Grammar: A First Course*, Cambridge: Cambridge University Press.

—— (1997) *Syntactic Theory and the Structure of English: A Minimalist Approach*, Cambridge: Cambridge University Press.

—— (2004) *Minimalist Syntax*, Cambridge: Cambridge University Press.

Rampton, Ben (1995) *Crossing: Language and Ethnicity Among Adolescents*, London: Longman.

Rauh, G. (ed.) (1983) *Essays on Deixis*, Tübingen: Gunter Narr Verlag.

Renkema, J. (2004) *Introduction to Discourse Studies*, Philadelphia, PA: Benjamins.

Richards, Jack C., Platt, John and Platt, Heidi (1992) *Dictionary of Language Teaching and Applied Linguistics* (2nd edn), London: Longman.

Roach, Peter (1991) *English Phonetics and Phonology: A Practical Course* (2nd edn), Cambridge: Cambridge University Press.

Robins, R.H. (1997) *A Short History of Linguistics* (4th edn), London: Longman.

Robinson, Andrew (1995) *The Story of Writing*, London: Thames & Hudson.

Robson, Mark and Stockwell, Peter (2005) *Language in Theory: A Resource Book for Students*, London: Routledge.

Romaine, Suzanne (1988) *Pidgin and Creole Languages*, London: Longman.

—— (1994) *Language in Society: An Introduction to Sociolinguistics*, Oxford: Oxford University Press.

—— (1995) *Bilingualism* (2nd edn), Oxford: Blackwell.

Ronen, Ruth (1994) *Possible Worlds in Literary Theory*, Cambridge: Cambridge University Press.

Ryan, Marie-Laure (1991) *Possible Worlds, Artificial Intelligence and Narrative Theory*, Bloomington, IN: Indiana University Press.

Sadock, Jerrold (1991) *Autolexical Syntax: A Theory of Parallel Grammatical Representations*, Chicago, IL: University of Chicago Press.

Saeed, John I. (1997) *Semantics*, Oxford: Blackwell.

Sampson, Geoffrey (1975) *The Form of Language*, London: Weidenfeld & Nicolson.

—— (1980) *Schools of Linguistics*, London: Hutchinson.

—— (1985) *Writing Systems*, London: Hutchinson.

—— (1997) *Educating Eve: The 'Language Instinct' Debate*, London: Cassell.

Sampson, Geoffrey and McCarthy, Diana (eds) (2005) *Corpus Linguistics: Readings in a Widening Discipline*, London: Continuum.

Saville-Troike, M. (2003) *The Ethnography of Communication* (3rd edn), Oxford: Blackwell.

Schank, Roger C. (1982) *Dynamic Memory: A Theory of Reminding and Learning in Computers and People*, Cambridge: Cambridge University Press.

—— (1986) *Explanation Patterns*, Hillsdale, NJ: Lawrence Erlbaum.

Schank, Roger C. and Abelson, Robert (1977) *Scripts, Plans, Goals and Understanding*, Hillsdale, NJ: Lawrence Erlbaum.

Schiffrin, Deborah (1994) *Approaches to Discourse*, Oxford: Blackwell.

Schmitt, Norbert (ed.) (2002) *An Introduction to Applied Linguistics*, London: Arnold.

Schmitt, Norbert and McCarthy, Michael (1997) *Vocabulary: Description, Acquisition and Pedagogy*, Cambridge: Cambridge University Press.

Sebba, Mark (1997) *Contact Languages: Pidgins and Creoles*, London: Macmillan.

Sebeok, Thomas (1984) *Encyclopedic Dictionary of Semiotics* (3 vols), Berlin: Mouton de Gruyter.

—— (1994) *An Introduction to Semiotics*, London: Pinter.

Sells, Peter (1985) *Lectures on Contemporary Syntactic Theories*, Stanford, CA: CSLI.

Semino, Elena (1997) *Language and World Creation in Poems and Other Texts*, London: Longman.

Shockey, Linda (2003) *Sound Patterns of Spoken English*, Oxford: Blackwell.

Shuy, Roger W. (2005) *Creating Language Crimes: How Law Enforcement Uses (and Misuses) Language*, Oxford: Oxford University Press.

—— (2006) *Linguistics in the Courtroom: A Practical Guide*, Oxford: Oxford University Press.

Siewierska, Anna (1991) *Functional Grammar*, London: Routledge.

Silverman, David (1993) *Interpreting Qualitative Data*, London: Sage.

Simpson, Paul (1993) *Language, Ideology and Point of View*, London: Routledge.

—— (1996) *Language through Literature: An Introduction*, London: Routledge.

—— (2004) *Stylistics: A Resource Book for Students*, London: Routledge.

Sinclair, John (1991) *Corpus, Concordance and Collocation*, Oxford: Oxford University Press.

Sinclair, John and Carter, Ronald (eds) (2004) *Trust the Text: Language, Corpus and Discourse*, London: Routledge.

Sinclair, John and Coulthard, Malcolm (1975) *Towards an Analysis of Discourse: The English Used by Teachers and Pupils*, Oxford: Oxford University Press.

Sloane, Thomas O. (ed.) (2001) *Encyclopedia of Rhetoric*, Oxford: Oxford University Press.

Smith, Cath (1990) *Signs Make Sense: A Guide to British Sign Language*, London: Souvenir Press.

Sommerstein, Alan H. (1977) *Modern Phonology*, London: Arnold.

Sperber, Dan and Wilson, Deirdre (1995) *Relevance: Communication and Cognition* (2nd edn), Oxford: Blackwell Publishers.

Stainton, Robert J. (1996) *Philosophical Perspectives on Language*, Peterborough, OR: Broadview.

Steinberg, Danny D. (1993) *An Introduction to Psycholinguistics*, London: Longman.

Stillings, Neil A. (1987) *Cognitive Science: An Introduction*, Cambridge, MA: MIT Press.

Stockwell, Peter (2002a) *Sociolinguistics: A Resource Book for Students*, London: Routledge.

—— (2002b) *Cognitive Poetics: An Introduction*, London: Routledge.

—— (2003) 'Schema Poetics and Speculative Cosmology', *Language and Literature* 12(3): 252–71.

—— (2007) *Texture: A Cognitive Aesthetics of Reading*, Edinburgh: Edinburgh University Press.

Sturrock, John (1993) *Structuralism* (2nd edn), London: Fontana.

Szemerényi, Oswald J.L. (1996) *Introduction to Indo-European Linguistics*, Oxford: Clarendon Press.

Tannen, Deborah (1991) *You Just Don't Understand: Women and Men in Conversation*, London: Virago.

Tarleton, R. (1988) *Learning and Talking: A Practical Guide to Oracy Across the Curriculum*, London: Routledge.

Taylor, John R. (2003) *Linguistic Categorization*, Oxford: Oxford University Press.

Tench, Paul (1996) *The Intonation Systems of English*, London: Cassell.

Thibault, Paul J. (1994) 'Intertextuality', in R.E. Asher and J.M.Y. Simpson (eds), *Encyclopedia of Language and Linguistics*, Oxford: Pergamon, Vol. IV, pp. 1751–4.

Thomas, Jenny (1995) *Meaning in Interaction*, London: Longman.

Thompson, Geoff (2004) *Introducing Functional Grammar* (2nd edn), London: Arnold.

Thornborrow, Joanna and Wareing, Shân (1998) *Patterns in Language: An Introduction to Language and Literary Style*, London: Routledge.

Tobin, Yishai (1990) *Semiotics and Linguistics*, London: Longman.

Tognini-Bonelli, Elena (2001) *Corpus Linguistics at Work*, Amsterdam: Benjamins.

Toolan, Michael (1988) *Narrative: A Critical Linguistic Introduction*, London: Routledge.

—— (1994a) 'Narrative: Linguistic and Structural Theories', in R.E. Asher and J.M.Y. Simpson (eds), *Encyclopedia of Language and Linguistics*, Oxford: Pergamon, vol. V, pp. 2679–96.

—— (1994b) 'Narrative, Natural', in R.E. Asher and J.M.Y. Simpson (eds), *Encyclopedia of Language and Linguistics*, Oxford: Pergamon, Vol. V, pp. 2696–2701.

—— (1996) *Total Speech: An Integrational Linguistic Approach to Language*, Durham, NC: Duke University Press.

Trask, R.L. (1994) *Language Change*, London: Routledge.

—— (1995) *Language: The Basics*, London: Routledge.

—— (1996) *Historical Linguistics*, London: Arnold.

Trudgill, Peter (1995) *Sociolinguistics* (2nd edn), London: Penguin.

Trudgill, Peter and Hannah, Jean (1994) *International English: A Guide to the Varieties of Standard English* (3rd edn), London: Arnold.

Turing, Alan (1950) 'Computing Machinery and Intelligence', *Mind* 59 (236, October): 433–60.

Turner, G.W. (1973) *Stylistics*, London: Penguin.

Ungerer, F. and Schmid, H.-J. (1996) *An Introduction to Cognitive Linguistics*, London: Longman.

Valli, Clayton and Lucas, Ceil (2001) *The Linguistics of American Sign Language: An Introduction* (3rd edn), Washington, DC: Gallaudet University Press.

van Peer, Willie (1986) *Stylistics and Psychology: Investigations of Foregrounding*, London: Croom Helm.

—— (1994) 'Text', in R.E. Asher and J.M.Y. Simpson (eds), *Encyclopedia of Language and Linguistics*, Oxford: Pergamon, Vol. IX, pp. 4564–8.

van Valin, Robert (2001) *An Introduction to Syntax*, Cambridge: Cambridge University Press.

van Valin, Robert D. and LaPolla, Randy (1997) *Syntax: Structure, Meaning and Function*, Cambridge: Cambridge University Press.

Verschueren, Jef (1999) *Understanding Pragmatics*, London: Arnold.

Wales, Katie (2001) *A Dictionary of Stylistics* (2nd edn), London: Pearson.

Wallman, Joel (1992) *Aping Language*, Cambridge: Cambridge University Press.

Wardhaugh, Ronald (2005) *An Introduction to Sociolinguistics* (5th edn), Oxford: Blackwell.

—— (1987) *Languages in Competition*, Oxford: Blackwell.

Watts, Richard, Ide, Sachiko and Ehlich, Konrad (eds) (2005) *Politeness in Language: Studies in its History, Theory, and Practice* (2nd edn), New York: Mouton de Gruyter.

Weinreich, Uriel, Labov, William and Herzog, Marvin I. (1968) 'Empirical Foundations for a Theory of Language Change', in W.P. Lehmann and Yakov Malkiel (eds) *Directions for Historical Linguistics*, Austin, TX: University of Texas Press, pp. 95–188.

Wells, John (1982) *Accents of English* (3 vols), Cambridge: Cambridge University Press.

Wenger, E. (1998) *Communities of Practice*, Cambridge: Cambridge University Press.

Wengraf, T. (2001) *Qualitative Social Interviewing: Biographic Narrative and Semi-Structured Methods.* London: Sage.

Werth, Paul (1999) *Text Worlds: Representing Conceptual Space in Discourse*, London: Longman.

Whaley, Lindsay J. (1997) *Introduction to Typology: The Unity and Diversity of Language*, London: Sage.

Whorf, Benjamin Lee (1956) *Language, Thought and Reality: Selected Writings of Benjamin Lee Whorf*, ed. by J.B. Carroll, Cambridge, MA: MIT Press.

Wierzbicka, Anna (1996) *Semantics: Primes and Universals*, Oxford: Oxford University Press.

Wodak, Ruth (1996) *Disorders of Discourse*, London: Longman.

Wodak, Ruth and Chilton, Paul (2005) *Methods of Critical Discourse Analysis*. London: Sage.

Wolf, Florian and Gibson, Edward (2006) *Coherence in Natural Language: Data Structures and Applications*, Cambridge, MA: MIT Press.

Wooffitt, R. (2005) *Conversation Analysis and Discourse Analysis: A Comparative and Critical Introduction*, London: Sage.

Wright, S. (2004) *Language Policy and Language Planning: From Nationalism to Globalisation*, Basingstoke: Palgrave.

Yip, Moira (2002) *Tone*, Cambridge: Cambridge University Press.

Yule, George (1996) *Pragmatics*, Oxford: Oxford University Press.

Zentella, A.C. (1997) *Growing up Bilingual*, Oxford: Blackwell.

Index

Note: page numbers in **bold** indicate the entry for a subject.

351

Lightning Source UK Ltd.
Milton Keynes UK
UKOW05f0413010317
295606UK00016B/171/P